Francesco d'Assisi, Saint

The little flowers of St. Francis ~~a Th~~...

EVERYMAN, I will go with thee,

and be thy guide,

In thy most need to go by thy side

SAINT FRANCIS OF ASSISI

Born in 1181–2, his father Pietro Bernadone being a cloth merchant. After being taken a prisoner of war at Perugia in 1202 and an attempt to fight in the papal army in 1206, he renounced his former wayward life and embraced a life of evangelical poverty. With his first twelve followers he received approval of his Order from Pope Innocent III in 1209. The final *Rule* of his Order was approved by Pope Honorius III in 1223. In 1219 he visited Syria and the Holy Land. When he was half blind in 1225 he composed his famous *Canticle of the Sun*. He died in 1226 and was canonized two years later.

The Little Flowers of St. Francis

The Mirror of Perfection

St. Bonaventure's Life of St. Francis

INTRODUCTION BY

FR HUGH McKAY, O.F.M., D.D.

With a postscript on
The Mirror of Perfection and *The Life of St Francis* by

FR ERIC DOYLE, O.F.M., S.T.D.

DENT: LONDON

EVERYMAN'S LIBRARY

DUTTON: NEW YORK

Printed in Great Britain by
Biddles Ltd, Guildford, Surrey
and bound at the
Aldine Press · Letchworth · Herts
for
J. M. DENT & SONS LTD
Aldine House · Albemarle Street · London
This edition was first published in
Everyman's Library in 1910
Last reprinted 1975

Published in the U.S.A. by arrangement
with J. M. Dent & Sons Ltd

No. 485 Hardback ISBN 0 460 00485 9

INTRODUCTION

The Little Flowers

AUTHORSHIP. Luke Wadding, the Irish Franciscan historian of the seventeenth century, believed that the author of the *Fioretti* was a certain Friar Ugolino da Santa Maria in Monte, in the Marches of Ancona. He also claimed that the title of the original work in Latin was *Floretum.* No certain evidence for this Latin work has come to light; but in 1902 M. Paul Sabatier published another Latin work entitled *Actus Beati Francisci et Sociorum eius*, and this was followed by Dr A. G. Little's text which now bears his name. This Latin document containing stories about St Francis and his followers had seventy-six chapters, of which fifty-two or fifty-three reappear in an abbreviated guise in the Italian *Fioretti*. Today, therefore, the common opnioin is that the *Fioretti* are derived, with modifications, from the *Actus Beati Francisci* and not from some hitherto undiscovered Latin *Floretum.*

In its earliest form the *Fioretti* contained only two parts. There were fifty-three chapters, together with Five Considerations on the glorious Stigmata of St Francis. These Considerations were, in fact, adaptations and additions borrowed from other sources. To these, in later editions, other translations from Latin works have been joined, such as 'The Life of Brother Juniper' and 'The Life of Brother Giles'. These two lives were based, with modifications, on *The Chronicle of the Twenty-four Generals*, completed in 1373, but incorporating material derived ultimately from Bro. Leo himself. It should, however, be understood that these additions are found in a Tuscan manuscript of the late fifteenth century, but that neither in their authorship, nor origin, nor translator, have they anything in common with the *Fioretti*.

Wadding seems to have been on safer ground in ascribing the authorship of the *Fioretti* to Ugolino da Santa Maria. His name occurs three times in the *Actus*. In the story of the Stigmata as told by Bro. Leo we read: 'This history, Fra Giacamo da Massa had from the mouth of Fra Leone, and Fra Ugolino had from the mouth of the said Fra

Giacamo and I wrote from the mouth of Fra Ugolino, a man in all respects worthy of faith' (*Actus*, ed. Sabatier, IX). Furthermore in the tale of Bro. Simon's unfranciscan asperity in dealing with the crows which disturbed his prayers, we find these words: 'And I, Brother Ugolino, stayed there three years, and saw with certainty that the said miracle was known both to laymen and Friars of the whole custody.' Elsewhere the writer speaks of himself as an associate of Fra Giovanni della Verna (*Actus*, LI, LII, LIV, LVIII). There is every reason for supposing that Ugolino is the author of the *Actus*, but that he had a collaborator—the 'ego qui scripsi' friar—who received the account of the Stigmata from Ugolino. This Ugolino makes it clear that he depends for much of his material on the oral traditions of James de Massa, who was a personal friend of people like Bros. Leo, Giles, and Masseo and Clare of Assisi. We may sum up then by saying that the *Actus-Fioretti* is largely the product of oral tradition handed down in the first instance by the intimate friends of St Francis himself to their immediate disciples, such as John of La Verna. This in turn reached the ears of Ugolino and was then committed to writing by him and some other collaborator. Unfortunately nothing more is known of Ugolino with any certainty. As for the translator of the *Actus* into the Italian of the *Fioretti*, internal evidence of style and language makes it plausible to believe that he must have been a friar from Tuscany living in the second half of the fourteenth century.

It has often been remarked that the stories of the *Fioretti* are divided into two main groups. In the first group (Chapters I–XXXVIII), the stories centre upon St Francis himself and his companions. In the second, (Chapters XLII–LII), the interest shifts to friars of a later date, living in the Marches of Ancona. These were contemporaries of the author of the original *Actus*. Sandwiched between these two groups is a literary intermezzo dealing with the lives of St Antony of Padua (Chapters XXXIX–XL) and Bro. Simon of Assisi (Chapter XLI). There is a change of tone and colour in the second group, which extol the virtues of the friars in the Province of Ancona. 'The Province of Ancona was of old, even as the sky with stars, adorned with holy and exemplary friars, who, like the luminaries of heaven, have illumined and adorned the Order of St Francis and the world with examples and with teaching' (Chapter XLII). Some like Bro. Pacificus belong to the early days of the Franciscan adventure, while others such as Conrad of Offida and John of La Verna are contemporaries of Ugolino himself. There can indeed be no question of their holiness. They are pugnacious upholders of poverty, they are lovers of solitude, men of great austerity, but for the most part the geniality, the childlike exuberance and sheer poetry of the earliest companions is less pronounced. They are obviously great and holy Franciscans, but the freshness, the vivacity, the intense individuality of the early stories have given place to men of ecstasies and contemplation. This concentration on a purely contemplative life was in fact one of two seemingly contradictory tendencies in St Francis himself—for his great desire for solitude and contemplation struggled with his equally great desire to preach the Gospel by word and example. In answer to St Clare's prayer this dilemma was solved once and for all, at least in principle, and while remaining one of the world's great mystics, he devoted himself untiringly to the external apostolate both in Italy and abroad. Though the dilemma was solved in principle, these divergent tendencies have always remained in the Order and become involved with questions of poverty in matters of buildings, libraries and other things necessary to a share in every sphere of the Church's life. They have, historically speaking, led to all kinds of factions and reforms in the course of time. But Padre Gemelli reminds us there is no need to take a purely pessimistic view of these upheavals and conflicting tendencies. 'It has been like the internal growth of tissues,' he says; 'cells become ripe, separate, and die. Something dies and something changes, but death is only apparent and the change momentary, for the cells renew themselves, recompense themselves once more to form the body to which they belong, in which they were born and live. United by this common bond of love for God and all His creatures, Franciscan idealism has developed throughout the centuries along lines of piety, thought and action.'

HISTORICITY. One question still remains to be answered: Have these wonderful stories of the *Fioretti* any authentic historical value? Professor Gardiner believes that in spite of embellishments and legendary elaborations there is much of genuine historical value in the stories of the first group, for Ugolino had before him not only written sources but also reliable and primitive oral tradition coming straight from the saint's first followers. In cases of doubt, e.g. in the author's extremely biased comments on Bro. Elias and St Bonaventure, we can counter-check their historical value by comparison with other historical sources of the saint's life, particularly with those of Celano and St Bonaventure. Some will prefer to give a purely symbolical meaning to the conversion of Bro. Wolf of Gubbio, but there is no need to jettison other stories of St Francis' power over birds and beasts. St Bonaventure has a whole chapter of such episodes (*Legenda Maior*, Chapter VIII) and his preaching to the birds goes back to Bro. Masseo himself, and an English writer, Roger of Wendover, could mention it as early as 1236.

SCOPE AND SPIRIT. 'In this book are contained certain Little Flowers—to wit, miracles and pious examples of the glorious servant of Christ, St Francis, and of some of his holy companions: to the glory and praise of Jesus Christ. Amen.' This introduction to the first chapter of the *Fioretti* shows the scope and spirit of the book. Whatever accretions or legendary material have crept in here and there to heighten the colours of St Francis' portrait, they are undoubtedly in keeping with the total impression which St Francis made upon the world of his day. The special challenge of St Francis is that we have a saint whose whole life was a poem, and it is the genius of the *Fioretti* to have met that challenge so simply and so successfully. Without blunting or smudging the outline of his natural gifts, we see the power of God's grace not merely bestowing holiness of mind and heart—that is common to all saints—but bestowing the sheer beauty of holiness, so that our love of the saint is fused with our love of the man. In its pages he charms us by his grace, his kindness, his poetic insight and the limpid simplicity and fervour of his love for Christ. We see his passionate love of poverty and the struggles of his early followers to keep that ideal untarnished. We know from other sources that Francis preached to the cardinals of the Roman Curia. It is the *Fioretti* which gives the unforgettable picture of him preaching to the birds. 'Beware my little sisters of the sin of ingratitude, and study always to give praise to God. As he said these words, all the birds began to open their beaks, to stretch their necks, to spread their wings and reverently bow their heads to the ground, endeavouring by their motions and by their songs to manifest their joy to St Francis. And the saint rejoiced with them' (Chapter XVI). All created things were love-tokens, sacramental things scattered through the world from the hand of his heavenly Father. But a man who nursed lepers knew the reality of pain and suffering, and a man who went through the mystic suffering of La Verna was no pretty sentimental pantheist.

So the stories about such a saint and his companions breathe the subtle perfume of wild flowers. They conjure up memories of the Umbrian valley with its rocky hermitages, its twisting streets on the hillside, its poplar trees, its sun-bathed vineyards, and La Verna rising up out of the morning mist. We catch a glimpse of San Damiano with its memories of St Clare and her pure love of St Francis. A procession of his followers moves before our eyes—sheltering in some shed or poor little abandoned church—men who seemed to have absorbed from Francis some special Franciscan gift of soul. There is Bro. Masseo, handsome, stately and eloquent; Bro. Bernard of Quintavalle, first follower, unswervingly faithful to his ideals of highest poverty; Bro. Leo, 'little lamb of God', sharer of the saint's most intimate secrets, trudging with him through the snow, and listening with, I am sure, a sinking heart, to Francis discoursing on perfect joy! There is Bro. Angelo, the knight of Rieti, loved by Francis for his gentle courtesy; Bro. Giles, mystical and shrewd enough to deflate pomposity and pride with a touch of innocent malice; Bro. Pacificus, who had been a great poet and musician before joining the Order; and Brother Juniper, the favourite of children everywhere.

1963. HUGH McKAY, O.F.M.

[1] *Analekten zur Geschichte des Franciscus von Assisi*, 1904.

The Mirror of Perfection

When M. Paul Sabatier published the *Speculum Perfectionis* (the Latin title of this work) in 1898, he was convinced that he had discovered the most ancient Franciscan source, composed, so he believed, by Brother Leo, one of St Francis's most intimate companions, about a year or so after the Saint's death in 1226. Had Sabatier's dating been correct, there would have been little room for doubt about the Saint's intentions for his Order. It was soon discovered, however, that his conclusions were based on a scribal error and that *The Mirror of Perfection* did not belong to the thirteenth century at all, but was a compilation dating from about 1318. While this date puts the work almost a century after the death of the Saint, it in no way detracts from its importance as a most precious source for an understanding of the mind of St Francis.

At the General Chapter of the Order held in Genoa in 1244 an invitation was issued to the friars who had known St Francis to put down all they could recall about his life and the early days of the Order. This proved to be one of the most fruitful decisions made by the Order in the thirteenth century. Among those who responded with their memories and reminiscences of the Saint were Brothers Leo, Angelo and Ruffino, the Saint's closest companions during his life. This material formed the basis of Celano's *Second Life* which appeared in the sad and troubled years of the late 1240s, when divisions had already crystallized on the interpretation of St Francis's intentions. One side favoured a more 'lax' view of observance; the other deplored the mitigations of the *Rule*, longed for a return to the simplicity of earlier days and placed the *Testament* of St Francis above any declaration on the *Rule*. Celano's *Second Life* shows the author to have been firmly among the latter.

These materials used by Celano were also the sources of *The Mirror of Perfection*. The attitude and intention of the work are made clear from the very first chapter where the Lord's words to Francis are strongly emphasized: 'I will that the Rule should thus be observed to the letter, without a gloss, without a gloss' (*Mirror of Perfection*, I, 1).

The Mirror of Perfection, then, belongs to that literature which looked back with nostalgia to the period of glorious freedom and simplicity when the Order was in its infancy.

It was a life of striving for Gospel perfection and holiness, largely unstructured and unfettered, in which the friars as poor, itinerant preachers moved from city to city in pairs, proclaiming the love and peace of God the Great King. This needed no fine learning, no privilege, no great and imposing buildings, but only a generous heart and a burning love of the Crucified Saviour. Perhaps the vision was too idyllic to last in any circumstances; that it was the mind of St Francis *The Mirror of Perfection* leaves us in no doubt at all.

St Bonaventure's Life of St Francis

St Bonaventure, the author of the *Legenda Maior* (the Latin title of this work), was born about 1217 at Bagnorea, a small city near Orvieto in Italy. Although he never met St Francis, he came under his influence at a very early age, for he tells us himself that he was cured from a fatal illness in his childhood through the Saint's intercession. After his early studies he went to Paris where he entered the Franciscan Order in 1243. While pursuing his academic career he was elected Minister General of the Franciscan Order in 1257, the eighth from St Francis to hold that office. He was made Cardinal and consecrated Bishop of Albano in 1273, having refused earlier, it is recorded, to accept the Archbishopric of York. He died at the Council of Lyons in July 1274.

St Bonaventure was one of the great scholastics of the thirteenth century and he ranks with St Thomas Aquinas as one of the most brilliant minds of the entire Middle Ages.

At the General Chapter he held at Narbonne in 1260 he was requested to write a life of St Francis in order to bring to an end the bitter controversies among the friars about the Saint's ideals and intentions. He wrote the *Legenda Maior* and the *Legenda Minor* (a shorter version for liturgical use) in 1261 and these were approved later at the General Chapter at Pisa in 1263. At a subsequent Chapter held at Paris in 1266 it was decreed that all other *Lives* were to be destroyed. Thus it was hoped that by making St Bonaventure's *Life of St Francis* the standard and official version, the various factions in the Order, especially the Spirituals, would be deprived of ammunition in the battle about St Francis. For one reason or another the decree was evidently disobeyed. Had it been obeyed we should have lost for ever Celano's two *Lives* and a great deal more material besides, and our knowledge of the Poverello of Assisi would have been infinitely the poorer.

St Bonaventure's *Life of St Francis* is a most beautifully written account of the Saint's spiritual progress from the first moment of his conversion. It gives a picture of St Francis by an author who evidently loved and revered him. But it is also a book with a motive. St Bonaventure omits controversial matters and his intention is clearly to pacify and satisfy all parties concerned. One hates to say he compromised. He was dealing with a delicate, not to say explosive, situation. Though his efforts were for a time successful, in the end they failed as the subsequent sad history of the Order bears witness. Perhaps the chief value of the book is the comfort and consolation it gives to scholars that, being the work of a very learned friar who became himself a saint, they may after all be true and real Franciscans.

1973. ERIC DOYLE, O.F.M.

BIBLIOGRAPHICAL NOTE

THE writings of St Francis himself have been published in a critical edition by the Franciscans of Quaracchi, 1904. There are English translations by a Religious of the Order, 1882 (2nd edition, 1890), and by Fr Paschal Robinson, 1906.

Early sources for the life of the saint and of his companions are as follows: Thomas of Celano, first life, 1228–9; second life, 1244–7; St Bonaventure, *Legenda Maior* (printed as 'The Life of St Francis' in the present volume), 1260–3; *Speculum Perfectionis* ('The Mirror of Perfection'), *c.* 1318; ed. P. Sabatier, 1898; definitive edition by A. G. Little, 1902; *Legenda Trium Sociorum* (Bros. Leo, Rufino and Angelo), 1244–7; translated by Miss E. Gurney Salter (Temple Classics), 1902; *Fioretti* ('Little Flowers'; *see* Introduction to the present volume). *See also* H. Boehmer, *Analekten zur Geschichte des Franciscus von Assisi*, 1904; W. Goetz, *Die Quellen zur Geschichte Hl. Franciscus von Assisi*, 1904; B. Bughetti, 'Alcune Idee Fondamentali sui Fioretti', in *Archivum Franciscanum Historicum*, XIII, 1920; A. Goffin: *I Fioretti: les petites fleurs de la vie du petit pauvre de Jésus-Christ, Saint François d'Assise, traduction, introduction et notes*, 1927; J. R. H. Moorman, *Sources for the Life of St Francis*, 1940; A. Vicinelli, *Gli Scritti di San Francesco e 'I Fioretti'*, 1955; *The Writings of St Francis of Assisi*, translated by Benen Fahy, O.F.M., with introduction and notes by Placid Hermann, O.F.M., 1963.

The following modern biographies and other Franciscan studies are also of value: P. Sabatier, *Life of St Francis of Assisi* (translated by Louise Seymour Houghton), 1894; J. A. Jackman, *The Seraph of Assisi*, 1898; F. Vernet, *The Inner Life of St Francis*, 1900; Paschal Robinson, *The Real St Francis of Assisi*, 1904; L. L. Dubois, *St Francis of Assisi, Social Reformer*, 1906; Paschal Robinson, *A Short Introduction to Franciscan Literature*, 1907; C. Goff, *Assisi of St Francis, and Influence of the Franciscan Legend on Italian Art*, etc., 1908; Fr Cuthbert, O.F.M., *Life of St Francis*, 1912 (3rd edition, 1921), and *Romanticism of St Francis*, 1915 (2nd edition, 1924); A. G. Little, *A Guide to Franciscan Studies*, 1920; G. K. Chesterton, *St Francis of Assisi*, 1923; A. K. Campbell, *In Praise of St Francis*, 1934; Agostino Gemelli, O.F.M., *The Franciscan Message to the World* (translated and adapted by H. L. Hughes), 1934; Etienne Gilson, *The Philosophy of St Bonaventure* (translated by Illtyd Trethowan and F. J. Sheed), 1940; A. G. Little, *Franciscan Papers, Lists and Documents*, 1943; J. R. H. Moorman, *Early Franciscan Art and Literature*, 1943; S. F. Wicks, *The Friends of St Francis*, 1952; A. Terzi, *S. Francesco d'Assisi a Roma*, 1956; L. Sherley-Price, *Lent with St Francis*, 1958, and *St Francis od Assisi*, 1959; M. D. Lambert, *Franciscan Poverty—The Doctrine of the Absolute Poverty of Christ and the Apostles in the Franciscan Order, 1210–1323*, 1961; Placid Hermann, O.F.M., *The Way of St Francis*, Chicago, 1964; J. Guy Bougerol, O.F.M., *Introduction to the Works of St Bonaventure* (translated by J. de Vinck), New Jersey, 1964; Ephrem Longpré, O.F.M., *François d'Assise et son expérience spirituelle*, Paris, 1966; John Moorman, *A History of the Franciscan Order from its Origins to the Year 1517*, Oxford, 1968; *Scripta Leonis, Rufini et Angeli Sociorum S. Francisci* (edited and translated by Rosalind B. Brooke), Oxford, 1970; John Holland Smith, *Francis of Assisi*, 1972.

THE LITTLE FLOWERS OF ST. FRANCIS

CHAPTER I

IN THE NAME OF OUR LORD JESUS CHRIST, THE CRUCIFIED, AND OF HIS MOTHER THE VIRGIN MARY. IN THIS BOOK ARE CONTAINED CERTAIN LITTLE FLOWERS, MIRACLES, AND DEVOUT EXAMPLES OF CHRIST'S POOR LITTLE ONE, ST. FRANCIS, AND OF SOME OF HIS COMPANIONS; TO THE PRAISE OF JESUS CHRIST. AMEN

IT is first to be considered that the glorious St. Francis in all the acts of his life was conformable to Christ the Blessed. And that even as Christ, at the beginning of His mission, chose twelve Apostles who were to despise all worldly things and follow Him in poverty and in the other virtues, so St. Francis in the beginning chose for the foundation of his Order twelve companions who were possessed of naught save direst poverty. And even as one of the twelve Apostles of Christ, being reproved by God, went and hanged himself by the neck, so one of the twelve companions of St. Francis, whose name was Friar [1] John della Cappella, became a renegade and at last hanged himself by the neck. Now these things are a great warning to the elect, and matter for humility and fear when they consider that none is certain of persevering to the end in God's grace. And even as those holy Apostles were, above all, wondrous in their holiness and humility and filled with the Holy Ghost, so those most holy companions of St. Francis were men of such saintliness that, since the days of the Apostles, the world hath never beheld men so wondrously holy. For one among them was rapt, like St. Paul, up to the third heaven, and he was Friar Giles; another, to wit, Friar Philip, was touched on the lips by an angel with a coal of fire, even as the prophet Isaiah was; another, to wit, Friar Silvester, spake with God as one friend speaketh with another, after the

[1] The Italian text distinguishes between *frate*—"friar" or "brother" in its religious sense—and *fratello*—"brother" in its ordinary sense.

manner of Moses; another by the purity of his mind soared as far as the light of the Divine Wisdom, even as did the Eagle, that is to say, John the Evangelist, and he was Friar Bernard, humblest of men, who was wont to expound the Holy Scriptures most profoundly; yet another was sanctified by God and canonised in heaven while yet he lived in the world, and he was Friar Rufus, a nobleman of Assisi. And thus were all distinguished by singular marks of holiness, as will be made clear hereafter.

CHAPTER II

OF FRIAR BERNARD OF QUINTAVALLE, THE FIRST COMPANION OF ST. FRANCIS

THE first companion of St. Francis was Friar Bernard of Assisi, that was converted after this manner: St. Francis, while yet in the secular habit, albeit he had renounced the world, was wont to go about in meanest guise and so mortified by penance that by many he was held to be a fool, and was mocked and hunted as a madman and pelted with stones and filthy mire both by his kinsfolk and by strangers; but he, even as one deaf and dumb, went his way enduring every insult and injury patiently. Now Bernard of Assisi, who was one of the noblest and richest and wisest of that city, began to consider wisely concerning St. Francis and his exceeding contempt of this world and his long-suffering under injury; and that, albeit for two years he had been thus hated and despised by all men, yet did he ever seem more steadfast. And he began to ponder these things and to say within himself, "Of a surety this friar hath great grace from God." And he invited St. Francis to sup and lodge with him; and St. Francis accepted and supped and tarried the night. And then Bernard determined in his heart to contemplate his holiness: wherefore he had a bed made ready for him in his own chamber wherein by night a lamp ever burned. And St. Francis, to conceal his holiness, flung himself on his bed immediately he entered his chamber and feigned to sleep: and Bernard likewise, after a little while, lay down in his bed and began to snore loudly, as one wrapped in deepest slumber. Wherefore St. Francis, verily believing that Bernard slept, arose, in the stillness of the night, from his bed and knelt down to pray; lifting his eyes and hands to heaven he cried with great devotion and fervour, "My God, my God!" And so saying and weeping bitter tears, he prayed until morning, ever repeating, "My God, my God!" and naught else. And St. Francis said this, while contemplating and marvelling at the excellency of the Divine Majesty that had deigned to stoop down to this perishing world, and, through His poor little one, St. Francis, had resolved to bring healing salvation to his soul and to others. And therefore, illumined by the Holy Ghost or by the spirit of prophecy, he foresaw the great things that God was to work through him and his Order. And considering his own insufficiency and little worth he called on God Almighty and prayed that of His compassion He would supply, aid, and complete that which he of his own frailty could not achieve. Now Bernard, when he beheld these most devout acts of St. Francis by the light of the lamp, and had reverently considered the words he uttered, was moved and inspired by the Holy Ghost to change his manner of life; wherefore when morning was come he called St. Francis to him and spake thus, "Friar Francis, I have fully determined in my heart to forsake the world and obey thee in all things thou commandest me." When St. Francis heard this he rejoiced in spirit and said, "Bernard, this that you [1] tell is a work so great and so difficult that it behoves us to seek counsel of our Lord Jesus Christ and pray that it may please Him to reveal His will concerning this thing, and teach us how we may put it into execution. Therefore we will go together to the bishop's house, where a good priest dwells, and mass shall be said, and then we will remain in prayer until tierce, beseeching God that He will point out to us in three openings of the mass book the way it pleaseth Him we should choose." Bernard answered that this pleased him much. Whereupon they set forth and went to the bishop's house, and after they had heard mass and had remained in prayer until tierce, the priest, at the entreaty of St. Francis, took the book, and having made the sign of holy cross, opened it thrice in the name of our Lord Jesus Christ. And at the first opening he happened on those words that Christ in the gospel spake to the young man who asked concerning the perfect way, "If thou wilt be perfect, go and sell that thou hast and give to the poor and follow Me." In the second opening occurred those words that Christ spake to the Apostles when He sent them to preach, "Take nothing for your journey, neither staves nor

[1] *Voi* (you) instead of the more familiar *tu* (thou). The more reverent, *voi*, is used by Dante only in addressing spirits of great dignity, *e.g.* Brunetto Latino, Cacciaguida, and a very few others.

scrip, neither shoes nor money," desiring by this to teach them that all trust for their livelihood should be placed in God, and all their mind intent on preaching the holy gospel. In the third opening were found those words which Christ spake, "If any man will come after Me, let him take up his cross and follow Me." Then said St. Francis to Bernard, "Behold the counsel that Christ giveth us. Go, therefore, do faithfully what thou hast heard, and blessed be the name of our Lord Jesus Christ, who hath deigned to reveal to us the life evangelical." Hearing this, Bernard departed and sold all he had (for he was very rich), and with great joy distributed all to widows and orphans, to prisoners and hospitals and pilgrims; and in all these things St. Francis helped him faithfully and carefully. And one whose name was Silvester, when he saw that St. Francis gave and caused to be given so much money to the poor, was constrained by avarice, and said to St. Francis, "Thou didst not pay me fully for the stones thou boughtest of me to repair the church, and therefore now thou hast money, pay me." Then St. Francis, marvelling at his avarice, and as a true follower of the gospel desiring not to contend with him, thrust his hands in Bernard's bosom, and with hands full of money placed them in Silvester's bosom, saying, that if he would have more, more should be given him. And Silvester, satisfied with this, departed and returned home, but in the evening, pondering on what he had done that day and on the fervour of Bernard and the holiness of St. Francis, he reproved himself for his avarice. And that night following and two other nights he had from God this vision: he beheld a cross of gold issue from the mouth of St. Francis, the top whereof touched heaven, and the arms stretched from the east as far as the west. Because of this vision he gave up all he had for love of God, and became a friar minor, and such holiness and grace had he in the Order that he spake with God even as one friend with another, according as St. Francis proved and as will be related hereafter. Bernard likewise was so filled with God's grace that in contemplation he was often taken up to God. And St. Francis was wont to say of him that he was worthy of all reverence and had founded this Order, for he was the first who had forsaken the world, holding back nothing, but giving all to Christ's poor, and the first who began his evangelic poverty by offering himself naked to the arms of the Crucified, to whom be all praise and glory world without end. Amen.

CHAPTER III

HOW ST. FRANCIS, BY REASON OF AN EVIL THOUGHT HE CHERISHED AGAINST FRIAR BERNARD, COMMANDED THE SAID FRIAR THAT HE SHOULD TREAD THRICE ON HIS NECK AND MOUTH

ST. FRANCIS, the most devout servant of the Crucified, had grown almost blind by the rigour of his penance and incessant weeping, so that he saw but ill; and once on a time he departed from the place where he was, and went to a place where Friar Bernard was in order to speak with him of divine things. Being arrived there, he found that Friar Bernard was at prayer in the wood, wholly lifted up and united with God. Then St. Francis went forth into the wood and called him. "Come," said he, "and speak with this blind man." And Friar Bernard answered him not a word; for being a man great in contemplation, his soul was lifted up and raised to God. And forasmuch as Friar Bernard was possessed of singular grace in discoursing of God, even as St. Francis had proved many times, great was his desire to speak with him. After some while he called him a second and a third time in that same wise, and no time did Friar Bernard hear him: therefore he neither answered nor came to him; whereat St. Francis departed somewhat disconsolate, marvelling within himself and grieving that Friar Bernard, being called thrice, had not come to him. St. Francis turned away with these thoughts in his mind, and when he was gone some little distance he said to his companion, "Tarry for me here." And he went aside hard by into a solitary place and prostrated himself in prayer, beseeching God to reveal to him why Friar Bernard answered him not; and remaining thus in prayer there came to him a voice from God, saying, "O poor little one, wherefore art thou troubled? Ought a man to forsake God for His creature? When thou didst call, Friar Bernard was united with Me, and therefore could neither come to thee nor answer thee. Marvel thou not if he could not respond, for he was so lifted out of himself that of thy words he heard none." St. Francis, having heard these words from God, straightway returned with great haste towards Friar Bernard, in order to accuse himself humbly before him of the evil thoughts he had nursed concerning him. And Friar Bernard, beholding him come towards him, drew nigh and cast himself at his feet; and then St. Francis made him rise up, and with great humility related to him the thoughts he had had and the tribulation he had suffered concerning him, and how that God had answered his prayer. And thus he concluded, "I command thee by holy obedience that thou do whatsoever I command thee." Friar Bernard, fearing lest St. Francis might lay on him some excess of penance, as he was wont to do, desired with all sincerity to escape such obedience, and answered him thus, "I am ready to do your obedience if you will promise to do what I shall command you." And St. Francis gave him the promise. Then said Friar Bernard, "Say on, father; what would you that I do?" And St. Francis answered him, saying, "I command thee by holy obedience that, in order to punish the arrogance and rashness of my heart, thou shalt now, even as I lay me supine on the ground, set one foot on my neck and the other on my mouth, and so pass thrice from one side to the other, reviling and crying shame on me; and especially shalt thou say, 'Lie there, churl, son of Peter Bernadone! whence cometh such pride to thee, thou that art so vile a creature?'" Friar Bernard hearing this, albeit it was very hard to do, performed, in holy obedience, what St. Francis had commanded him, with all the gentleness he could. This done, St. Francis said, "Now command thou me what thou wouldest I should do, for I have promised thee holy obedience." Then said Friar Bernard, "I command thee by holy obedience, that every time we are together thou rebuke and correct me harshly for all my faults." Whereupon St. Francis marvelled greatly, for Friar Bernard was of such exceeding sanctity that he held him in great reverence and in no wise worthy of reproof. And thenceforth St. Francis was careful to avoid being much with him, because of the said obedience, lest it befell that he utter one word of reproof against him, that he knew to be of such great holiness. But when he desired to see him, or indeed to hear him speak of God, he made haste to leave him and depart from him, and a goodly thing it was to behold, what great charity and reverence and humility St. Francis, the father, used towards Bernard, his first-born son, when he spake with him. To the praise and glory of Christ Jesus and of the poor little Francis. Amen.

CHAPTER IV

HOW THE ANGEL OF GOD PUT A QUESTION TO FRIAR ELIAS, WARDEN OF THE FRIARY[1] IN THE VALE OF SPOLETO, AND BECAUSE FRIAR ELIAS ANSWERED HIM HAUGHTILY, DEPARTED AND WENT ALONG THE WAY TO ST. JAMES'S, WHERE HE FOUND FRIAR BERNARD AND TOLD HIM THE STORY

At the first beginning of the Order, when there were but few friars and their friaries were not yet established, St. Francis repaired for his devotions to St. James's of Compostella in Galicia, and took a few friars with him, one of whom was Friar Bernard. And as they journeyed thus together, he found a poor sick man in a village by the way. Filled with compassion, he said to Friar Bernard, "Son, I desire that thou remain here to tend this sick man;" and Friar Bernard humbly kneeling and bowing his head, reverently received the holy father's obedience and remained in that place: and St. Francis and the other companions went their way to St. James's. Arrived there, they passed the night in prayer in the church of St. James, where it was revealed to St. Francis that he was to establish many friaries throughout the world; for his Order was to spread and grow into a great multitude of friars: whereat, according to this revelation, St. Francis began to establish friaries in those lands. And as St. Francis was returning by the way he came, he found Friar Bernard, and the sick man with whom he had left him healed perfectly; whereupon St. Francis gave Friar Bernard leave to go the following year to St. James's. And St. Francis returned to the vale of Spoleto, and he and Friar Masseo and Friar Elias and others abode in a wilderness; and each took heed not to vex or disturb St. Francis in his prayers, because of the great reverence they bore him, and because they knew that God revealed great things to him in his prayers. It fell out one day, while St. Francis was in the wood at prayer, that a fair youth, apparelled as for a journey, came to the door of the friary and knocked so impatiently and loudly and for so long a time that the friars marvelled much at so unwonted a knocking. Friar Masseo went and opened the door, and said to the youth, "Whence comest thou, my son; it seemeth thou

[1] *Luogo, luogo dei frati:* literally, "place of the friars." I have rendered this "friary" as well as the term *convento*, used by the Franciscans when in later times their poor hovels and caves were exchanged for edifices of brick and stone.

hast never been here before, so strangely hast thou knocked." The youth answered, "And how then ought one to knock?" Friar Masseo said, "Knock three times, one after the other, slowly; then tarry so long as the friar may say a paternoster and come to thee: and if in this space of time he come not, knock once again." The youth answered, "I am in great haste, and therefore I knock thus loudly. I have to go a journey, and am come here to speak with Friar Francis; but he is now in the wood in contemplation, and I would not disturb him; but go and send Friar Elias to me, for I would ask him a question, and he is very wise." Friar Masseo goes and bids Friar Elias haste to that youth; and he takes offence and will not go. Whereat Friar Masseo knows not what to do, nor what answer to make to that youth; for if he said, "Friar Elias cannot come," he lied; if he said he was in evil humour, he feared to set a bad example. And while Friar Masseo was thus laggard in returning, the youth knocked yet again, even as before. Friar Masseo came back to the door and said to the youth, "Thou hast not observed my instructions in knocking." The youth answered, "Friar Elias will not come to me; but go thou and say to Friar Francis that I am come to speak with him; but since I would not disturb him in his prayers, bid him send Friar Elias to me." And then Friar Masseo went to St. Francis, that was praying in the wood with his face lifted up to heaven, and gave him the youth's message and Friar Elias's reply. And that youth was an angel of God in human form. Then St. Francis, changing neither his position nor lowering his face, said to Friar Masseo, "Depart and bid Friar Elias by obedience go to that youth." Now Friar Elias, when he heard the command of St. Francis, went in great fury to the door and flung it open with great violence and noise, saying to the youth, "What wouldst thou?" The youth answered, "Beware, friar, lest thou be angry as thou seemest, for anger hindereth much the soul and cloudeth the perception of truth." Friar Elias said, "Tell me, what wouldst thou of me?" The youth answered, "I ask thee if it be lawful for observers of the holy gospel to eat whatsoever is placed before them, according as Christ said to His disciples; and I likewise ask thee whether it be lawful for any man to command things contrary to evangelical liberty." Friar Elias answered proudly, "This know I well, but I will not answer thee: go thy ways." Said the youth, "I could answer this question better than thou." Then Friar Elias slammed the door in a great rage and departed. And then he began to ponder the said question and to doubt within himself, and he could not solve it; for he was vicar of the Order, and had ordered and made a rule outside the gospel and outside the Rule of St. Francis, to wit, that no friar of the Order should eat flesh: therefore the said question was aimed against him. Whereupon, unable to get clear with himself, he began to consider the youth's modesty, and that he had told him he could answer the question better than he, and Friar Elias returned to the door and opened it, to ask the youth concerning the aforesaid question. But he had already departed, for the pride of Friar Elias made him unworthy to speak with angels. This done, St. Francis, to whom all had been revealed by God, returned from the wood, and loudly and severely reproved Friar Elias, saying, "Thou dost ill, proud friar, that chasest away the holy angels from us that come to teach us. I tell thee, much do I fear lest thy pride make thee end thy days outside this Order.". And so it befell thereafter even as St. Francis had said, for he died outside the Order. On that same day, at the very hour he departed, the angel appeared in that same form to Friar Bernard, who was walking along the bank of a great river, on his way back from St. James's, and gave him salutation in his own tongue, saying, "Hail, good friar, the peace of God be with thee!" And Friar Bernard marvelled greatly, and considering the comeliness of the youth and the salutation of peace in the mother tongue and his glad countenance, questioned him thus: "Whence comest thou, good youth?" The angel answered, "I come from such a place, where St. Francis dwells, and I went to speak with him, but could not, for he was in the wood contemplating divine things, and I would not disturb him. And in that same house dwell Friar Masseo and Friar Giles and Friar Elias; and Friar Masseo taught me how to knock at the door after the manner of a friar, but Friar Elias, because he would not answer a question I propounded to him, repented and desired thereafter to hear and see me; and he could not." Having spoken these words the angel said to Friar Bernard, "Wherefore dost thou not pass over yonder?" Friar Bernard answered, "Because I dread danger from the depth of the water I see." Said the angel, "Let us pass over together; fear not:" and he takes his hand and in the twinkling of an eye places him on the other side of the river. Then Friar Bernard knew that he was the angel of God, and with great reverence and joy said in a loud voice, "O blessed angel of God, tell me, what is thy name?" The angel answered, "Wherefore askest thou my name, that is marvellous?" This said, the angel vanished, and left Friar Bernard much consoled, so much that he went all that journey with great joyfulness; and he marked the day and the hour of the angel's appearance. And reaching the friary, where St. Francis was with the aforesaid companions, he related to them all things in the order of their happening; and they knew of a surety that that same angel had appeared to them and to him on that very day and at that very hour.

CHAPTER V

HOW THE HOLY FRIAR BERNARD OF ASSISI WAS SENT BY ST. FRANCIS TO BOLOGNA, AND THERE ESTABLISHED A FRIARY

Forasmuch as St. Francis and his companions were called and chosen by God to bear the cross of Christ in their hearts and in their works, and to preach it with their tongues, they seemed and truly were, men crucified, so far as regarded their dress, the austerity of their lives, their acts, and their deeds; and therefore they desired rather to endure shame and reproach for love of Christ than worldly honour, or reverence, or praise from men. Yea, they rejoiced in contumely, and were afflicted by honour; they went about the world as pilgrims and strangers, bearing naught with them save Christ crucified. And because they were true branches of the true vine, which is Christ, they brought forth great and good fruit in the souls they won to God. It came to pass in the beginning of the Order that St. Francis sent Friar Bernard to Bologna, that he might bring forth fruit to God there, according to the grace God had given him. And Friar Bernard, having made the sign of holy cross, departed in holy obedience and came to Bologna. And when the children beheld him in a ragged and mean habit they mocked him and reviled him loudly as were he a fool. And Friar Bernard suffered all things patiently and joyfully for the love of Christ. Aye, and in order that he might be the more derided he set himself openly in the market-place of the city; and as he sat there many children and men gathered around him, and one plucked at his cowl from behind, and another in front; one cast dust at him, and another stones; one pushed him on this side, and another on that; but Friar Bernard, neither uttering complaint nor changing his position, abode there patient and glad: and for many days he returned to that same place, solely to endure the like things. And since patience is a work of perfection and proof of virtue, a wise doctor of laws, on beholding Friar Bernard's exceeding great constancy and virtue, and how he could not be provoked during many days by any hurt or insult, said within himself, "It is impossible but that this must be a holy man." And drawing nigh to him, spake to him thus, "Who art thou, and wherefore art thou come hither?" And for answer Friar Bernard put his hand in his bosom and drew forth the Rule of St. Francis and gave it him that he might read. And when he had read it and had considered its lofty perfection, he turned to the companions with greatest amazement and admiration, and said, "Verily this is the most exalted state of the religious life whereof I ever heard: therefore this man and his companions are the most saintly men in this world, and he who revileth him is the greatest of sinners; for he is worthy of highest honour since he is the true friend of God." Then said he to Friar Bernard, "If you would take a place wherein you might conveniently serve God, I fain would give it you for the salvation of my soul." Friar Bernard answered him, "Master, I believe this offer is an inspiration from our Lord Jesus Christ, and therefore willingly do I accept it for the honour of Christ." Then the said judge led Friar Bernard to his home with great love and joy: and he gave him the promised place, and furnished and completed it at his own cost: and thenceforth he became to him as a father, and was the diligent upholder of Friar Bernard and his companions. And Friar Bernard began to be so greatly honoured by all men, that any one who could touch or behold him held himself blessed. But he, as a true disciple of Christ and of the lowly Francis, fearing lest the honours of this world might hinder the peace and salvation of his soul, departed one day and returned to St. Francis, and spake to him thus, "The place has been taken in the city of Bologna; send friars thither to abide and maintain it, for I have no profit there; nay, I fear, by reason of the too great honour done to me, lest I lose more than I should gain." Then St. Francis, having heard all things in order that God had wrought there through Friar Bernard, gave thanks to God who thus began to spread abroad the poor little disciples of the cross: and then he sent some of his companions to Bologna and to Lombardy, who established many friaries in divers places.

CHAPTER VI

HOW ST. FRANCIS BLESSED THE HOLY FRIAR BERNARD AND APPOINTED HIM TO BE HIS VICAR WHEN HE SHOULD PASS FROM THIS LIFE

Friar Bernard was of such holiness that St. Francis bore him great reverence and ofttimes praised him. St. Francis being on a day devoutly at prayer, it was revealed to him of God that Friar Bernard, by divine permission, was to endure many and grievous assaults from devils, wherefore St. Francis, that had great compassion on the said Friar Bernard and loved him as a son, prayed many days in tears, commending him to Christ Jesus, and entreating God that victory over the devil might be vouchsafed to him. And one day while St. Francis was thus devoutly praying, God answered him, saying, "Francis, fear not; for all the temptations whereby Friar Bernard shall be assailed are permitted by God as an exercise of virtue and crown of merit; and at the last he shall gain the victory over all his enemies, for he is one of the ministers of the kingdom of heaven." At which answer St. Francis rejoiced greatly and gave thanks to God; and from that hour he bore greater love and reverence to Friar Bernard. And this he showed not only in his life, but also at his death, for when St. Francis came to die, after the manner of the holy patriarch Jacob, with his devout children standing around him, all sorrowing and weeping at the departure of so loving a father, he asked, "Where is my first-born? Come nigh to me, my son, that my soul may bless thee ere I die." Then Friar Bernard said secretly to Friar Elias, that was vicar of the Order, "Father, go to the right hand of the saint that he may bless thee." And Friar Elias drew nigh to his right hand, and St. Francis, that had lost his sight through excess of weeping, placed his right hand on Friar Elias's head, and said, "This is not the head of my first-born, Friar Bernard." Then Friar Bernard went to his left hand, and St. Francis moved his hands over in the form of a cross, and placed his right hand on Friar Bernard's head and his left on Friar Elias's head, and said to Friar Bernard, "God the Father and our Lord Jesus Christ bless thee with all spiritual and celestial blessings. Thou art the first-born, chosen in this holy Order to give evangelical example, and to follow Christ in evangelical poverty, for not only gavest thou thine own substance and didst distribute it wholly and freely to the poor for love of Christ, but thou didst offer thyself also to God in this Order, a sacrifice of sweetness. Blessed be thou therefore by our Lord Jesus Christ and by me, poor little one, His servant, with blessings everlasting, walking and standing, watching and sleeping, living and dying. Let him that blesseth thee be filled with blessings, and he who curseth thee go not unpunished. Be thou lord over thy brethren and let all the friars obey thy commands; whosoever thou wilt, let him be received into this Order; let no friar have lordship over thee, and be it lawful to thee to go and to abide wheresoever it may please thee." And after the death of St. Francis, the friars loved and revered Friar Bernard as a venerable father; and when he was nigh unto death, many friars came to him from divers parts of the earth, among whom was that angelic and divine Friar Giles; and he, beholding Friar Bernard, cried with great joy, "*Sursum corda*, Friar Bernard, *sursum corda!*" and Friar Bernard secretly bade a friar prepare for Friar Giles a place meet for contemplation; and this was done. Now Friar Bernard being come to the last hour of death, had himself raised up and spake to the friars that stood around him, saying, "Brethren, most dear, I will not say many words to you, but ye must consider that this religious state wherein I have lived, ye live; and such as I am now, ye shall be also, and this I know in my soul—that not for a thousand worlds such as this would I have renounced the service of our Lord Jesus Christ for that of any other lord, and I do now accuse me of all my offences, and confess my sins to Jesus my Saviour, and to you. I beseech you, dearest brothers mine, that ye love one another." And after these words and other good exhortations he lay back in his bed, and his countenance shone with exceeding great joy; whereat all the friars marvelled greatly; and in that joy his most holy soul departed from this present life, crowned with glory, to the blessed life of the angels.

CHAPTER VII

HOW ST. FRANCIS KEPT LENT ON AN ISLAND IN THE LAKE OF PERUGIA, WHERE HE FASTED FORTY DAYS AND FORTY NIGHTS, AND ATE NO MORE THAN HALF A LOAF

FORASMUCH as St. Francis, the true servant of Christ, was in certain things well-nigh another Christ given to the world for the salvation of souls, it was the will of God the Father that in many of his acts he should be conformable and like unto His Son Jesus Christ, even as he showed to us in the venerable company of the twelve companions and in the wondrous mystery of the sacred stigmas, and in the continuous fast of the holy Lent, which he kept in this wise. St. Francis was once lodging on carnival day in the house of one of his devout followers on the shores of the lake of Perugia, and was inspired by God to go and pass that Lent on an island in the lake; wherefore St. Francis prayed his disciple to carry him in his little bark to an island, whereon no man dwelt, and this on the night of Ash Wednesday, to the end that none should perceive it. And he by the great love and devotion he bore to St. Francis satisfied diligently his desire, and carried him to the said island, St. Francis taking with him naught save two small loaves. And when he had reached the island, and his friend was about to depart and return to his home, St. Francis prayed him earnestly to reveal to no man where he was nor to come for him before Holy Thursday, and so the friend departed and St. Francis remained alone. And finding no house wherein he could take shelter, he crept into a very dense thicket of thorn and other bushes fashioned after the manner of a lair or a little hut: and in this place he betook himself to prayer and to the contemplation of divine things. And there he abode the whole of Lent, eating and drinking naught save the half of one of those small loaves, even as his devout friend perceived when he returned for him on Holy Thursday: for of the loaves he found one whole and the other half eaten. And it was believed that St. Francis ate this through reverence for the fasting of Jesus Christ, who fasted forty days and forty nights without taking any bodily food; for with this half-loaf he cast the venom of vain-glory from him while following the example of Christ in the fast of forty days and forty nights. And God wrought many miracles thereafter in that same place where St. Francis had endured so marvellous an abstinence, because of his merits: wherefore folk began to build houses and to dwell there. And in brief time a fair town[1] was built there, and there also is the friary that is called of the island; and to this day the men and women of that town hold the place where St. Francis kept Lent in great devotion and reverence.

CHAPTER VIII

HOW ST. FRANCIS SET FORTH TO FRIAR LEO, AS THEY JOURNEYED TOGETHER, WHERE PERFECT JOY WAS TO BE FOUND

One winter's day, as St. Francis was going from Perugia with Friar Leo to St. Mary of the Angels, suffering sorely from the bitter cold, he called Friar Leo, that was going before him, and spake thus, "Friar Leo, albeit the friars minor in every land give good examples of holiness and edification, nevertheless write and note down diligently that perfect joy is not to be found therein." And St. Francis went his way a little farther, and called him a second time, saying, "O Friar Leo, even though the friar minor gave sight to the blind, made the crooked straight, cast out devils, made the deaf to hear, the lame to walk, and restored speech to the dumb, and, what is a yet greater thing, raised to life those who have lain four days in the grave; write—perfect joy is not found there." And he journeyed on a little while, and cried aloud, "O Friar Leo, if the friar minor knew all tongues and all the sciences and all the Scriptures, so that he could foretell and reveal not only future things, but even the secrets of the conscience and of the soul; write—perfect joy is not there." Yet a little farther went St. Francis, and cried again aloud, "O Friar Leo, little sheep of God, even though the friar minor spake with the tongue of angels and knew the courses of the stars and the virtues of herbs, and were the hidden treasures of the earth revealed to him, and he knew the qualities of birds, and of fishes, and of all animals, and of man, and of trees, and stones, and roots, and waters; write—not there is perfect joy." And St. Francis went on again a little space, and cried aloud, "O Friar Leo, although the friar minor were skilled to preach so well that he should convert all the infidels

[1] *Castello*. See Petrocchi, *Nuovo diz. universale de lingua ital.: piccolo paese con mura.*

to the faith of Christ; write—not there is perfect joy." And when this fashion of talk had endured two good miles, Friar Leo asked him in great wonder and said, " Father, prithee in God's name tell me where is perfect joy to be found? " And St. Francis answered him thus, " When we are come to St. Mary of the Angels, wet through with rain, frozen with cold, and foul with mire and tormented with hunger; and when we knock at the door, the doorkeeper cometh in a rage and saith, 'Who are ye?' and we say, 'We are two of your friars,' and he answers, 'Ye tell not true; ye are rather two knaves that go deceiving the world and stealing the alms of the poor; begone!' and he openeth not to us, and maketh us stay outside hungry and cold all night in the rain and snow; then if we endure patiently such cruelty, such abuse, and such insolent dismissal without complaint or murmuring, and believe humbly and charitably that that doorkeeper truly knows us, and that God maketh him to rail against us; O Friar Leo, write—there is perfect joy. And if we persevere in our knocking, and he issues forth and angrily drives us away, abusing us and smiting us on the cheek, saying, 'Go hence, ye vile thieves, get ye gone to the workhouse; here ye shall neither eat nor lodge;' if this we suffer patiently with love and gladness; write, O Friar Leo—this is perfect joy. And if, constrained by hunger and by cold, we knock once more and pray with many tears that he open to us for the love of God and let us but come inside, and he more insolently than ever crieth, 'These be impudent rogues, I will pay them out as they deserve;' and issues forth with a big knotted stick and seizes us by our cowls and flings us on the ground and rolls us in the snow, bruising every bone in our bodies with that heavy stick—if we, thinking on the agony of the blessed Christ, endure all these things patiently and joyously for love of Him; write, O Friar Leo, that here and in this perfect joy is found. And now, Friar Leo, hear the conclusion. Above all the grace and the gifts of the Holy Spirit that Christ giveth to His beloved is that of overcoming self, and for love of Him willingly to bear pain and buffetings and revilings and discomfort; for in none other of God's gifts, save these, may we glory, seeing they are not ours, but of God. Wherefore the Apostle saith, 'What hast thou that is not of God, and if thou hast received it of Him, wherefore dost thou glory as if thou hadst it of thyself?' But in the cross of tribulation and of affliction we may glory, because this is ours. Therefore the Apostle saith, 'I will not glory save in the cross of our Lord Jesus Christ.' "

CHAPTER IX

HOW ST. FRANCIS TAUGHT FRIAR LEO HOW TO ANSWER HIM, AND FRIAR LEO COULD NEVER SAY AUGHT SAVE THE CONTRARY OF THAT WHICH ST. FRANCIS BADE HIM ANSWER

In the early days of the Order, St. Francis and Friar Leo were once in a friary where no book could be found wherefrom the divine offices might be said, and when the hour of matins was come St. Francis said to Friar Leo, "Dearest, we have no breviary to say matins from; but in order that we may spend the time in praise of God, I will speak and thou shalt answer me as I teach thee, and beware lest thou change one of the words I teach thee. I will say thus, 'O Friar Francis, thou hast done so many evil deeds and committed so many sins in the world that thou art deserving of hell;' and thou, Friar Leo, shalt answer, 'Truly thou dost merit the deepest hell.'" And Friar Leo said, with dove-like simplicity, "Willingly, father; do thou begin in God's name." Then St. Francis began to say, "O Friar Francis, thou hast done so many evil deeds and hast committed so many sins in the world that thou art deserving of hell." And Friar Leo answers, "God will perform so many good works through thee that thou shalt go to paradise." Saith St. Francis, "Say not so, Friar Leo, but when I say, 'O Friar Francis, thou hast committed so many iniquities against God that thou art worthy of being cursed by God,' do thou answer thus, 'Verily thou art worthy of being numbered among the accursed.'" And Friar Leo answers, "Willingly, father." Then St. Francis, with many tears and sighs and smitings of the breast, said with a loud voice, "O Lord God of heaven and earth, I have committed so many sins and iniquities against Thee that I am wholly worthy of being cursed by Thee." And Brother Leo answers, "O Friar Francis, God will do in such wise that among the blessed thou shalt be singularly blessed." St. Francis, marvelling that Friar Leo ever answered contrary to that which he had charged him, rebuked him thus, saying, "Wherefore answerest thou not as I teach thee? I command thee by holy obedience that thou answer as I teach thee. I will say thus, 'O Friar Francis, little wretch, thinkest thou God will have mercy on thee, seeing thou hast committed so many sins against the Father of mercies and God of all consolations that thou art not worthy to find mercy?' And thou, Friar Leo, little sheep, shalt answer, 'In no wise art thou worthy of finding mercy.'" But when St. Francis said, "O Friar Francis, little wretch," *et cetera*, lo, Friar Leo answered, "God the Father, whose mercy is infinite, far exceeding thy sins, will show great mercy to thee, and will add likewise many graces thereto." At this answer St. Francis, sweetly angry and meekly perturbed, said to Friar Leo, "Wherefore hast thou had the presumption to act counter to obedience, and so many times hast answered the contrary of what I told thee and charged thee?" Friar Leo answers, with deep humility and reverence, "God knoweth, my father; for I have purposed in my heart each time to answer as thou hast commanded me; but God maketh me to speak as it pleaseth Him, and not as it pleaseth me." Whereat St. Francis marvelled, and said to Friar Leo, "I pray thee most dearly, answer me this once as I have charged thee." Said Friar Leo, "Say on, in God's name, for of a surety this time I will answer as thou desirest." And St. Francis said, in tears, "O Friar Francis, little wretch, thinkest thou God will have mercy on thee?" *et cetera*. And Friar Leo answers, "Nay, rather great grace shalt thou receive of God, and He will exalt thee and glorify thee everlastingly, because he that humbleth himself shall be exalted; and naught else can I say, for God speaketh by my mouth." And so in this lowly disputation, with many tears and much spiritual consolation, they watched until the dawn.

CHAPTER X

HOW FRIAR MASSEO, HALF IN JEST, SAID TO ST. FRANCIS THAT THE WHOLE WORLD WAS FOLLOWING AFTER HIM; AND ST. FRANCIS ANSWERED THAT BY GOD'S GRACE IT WAS SO TO THE CONFUSION OF THE WORLD

WHILE St. Francis was abiding at the friary of the Porziuncula with Friar Masseo of Marignano, a man of great holiness and discernment and grace in discoursing of God, and therefore much beloved of him, he was returning one day from prayer in the wood, and was already on the point of issuing therefrom, when Friar Masseo, desiring to prove his humility, made towards him and said, half jestingly, "Why after thee? Why after thee? Why after thee?" And St. Francis answered, "What meanest thou?" Said Friar Masseo, "I mean why doth all the world follow after thee, and why doth every man desire to see thee and to hear thee and to obey thee? Thou art not fair to look upon; thou art not a man of great parts; thou art not of noble birth. Whence cometh it, then, that all the world followeth after thee?" When St. Francis heard this he rejoiced exceedingly in spirit, and raising his face to heaven, remained for a great space with his soul uplifted to God. And then, returning to himself, he knelt down and gave praise and thanks to God. Then with great fervour of spirit he turned to Friar Masseo and said, "Wouldst thou know why after me? Wouldst thou know why after me? Wouldst thou know why after me? Know that this I have from those eyes of the most high God, that everywhere behold the righteous and the wicked, and forasmuch as those most holy eyes have beheld among sinners none more vile, more imperfect, nor a greater sinner than I, therefore since He hath found no viler creature on earth to accomplish the marvellous work He intendeth, He hath chosen me to confound the nobility, the majesty, the might, the beauty, and the wisdom of the world; in order to make manifest that every virtue and every good thing cometh from Him the Creator, and not from the creature, and that none may glory before Him: but that he that glories shall glory in the Lord, to whom belong all glory and all honour for ever and ever." Then Friar Masseo waxed sore afraid at this lowly answer given with great fervour, and knew of a surety that St. Francis was grounded in humility.

CHAPTER XI

HOW ST. FRANCIS MADE FRIAR MASSEO TURN ROUND AND ROUND MANY TIMES, AND THEN WENT HIS WAY TO SIENA

On a day as St. Francis was journeying with Friar Masseo, the said Friar Masseo went a little in front of him; and when they reached a point where three ways met—one leading to Florence, another to Siena, and a third to Arezzo—Friar Masseo said, "Father, which road ought we to follow?" St. Francis answered, "That which God willeth." Said Friar Masseo, "And how shall we know the will of God?" St. Francis answered, "By the token I shall show thee: wherefore I command thee by the merit of holy obedience that at this parting of the ways, and on the spot where thou now standest, thou shalt turn round and round as children do, and shalt not cease turning until I bid thee." Then Friar Masseo began to turn round and round, and continued so long that by reason of the giddiness which is wont to be begotten by such turning, he fell many times to the ground; but, as St. Francis did not bid him stay, he rose up again, for faithfully he desired to obey him. At length, when he was turning lustily, St. Francis cried, "Stay; stir not!" And he stayed. Then St. Francis asked him, "Towards which part is thy face turned?" Friar Masseo answers, "Towards Siena." Said St. Francis, "That is the road God wills we should go." And as they walked by the way, Friar Masseo marvelled that St. Francis had made him turn around and around even as a child doth, in the presence of secular folk that were passing by: yet for very reverence he dared say naught thereof to the holy father. As they drew nigh to Siena the people of that city, hearing of the advent of the saint, made towards him; and in their devotion they carried the saint and his companion shoulder high as far as the bishop's house, so that they never touched ground with their feet. Now in that same hour certain men of Siena were fighting among themselves, and already two of them had been slain. When St. Francis came among them he preached with such great devotion and sanctity that he brought the whole of them to make peace and to dwell in great unity and concord together. Wherefore, when the bishop of Siena heard of the holy work that St. Francis had accomplished, he invited him to his house, and received him that day and that night also with the greatest honour. And the following morning St. Francis, who in all his works sought but the glory of God, arose betimes and with true humility departed with his companion without the knowledge of the bishop. Wherefore the said Friar Masseo went murmuring within himself by the way, and saying, "What is this that holy man hath done? Me he made to turn round and round as a child, and to the bishop who did him so much honour he said naught, not even a word of thanks:" and it seemed to Friar Masseo that St. Francis had borne himself indiscreetly. But soon, by divine inspiration, Friar Masseo bethought him and reproved himself in his heart, and said, "Friar Masseo, thou art over-proud, thou that judgest the ways of God, and for thy indiscreet pride art worthy of hell. For yesterday Friar Francis wrought such holy works, that they could not have been more marvellous if the angel of God had done them. Wherefore if he should command thee to cast stones, thou shouldst obey him; for what he hath wrought in this city hath been by divine operation, even as is manifest in the good that followeth thereafter; because had he not made peace among those that were fighting, not only would many bodies have been slain by the knife (even as had already begun to come to pass), but many souls likewise would have been dragged to hell by the devil. Therefore art thou very foolish and proud, thou that murmurest at these things which manifestly proceed according to the will of God." Now all these things that this friar was saying in his heart were revealed by God to St. Francis, wherefore St. Francis drew nigh to him and said, "Hold fast to those things thou art now thinking, for they are good and profitable, and inspired by God; but thy first murmurings were blind and vain and proud, and instigated by the evil one." Then did Friar Masseo perceive clearly that St. Francis knew the secrets of his heart, and he understood that of a surety the Spirit of divine wisdom governed the holy father in all his works.

CHAPTER XII

HOW ST. FRANCIS APPOINTED FRIAR MASSEO TO BE DOORKEEPER, ALMONER, AND COOK: THEN AT THE ENTREATIES OF THE OTHER FRIARS REMOVED HIM

St. Francis, desiring to humble Friar Masseo in order that by reason of the many gifts and graces God had bestowed on him he should not be puffed up with vainglory, but by virtue of humility should increase from virtue to virtue, said to him on a day when he was dwelling with his first companions in a solitary place—those truly holy companions whereof Friar Masseo was one,—"O Friar Masseo, all these thy companions have the gift of contemplation and of prayer; but thou hast the gift of preaching the word of God to the satisfaction of the people. Therefore I desire that thou take upon thee the offices of doorkeeper, of almoner, and of cook, in order that thy companions may give themselves up to contemplation; and when the other friars are eating, thou shalt eat outside the door of the friary, so that thou mayst satisfy with some sweet words of God those who come to the convent, ere they knock; and so that no other friar than thou have need to go outside. And this do through the merit of holy obedience." Then Friar Masseo drew back his cowl and inclined his head and humbly received and fulfilled this command, and for many days he discharged the offices of doorkeeper, and almoner, and cook. Whereat the companions, even as men illumined by God, began to feel great remorse in their hearts, considering that Friar Masseo was a man of as great perfection as they were, or even greater; and yet on him was laid the whole burden of the convent, and not on them. Wherefore, moved by one desire, they went with one accord and entreated the holy father to be pleased to distribute those offices among them; for in no wise could they endure in their conscience that Friar Masseo should bear so many burdens. When St. Francis heard this he gave heed to their prayers and consented to their desire, and calling Friar Masseo he thus spake to him, "Friar Masseo, thy companions would have a share in the offices wherewith I have charged thee: it is therefore my will that the said offices be divided." Says Friar Masseo, with great humility and meekness, "Father, whatsoever thou layest upon me, either all or part, that I hold to be wholly done of God." Then St. Francis, beholding the love of them and the humility of Friar Masseo, preached a wondrous sermon touching most holy humility, admonishing them that the greater the gifts and graces that God bestows upon us, the greater ought our humility to be; for without humility no virtue is acceptable to God. And when he had made an end of his sermon he apportioned the offices among them with the greatest loving-kindness.

CHAPTER XIII

HOW ST. FRANCIS AND FRIAR MASSEO SET DOWN THE BREAD THEY HAD BEGGED ON A STONE BESIDE A SPRING, AND ST. FRANCIS GREATLY PRAISED POVERTY. THEN HE PRAYED UNTO GOD AND ST. PETER AND ST. PAUL THAT THEY WOULD INSPIRE HIM WITH THE LOVE OF HOLY POVERTY; AND HOW ST. PETER AND ST. PAUL APPEARED TO HIM

THE wondrous servant and follower of Christ, to wit, St. Francis, to the end that he might conform himself to Christ perfectly in all things (who, according to the gospel, sent His disciples two by two unto all those cities and places whither He was to go), gathered together twelve companions and sent them forth after the example of Christ two by two to preach throughout the world. And St. Francis, that he might give them an example of true obedience, himself set forth first, after the example of Christ, who began to do before He began to teach. Wherefore, having assigned to his companions the other quarters of the world, he took Friar Masseo with him as his companion and went his way towards the land of France. And journeying one day they came to a city sore a-hungered, and went, according to the Rule, begging bread for love of God: and St. Francis took one street and Friar Masseo another. But forasmuch as St. Francis was a man of mean appearance and short of stature, and therefore looked down upon as a poor vile creature by those who knew him not, he collected naught save a few mouthfuls of dry crusts; but to Friar Masseo many large pieces of bread and even whole loaves were given, for he was fair and tall of body. And after they had begged their food, they met to eat together at a place outside the city where was a fair fountain, and beside it a fair broad stone, whereon each laid the alms he had collected. Now when St. Francis saw that the bread and loaves brought by Friar Masseo were finer and larger than his own, he showed forth joy exceeding great, and spake thus, "O Friar Masseo, we are not worthy of so great a treasure." And having repeated these words many times, Friar Masseo answered, "Dearest father, how can that be called a treasure where there is poverty so great and such lack of needful things? Here is neither cloth, nor knife, nor trencher, nor bowl, nor house, nor table, nor man-servant, nor maid-servant." Then said St. Francis, "And this is what I hold to be a great treasure: where there is no dwelling made by human hands, but all is prepared for us by divine providence, even as is made manifest by the bread we have collected on this table of stone so fair and this fountain so clear. Therefore I desire that we pray unto God that He may make us love with all our hearts this noble treasure of holy poverty that hath God for its servitor." After these words they refreshed their bodies, and having made their prayer, rose up and journeyed on to France. And when they came to a church, St. Francis said to his companion, "Let us enter into this church to pray." And St. Francis goes behind the altar and kneels down in prayer. And as he prayed he was inspired by the divine presence with fervour so exceeding great that his whole soul was inflamed with love for holy poverty; in such wise that what with the hue of his face and the strange yawning of his mouth, it seemed as if flames of love were bursting from him. And coming thus aflame towards his companion, he spake thus to him, "Ah, ah, ah, Friar Masseo; give thyself to me." And this he said thrice; and the third time St. Francis lifted up Friar Masseo into the air with his breath, and cast him away from him the length of a tall spear; whereat Friar Masseo was filled with great amaze. And he afterwards related to his companions that when St. Francis thus lifted him up and cast him from him with his breath, he felt such great sweetness in his soul, and such deep consolation from the Holy Spirit, that never in his life had he felt the like. This done, St. Francis said, "Dearest companion, go we now to St. Peter and St. Paul and pray them to teach us and aid us to possess this boundless treasure of holiest poverty; for it is a treasure of such exceeding worth and so divine that we are unworthy to possess it in our vile vessels. Yea! this is that celestial virtue whereby all earthly and transitory things are trodden under foot and whereby every hindrance is removed from the soul that she may be freely conjoined with the eternal God. This is the virtue that maketh the soul, while yet on earth, have communion with the angels in heaven; that companioned Christ on the cross; with Christ was buried; with Christ rose again, and with Christ ascended into heaven. It is this virtue also that easeth the flight into heaven of those souls that love it; for it guards the armour of true humility and charity. Therefore let us pray unto the most holy Apostles of Christ, who were perfect lovers of this pearl evangelical, to obtain for us this grace from our Lord Jesus Christ: that He in His holy mercy may vouchsafe to us to grow worthy to be true lovers and followers and humble disciples of the most precious and most lovable gospel poverty." Thus discoursing, they came to Rome and entered St. Peter's church; and St. Francis set himself to pray in one corner of the church, and Friar Masseo in another. And as St. Francis remained in prayer a long while, with many tears and great devotion, the holy Apostles Peter and Paul appeared to him in great splendour, and said, "Forasmuch as thou askest and desirest to serve that which Christ and His holy Apostles served, our Lord Jesus Christ sendeth us to thee to announce that thy prayer is heard, and that God granteth to thee and to thy followers the perfect treasure of holiest poverty. And from Him also we say unto thee, that whosoever, following thy example, shall pursue this desire perfectly, he is assured of the blessedness of life eternal; and thou and all thy followers shall be blessed of God." These words said, they vanished, leaving St. Francis filled with consolation; who, rising from prayer, returned to his companion and asked him if God had revealed aught to him; and he answered, "Nay." Then St. Francis told him how the holy apostles had appeared to him, and what they had revealed. Whereupon each of them, filled with joy, purposed to return to the vale of Spoleto, and renounce the journey into France.

CHAPTER XIV

HOW, WHILE ST. FRANCIS AND HIS FRIARS WERE DISCOURSING OF GOD, HE APPEARED IN THEIR MIDST

In the early days of the Order, as St. Francis was communing with his companions and discoursing of Christ, he, in fervour of spirit, bade one of them open his lips in God's name and speak what the Holy Ghost would inspire him to say concerning God. This friar having fulfilled his behest and discoursed wondrously of God, St. Francis laid silence upon him, and gave a like command to another friar. He also having obeyed and spoken subtly of God, St. Francis in like manner laid silence upon him, and bade a third speak of God; and he likewise began to discourse so profoundly of the hidden things of God that St. Francis knew of a surety that he, together with the other two, had spoken by the Holy Ghost; and this was shown forth also by example and by a clear token; for while they were thus speaking the blessed Christ appeared in the midst of them in the similitude and form of a most fair youth, and blessed them and filled them with so much grace and sweetness that they all were rapt out of themselves, and lay as though dead and insensible to the things of this world. And when they returned to themselves, St. Francis said to them, "Brothers mine, most dear, give thanks to God, who hath willed to reveal the treasures of divine wisdom through the lips of the simple; for God is He that openeth the mouths of the dumb, and the tongues of the simple He maketh to speak great wisdom."

CHAPTER XV

HOW ST. CLARE ATE WITH ST. FRANCIS AND HIS FELLOW-FRIARS AT ST. MARY OF THE ANGELS

When St. Francis was at Assisi he visited St. Clare many times and gave her holy instruction, and she having great desire to eat once with him did entreat him thereof many times, but never would he grant her this consolation. Whereupon his companions, beholding St. Clare's desire, spake to St. Francis and said, "Father, it seemeth to us too severe a thing and not in accord with divine charity that thou grantest not the prayer of Sister Clare, that is a virgin so holy and so beloved of God, in so small a grace as to eat with thee; above all, when we consider that through thy preaching she forsook the pomps and riches of this world. Nay, had she asked even greater grace of thee thou shouldst grant it to her, thy spiritual plant." Then St. Francis answered, "Doth it seem good to you that I should grant her prayer?" His companions made answer, "Father, even so, for it is meet that thou grant her this grace and give her consolation." Then said St. Francis, "Since it seemeth good to you, even so it seemeth good to me. But that she may be the more consoled, I desire that this repast be made in St. Mary of the Angels; for long hath she been shut up in St. Damian's, and it will profit her to behold the friary of St. Mary, where her hair was shorn and she became the spouse of Jesus Christ: there will we break bread together in the name of God." And when the appointed day came, St. Clare came forth from the convent with one companion, and accompanied by the companions of St. Francis, journeyed to St. Mary of the Angels; and having devoutly saluted the Virgin Mary, before whose altar she had been shorn and veiled, the companions conducted her around to see the friary of St. Mary's until the hour of the repast was come. Meanwhile St. Francis made ready the table on the bare ground, as he was wont to do. And the hour for dinner being come, St. Francis and St. Clare, and one of the companions of St. Francis and the companion of St. Clare, seated themselves together; and all the other companions of St. Francis then humbly took their places at the table. And for the first dish St. Francis began to discourse of God so sweetly, so loftily, and so wondrously that a bounteous measure of divine grace descended upon them and they were all rapt in God. And being thus ravished, with eyes and hands lifted up to heaven, the men of Assisi and of Bettona, and the men of the country round about, beheld St. Mary of the Angels and the whole friary and the wood that was around about it brightly flaming; and it seemed as 'twere a great fire that was devouring the church and the friary and the wood together: wherefore the men of Assisi, verily believing that everything was in flames, ran down thither with great haste to quench the fire. But when they came to the friary and found nothing burning, they entered within and beheld St. Francis with St. Clare and all their companions seated around that humble table and rapt in the contemplation of God. Wherefore they understood that truly the fire had not been a material fire, but a divine fire which God had miraculously made to appear in order to show forth and signify the fire of divine love wherewith the souls of these holy friars and holy nuns did burn: and they departed with great consolation in their hearts and with holy edification. Then after a long space St. Francis and St. Clare, together with the companions, returned to themselves, and feeling well comforted with spiritual food, took little heed of corporeal food; and thus that blessed repast being ended, St. Clare, well companioned, returned to St. Damian's. And when the sisters beheld her they had great joy, for they feared lest St. Francis had sent her to rule over some other convent, even as he had already sent Sister Agnes, her holy sister, to rule, as abbess, over the convent of Monticelli at Florence. For on a time St. Francis had said to St. Clare, "Make thee ready if it so be that I must needs send thee to another convent." And she, even as a daughter of holy obedience, had answered, "Father, behold I am ever ready to go whithersoever thou wilt send me." Therefore the sisters rejoiced greatly when they had her back again, and thenceforth St. Clare abode there much consoled.

CHAPTER XVI

HOW ST. FRANCIS HAD COUNSEL FROM ST. CLARE AND FROM THE HOLY FRIAR SILVESTER, TO WIT, THAT HE WAS TO CONVERT MUCH PEOPLE: AND HOW HE STABLISHED THE THIRD ORDER AND PREACHED TO THE BIRDS AND MADE THE SWALLOWS HOLD THEIR PEACE

St. Francis, humble servant of God, short time after his conversion, having gathered together many companions and received them into the Order, fell into great perplexity and doubt touching what it behoved him to do—whether to be wholly intent on prayer, or sometimes to preach. And greatly he desired to know the will of God touching these things. But since the holy humility wherewith he was filled suffered him not to lean overmuch on his own judgment, nor on his own prayers, he bethought him to seek the divine will through the prayers of others. Wherefore he called Friar Masseo to him and spake to him thus, "Go to Sister Clare and bid her from me that she and some of the most spiritual of her companions pray devoutly unto God, that He may be pleased to reveal to me which is the more excellent way: whether to give myself up to preaching or wholly to prayer; then go to Friar Silvester and bid him do the like." Now he had been in the world and was that same Friar Silvester that beheld a cross of gold issue from the mouth of St. Francis, the length whereof was high as heaven, and the breadth whereof reached to the uttermost parts of the earth. And this Friar Silvester was a man of such great devotion and holiness that whatsoever he asked of God he obtained, and the same was granted to him; and ofttimes he spake with God, wherefore great was the devotion of St. Francis to him. Friar Masseo went forth and gave his message first to St. Clare, as St. Francis had commanded, and then to Friar Silvester, who no sooner had heard the command than he straightway betook himself to prayer, and when he had received the divine answer, he returned to Friar Masseo and spake these words, "Thus saith the Lord God, 'Go to Friar Francis and say unto him that God hath not called him to this state for himself alone, but that he may bring forth fruit of souls and that many through him may be saved.'" Friar Masseo, having received this answer, returned to Sister Clare to learn what answer she had obtained of God; and she answered that she and her companions had received the selfsame response from God that Friar Silvester had. And Friar Masseo returned with this answer to St. Francis, who greeted him with greatest charity, washing his feet and setting meat before him. And St. Francis called Friar Masseo, after he had eaten, into the wood, and there knelt down before him, drew back his cowl, and making a cross with his arms, asked of him, "What doth my Lord Jesus Christ command?" Friar Masseo answers, "Thus to Friar Silvester and thus to Sister Clare and her sisterhood hath Christ answered and revealed His will: that thou go forth to preach throughout the world, for He hath not chosen thee for thyself alone, but also for the salvation of others." Then St. Francis, when he had heard these words and learned thereby the will of Christ, rose up and said with great fervour, "Let us then go forth in God's name." And with him he took Friar Masseo and Friar Agnolo, holy men both, and setting forth with great fervour of spirit and taking heed neither of road nor path, they came to a city called Saburniano. And St. Francis began to preach, first commanding the swallows to keep silence until his sermon were ended; and the swallows obeying him, he preached with such zeal that all the men and women of that city desired in their devotion to follow after him and forsake the city. But St. Francis suffered them not, saying, "Be not in haste to depart, for I will ordain what ye shall do for the salvation of your souls." And then he bethought him of the third Order which he stablished for the universal salvation of all people. And so, leaving them much comforted and well disposed to penitence, he departed thence and came to a place between Cannara and Bevagna. And journeying on in that same fervour of spirit, he lifted up his eyes and beheld some trees by the wayside whereon were an infinite multitude of birds; so that he marvelled and said to his companions, "Tarry here for me by the way and I will go and preach to my little sisters the birds." And he entered into the field and began to preach to the birds that were on the ground; and anon those that were on the trees flew down to hear him, and all stood still the while St. Francis made an end of his sermon; and even then they departed not until he had given them his blessing. And according as Friar Masseo and Friar James of Massa thereafter related, St. Francis went among them, touching them with the hem of his garment, and not one stirred. And the substance of the sermon St. Francis preached was this, "My little sisters the birds, much are ye beholden to

God your Creator, and always and in every place ye ought to praise Him for that He hath given you a double and a triple vesture; He hath given you freedom to go into every place, and also did preserve the seed of you in the ark of Noe, in order that your kind might not perish from the earth. Again, ye are beholden to Him for the element of air which He hath appointed for you; moreover, ye sow not, neither do ye reap, and God feedeth you and giveth you the rivers and the fountains for your drink; He giveth you the mountains and the valleys for your refuge, and the tall trees wherein to build your nests, and forasmuch as ye can neither spin nor sew God clotheth you, you and your children: wherefore your Creator loveth you much, since He hath dealt so bounteously with you; and therefore beware, little sisters mine, of the sin of ingratitude, but ever strive to praise God." While St. Francis was uttering these words, all those birds began to open their beaks, and stretch their necks, and spread their wings, and reverently to bow their heads to the ground, showing by their gestures and songs that the holy father's words gave them greatest joy: and St. Francis was glad and rejoiced with them, and marvelled much at so great a multitude of birds and at their manifold loveliness, and at their attention and familiarity; for which things he devoutly praised the Creator in them. Finally, his sermon ended, St. Francis made the sign of holy cross over them and gave them leave to depart; and all those birds soared up into the air in one flock with wondrous songs, and then divided themselves into four parts after the form of the cross St. Francis had made over them; and one part flew towards the east; another towards the west; the third towards the south, and the fourth towards the north. And each flock sped forth singing wondrously, betokening thereby that even as St. Francis, standard-bearer of the cross of Christ, had preached to them and had made the sign of the cross over them, according to which they had divided themselves, singing, among the four quarters of the world, so the preaching of Christ's cross, renewed by St. Francis, was, through him and his friars, to be borne throughout the whole world; the which friars possessing nothing of their own in this world, after the manner of birds, committed their lives wholly to the providence of God.

CHAPTER XVII

HOW A LITTLE BOY FRIAR, WHILE ST. FRANCIS WAS PRAYING BY NIGHT, BEHELD CHRIST AND THE VIRGIN MARY AND MANY OTHER SAINTS DISCOURSING WITH HIM

A BOY most pure and innocent was received into the Order, during the life of St. Francis, in a convent so small that the friars were of necessity constrained to sleep two in a bed. And St. Francis once came to the said convent, and at even, after compline, lay down to rest that he might rise up to pray in the night while the other friars slept, as he was wont to do. The said boy having set his heart on spying out diligently the ways of St. Francis, lay down to sleep beside St. Francis that he might understand his holiness, and chiefly what he did by night when he rose up; and in order that sleep might not beguile him, he tied his own cord to the cord of St. Francis, that he might feel when he stirred: and of this St. Francis perceived naught. But by night, during the first sleep, when all the friars were slumbering, St. Francis arose and found his cord thus tied; and he loosed it so gently that the boy felt it not, and went forth alone into the wood near the friary, and entered into a little cell there and betook himself to prayer. After some space the boy awoke, and finding his cord loosed, and St. Francis risen, he rose up likewise and went seeking him, and finding the door open which led to the wood, he thought St. Francis had gone thither, and he entered the wood. And coming nigh unto the place where St. Francis was praying, he began to hear much talking; and as he drew closer to see and understand what he heard, he beheld a wondrous light that encompassed St. Francis, wherein were Christ and the Virgin Mary, and St. John the Baptist, and the Evangelist, and an infinite multitude of angels that were speaking with St. Francis. Seeing and hearing this, the boy fell lifeless to the earth. And the mystery of that holy apparition being ended, St. Francis, as he returned to the house, stumbled with his foot against the boy, who lay as one dead, and in compassion lifted him up and carried him in his arms, even as the good shepherd doth his sheep. And then learning from him how he had beheld the said vision, St. Francis commanded him to tell it to no man, to wit, so long as he should live, and the boy increasing daily in the great grace of God and in devotion to St. Francis, became a valiant man in the Order, and after the death of St. Francis revealed the said vision to the friars.

CHAPTER XVIII

OF THE WONDROUS CHAPTER THAT ST. FRANCIS HELD AT ST. MARY OF THE ANGELS, WHERE MORE THAN FIVE THOUSAND FRIARS WERE ASSEMBLED

FRANCIS, faithful servant of Christ, once held a Chapter-General at St. Mary of the Angels, where more than five thousand friars were gathered together. Now St. Dominic, head and founder of the Order of preaching friars, who was then journeying from Burgundy to Rome, came thither, and hearing of the congregation of the Chapter that St. Francis was holding in the plain of St. Mary of the Angels, he went with seven friars of his Order to see. And there was likewise at the said Chapter a cardinal who was most devoted to St. Francis, the which cardinal he had foretold should one day become pope: [1] even as it came to pass. This cardinal had journeyed diligently to Assisi from Perugia, where the papal court was, and every day he came to behold St. Francis and his friars, and sometimes sang the mass, and sometimes preached the sermon to the friars in Chapter; and the said cardinal was filled with the greatest joy and devotion when he came to visit that holy assembly. And beholding the friars sitting on that plain, around St. Mary's, company by company, here forty, there a hundred, there eighty together, all engaged in discoursing of God, or at prayer, or in tears, or in works of charity, and all so silent and so meek that no sound nor discord was heard, and marvelling at so great and orderly a multitude, he said with great devotion and tears, "Verily this is the camp and the army of the knights of God." In so mighty a host was heard neither vain words nor jests, but wheresoever a company of friars was assembled together, there they prayed, or said the office, or bewailed their sins, or the sins of their benefactors, or discoursed of the salvation of souls. For shelter they made them little wicker cots of willow and of rush matting, divided into groups according to the friars of the divers provinces: and therefore that Chapter was called the Chapter of the wicker cots or of the mats. Their couch was the bare earth,

[1] Cardinal Hugolin, who became Gregory IX.

with a little straw for some: their pillows were blocks of stone or of wood. For which cause so great was the devotion of whosoever heard or saw them, so great the fame of their sanctity, that many counts and barons, and knights and other noblemen, and many priests likewise, and cardinals and bishops, and abbots and other clerks, came from the papal court, which then was at Perugia, and from the vale of Spoleto, to behold that great assembly, so holy and so humble, and so many saintly men together, the like whereof the world had never known before. And chiefly they came to behold the head and most holy father of that saintly folk, who had snatched so fair a prey from the world, and had gathered together so fair and devout a flock to follow the footprints of the true Shepherd Jesus Christ. The Chapter-General then being assembled together, St. Francis, holy father of all and general minister, expounded the word of God in fervour of spirit and preached unto them in a loud voice whatsoever the Holy Spirit put into his mouth. And for the text of his sermon he took these words, "My children, great things have we promised unto God: things exceeding great hath God promised unto us, if we observe those we have promised unto Him: and of a surety do we await those things promised unto us. Brief is the joy of this world; the pain that cometh hereafter is everlasting: small is the pain of this life; but the glory of the life to come is infinite." And on these words he preached most devoutly, comforting the friars and moving them to obedience and to reverence of Holy Mother Church, to brotherly love and to pray to God for all men, to be patient under the adversities of this world, temperate in prosperity, observant of purity and angelic chastity, to live in peace and concord with God and with men and with their own conscience, and in the love and practice of most holy poverty. And then he spake and said, "I command you by the merit of holy obedience, all you that are here assembled, that none of you have care nor solicitude for what he shall eat nor what he shall drink, nor for aught necessary for the body, but give ye heed solely to prayer and to the praise of God: lay upon Him all solicitude for your body; for He hath special care of you." And all and sundry received this commandment with glad hearts and with joyful countenances: and the sermon of St. Francis being ended, all prostrated themselves in prayer. Whereat St. Dominic, that was present at all these things, marvelled mightily at the commandment of St. Francis and deemed it rash; for he knew not how so great a multitude could be governed while taking no thought or care for the things necessary to the body. But the chief Shepherd, Christ the blessed, being willed to show what care He hath for His sheep and His singular love for His poor ones, anon moved the hearts of the people of Perugia, of Spoleto, of Foligno, of Spello, and of Assisi, and of the other cities round about, to bring wherewithal to eat and to drink to that holy congregation. And lo, there came quickly from the aforesaid cities, men with sumpter mules and horses and carts, loaded with bread and wine, with beans and cheese and other good things to eat, according to the needs of Christ's poor ones. Besides this they brought napery and pitchers, and bowls and glasses, and other vessels needful for so great a multitude; and blessed he that could bring the heaviest load or serve most diligently, so that knights and barons also and other noblemen, who had come to look on, served them with great humility and devotion. Wherefore St. Dominic, beholding all these things and knowing of a truth that divine providence wrought in them, humbly owned that he had falsely judged St. Francis of rashness, and drawing nigh to him knelt down and humbly confessed his fault, and added, "Verily, God hath especial care of these His poor little ones, and I knew it not: henceforth I promise to observe holy gospel poverty, and in God's name do curse all the friars of my Order that shall dare to possess things of their own." And St. Dominic was much edified by the faith of the most holy St. Francis, and by the obedience and poverty of so great and well ordered an assembly, and by the divine providence and the rich abundance of all good things. Now in that same Chapter it was told St. Francis that many friars were wearing breastplates of iron[1] next their skins, and iron rings, whereby many grew sick even unto death and were hindered in their prayers. Whereat St. Francis, as a wise father, commanded by holy obedience that whosoever had these breast-plates or iron rings should remove them and lay them

[1] *Cuoretto.* The sense of this word is doubtful. A note to Cesari's text interprets "a kind of metal cilice in the form of a heart." The Upton fathers render "leather bands with sharp points;" Cardinal Manning has "small hearts of iron." Prof. Arnold in his admirable translation gives "shirts of mail." A shirt of mail was, however, an expensive harness in the Middle Ages, and a gathering of mendicant friars, 500 of whom were possessed of shirts of mail, is hardly credible. Petrocchi, *Nuovo diz. universale*, interprets, *specie di cilizio*, "a kind of cilice," and Johann Jörgensen, the Danish translator, has *Bodsskjorte*, "penitential shirt." A reference to the Latin original gives *loricam*, and since a well-known eleventh-century Italian hermit, S. Domenico lorato, was thus called by reason of the iron cuirass he wore next his skin, I have small doubt that *cuoretto* should be rendered "breastplate." The friars could easily have begged old breast-plates for penitential purposes.

before him, and thus did they; and there were numbered full five hundred breast-plates, and many more rings, either for the arm or for the loins, so that they made a great heap; and St. Francis bade them be left there. After the Chapter was ended St. Francis heartened them all to good works, and taught them how they should escape without sin from this wicked world; then dismissed them with God's blessing and his own to their provinces, all consoled with spiritual joy.

CHAPTER XIX

HOW THE VINEYARD OF THE PARISH PRIEST OF RIETI, IN WHOSE HOUSE ST. FRANCIS PRAYED, WAS STRIPPED OF ITS GRAPES BY REASON OF THE MULTITUDE OF PEOPLE THAT CAME TO SEE HIM; AND HOW THAT VINEYARD BROUGHT FORTH MIRACULOUSLY MORE WINE THAN EVER BEFORE, ACCORDING TO THE PROMISE OF ST. FRANCIS. AND HOW GOD REVEALED TO ST. FRANCIS THAT PARADISE SHOULD BE HIS PORTION WHEN HE DEPARTED THIS LIFE

St. Francis being on a time sorely afflicted in his eyes, was invited by a letter from Cardinal Hugolin, protector of the Order, to come to Rieti, where excellent physicians for the eyes then dwelt, for he loved him tenderly. When St. Francis received the cardinal's letter he went first to St. Damian's, where St. Clare, the most devout spouse of Christ was, to give her some consolation; then he would go his way to the cardinal at Rieti. And the night after he came thither his eyes worsened so that he saw no light at all. Wherefore, being unable to depart, St. Clare made him a little cell of reeds wherein he might the better find repose. But St. Francis, what with the pain of his eyes and what with the multitude of mice that tormented him, could not rest a moment night or day. And after enduring that pain and tribulation many days, he began to bethink him and to understand that this was a divine scourge for his sins; and he began to thank God with all his heart and with his mouth, and then crying with a loud voice, said, "My Lord, worthy am I of all this and far worse. My Lord Jesus Christ, good Shepherd, that in Thy mercy hast laid upon us sinners divers corporeal pains and anguish, grant to me, Thy little sheep, such virtue and grace that for no sickness or anguish or suffering I may depart from Thee."

And as he prayed there came to him a voice from heaven saying, "Francis, answer Me: If all the earth were gold, and all the sea and fountains and rivers were balm, and all the mountains and hills and rocks were precious stones, and thou shouldst find another treasure as much nobler than these things as gold is nobler than clay, and balm than water, and precious stones than mountains and rocks, and if that nobler treasure were given thee for thine infirmity, oughtest thou not to be right glad and right joyful?" St. Francis answers, "Lord, I am unworthy of so precious a treasure." And the voice of God said to him, "Rejoice, Francis, for that is the treasure of life eternal, which I have laid up for thee, and from this hour forth I do invest thee therewith: and this sickness and affliction is a pledge of that blessed treasure." Then St. Francis with exceeding great joy called his companion and said, "Go we to the cardinal." And first consoling St. Clare with holy words and humbly taking leave of her, he went his way towards Rieti. And when he drew nigh to the city, so great a multitude of people came forth to meet him that he would not enter therein, but went to a church that was perchance two miles distant therefrom. When the citizens heard that he was at the said church, they ran thither to behold him in such numbers that the vineyard of the said church was utterly despoiled, and all the grapes were plucked: whereat the priest, sorely grieved in his heart, repented that he had received St. Francis in his church. Now that priest's thoughts being revealed by God to St. Francis, he called him aside and said to him, "Dearest father, how many measures of wine doth this vineyard yield thee a year when the yield is highest?" He answered, "Twelve measures." Says St. Francis, "Prithee, father, suffer me patiently to sojourn here yet a few days, for I find much repose here; and for the love of God and of me, poor little one, let every man gather grapes from thy vineyard, and I promise thee, in the name of my Lord Jesus Christ, that every year thy vineyard shall yield thee twenty measures of wine." And St. Francis tarried there because of the great harvest of souls manifestly gathered from the folk that came thither; whereof many departed inebriated with divine love and forsook the world. The priest had faith in the promise of St. Francis, and surrendered the vineyard freely to those that came thither: and the vineyard was all wasted and stripped, so that scarce a bunch of grapes remained. Marvellous to tell, the vintage season comes, and lo, the priest gathers the few bunches that were left and casts them into the wine-press and treads them, and, according to the promise of St. Francis, he harvested twenty measures of excellent wine. In this miracle was manifestly seen that, since by the merits of St. Francis the vineyard, stripped of its grapes, gave forth abundance of wine, so Christian folk, barren of virtue through sin, ofttimes abounded in good fruit of penitence through the merits and teaching of St. Francis.

CHAPTER XX

TOUCHING A MOST BEAUTIFUL VISION THAT A YOUNG FRIAR SAW, WHO SO HATED HIS HABIT THAT HE WAS MINDED TO CAST IT OFF AND FORSAKE THE ORDER

A YOUTH of very noble birth and gently nurtured entered the Order of St. Francis; and after some days, at the instigation of the devil, began to hold the habit he wore in such abomination that it seemed to him of vilest sackcloth. The sleeves thereof he held in horror; he hated the cowl, and the length and coarseness thereof seemed to him an intolerable burden. And his dislike of the Order increasing also, he finally determined to quit the habit and return to the world. Now he was already wonted, even as he had been taught by his master, to kneel down with great reverence and draw off his cowl and cross his arms on his breast and prostrate himself whensoever he passed before the altar of the friary, where the body of Christ was reserved. Now it befell on the night when he was minded to depart and leave the Order, that it behoved him to pass before the altar of the convent: and passing there he knelt down as was his wont and did reverence. And suddenly he was rapt in spirit, and a wondrous vision was shown him by God; for he beheld, as it were, a countless multitude of saints pass before him, after the manner of a procession, two by two, clad in most fair and precious raiment; and the countenances and hands of them shone like the sun; and they paced to the chants and music of angels. And amid these saints were two more nobly arrayed and adorned than all the others; and they were encompassed with such brightness that he who beheld them was filled with great amaze; and well-nigh at the end of the procession he beheld one adorned so gloriously that he seemed a new-made knight, more honoured than the others. This youth, beholding the said vision, marvelled greatly, and knew not what that procession betokened, yet dared not ask, and remained dazed with the sweetness thereof. And, nevertheless, when all the procession was passed, he took courage and ran after the last of them, and asked, saying, " O beloved, prithee of your courtesy tell me who be they so marvellously arrayed that walk in this venerable procession? " They answered, " Know, my son, that we are all friars minor, who now are coming from the glory of paradise." Then asked he thus, " Who be those two that shine more brightly than the others? " They answered, " Those are St. Francis and St. Anthony; and he the last of all whom thou sawest thus honoured is a holy friar that newly died, whom we are leading in triumph to the glory of paradise, for that he hath fought valiantly against temptation and persevered unto the end; and these fair garments of fine cloth we wear, are given to us by God in lieu of the coarse tunics we wore in the Order; and the glorious brightness that thou beholdest is given to us by God for the humility and patience, and for the holy poverty and obedience and chastity we kept even to the last. Therefore, my son, be it not hard to thee to wear the sackcloth of the Order, that is so fruitful, because, if clothed in the sackcloth of St. Francis, thou for love of Christ despise the world and mortify thy flesh and valiantly fight against the devil, thou, with us, shalt have a like raiment and exceeding brightness of glory." These words said, the youth returned to himself, and heartened by this vision, cast away from him all temptation, and confessed his fault before the warden and the friars; and thenceforth he desired the bitterness of penitence and the coarseness of the habit, and ended his life in the Order in great sanctity.

CHAPTER XXI

OF THE MOST HOLY MIRACLE THAT ST. FRANCIS WROUGHT WHEN HE CONVERTED THE FIERCE WOLF OF GUBBIO

In the days when St. Francis abode in the city of Gubbio, a huge wolf, terrible and fierce, appeared in the neighbourhood, and not only devoured animals but men also; in such wise that all the citizens went in great fear of their lives, because ofttimes the wolf came close to the city. And when they went abroad, all men armed themselves as were they going forth to battle; and even so none who chanced on the wolf alone could defend himself; and at last it came to such a pass that for fear of this wolf no man durst leave the city walls. Wherefore St. Francis had great compassion for the men of that city, and purposed to issue forth against that wolf, albeit the citizens, with one accord, counselled him not to go. But he, making the sign of holy cross, and putting all his trust in God, set forth from the city with his companions; but they, fearing to go farther, St. Francis went his way alone towards the place where the wolf was. And lo! the said wolf, in the sight of much folk that had come to behold the miracle, leapt towards St. Francis with gaping jaws; and St. Francis, drawing nigh, made to him the sign of most holy cross and called him, speaking thus, "Come hither, friar wolf; I command thee in the name of Christ that thou do hurt neither to me nor to any man." Marvellous to tell! no sooner had St. Francis made the sign of holy cross than the terrible wolf closed his jaws and stayed his course; no sooner was the command uttered than he came, gentle as a lamb, and laid himself at the feet of St. Francis. Then St. Francis speaks to him thus, "Friar wolf, thou workest much evil in these parts, and hast wrought grievous ill, destroying and slaying God's creatures without His leave; and not only hast thou slain and devoured the beasts of the field, but thou hast dared to destroy and slay men made in the image of God; wherefore thou art worthy of the gallows as a most wicked thief and murderer: all folk cry out and murmur against thee, and all this city is at enmity with thee. But, friar wolf, fain would I make peace with them and thee, so that thou injure them no more; and they shall forgive thee all thy past offences, and neither man nor dog shall pursue thee more." Now when St. Francis had spoken these words, the wolf, moving his body and his tail and his ears, and bowing his head, made signs that he accepted what had been said, and would abide thereby. Then said St. Francis, "Friar wolf, since it pleaseth thee to make and observe this peace, I promise to obtain for thee, so long as thou livest, a continual sustenance from the men of this city, so that thou shalt no more suffer hunger, for well I ween that thou hast wrought all this evil to satisfy thy hunger. But after I have won this favour for thee, friar wolf, I desire that thou promise me to do hurt neither to man nor beast. Dost thou promise me this?" And the wolf bowed his head and gave clear token that he promised these things. And St. Francis said, "Friar wolf, I desire that thou pledge thy faith to me to keep this promise, that I may have full trust in thee." And when St.

Francis held forth his hand to receive this pledge, the wolf lifted up his right paw and gently laid it in the hand of St. Francis, giving him thereby such token of good faith as he could. Then said St. Francis, " Friar wolf, I command thee in the name of Jesus Christ to come with me; fear naught, and we will go and confirm this peace in the name of God." And the wolf, obedient, set forth by his side even as a pet lamb; wherefore, when the men of the city beheld this, they marvelled greatly. And anon this miracle was noised about the whole city, and all folk, great and small, men and women, old and young, flocked to the market-place to see the wolf with St. Francis. And when all the people were gathered together there, St. Francis stood forth and preached to them, saying, among other things, how that for their sins God had suffered such calamities to befall them, and how much more perilous were the flames of hell which the damned must endure everlastingly than was the ravening of a wolf that could only slay the body; and how much more to be feared were the jaws of hell, since that for fear of the mouth of a small beast such multitudes went in fear and trembling. " Turn ye, then, dearest children, to God, and do fitting penance for your sins, and so shall God free you from the wolf in this world and from eternal fire in the world to come." And having made an end of his sermon, St. Francis said, " Hark ye, my brethren, friar wolf, here before you, hath promised and pledged his faith to me never to injure you in anything whatsoever, if you will promise to provide him daily sustenance; and here stand I, a bondsman for him, that he will steadfastly observe this pact of peace." Then the people with one voice promised to feed him all his days. And St. Francis, before all the people, said to the wolf, " And thou, friar wolf, dost promise to observe the conditions of this peace before all this people, and that thou wilt injure neither man nor beast nor any living creature? " And the wolf knelt down and bowed his head, and with gentle movements of tail and body and ears, showed by all possible tokens his will to observe every pact of peace. Says St. Francis, " I desire, friar wolf, that even as thou didst pledge thy faith to me without the city gates to hold fast to thy promise, so here, before all this people, thou shalt renew thy pledge, and promise thou wilt never play me, thy bondsman, false." Then the wolf, lifting up his right paw, placed it in the hand of St. Francis. Whereat, what with this act and the others aforesaid, there was such marvel and rejoicing among all the people—not only at the strangeness of the miracle, but because of the peace made with the wolf—that they all began to cry aloud to heaven, praising and blessing God, who had sent St. Francis to them, by whose merits they had been freed from the cruel wolf. And the said wolf lived two years in Gubbio, and was wont to enter like a tame creature into the houses from door to door, doing hurt to no one and none doing hurt to him. And he was kindly fed by the people; and as he went about the city never a dog barked at him. At last, after two years, friar wolf died of old age; whereat the citizens grieved much, for when they beheld him going thus tamely about the city, they remembered better the virtues and holiness of St. Francis.

CHAPTER XXII

HOW ST. FRANCIS TAMED THE WILD TURTLE DOVES

A CERTAIN youth one day, having snared many turtle doves, was taking them to market when St. Francis met him. And St. Francis, who ever had singular compassion for gentle creatures, gazed upon those doves with a pitying eye, and said to the youth, "O good youth, prithee give them to me, lest birds so gentle, that chaste, humble, and faithful souls are compared to them in the scriptures, fall into the hands of cruel men who would kill them." Straightway the youth, inspired by God, gave them all to St. Francis, who received them into his bosom and began to speak sweetly to them, "O my little sisters, ye simple doves, innocent and chaste, wherefore suffer yourselves to be caught? Now will I rescue you from death, and make nests for you, that ye may be fruitful and multiply, according to the commandments of our Creator." And St. Francis went and made nests for them all; and they took to the nests and began to lay eggs and rear their young before the eyes of the friars: and thus they abode tamely and grew familiar with St. Francis and the other friars, as if they had been chickens ever fed by their hands: nor did they depart until St. Francis gave them leave with his blessing. And he said to the youth that had given them to him, "Son, thou shalt yet be a friar in this Order and serve Jesus Christ in grace." And so it befell, for the said youth became a friar and lived in the Order with great holiness.

CHAPTER XXIII

HOW ST. FRANCIS DELIVERED A SINFUL FRIAR FROM THE POWER OF THE DEVIL

It fell out on a time as St. Francis was at prayer in the friary of the Porziuncula, that he beheld by divine revelation the whole house surrounded and besieged by devils in the similitude of a mighty army. But they could not enter within because those friars were of such holiness that no evil spirit could come nigh them. And as the enemy lay in wait, one of the friars on a day quarrelled with another, and thought in his heart how he might accuse him and be avenged. Wherefore, while he nursed this evil thought, the devil saw the way open and entered into the friary and sat on the friar's shoulder. But the compassionate and vigilant shepherd that ever watched over his flock, seeing the wolf had entered the fold to devour his lamb, let that friar be called to him, and commanded him straightway to reveal the venom of hatred he had conceived towards his neighbour, whereby he had fallen into the power of the enemy of mankind. The friar, affrighted when he perceived that the holy father had thus read his heart, revealed all the venom and malice he had borne in his breast, and confessed his sin and humbly craved mercy and penance. This done, and his penance being accepted, he was assoiled of his sin, and straightway the devil departed in the presence of St. Francis. And the friar, thus delivered from the power of the cruel fiend through the loving-kindness of the good shepherd, gave thanks to God, and returned chastened and admonished to the fold of the holy pastor, and ever after lived in great sanctity.

CHAPTER XXIV

HOW ST. FRANCIS CONVERTED THE SOLDAN OF BABYLON TO THE TRUE FAITH

St. Francis, stirred by zeal for the faith of Christ and by the desire of martyrdom, voyaged on a time over the seas with twelve of his holiest companions, to fare straight to the Soldan of Babylon;[1] and when they came to the land of the Saracens,

[1] Old Cairo.

where the passes were guarded by certain men so cruel that never a Christian who journeyed that way escaped death at their hands, by the grace of God they escaped, and were not slain; but seized and beaten, they were led in bonds before the Soldan. And standing before him, St. Francis, taught by the Holy Ghost, preached the faith of Christ so divinely that for his faith's sake he even would have entered the fire. Whereat the Soldan began to feel great devotion towards him, as much for the constancy of his faith as for his contempt of the world (for albeit he was very poor, he would accept no gift), and also for the fervour of martyrdom he beheld in him. From that time forth the Soldan heard him gladly, and entreated him many times to come back, granting to him and to his companions freedom to preach wheresoever it might please them; and he gave them also a token, so that no man should do them hurt. Having therefore received this licence, St. Francis sent forth those chosen companions, two by two, in divers parts, to preach the faith of Christ to the Saracens. And himself, with one of them, chose a way, and journeying on he came to an inn to rest. And therein was a woman, most fair in body but foul in soul, who, accursed one, did tempt him to sin. And St. Francis, saying he consented thereto, she led him into a chamber. Said St. Francis, "Come with me." And he led her to a fierce fire that was kindled in that chamber, and in fervour of spirit stripped himself naked and cast himself beside that fire on the burning hearth; and he invited her to go and strip and lie with him on that bed, downy and fair. And when St. Francis had lain thus for a great space, with a joyous face, being neither burned nor even singed, that woman, affrighted and pierced to the heart, not only repented of her sin and of her evil intent, but likewise was wholly converted to the faith of Christ; and she waxed so in holiness that many souls were saved through her in those lands.

At last, when St. Francis saw he could gather no more fruit in those parts, he prepared by divine admonition to return to the faithful with all his companions; and having assembled them together, he went back to the Soldan and took leave of him. Then said the Soldan to him, "Friar Francis, fain would I convert me to the faith of Christ, but I fear to do so now, for if this people heard thereof they would surely slay thee and me and all thy companions; and forasmuch as thou canst yet work much good, and as I have certain affairs of great moment to despatch, I will not be the cause of thy death and of mine. But teach me how I may be saved; lo, I am ready to do whatsoever thou layest upon me." Then said St. Francis, "My lord, now must I depart from you, but after I am returned to mine own country and by the grace of God have ascended to heaven, after my death, as it may please God, I will send thee two of my friars, at whose hands thou shalt receive the holy baptism of Christ and be saved, even as my Lord Jesus Christ hath revealed to me. And do thou meanwhile get thee free from all hindrance, so that when the grace of God shall come upon thee thou shalt find thyself well disposed to faith and devotion." Thus he promised and thus he did. This said, St. Francis returned with that venerable college of his holy companions, and after some years he gave up his soul to God by the death of the body. And the Soldan, being fallen sick, awaits the promise of St. Francis, and stations guards at certain of the passes, and commands them that if two friars appear in the habit of St. Francis, they shall straightway be led before him. At that very hour St. Francis appeared to two friars, and bade them tarry not, but hasten to the Soldan and compass his salvation, according as he had promised. And anon the friars set forth, and having crossed the pass, were led by the said guards before the Soldan. And when the Soldan beheld them he was filled with great joy, and said, "Now do I truly perceive that God hath sent his servants to me for my salvation, according to the promise St. Francis made to me by divine inspiration." And when he had received instruction from those friars in the faith of Christ and holy baptism, he, being born again in Christ, died of that sickness, and his soul was saved through the merits and the prayers of St. Francis.

CHAPTER XXV

HOW ST. FRANCIS MIRACULOUSLY HEALED A LEPER, BODY AND SOUL, AND WHAT THAT SOUL SAID TO HIM ON HER WAY TO HEAVEN

St. Francis, true disciple of Christ, while he lived in this miserable life, strove with all his might to follow Christ, the perfect Master; wherefore it befell many times, by divine power, that the souls of those, whose bodies he healed, were also healed at the selfsame hour, even as we read of Christ. And he not only served lepers gladly, but had also ordained that the friars of his Order, as they went about the world, should serve lepers for love of Christ, who for our sakes was willing to be accounted a leper. Now it befell on a time, in a friary nigh unto where St. Francis then was dwelling, that the friars were serving lepers and other sick folk in a lazar-house, among whom was a leper, so froward, so intolerable, and so insolent, that all believed of a surety he was possessed of the devil; and so in sooth it was, for he reviled so shamefully with words, and belaboured whosoever was tending him, and, what is worse, did foully blaspheme the blessed Christ and His most holy Mother the Virgin Mary, so that in no wise could one be found willing or able to serve him. And albeit the friars strove to bear patiently the injuries and insults heaped upon themselves, in order to increase the merit of their patience, nevertheless, their consciences were unable to endure those uttered against the Christ and His Mother: so they resolved to forsake the said leper, but would not until they had signified all things in due order to St. Francis, who was then dwelling in a friary hard by. And when they had signified these things to him, St. Francis came to this perverse leper, and drawing nigh, gave him salutation, saying, " God give thee peace, my dearest brother." The leper answers, " What peace can I have from God, who hath taken peace from me and all good things, and hath made me all rotten and stinking? " And St. Francis said, " My son, have patience, for the infirmities of the body are given to us by God in this world for the salvation of souls; inasmuch as they are of great merit when they are endured patiently." The sick man answers, " And how can I bear patiently this continual pain that afflicts me day and night? And not only am I afflicted by my sickness, but the friars thou gavest to serve me do even worse, and serve me not as they ought." Then St. Francis, knowing by divine revelation that this leper was possessed of the evil spirit, went aside and betook himself to prayer, and devoutly prayed God for him. His prayer ended, he returns to the leper and bespeaks him thus, " My son, I will serve thee, even I, since thou art not content with the others." And the leper answers, " So be it; but what canst thou do more than the others? " St. Francis answers, " Whatsoever thou wilt, that will I do." Says the leper, " I will that thou wash me all over, for I stink so foully that I cannot abide myself." Then St. Francis made quickly water boil, with many sweet-smelling herbs therein; then did strip the leper and began to wash him with his own hands, while another friar poured water over him. And by miracle divine, wherever St. Francis touched him with his holy hands the leprosy departed, and the flesh became perfectly whole. And even as the flesh began to heal, the soul began to heal also; whereupon the leper, seeing the leprosy on the way to leave him, began to have great compunction and repentance for his sins; and bitterly he began to weep; so that while the body was outwardly cleansed of the leprosy by the washing with water, the soul within was cleansed of sin by amendment and tears. And being wholly healed, as well in body as in soul, he humbly confessed his sins, and weeping, said with a loud voice, "Woe unto me, who am worthy of hell for the insults and injuries I have put upon the friars in word and deed, and for my perversity and blasphemies against God." Wherefore a fortnight long he persevered in bitter weeping for his sins and in craving mercy of God, confessing himself unto the priest with a whole heart. And when St. Francis beheld so clear a miracle that God had wrought by his hands, he gave thanks to God, and departing thence, journeyed into a very far country; for through humility he desired to flee all vainglory, and in all his works sought the honour and glory of God, and not his own. Then as it pleased God, the said leper, being healed in body and soul, fell sick of another infirmity a fortnight after his repentance; and, armed with the sacraments of the church, died a holy death. And his soul, on her way to paradise, appeared in the air to St. Francis, who was at prayer in a wood, and said to him, "Knowest thou me?" "Who art thou?" said St. Francis. "I am the leper whom the blessed Christ healed through thy merits, and this day am going to life everlasting; wherefore I render thanks to God and to thee. Blessed be thy soul and thy body; blessed thy holy words and deeds, because through thee many souls shall be saved in the world: and know that not a day passeth in the world but that the holy angels and the other saints give thanks to God for the holy fruits that thou and thy Order bring forth in divers parts of the world. Therefore be comforted, and give thanks to God and abide with His blessing." These words said, the soul passed into heaven, and St. Francis remained much comforted.

CHAPTER XXVI

HOW ST. FRANCIS CONVERTED THREE MURDEROUS ROBBERS THAT BECAME FRIARS; AND OF THE MOST NOBLE VISION THAT ONE OF THEM BEHELD WHO WAS A MOST HOLY FRIAR

St. Francis on a time was journeying through the wilderness of Borgo San Sepolcro, and as he passed by a stronghold, called Monte Casale, a noble and delicate youth came to him and said, "Father, fain would I become one of your friars." St. Francis answers, "Son, thou art but a delicate youth and of noble birth, peradventure thou couldst not endure our poverty and our hardships." And the youth said, "Father, are ye not men as I am? Since ye then endure these things, even so can I by the grace of Jesus Christ." St. Francis, well pleased with this answer, gave him his blessing, and anon received him into the Order, and gave him for name Friar Angel. And this youth waxed so in grace that short time after St. Francis made him warden of the friary called of Monte Casale. Now in those days three famous robbers who infested that country and wrought much evil therein, came to the said friary and besought the said warden, Friar Angel, to give them food to eat; and the warden answered them in this wise, rebuking them harshly, "Ye robbers and cruel manslayers, are ye not ashamed to steal the fruit of others' labours, but, frontless and insolent, would seek likewise to devour the alms bestowed on God's servants? Ye are not worthy even to walk this earth, for ye reverence neither man nor the God that created you; get ye gone, then, and be seen here no more." Whereat they, perturbed, departed in great fury. And lo, St. Francis appeared outside the friary, his wallet filled with bread, and carrying a small vessel of wine, that he and his companion had begged. And when the warden related to him how he had driven the robbers away, St. Francis chid him severely, saying he had borne himself cruelly, since sinners were better drawn to God by gentleness than by cruel reproof. "Wherefore our Master, Jesus Christ, whose gospel we have promised to observe, saith, that the whole need not a physician, but they that are sick, and that He had not come to call the just but sinners to repentance; and therefore many times He ate with them. Forasmuch as thou hast done contrary to charity and contrary to Christ's holy gospel, I command thee by holy obedience that thou straightway take this wallet of bread that I have begged and this vessel of wine, and go diligently after them over hill and valley until thou find them, and give them all this bread and wine from me: then kneel thee down before them and confess humbly thy fault of cruelty, and entreat them for my sake to work evil no more, but to fear God and offend Him no more; and say that if they will do this I promise to provide for all their needs, and give them continually enough to eat and to drink. And when thou hast done this, return humbly hither." While the said warden went to do this bidding, St. Francis betook himself to prayer, and besought God that He would soften the hearts of those robbers and convert them to repentance. The obedient warden overtakes them and gives them the bread and wine, and does and says what St. Francis had commanded him. And it pleased God that those robbers, as they ate of the alms of St. Francis, began to say to one another, "Woe unto us, wretched and hapless! what hard torments await us in hell! For we go about not only robbing our neighbours, beating and wounding them, but do slay them likewise; and so many evil deeds and wicked works notwithstanding, we have neither remorse of conscience nor fear of God; and lo, this holy friar hath come to us, and for a few words wherewith he justly rebuked our wickedness, hath humbly confessed to us his fault; and moreover, hath brought us bread and wine and promise so bounteous from the holy father: verily these are God's holy friars that merit His paradise, and we are children of eternal wrath that deserve the pains of hell, and each day do increase our doom; yea, we know not whether for the sins we have committed to this day we may return to the mercy of God." These and the like words being spoken by one of them, the others said, "Of a surety thou speakest sooth, but look ye, what must we do?" "Go we," said one, "to St. Francis, and if he give us hope that we may find mercy from God for our sins, let us do whatsoever he command us, and so may we deliver our souls from the torments of hell." Now this counsel was pleasing to the others, and thus all three being in accord, they came in haste to St. Francis and spake to him thus, "Father, we for our many wicked sins believe we cannot return to the mercy of God; but if thou have some hope that God in His mercy will receive us, lo, we are ready to do thy bidding and to do penance with thee." Then St. Francis received them with loving-kindness and comforted them with many examples, and made them confident of God's mercy, promising he would surely obtain it for them from God. He told them that the mercy of God was infinite, and that, according to the gospel, even if our sins were infinite, His mercy was yet greater than our sins; and that the Apostle St. Paul hath said, "Christ the blessed came into the world to save sinners." Hearing these words and the like teachings, the said three robbers renounced the devil and all his works, and St. Francis received them into the Order, and they began to do great penance. And two of them lived but a brief space after their conversion and went to paradise; but the third lived on, and, pondering on his sins, gave himself up to do such penance during fifteen unbroken years that, besides the common lenten fasts which he kept with the other friars, he fasted three days of the week on bread and water; he went ever barefoot, with naught on his back but a single tunic, nor ever slept after matins. In the meantime St. Francis passed from this miserable life; and this friar through many years continued his penance, when lo, one night after matins, so sore a temptation to sleep came upon him, that in no wise could he resist it, nor watch as he was wont to do. At length, unable to overcome his drowsiness, or to pray, he lay on his bed to sleep. No sooner had he laid down his head than he was rapt and led in spirit to the top of a very high mountain over a steep place, and on this side and on that were broken and jagged rocks and monstrous crags that jutted forth from the rocks; wherefore this steep place was frightful to behold. And the angel that was leading this friar pushed him and flung him down that steep place; and as he fell he was dashed from rock to rock and from crag to crag until he fell to the bottom of the abyss, his limbs all broken and shattered to pieces, according as it seemed to him. And lying thus mangled on the ground, he that led him said, "Rise up, for it behoves thee to go a yet greater journey." The friar answered, "Methinks thou art a most foolish and cruel man; for thou seest I am well-nigh dead of my fall, which has dashed me to pieces, and thou yet biddest me rise up." And the angel drew nigh and, touching him, made all his members whole again and healed his wounds. And then he showed him a great plain, full of sharp and pointed stones and thorns and briars, and told him he must needs run across all this plain and pass over it with naked feet until he came to the end; there he would behold a fiery furnace wherein he must enter. And the friar having passed over all the plain with great pain and anguish, the angel said to him, "Enter yon furnace, for this it behoves thee now to do." He answers, "Alas! how cruel a guide art thou, that seest I am nigh unto death, because of this horrible plain; and now for repose thou biddest me enter this fiery furnace." And as he gazed, he beheld many devils around the furnace with iron forks in their hands, wherewith, seeing him slow to enter, they thrust him into the furnace. Having entered the furnace, he gazed around and beheld one that had been his boon companion, who was all a-burning; and he asked of him, "O hapless comrade, how camest thou here?" And he answered and said, "Go a little farther and thou shalt find my wife, thy gossip; she will tell thee the cause of our damnation." And as the friar passed on, lo, the said gossip appeared, all aflame and enclosed in a fiery measure of corn; and he asked her, saying, "O gossip, hapless and wretched, why art thou in so cruel a torment?" And she answered, "Because at the time of the great famine that St. Francis had foretold, my husband and I gave false measure of corn and wheat; therefore do I burn in this measure." These words said, the angel who was leading the friar thrust him out of the furnace and said to him, "Make thee ready for a horrible journey thou hast to take." And he, lamenting, said, "O guide most cruel, that hast no compassion on me, thou seest I am well-nigh all burned in this furnace, and yet wouldst lead me on a perilous and horrible journey." And the angel touched him, and made him whole and strong. Then he led him to a bridge, which could not be crossed without great peril, for it was very frail and narrow and slippery and without a rail at the sides; and beneath it flowed a terrible river, filled with serpents and dragons and scorpions, that it gave forth a great stench. And the angel said to him, "Pass over this bridge; at any cost thou must pass over." And the friar answers, "And how shall I cross without falling into this perilous river?" Says the angel, "Follow after me, and set thy foot where thou seest me place mine; so shalt thou pass over well." This friar passes behind the angel as he had shown him, until he reached the middle of the bridge, and as he stood thus on the crown of the bridge the angel flew away, and departing from him, went to the top of a most high mountain far away beyond the bridge. And the friar considered well the place whither the angel had flown; but, left without a guide and gazing below him, he beheld those terrible beasts with their heads out of the water and with open jaws ready to devour him if peradventure he should fall; and he trembled so that in no wise knew he what to do, nor what to say; for he could neither turn back nor go forward. Wherefore, beholding himself in such great tribulation, and that he had no other refuge save in God, he stooped down and clasped the bridge, and with his whole heart and in tears he commended himself to God, and prayed that of His most holy mercy he would succour him. His prayer ended, himseemed to put forth wings, whereat with great joy he waited until they grew, that he might fly beyond the bridge whither the angel had flown. But after a while, by the great desire he had to pass beyond this bridge, he set himself to fly, and because his wings were not yet fully grown, he fell upon the bridge and his wings dropped from him; whereat he clasped the bridge again, and commended himself as before to God. And his prayer ended, again himseemed to put forth wings; but, as before, he waited not until they had fully grown, and setting himself to fly before the time, he fell again on the bridge, and his wings dropped. Wherefore, seeing these things, and that he had fallen, through his untimely haste to fly, he began to say within himself, "Of a surety, if I put forth wings a third time, I will wait until they be so great that I may fly without falling again." And pondering these things, lo, himseemed yet a third time to put forth wings; and waiting a great space, until they were well grown, himseemed with the first and second and third putting forth of wings that he had waited full a hundred and fifty years or more. At length he lifted him up this third time, and with all his might took wing and flew on high as far as the place whither the angel had flown. And knocking at the door of the palace wherein the angel was, the doorkeeper asked of him, "Who art thou that comest here?" He answered, "I am a friar minor." Says the doorkeeper, "Tarry a while, for I will bring St. Francis hither, to see if he know thee." As he went his way to St. Francis, this friar began to gaze on the marvellous walls of the palace; and lo, these walls appeared translucent and of such exceeding brightness that he beheld clearly the choirs of the saints and all that was doing within. And standing thus amazed at this vision, lo, St. Francis cometh, and Friar Bernard, and Friar Giles; and after these, so great a multitude of sainted men and women that had followed the example of his life, that they seemed wellnigh countless; and St. Francis came forth and said to the doorkeeper, "Let him enter, for he is one of my friars." And no sooner had he entered therein than he felt such great consolation and such sweetness that he forgot all the tribulations he had suffered, even as if they had not been. And then St. Francis led him in and showed him many marvellous things, and thus bespake him, "Son, needs must thou return to the world and abide there seven days, wherein thou shalt make thee ready diligently and with great devotion; for after these seven days I will come for thee, and then shalt thou enter with me this abode of the blessed." Now St. Francis was arrayed in a wondrous garment, adorned with fairest stars, and his five stigmas were like unto five beauteous stars, of such exceeding splendour that the whole palace was illumined with their beams. And Friar Bernard's head was crowned with fairest stars, and Friar Giles was aureoled with wondrous light; and many other friars he knew among them that in the world he had never seen. Then taking leave of St. Francis he returned, albeit with laggard steps, to the world again. And when he awoke and returned to himself and came to his wits again, the friars were chanting prime; so that he had been in that vision but from matins to prime, albeit it had seemed to him that he had remained therein many years. And having related to the warden all this vision in due order, he began, within seven days, to sicken of a fever; and on the eighth day St. Francis came for him, according to his promise, with a great multitude of glorious saints, and led his soul to life everlasting in the realms of the blessed.

CHAPTER XXVII

HOW ST. FRANCIS CONVERTED TWO SCHOLARS AT BOLOGNA THAT BECAME FRIARS, AND THEN DELIVERED ONE OF THEM FROM A GREAT TEMPTATION

Once on a time when St. Francis came to the city of Bologna all the people of the city ran forth to behold him, and so great was the press that the folk could with great difficulty reach the market-place; and the whole place being filled with men and women and scholars, lo, St. Francis stood up on high in the midst of them and began to preach what the Holy Ghost taught him. And so wondrously he preached that he seemed to speak with the voice of an angel rather than of a man; his celestial words seemed to pierce the hearts of those that heard them, even as sharp arrows, so that during his sermon a great multitude of men and women were converted to repentance. Among whom were two students of noble birth from the Marches of Ancona, the one named Pellegrino, the other Rinieri: and being touched in their hearts by divine inspiration through the said sermon, they came to St. Francis saying they desired wholly to forsake the world and be numbered among his friars. Then St. Francis, knowing by divine revelation that they were sent of God and were to lead a holy life in the Order, and considering their great fervour, received them joyfully, saying, "Thou, Pellegrino, keep the way of humility in the Order, and do thou, Friar Rinieri, serve the friars;" and thus it was: for Friar Pellegrino would never go forth as a priest but as a lay brother, albeit he was a great clerk and learned in the canon law. And by reason of this humility he attained to great perfection of virtue; in such wise that Friar Bernard, first-born of St. Francis, said of him, that he was one of the most perfect friars in this world. Finally, the said Friar Pellegrino passed from his blessed life, full of virtue, and wrought many miracles before his death and after. And the said Friar Rinieri, devoutly living in great holiness and humility, faithfully served the friars, and was much beloved of St. Francis. Being afterwards chosen minister of the province of the Marches of Ancona, he ruled it a long time with great peace and discretion. After a while God suffered a sore temptation to arise in his soul; whereat, in anguish and tribulation, he afflicted himself mightily with fastings and scourgings, with tears and prayers, both day and night. Nevertheless, he could not banish that temptation, but ofttimes was in great despair because he deemed himself forsaken by God. In this great despair he resolved, as a last remedy, to go to St. Francis, thinking thus within himself, "If St. Francis meet me with a kindly countenance, and show me affection, as he is wont to do, I believe that God will yet have compassion on me: but if not it shall be a token that I am forsaken of God." Thereupon he set forth and went to St. Francis, who at that time lay grievously sick in the bishop's palace at Assisi; and God revealed to him all the manner of that temptation, and of the state of the said Friar Rinieri, and his coming. And straightway St. Francis calls Friar Leo and Friar Masseo, and says to them, "Go ye quickly and meet my most dear son, Friar Rinieri, and embrace him for me and salute him, and say unto him that among all the friars that are in the world, him I love with singular love." They go forth and find Friar Rinieri by the way and embrace him, saying unto him what St. Francis had charged them to say. Whereupon such great consolation and sweetness filled his soul that he was well-nigh beside himself with joy, and giving thanks to God with all his heart he journeyed on and reached the place where St. Francis lay sick. And albeit St. Francis was grievously sick, nevertheless, when he heard Friar Rinieri coming, he rose up from his bed and went towards him and embraced him most sweetly and spake to him thus, " Friar Rinieri, dearest son, thee I love above all the friars in this world; thee I love with singular love: " and these words said, he made the sign of most holy cross on his brow and there did kiss him Then he said to him, " Son most dear, God hath suffered this sore temptation to befall thee for thy great gain of merit: but if thou desire this gain no longer, have it not." Marvellous to tell! no sooner had St. Francis uttered these words than all temptation departed from him, even as if he ne'er had felt it in his life: and he remained fully comforted.

CHAPTER XXVIII

OF THE DIVINE ECSTASY THAT CAME TO FRIAR BERNARD WHEREBY HE REMAINED FROM MORN TO NOON INSENSIBLE TO OUTWARD THINGS

How large a measure of grace God oft bestowed on poor followers of the gospel that forsook the world for love of Christ was shown forth in Friar Bernard of Quintavalle, who, after having put on the habit of St. Francis, was rapt many times in God through contemplation of celestial things. Among others, it befell on a time that when he was in church hearing mass, and with his whole mind lifted up to God, he became so absorbed and rapt in God that he perceived not when the body of Christ was elevated, nor knelt down, nor drew off his cowl as the other friars did: but without moving his eyes, stood with fixed gaze, insensible to outward things from morn till noon. And after noon, returning to himself, he went about the friary crying with a voice of wonder, " O friars, O friars, O friars, there is no man in this country, were he ever so great or so noble, but if he were promised a beautiful palace filled with gold would not find it easy to carry a sack full of dung in order to win that treasure so noble." To this celestial treasure, promised to those that love God, the aforesaid Friar Bernard had his mind so lifted up that for full fifteen years he ever went with his mind and his countenance raised to heaven; during which time he never satisfied his hunger at table, albeit he ate a little of that which was placed before him: for he was wont to say that perfect abstinence did not consist in foregoing that which a man did not relish, but that true abstinence lay in using temperance in those things that were of pleasant savour in the mouth; and thereby he attained to such degree of clearness and light of understanding that even great doctors had recourse to him for the solution of the knottiest questions and of difficult passages in the Scriptures, and he resolved all their difficulties. And forasmuch as his mind was wholly loosed and detached from earthly things, he, like the swallows, soared high by contemplation: wherefore, sometimes twenty days, sometimes thirty, he dwelt alone on the tops of the highest mountains, contemplating divine things. For which cause Friar Giles was wont to say of him, that on no other man was this gift bestowed as it was on Friar Bernard; to wit, that he should feed flying, as the swallows did. And for this excellent grace that he had from God, St. Francis willingly and oft spake with him, both day and night; so that sometimes they were found together in the wood, rapt in God, the whole night long, whither they had both withdrawn to discourse of God.

CHAPTER XXIX

HOW THE DEVIL IN THE FORM OF THE CRUCIFIED APPEARED MANY TIMES TO FRIAR RUFFINO AND TOLD HIM HE WAS LOSING THE GOOD HE WAS PRACTISING BECAUSE HE WAS NOT OF THE ELECT. WHEREAT ST. FRANCIS, KNOWING THIS BY REVELATION FROM GOD, MADE FRIAR RUFFINO WARE OF THE ERRORS WHERETO HE HAD GIVEN CREDENCE

Friar Ruffino, one of the noblest gentlemen of the city of Assisi, and the companion of St. Francis, a man of great holiness, was once mightily assailed and tempted in soul touching predestination; whereby he became full of sadness and melancholy; for the devil put it into his heart that he was damned, and not among those predestined to eternal life; and that he was losing all his work in the Order. And this temptation lasting many days, he, for very shame, did not reveal it to St. Francis; nevertheless he ceased not to pray nor to observe the usual fasts: whereat the enemy began to heap trial upon trial upon him, and ever and above the battle within did likewise assail him outwardly with false visions. Wherefore he appeared to him once in the form of the Crucified, and said to him, "O Friar Ruffino, wherefore afflict thyself with penance and prayer, seeing thou art not among those predestined to life eternal? Believe me, for I know whom I have elected and predestined, and heed not the son of Peter Bernadone if he tell thee contrary; and moreover, question him not concerning this matter, for neither he nor any man knoweth; none save Me, that am the Son of God: therefore believe that of a surety thou art numbered among the damned; and the son of Peter Bernadone, thy father, and his father also are damned, and whosoever followeth him is beguiled." These words said, Friar Ruffino began to be so overcast by the prince of darkness that already he lost all the faith and love he had had for St. Francis, and cared not to tell him aught of his condition. But that which Friar Ruffino told not the holy father was revealed to him by the Holy Spirit; whereat St. Francis, beholding in spirit the great peril of the said friar, sent Friar Masseo for him; to whom Friar Ruffino answered, murmuring, "What have I to do with Friar Francis?" Then Friar Masseo, filled with divine wisdom, and knowing the wiles of the devil, said, "O Friar Ruffino, knowest thou not that St. Francis is like unto an angel of God that hath illumined so many souls in this world and from whom we have received the grace of God? Therefore I desire that thou, by all means, come with me to him, for clearly do I perceive thou art beguiled by the devil." This said, lo, Friar Ruffino set forth and went to St. Francis; and St. Francis beholding him coming from afar, began to cry, "O naughty Friar Ruffino, to whom hast thou given credence?" And when Friar Ruffino was come to him, St. Francis related all the temptation he had suffered from the devil in due order, both within and without, and showed to him clearly that he who had appeared to him was the devil and not Christ, and that in no wise should he consent unto his suggestions; but that "whenever the devil saith again to thee: 'Thou art damned,' answer him thus: 'Open thy mouth and I will drop my dung therein.' And let this be a token to thee that he is the devil and not Christ; and when thou hast thus answered he will forthwith flee from thee. By this token also shalt thou know that it was the devil: for that he hardened thy heart against all good, which thing is his own proper office; but the blessed Christ never hardeneth the heart of the man of faith, rather doth He soften it according as He speaketh by the mouth of the prophet: 'I will take away the stony heart out of their flesh, and will give them an heart of flesh.'" Then Friar Ruffino, seeing that St. Francis had told him all the circumstance of his temptation, was melted by his words, and began to weep bitterly and to give praise to St. Francis, humbly confessing his fault in that he had hidden his temptation from him. And thus he remained fully consoled and comforted by the holy father's admonitions and wholly changed for the better. Then at the last St. Francis said to him, "Go, my son, confess thee, and cease not the exercise of thy wonted prayers, and know of a surety that this temptation shall be of great profit and consolation to thee, and in brief time shalt thou prove it." Friar Ruffino returns to his cell in the wood, and being at prayer with many tears, lo, the enemy comes in the form of Christ, according to outward similitude, and saith to him, "O Friar Ruffino, did I not tell thee thou shouldst not believe the son of Peter Bernadone, and shouldst not weary thee in tears and prayers, seeing thou art damned? What doth it profit thee to afflict thyself while thou art yet alive, seeing that when thou diest thou shalt be damned?" And anon Friar Ruffino answered the devil and said, "Open thy mouth and I will drop my dung therein." Whereupon the devil straightway departed in great wrath, and with such tempest and ruin of stones from Mount Subasio hard by, that the thunder of the falling rocks endured a great space; and so mightily did they smite one against the other as they rolled down that they kindled horrible sparks of fire through the vale below: and at the terrible noise they made, St. Francis and his companions issued forth from the friary in great amaze to behold what strange thing had befallen; and to this very day that mighty ruin of rocks may be seen. Then did Friar Ruffino manifestly perceive that he who had beguiled him was the devil, and returning to St. Francis flung himself again on the ground and confessed his fault. And St. Francis comforted him with sweet words, and sent him forth all consoled to his cell; wherein, while he remained in devoutest prayers, the blessed Christ appeared to him and kindled his whole soul with divine love, and said, "Well didst thou, My son, to believe in Friar Francis; for he who afflicted thee was the devil; but I am Christ thy Master, and to make thee full sure I give thee this token: that while thou livest thou shalt feel neither sadness nor melancholy." This said, Christ departed, leaving him in such gladness and sweetness of spirit and elevation of mind, that day and night he was absorbed and rapt in God. And thenceforth was he so confirmed in grace and in certainty of salvation that he became wholly changed into another man, and would have remained both day and night in prayer and in contemplation of divine things, if the friars had suffered him. Wherefore St. Francis said of him, that Friar Ruffino was canonised by Christ in this life, and that save in his presence he would not hesitate to call him Saint Ruffino, albeit he still was living on the earth.

CHAPTER XXX

OF THE FAIR SERMON THAT ST. FRANCIS AND FRIAR RUFFINO PREACHED AT ASSISI

THE said Friar Ruffino was by his continual contemplation so absorbed in God that he grew dumb and almost insensible to outward things, and spake very seldom, and, moreover, had no longer grace, nor courage, nor eloquence in preaching. None the less St. Francis on a time bade him go to Assisi and preach to the people what God should inspire him to say. Whereat Friar Ruffino answered and said, "Reverend father, prithee forgive me and send me not, for thou knowest I lack the gift of preaching, and am simple and unlearned." Then said St. Francis, "Forasmuch as thou hast not obeyed quickly, I command thee by holy obedience that thou go to Assisi naked, and clothed only in thy breeches, and enter into a church and preach to the people." At his command Friar Ruffino strips himself and goes forth to Assisi and enters a church; and having made his reverence to the altar ascends the pulpit and begins to preach. Whereat the children and the men of Assisi began to laugh and said, "Now look ye, these friars do such penance that they grow foolish and lose their wits." Meanwhile, St. Francis, bethinking him of the ready obedience of Friar Ruffino, that was one of the noblest gentlemen of Assisi, and of the hard command he had laid upon him, began to upbraid himself, saying, "Whence, O son of Peter Bernadone, thou sorry churl, whence such great presumption that thou commandest Friar Ruffino, one of the noblest gentlemen of Assisi, to go and preach to the people like a crazy man? By God's grace thou shalt prove in thyself what thou commandest others to do." And straightway in fervour of spirit he stripped himself in like manner and set forth for Assisi; and with him he took Friar Leo, who carried his and Friar Ruffino's habits. And the men of

Assisi, beholding him in like plight, mocked him, deeming that he and Friar Ruffino were crazy from excess of penance. St. Francis enters the church, where Friar Ruffino was preaching thus, " O dearest brethren, flee from the world and forsake sin, make restoration to others if ye would escape from hell; keep God's commandments and love God and your neighbour if ye would go to heaven; do penance if ye would possess the kingdom of heaven." Then St. Francis mounted the pulpit and began to preach so wondrously of the contempt of the world, of holy penance, of voluntary poverty, and of the desire for the heavenly kingdom, and of the nakedness and shame of the passion of our Lord Jesus Christ, that all they that were present at the sermon, men and women, in great multitudes, began to weep bitterly with wondrous devotion and contrition of heart; and not only there, but throughout the whole of Assisi, was such bewailing of the passion of Christ that the like had never been known before. And the people being thus edified and consoled by this act of St. Francis and of Friar Ruffino, St. Francis clothed himself and Friar Ruffino again; and thus re-clad they returned to the friary of the Porziuncula, praising and glorifying God, who had given them the grace to vanquish themselves by contempt of self, and to edify Christ's little sheep by good example, and to show forth how much the world is to be despised. And on that day the devotion of the people towards them increased so greatly that he who could touch the hem of their garments deemed himself blessed.

CHAPTER XXXI

HOW ST. FRANCIS KNEW THE SECRETS OF THE CONSCIENCES OF HIS FRIARS IN ALL THINGS

EVEN as our Lord Jesus Christ saith in the gospel, " I know My sheep, and Mine own know Me," etc., so the blessed father St. Francis, like a good shepherd, knew all the merits and the virtues of his companions by divine revelation, and likewise their failings: by which means he knew how to provide the best remedy for each, to wit, by humbling the proud, exalting the humble, reproving vice, and praising virtue, even as may be read in the wondrous revelations he had, touching his first household. Among which it is found that St. Francis being on a time with his household in a friary discoursing of God, and

Friar Ruffino not being with them during that discourse, but in the wood absorbed in contemplation, lo, while they continued in their discourse of God, Friar Ruffino came forth from the wood and passed by somewhat afar from them. Then St. Francis, beholding him, turned to his companions and asked of them, saying, "Tell me, who think ye is the saintliest soul God hath in this world?" And they answered him, saying, they believed it was his own; and St. Francis said to them, "Dearest friars, I am of myself the most unworthy and vilest of men that God hath in this world; but, behold yon Friar Ruffino, that now cometh forth from the wood! God hath revealed to me that his soul is one of the three saintliest souls in this world: and truly I say unto you, that I would not doubt to call him St. Ruffino even while he yet liveth, for his soul is confirmed in grace, and sanctified and canonised in heaven by our Lord Jesus Christ." But these words St. Francis never spoke in the presence of the said Friar Ruffino. Likewise, how that St. Francis knew the failings of his friars is clearly manifest in Friar Elias, whom many times he chid for his pride; and in Friar John della Cappella, to whom he foretold that he was to hang himself by the neck; and in that friar whom the devil held fast by the throat when he was corrected for his disobedience; and in many other friars whose secret failings and virtues he clearly knew by revelation from Christ.

CHAPTER XXXII

HOW FRIAR MASSEO CRAVED FROM CHRIST THE VIRTUE OF HUMILITY

The first companions of St. Francis strove with all their might to be poor in earthly things and rich in virtue, whereby they attained to true celestial and eternal riches. It befell one day that while they were gathered together discoursing of God, a friar among them spake thus by way of example, "One there was, a great friend of God, that had much grace both for the active and for the contemplative life, and withal he was of such exceeding humility that he deemed himself the greatest of sinners. And this humility confirmed and sanctified him in grace and made him increase continually in virtue and in divine gifts, and never suffered him to fall into sin." Now Friar Masseo, hearing such wondrous things of humility, and knowing it to be a treasure of life eternal, began to be so kindled with love, and with desire for this virtue of humility, that in great fervour of spirit he lifted up his face to heaven and made a vow and steadfast aim never to rejoice again in this world until he felt the said virtue perfectly in his soul: and thenceforth he remained well-nigh continually secluded in his cell, mortifying himself with fasts, vigils, prayer, and bitter tears before God to obtain that virtue from Him, failing which he deemed himself worthy of hell—the virtue wherewith that friend of God of whom he had heard was so bounteously dowered. And Friar Masseo, being thus for many days filled with this desire, it fell out on a day that he entered the wood, and in fervour of spirit roamed about giving forth tears, sighs, and cries, and craving this virtue from God with fervent desire: and since God willingly granteth the prayers of humble and contrite hearts, there came a voice from heaven to Friar Masseo, as he thus strove, and called him twice, "Friar Masseo, Friar Masseo!" And he, knowing in spirit that it was the voice of Christ, answered thus, "My Lord." And Christ said to him, "What wouldst thou give to possess the grace thou askest?" Friar Masseo answered, "Lord, I would give the eyes out of my head." And Christ said to him, "And I will that thou have this grace and thine eyes also." This said, the voice vanished, and Friar Masseo remained filled with such grace of the yearned-for virtue of humility, and of the light of God, that from thenceforth he was ever blithe of heart. And many times he made a joyous sound like the cooing of a dove, "Coo, coo, coo." And with glad countenance and jocund heart he dwelt thus in contemplation; and withal, being grown most humble, he deemed himself the least of men in the world. Being asked by Friar James of Falterone wherefore he changed not his note in these his jubilations, he answered with great joyfulness, that when we find full contentment in one song there is no need to change the tune.

CHAPTER XXXIII

HOW ST. CLARE, BY COMMAND OF THE POPE, BLESSED THE BREAD THAT LAY ON THE TABLE, WHEREUPON THE SIGN OF THE HOLY CROSS APPEARED ON EVERY LOAF

St. Clare, most devout disciple of the cross of Christ and noble plant of St. Francis, was so filled with holiness that not only bishops and cardinals but the pope also, with great affection, desired to behold and to hear her, and ofttimes visited her in person. Among other times, the holy father once went to her convent to hear her discourse of divine and celestial things: and being thus together, holding divers discourses, St. Clare had the table laid and set loaves of bread thereon that the holy father might bless them. Whereupon, the spiritual discourse being ended, St. Clare knelt down with great reverence and besought him to be pleased to bless the bread placed on the table. The holy father answers, "Sister Clare, most faithful one, I desire that thou bless this bread, and make over it the sign of the most holy cross of Christ, to which thou hast wholly devoted thyself." And St. Clare saith, "Most holy father, pardon me, for I should merit too great reproof if, in the presence of the vicar of Christ, I, that am a poor, vile woman, should presume to give such benediction." And the pope gives answer, "To the end that this be not imputed to thy presumption, but to the merit of obedience, I command thee, by holy obedience, that thou make the sign of the most holy cross over this bread, and bless it in the name of God." Then St. Clare, even as a true daughter of obedience, devoutly blessed the bread with the sign of the most holy cross. Marvellous to tell! forthwith on all those loaves the sign of the cross appeared figured most beautifully. Then, of those loaves, a part was eaten and a part preserved, in token of the miracle. And the holy father, when he saw this miracle, partook of the said bread and departed, thanking God and leaving his blessing with St. Clare. In that time Sister Ortolana, mother of St. Clare, abode in the convent, and Sister Agnes, her own sister, both of them, together with St. Clare, full of virtue and of the Holy Spirit, and with many other nuns, to whom St. Francis sent many sick persons; and they, with their prayers and with the sign of the most holy cross, restored health to all of them.

CHAPTER XXXIV

HOW ST. LOUIS, KING OF FRANCE, WENT IN PERSON, IN THE GUISE OF A PILGRIM, TO PERUGIA TO VISIT THE SAINTLY FRIAR GILES

St. Louis, King of France, went on a pilgrimage to visit the holy places throughout the world, and hearing of the far-famed holiness of Friar Giles, who had been one of the first companions of St. Francis, purposed and set his heart wholly on visiting him in person: for which thing he came to Perugia, where the said friar then dwelt. And coming to the door of the friary as a poor unknown pilgrim, with but few companions, he asked with great importunity for Friar Giles, telling not the doorkeeper who he was. So the doorkeeper goes to Friar Giles and says, "There is a pilgrim at the door that asketh for you." And God inspired and revealed to him that this was the King of France. Whereat, anon he comes forth from his cell with great fervour and runs to the door; and asking naught, and never having seen each other before, they knelt down with great devotion, and embraced each other, and kissed with such affection as if for a long space they had been great friends together; yet, through all this, neither one nor the other spake, but they remained silently locked in each other's arms with those outward signs of loving charity. And after they had remained thus a great space, saying no word each to other, they both departed: St. Louis went his way and Friar Giles returned to his cell. Now as the king was setting forth, a friar asked of one of the king's companions who he might be that had so long embraced Friar Giles, and answer was made that he was Louis, King of France, who had come to see Friar Giles. And when the friar told this to the others they waxed mightily afflicted that Friar Giles had spoken no word with the king, and, making complaint, they cried, "O Friar Giles, wherefore hast thou been so churlish as to speak no word to so great and saintly a king, that hath come from France to see thee and to hear some good word from thee?" Friar Giles answered, "Dearest friars, marvel not thereat, for neither I to him nor he to me could utter one word; since, no sooner had we embraced together, than the light of wisdom revealed and manifested his heart to me and mine to him, and thus, by divine power, as we looked in each other's breasts, we knew better what I would say to him and he to me than if we had spoken with our mouths; and greater consolation had we than if we had sought to explain with our lips what we felt in our hearts. For, because of the defect of human speech, that cannot express clearly the mysteries and secrets of God, words would have left us disconsolate rather than consoled; know, therefore, that the king departed from me marvellously glad and consoled in spirit."

CHAPTER XXXV

HOW ST. CLARE, BEING SICK, WAS MIRACULOUSLY BORNE ON CHRISTMAS EVE TO THE CHURCH OF ST. FRANCIS, AND THERE HEARD THE OFFICE

St. Clare, being on a time grievously sick, so that she could in no wise go to say the office in church with the other nuns, and seeing that when the feast of the Nativity of Christ came all the others went to matins, while she remained in bed, grew ill at ease that she could not go with them and enjoy that spiritual consolation. But Jesus Christ, her spouse, not willing to leave her thus disconsolate, caused her to be miraculously borne to the church of St. Francis and to be present at the whole office of matins, and at the midnight mass; and moreover, she received the holy communion, and then was borne back to her bed. When the nuns returned to St. Clare, after the office at St. Damian's was over, they spake to her thus, "O Sister Clare, our mother, what great consolation have we had on this holy feast of the Nativity; would now it had pleased God that you had been with us!" And St. Clare answered, "Thanks and praise do I render to our blessed Lord Jesus Christ, my sisters, and dearest daughters, for at all the solemn offices of this most holy night, yea, and at even greater festivals have I been present with great consolation of soul, than ye have seen, for by the solicitude of my father, St. Francis, and by the grace of Jesus Christ, have I been present in the church of my venerable father, St. Francis; and with my bodily and spiritual ears have I heard all the office and the music of the organs that were played there, and in that same church have I partaken of the most holy communion. Wherefore rejoice ye that such grace hath been vouchsafed to me and praise our Lord Jesus Christ."

CHAPTER XXXVI

HOW ST. FRANCIS INTERPRETED A FAIR VISION THAT FRIAR LEO HAD SEEN

On a time when St. Francis lay grievously sick and Friar Leo was tending him, the said friar, being in prayer by the side of St. Francis, was rapt in ecstasy and led in spirit to a mighty torrent, wide and raging. And as he stood gazing on those who were crossing it, he beheld certain friars, bearing burdens, enter into this stream that anon were overthrown by the fierce buffetings of the waves and drowned; some reached as far as a third of the way across; others as far as the middle; yet others reached nigh over unto the shore. But all of them, by reason of the fury of the waters and the heavy burdens they bore on their backs, fell at last and were drowned. Friar Leo, beholding this, had compassion on them exceeding great, and straightway, as he stood thus, lo, there comes a great multitude of friars, bearing no burdens or load of any kind, in whom shone forth the light of holy poverty: and they entered this stream and passed over to the other side without peril: and when he had seen this, Friar Leo returned to himself. Then St. Francis, feeling in spirit that Friar Leo had seen a vision, called him to himself and asked touching the vision he had seen. And as soon as the aforesaid Friar Leo had told his vision in due order, St. Francis said, "What thou hast seen is true. The mighty stream is this world; the friars that were drowned therein are they that followed not the teachings of the gospel, and especially in regard to most high poverty; but they that passed over without peril are those friars that seek after no earthly or carnal thing, nor possess aught in this world; but, temperate in food and clothing, are glad, following Christ naked on the cross, and bear joyously and willingly the burden and sweet yoke of Christ and of most holy obedience. Therefore they pass with ease from this temporal life to life eternal."

CHAPTER XXXVII

HOW JESUS CHRIST THE BLESSED, AT THE PRAYER OF ST. FRANCIS, CAUSED A RICH AND NOBLE KNIGHT TO BE CONVERTED AND BECOME A FRIAR; WHICH KNIGHT HAD DONE GREAT HONOUR AND HAD MADE MANY GIFTS UNTO ST. FRANCIS

St. Francis, servant of Christ, coming late at eve to the house of a great and potent nobleman, was received and entertained by him, both he and his companion, as had they been angels of God, with the greatest courtesy and devotion; wherefore St. Francis loved him much, considering that on entering the house he had embraced him and kissed him affectionately; then had washed his feet and wiped them and humbly kissed them; and had kindled a great fire and made ready the table with much good food; and while he ate, did serve him zealously with joyful countenance. Now when St. Francis and his companion had eaten, this nobleman said, "Lo, my father, I proffer myself and my goods to you; how many times soever you have need of tunic or cloak or aught else, buy them and I will pay for you; nay, look you, I am ready to provide for all your needs, for by God's grace I am able so to do, inasmuch as I have abundance of all worldly goods; therefore, for love of God, that hath bestowed them on me, I willingly do good to His poor." St. Francis, beholding such great courtesy and loving-kindness in him, and his bounteous offerings, conceived for him love so great that when he afterwards departed from him he spake thus to his companion as they journeyed together, "Verily this noble gentleman, that is so grateful and thankful to God and so kind and courteous to his neighbour and to the poor, would be a good companion for our Order. Know, dearest friar, that courtesy is one of the attributes of God, who of His courtesy giveth His sun and His rain to the just and to the unjust: and courtesy is sister to charity, that quencheth hatred and kindleth love. And since I have found in this good man such divine virtue, fain would I have him for companion: therefore I will that one day we return to him, if haply God may touch his heart and bend his will to accompany us in the service of God. Meanwhile, pray we unto God that He may set this desire in his heart and give him grace to attain thereto." Marvellous to tell! a few days after St. Francis had made this prayer, God put these desires into this nobleman's heart, and St. Francis said to his companion, "Let us go, my brother, to the abode of that courteous gentleman, for I have a certain hope in God that, with the same bounty he hath shown in temporal things, he will give himself also, and will be our companion." And they went. And coming nigh unto his house, St. Francis said to his companion, "Tarry a while for me; I desire first to pray to God that He may prosper our way, and that it may please Jesus Christ to grant unto us, poor and weak men, the noble prey we think to snatch from the world by virtue of His most holy Passion." This said, he went forth to pray in a place where he might be seen of that same courteous gentleman. Now, as it pleased God, he, looking hither and thither, had perceived St. Francis most devoutly in prayer before Jesus Christ, who with great splendour had appeared to him and stood before him during the said prayer; and as he thus gazed he beheld St. Francis lifted up a great space bodily from the earth. Whereat he was so touched by God and inspired to forsake the world that he straightway came forth from his mansion and ran in fervour of spirit towards St. Francis, and coming to him, who still remained in prayer, knelt down at his feet, and with great instance and devotion prayed that it might please him to receive him and do penance with him together. Then St. Francis, seeing his prayer was heard of God, and that what he himself desired, that noble gentleman was craving with much importunity, lifted himself up, and in fervour and gladness of heart embraced and kissed him, devoutly giving thanks to God, who had increased his company by so great a knight. And that gentleman said to St. Francis, "What dost thou command me to do, my father? Lo, I am ready to do thy bidding and give all I possess to the poor, and thus disburdened of all worldly things to follow Christ with thee." Thus did he, according to the counsel of St. Francis, for he distributed all his goods among the poor, and entered the Order and lived in great penitence and holiness of life and godly conversation.

CHAPTER XXXVIII

HOW ST. FRANCIS KNEW IN SPIRIT THAT FRIAR ELIAS WAS DAMNED AND WAS TO DIE OUTSIDE THE ORDER: WHEREFORE, AT THE PRAYER OF FRIAR ELIAS, HE BESOUGHT CHRIST FOR HIM AND WAS HEARD

On a time when St. Francis and Friar Elias were dwelling in a friary together, it was revealed by God to St. Francis that Friar Elias was damned, and was to become a renegade and in the end, die outside the Order. Whereat St. Francis conceived so great a displeasure towards him that he never spake nor held converse with him; and if it befell that Friar Elias came towards him at any time, he turned aside and went another way that he might not encounter him; whereby Friar Elias began to perceive and comprehend that St. Francis was displeased with him. And desiring one day to know the cause thereof, he accosted St. Francis and would speak with him; and as St. Francis turned from him he gently held him back by force, and began to entreat him earnestly to be pleased to signify to him the reason why he thus shunned his company and forbore to speak with him. And St. Francis answered, "The cause is this: It hath been revealed to me by God that thou, for thy sins, shalt become a renegade and shalt die outside the Order; and God hath likewise revealed to me that thou art damned." Hearing these words, Friar Elias spake thus, "My reverend father, I pray thee for the love of Jesus Christ that for this cause thou shun me not, nor cast me from thee; but as a good shepherd, after the example of Christ, thou seek out and receive again the sheep that will perish except thou aid him, and that thou wilt pray to God for me, if haply He may revoke the sentence of my damnation; for it is written that God will remit the sentence, if the sinner amend his ways; and I have such great faith in thy prayers, that if I were in the midst of hell, and thou didst pray to God for me, I should feel some refreshment: wherefore yet again I beseech thee that thou commend me, a sinner, unto God, who came to save sinners, that He may receive me to His mercy-seat." This, Friar Elias said with great devotion and tears; whereat St. Francis, even as a compassionate father, promised he would pray for him. And praying most devoutly to God for him, he understood by revelation that his prayer was heard of

God in so far as concerned the revocation of the sentence of damnation passed on Friar Elias, and that at the last his soul should not be damned; but that of a surety he would forsake the Order and, outside the Order, would die. And so it came to pass. For when Frederick, King of Sicily, rebelled against the church and was excommunicated by the pope, he and whosoever gave him aid or counsel, the said Friar Elias, that was reputed one of the wisest men in the world, being entreated by the said King Frederick, went over to him, and became a rebel to the church and a renegade from the Order. Wherefore he was banned by the pope and stripped of the habit of St. Francis. And being thus excommunicate, behold he fell grievously sick; and his brother, a lay friar who had remained in the Order, and was a man of good and honest life, went to visit him, and among other things spake to him thus, "Dearest brother mine, it grieveth me sorely that thou art excommunicate and cast out of thine Order and even so shall die: but if thou seest any way or means whereby I may deliver thee from this peril, willingly will I undertake any toil for thee." Friar Elias answered, "Brother mine, no other way do I see but that thou repair to the pope and beseech him, for the love of God and of St. Francis His servant, at whose teachings I forsook the world, that he absolve me from his ban and restore to me the habit of the Order." And his brother answered that willingly would he labour for his salvation: and departing from him he went to the footstool of the holy father and humbly besought him that he would grant this grace to his brother, for love of Christ and of St. Francis His servant. And as it pleased God, the pope consented that he should return; and that if he found Friar Elias yet living, he should absolve him in his name from the ban and restore the habit to him. Whereat he departed joyfully, and returned in great haste to Friar Elias, and, finding him alive, but well-nigh at the point of death, absolved him from the ban; and Friar Elias, putting on the habit again, passed from this life, and his soul was saved by the merits of St. Francis and by his prayers, wherein Friar Elias had placed hope so great.

CHAPTER XXXIX

OF THE MARVELLOUS SERMON THAT ST. ANTHONY OF PADUA, A FRIAR MINOR, PREACHED IN THE CONSISTORY

THAT wondrous vessel of the Holy Spirit, St. Anthony of Padua, one of the chosen disciples and companions of St. Francis, he that St. Francis called his vicar, was once preaching in the consistory before the pope and the cardinals, in which consistory were men of divers nations, to wit, French, Germans, Sclavonians, and English, and divers other tongues throughout the world. Inflamed by the Holy Spirit, he expounded the word of God so effectually, so devoutly, so subtly, so sweetly, so clearly, and so wisely, that all they that were in the consistory, albeit they were of divers nations, clearly understood all his words distinctly, even as though he had spoken to each one of them in his native tongue; and all were filled with wonder, for it seemed that that miracle of old were renewed when the Apostles, on the day of Pentecost, spake, by the power of the Holy Spirit, in every tongue. And marvelling, they said one to another, "Is not he that preacheth a Spaniard? How then hear we all the tongue of our native land in his speech?" The pope likewise, considering and marvelling at the depth of his words, said, "Verily this friar is the ark of the covenant and the treasury of divine scriptures."

CHAPTER XL

OF THE MIRACLE THAT GOD WROUGHT, WHEN ST. ANTHONY, BEING AT RIMINI, PREACHED TO THE FISHES IN THE SEA

CHRIST the blessed, being pleased to show forth the great holiness of His most faithful servant, St. Anthony, and with what devotion his preaching and his holy doctrine were to be heard, one time, among others, rebuked the folly of infidel heretics by means of creatures without reason, to wit, the fishes; even as in days gone by, in the Old Testament, He rebuked the ignorance of Balaam by the mouth of an ass. Wherefore it befell, on a time when St. Anthony was at Rimini, where was a great multitude of heretics whom he desired to lead to the light of the true faith and to the paths of virtue, that he preached for many days and disputed with them concerning the faith of Christ and of the Holy Scriptures: yet they not only consented not unto his words, but even hardened their hearts and stubbornly refused to hear him. Wherefore St. Anthony, by divine inspiration, went one day to the bank of the river, hard by the seashore, and standing there on the bank of the river, between it and the sea, began to speak to the fishes after the manner of a preacher sent by God, "Hear the word of God, ye fishes of the sea and of the river, since the miscreant heretics scorn to hear it." And when he had thus spoken, anon there came towards the bank such a multitude of fishes, great and small, and middling, that never before in those seas, nor in that river, had so great a multitude been seen; and all held their heads out of the water in great peace and gentleness and perfect order, and remained intent on the lips of St. Anthony: for in front of him and nearest to the bank were the lesser fishes; and beyond them were those of middling size; and then behind, where the water was deepest, were the greater fishes. The fishes being then mustered in such order and array, St. Anthony began to preach to them solemnly, and spake thus, "Ye fishes, my brothers, much are ye bound, according to your power, to thank God our Creator, who hath given you so noble an element for your habitation; for at your pleasure have ye waters, sweet and salt, and He hath given you many places of refuge to shelter you from the tempests; He hath likewise given you a pure and clear element, and food whereby ye can live. God, your Creator, bountiful and kind, when He created you, commanded you to increase and multiply, and gave you His blessing; then, in the universal deluge and when all other animals were perishing, you alone did God preserve from harm. Moreover, He hath given you fins that ye may fare whithersoever it may please you. To you was it granted, by commandment of God, to preserve Jonah the prophet, and after the third day to cast him forth on dry land, safe and whole. Ye did offer the tribute money to Christ our Lord, to Him, poor little one, that had not wherewithal to pay. Ye, by a rare mystery, were the food of the eternal King, Christ Jesus, before the resurrection and after. For all those things much are ye held to praise and bless God, that hath given you blessings so manifold and so great; yea, more even than to any other of His creatures." At these and the like words and admonitions from St. Anthony, the fishes began to open their mouths and bow their heads, and by these and other tokens of reverence, according to their fashion and power, they gave praise to God. Then St. Anthony, beholding in the fishes such great reverence towards God their Creator, rejoiced in spirit, and said with a loud voice, "Blessed be God eternal, since the fishes in the waters honour Him more than do heretic men; and creatures without reason hear His word better than infidel men." And the longer St. Anthony preached, the greater the multitude of fishes increased, and none departed from the place he had taken. And the people of the city began to run to behold this miracle, among whom the aforesaid heretics were also drawn thither; and when they beheld a miracle so marvellous and manifest, they were pricked in their hearts, and cast themselves all at the feet of St. Anthony to hear his words. Then St. Anthony began to preach the catholic faith, and so nobly did he expound the faith that he converted all those heretics, and they turned to the true faith of Christ; and all the faithful were comforted and filled with joy exceeding great, and were strengthened in the faith. This done, St. Anthony dismissed the fishes, with God's blessing, and all they departed with wondrous signs of gladness, and the people likewise. And then St. Anthony sojourned in Rimini many days, preaching and gathering much spiritual fruit of souls.

CHAPTER XLI

HOW THE VENERABLE FRIAR SIMON DELIVERED A FRIAR FROM A GREAT TEMPTATION WHO FOR THIS CAUSE HAD DESIRED TO LEAVE THE ORDER

In the early days of the Order of St. Francis, and while the saint was yet alive, a youth of Assisi came to the Order that was called Friar Simon, whom God adorned and endowed with such grace and such contemplation and elevation of mind that all his life he was a mirror of holiness, even as I heard from those that were with him a long time. Very seldom was he seen outside his cell, and if at any time he was seen with the friars, he was ever discoursing of God. He had never been through the schools, yet so profoundly and so loftily spake he of God, and of the love of Christ, that his words seemed supernatural; wherefore one evening being gone into the wood with Friar James of Massa to speak of God, they spent all the night in that discourse; and when the dawn came it seemed to them they had been together but for a very brief space of time, as the said Friar James related to me. And the said Friar Simon received the divine and loving illuminations of God to such a degree of pleasantness and sweetness that ofttimes when he felt them coming he lay down on his bed; for the gentle sweetness of the Holy Spirit required of him, not only rest of soul, but also of body, and in divine visitations, such as these, he was many times rapt in God and became insensible to corporeal things. Wherefore on a time when he was thus rapt in God and insensible to the world, and burning inwardly with divine love, so that he felt naught of outward things with his bodily senses, a friar, desiring to have experience thereof and prove if it were verily as it seemed to be, went and took a coal of fire and laid it on his naked foot. And Friar Simon felt naught, nor made it any scar on the foot, albeit it remained there a great space, so great that it went out of itself. The said Friar Simon, when he sat down at table, before he partook of bodily food was wont to take to himself and give to others spiritual food, discoursing of God. By his devout speech a young man of San Severino was once converted, that in the world was a most vain and worldly youth, and of noble blood and very delicate of body; and Friar Simon receiving this youth into the Order, put aside his worldly vestments and kept them near himself, and he abode with Friar Simon to be instructed by him in the observances of the Order. Whereat the devil, that ever seeketh to thwart every good thing, set within him so mighty a thorn and temptation of the flesh that in no wise could he resist; wherefore he repaired to Friar Simon and said to him, "Restore to me my clothes that I brought from the world, for I can no longer endure the temptation of the flesh." And Friar Simon, having great compassion on him, spake to him thus, "Sit thou here, my son, a while with me." And he began to discourse to him of God, in such wise that all temptation left him; then after a time the temptation returned, and he asked for his clothes again, and Friar Simon drave it forth again by discoursing of God. This being done many times, at last the said temptation assailed him so mightily one night, even more than it was wont to do, that for naught in this world was he able to resist it; and he went to Friar Simon and demanded from him yet again all his worldly clothes, for in no wise could he longer remain. Then Friar Simon, according as he was wont to do, made him sit beside him; and as he discoursed to him of God, the youth leaned his head on Friar Simon's bosom for very woe and sadness. Then Friar Simon, of his great compassion, lifted up his eyes to heaven and made supplication to God; and as he prayed most devoutly for him, the youth was rapt in God and Friar Simon's prayers were heard: wherefore the youth returning to himself was wholly delivered from that temptation, even as though had he never felt it: yea, the fire of temptation was changed to the fire of the Holy Spirit, forasmuch as he had sat beside that burning coal, Friar Simon, who was all inflamed with the love of God and of his neighbour, in such wise that on a time, when a malefactor was taken that was to have both his eyes plucked out, the said youth for very pity went boldly up to the governor, and in full council and with many tears and devout prayers entreated that one of his own eyes might be plucked out, and one of the malefactor's, in order that the wretch might not be deprived of both. But the governor and his council, beholding the great fervour and charity of the friar, pardoned both of them. One day as Friar Simon was in the wood at prayer, feeling great consolation in his soul, a flock of rooks began to do him much annoy by their cawing: whereat he commanded them in the name of Jesus to depart and return no more; and the said birds departing thence were no more seen nor heard, neither in the wood nor in all the country round about. And the miracle was manifest over all the custody of Fermo wherein the said friary stood.

CHAPTER XLII

OF THE FAIR MIRACLES GOD WROUGHT THROUGH HIS HOLY FRIARS, FRIAR BENTIVOGLIA, FRIAR PETER OF MONTICELLO, AND FRIAR CONRAD OF OFFIDA; AND HOW FRIAR BENTIVOGLIA CARRIED A LEPER FIFTEEN MILES IN A VERY BRIEF TIME; AND HOW THE OTHER FRIAR SPAKE WITH ST. MICHAEL, AND HOW TO THE THIRD CAME THE VIRGIN MARY AND LAID HER SON IN HIS ARMS

THE province of the Marches of Ancona was adorned of old, after the manner of the starry firmament, with holy and exemplary friars who, like the shining lights of heaven, have adorned and illumined the Order of St. Francis and the world by their example and doctrine. Among others there was, in the early days, Friar Lucido Antico, that was truly lucent by his holiness and burning with divine charity, whose glorious tongue, informed of the Holy Spirit, brought forth marvellous fruit by his preaching. Another was Friar Bentivoglia of San Severino, who was seen by Friar Masseo to be lifted up in the air for a great space while he was at prayer in the wood; for which miracle the devout Friar Masseo, being then a parish priest, left his parish and became a friar minor; and he was of holiness so great that he wrought many miracles during his life and after his death, and his body lies at Murro. The aforesaid Friar Bentivoglia, when he sojourned alone at Ponte della Trave, tending and serving a leper, was commanded by his superior to depart thence and go to another friary that was fifteen miles away; and not being willing to forsake the leper, he laid hold of him, and with great fervour of charity lifted him on to his shoulder and carried him between dawn and sunrise the whole of those fifteen miles as far as the place whither he was sent, that was called Monte Sancino: which distance, even had he been an eagle, he could not have flown in so short a time; and in all that country was much wonder and amazement at this divine miracle. Another was Friar Peter of Monticello, who was seen by Friar Servodio of Urbino, then warden of the old friary of Ancona, to be lifted bodily up from the ground full five or six cubits, as far as the foot of the crucifix before which he was in prayer. And this Friar Peter, while keeping the forty days' fast of St. Michael the Archangel with great devotion, and being in church at prayer on the last day of that fast, was heard by a young friar speaking with St. Michael the Archangel, for he had hidden himself under the high altar to behold somewhat of his sanctity; and the words he spake were these. Said St. Michael, "Friar Peter, thou hast faithfully travailed for me, and in many ways hast afflicted thy body: lo, I am come to comfort thee, and that thou mayest ask whatsoever grace thou desirest I will promise to obtain it of God." Friar Peter answered, "Most holy prince of the host of heaven, and faithful zealot of divine love and compassionate protector of souls, this grace do I ask of thee: that thou obtain from God the pardon of my sins." St. Michael answered, "Ask some other grace, for this shall I obtain for thee right easily." But Friar Peter asking naught else, the archangel made an end, saying, "For the faith and devotion thou hast in me I will obtain this grace for thee and many others." And their discourse being ended, that endured a great space, the archangel Michael departed, leaving him comforted exceedingly. In the days of this holy Friar Peter lived the holy Friar Conrad of Offida, who, dwelling with him together at the friary of Forano in the custody of Ancona, went forth one day into the wood for divine contemplation; and Friar Peter secretly followed after him to see what should befall him. And Friar Conrad betook himself to prayer and most devoutly besought the Virgin Mary, of her great compassion, that she would obtain this grace from her blessed Son: to wit, that he might feel a little of that sweetness that St. Simeon felt on the day of Purification when he bore Jesus the blessed Saviour in his arms. And his prayer ended, the merciful Virgin Mary granted it. And lo, the Queen of Heaven appeared with resplendent clarity of light, with her blessed Son in her arms, and drawing nigh to Friar Conrad, laid her blessed Son in his arms, who, receiving Him, devoutly embraced and kissed Him, then clasping Him to his breast, was wholly melted and dissolved in love divine and unspeakable consolation: and Friar Peter likewise, who secretly beheld all these things, felt great sweetness and consolation in his soul. And when the Virgin Mary had departed from Friar Conrad, Friar Peter returned in haste to the friary that he might not be seen of him. But thereafter when Friar Conrad returned, all joyous and glad, Friar Peter said to him, "O celestial soul, great consolation hast thou had this day." Said Friar Conrad, "What sayest thou, Friar Peter? How knowest thou what I may have had?" "Full well I know, full well I know," said Friar Peter, "that the Virgin Mary with her blessed Son hath visited thee." Then Friar Conrad, who with true humility desired that this grace of God should be hidden, besought him to speak no word of these things. And so great thenceforth was the love between these two friars that they seemed to be of one heart and one mind in all things. And the said Friar Conrad on a time in the friary of Siruolo delivered a woman possessed of a devil by praying for her the whole night through, and being seen of her mother on the morrow, he fled lest he might be found and honoured by the people.

CHAPTER XLIII

HOW FRIAR CONRAD OF OFFIDA CONVERTED A YOUNG FRIAR THAT WAS A STUMBLING-BLOCK TO THE OTHER FRIARS. AND HOW AFTER THE SAID YOUNG FRIAR DIED HE APPEARED TO THE SAID FRIAR CONRAD AND ENTREATED HIM TO PRAY FOR HIM; AND HOW HE DELIVERED HIM BY HIS PRAYERS FROM THE MOST GRIEVOUS PAINS OF PURGATORY

THE said Friar Conrad of Offida, wondrous zealot of gospel poverty and of the Rule of St. Francis, was of so religious a life, and of such great merit before God, that Christ the blessed honoured him in his life and after his death with many miracles, among which, being come on a time to the friary of Offida as a guest, the friars prayed him for love of God and of his charity to admonish a young friar that was in the settlement, who bore himself so childishly, so disorderly and dissolutely, that he disturbed both old and young of that community during the divine offices, and cared little or naught for the observances of the Rule. Whereupon Friar Conrad, in compassion for that youth, and at the prayers of the friars, called the said youth apart one day, and in fervour of charity spake to him words of admonition, so effectual and so divine, that by the operation of divine grace he straightway became changed from a child to an old man in manners, and grew so obedient and benign and diligent and devout, and thereafter so peaceful and obedient, and so studious of every virtuous thing, that even as at first the whole community were perturbed because of him, so now all were content with him, and comforted, and greatly loved him. And it came to pass, as it pleased God, that some time after this conversion, the said youth died, whereat the said friars mourned; and a few days after his death, his soul appeared to Friar Conrad, while he was devoutly praying before the altar of the said friary, and saluted him devoutly as a father; and Friar Conrad asked him, "Who art thou?" And he answered and said, "I am the soul of that young friar that died these latter days." And Friar Conrad said, "O my dearest son, how is it with thee?" He answered, "By God's grace, and your teaching, 'tis well; for I am not damned, but for certain of my sins, whereof I lacked time to purge me sufficiently, I suffer grievous pains in purgatory; but I pray thee, father, that as of thy compassion thou didst succour me while I lived, so may it please thee to succour me now in my pains, and say some paternosters for me; for thy prayers are very acceptable before God." Then Friar Conrad consented kindly to his prayers and recited the paternoster, with the *requiem æternum*, once for him. Said that soul, "O dearest father, what great good and what great refreshment do I feel! Now, prithee recite it once again." And Friar Conrad recited it, and when it was repeated again, that soul said, "Holy father, when thou prayest for me I feel all my pains lightened, wherefore I beseech thee that thou cease not thy prayers for me." Then Friar Conrad, beholding his prayers availed that soul so much, said a hundred paternosters for her. And when they were recited, that soul said, "I thank thee, dearest father, in God's name, for the charity thou hast had for me: for by thy prayers am I freed from all the pains of purgatory, and am on my way to the kingdom of heaven." This said, the soul departed. Then Friar Conrad, to give joy and comfort to the friars, related to them all this vision in order; and thus the soul of that youth went to paradise through the merits of Friar Conrad.

CHAPTER XLIV

HOW THE MOTHER OF CHRIST AND ST. JOHN THE EVANGELIST APPEARED TO FRIAR PETER AND TOLD HIM WHICH OF THEM SUFFERED GREATEST PAIN AT THE PASSION OF CHRIST

In the days when the aforesaid Friar Conrad and Friar Peter abode together at the friary of Forano, in the district of Ancona—those two friars that were bright twin stars in the province of the Marches, and two most godly men—forasmuch as they seemed of one heart and one mind, they, in their love and charity, bound themselves together in this covenant: That they would reveal to each other in charity every consolation that God in His mercy bestowed on them. This covenant being made between them, it befell on a day when Friar Peter was at prayer and pondering most devoutly on the Passion of Christ, and how that the most blessed Mother of Christ, and John the Evangelist, the most beloved disciple, and St. Francis, were all painted at the foot of the cross, crucified in dolour of soul with Christ, a desire came upon him to know which of those three had suffered greatest sorrow in the Passion of Christ—the Mother that had begotten Him, or the disciple that had slept on His breast, or St. Francis, crucified with the wounds of Christ. And being thus absorbed in meditation, the Virgin Mary appeared to him, with St. John the Evangelist and St. Francis, clothed in noblest raiment of beatific glory; but St. Francis seemed arrayed in a fairer garment than St. John. And Peter being sore afraid at this vision, St. John comforted him and said to him, "Fear not, dearest brother, for we are come to console thee in thy doubt. Know then that the Mother of Christ and I sorrowed above all other creatures at the Passion of Christ; but after us St. Francis felt greater sorrow than any other: therefore thou seest him in such glory." And Friar Peter asked, "O holiest Apostle of Christ, wherefore doth the raiment of St. Francis seem fairer than thine?" St. John answered, "The reason is this: that in the world he wore viler garments than I." These words said, St. John gave Friar Peter a glorious robe that he bore in his hand, and said to him, "Take this robe which I have brought to give thee." And when St. John was about to clothe him with it, Friar Peter fell dazed to the ground and began to cry, "Friar Conrad, dearest Friar Conrad, succour me quickly; come and behold marvellous things." And at these holy words the saintly vision vanished. Then when Friar Conrad came he told him all things in order, and they gave thanks to God.

CHAPTER XLV

OF THE CONVERSION, LIFE, MIRACLES, AND DEATH OF THE HOLY FRIAR JOHN OF LA PENNA

One night, in the province of the Marches, a child, exceeding fair, appeared to Friar John of La Penna, when he was yet a lad in the world, and called him, saying, "John, go to the church of St. Stephen, where one of my friars minor is preaching; believe in his teaching and give heed to his words, for I have sent him thither; this done, thou shalt take a long journey and thou shalt come to me." Whereat, anon he rose up, and felt a great change in his soul, and going to St. Stephen's, he found a great multitude of men and women that were assembled there to hear the sermon. And he that was to preach there was a friar, called Friar Philip, who was one of the first friars that had come to the Marches of Ancona; and as yet few friaries were established in the Marches. Up climbs this Friar Philip to preach, and preaches most devoutly, and not in words of human wisdom; but by virtue of the spirit of Christ he announced the kingdom of life eternal. The sermon ended, the lad went to the said Friar Philip and said to him, "Father, if it please you to receive me into the Order, fain would I do penance and serve our Lord Jesus Christ." Friar Philip, beholding and knowing the wondrous innocence of the said lad and his ready will to serve God, spake to him thus, "Thou shalt come to me on such a day at Ricanati, and I will have thee received." Now the provincial Chapter was to be held in that city, wherefore the lad, being very guileless, thought this was the great journey he was to make, according to the revelation he had had, and then was to go to paradise; and this he thought to do straightway after he was received into the Order. Therefore he went and was received: and then, seeing his thought was not fulfilled, and hearing the minister say in the Chapter that whosoever would go to the province of Provence, through the merit of holy obedience, he would freely give him leave, there came to him a great desire to go thither, believing in his heart that that was the great journey he must take ere he went to paradise. But he was ashamed to say so, and confided at last in the aforesaid Friar Philip, that had had him received into the Order, and gently prayed him to obtain that grace for him, to wit, that he should go to the province of Provence. Then Friar Philip, beholding his innocency and his holy intent, obtained leave for him to go; whereupon Friar John set forth on his way with great joy, believing that, the journey accomplished, he would go to paradise. But it pleased God that he should remain in the said province five-and-twenty years in this expectancy and desire, a pattern of sanctity and walking in great godliness; and increasing ever in virtue and in the favour of God, and of the people, he was greatly loved by the friars and by the world. And Friar John, being one day devoutly in prayer, weeping and lamenting that his desire was not fulfilled and that his earthly pilgrimage was too prolonged, the blessed Christ appeared to him, at sight of whom his soul was all melted, and said to him, "My son, Friar John, ask of Me what thou wilt." And he answered, "My Lord, I know not what to ask of Thee save Thyself, for naught else do I desire; this alone I pray—that Thou forgive me all my sins, and give me grace to behold Thee once again when I may have a greater need of Thee." Said Christ, "Thy prayer is granted." After these words He departed, and Friar John remained all comforted. At last the friars of the Marches, hearing of the fame of his holiness, wrought so with the general of the Order that he bade him by obedience return to the Marches; and when Friar John received this command, joyously he set forth on his way, thinking that this journey being accomplished he should go to heaven, according to the promise of Christ. But when he was returned to the province of the Marches, he abode there yet thirty years, and none of his kinsfolk knew him: and every day he waited for the mercy of God and that He should fulfil the promise made to him. And during these years he filled the office of warden many times with great discretion, and through him God wrought many miracles. Now among other gifts he had of God was the spirit of prophecy. Wherefore, on a time when he was gone forth from the friary, one, his novice, was assailed by the devil and tempted so mightily that he consented to the temptation, and purposed within himself to leave the Order as soon as Friar John had returned. But this temptation and purpose being known to Friar John by the spirit of prophecy, he straightway returned to the friary and called the said novice to him and bade him confess: and before he confessed he related all the temptation to him in order, even as God had revealed it to him, and ended thus, "Son, forasmuch as thou didst wait for me, and wouldst not depart without my blessing, God hath granted thee this grace—that thou shalt never issue forth from this Order, but by divine grace shalt die in the Order." Then the said novice was strengthened in his good will, and remaining in the Order, became a holy friar. And all these things Friar Hugolin related to me. The said Friar John, that was a man of joyful and tranquil mind, spake but rarely, and was given to great meditation and devotion: and above all, after matins he never returned to his cell, but remained in church at prayer until the day broke. And he, being at prayer one night after matins, the angel of God appeared to him and said, "Friar John, thy journey is accomplished for which thou hast waited so long: therefore I announce to thee in God's name that thou mayst ask whatsoever grace thou desirest. And likewise I announce to thee that thou mayst choose which thou wilt—either one day in purgatory or seven days' pain on earth." And Friar John, choosing rather seven days' pain on earth, anon fell sick of divers infirmities; for a violent fever took him, and gout in his hands and feet, and colic, and many other ills; but what wrought him greatest pain was, that a devil stood before him, holding in his hand a great scroll, whereon were written all the sins he had ever done or thought, and spake to him thus " For those sins that thou hast done, either in thought, or word, or deed, thou art damned to the lowest depths of hell." And he remembered naught of good that he had ever done, nor that he was in the Order, nor ever had been therein; but he believed he was thus damned, even as the devil told him. Wherefore, when he was asked how it went with him, he answered, " Ill, for I am damned." The friars, seeing this, sent for an aged friar, whose name was Friar Matthew of Monte Rubbiano, that was a holy man and dear friend of this Friar John: and the said Friar Matthew, being come to him on the seventh day of his tribulation, gave him salutation and asked how it was with him. He answered, that it fared ill with him because he was damned. Then said Friar Matthew, "Rememberest thou not that many times thou hast confessed to me, and I have wholly absolved thee of thy sins? Rememberest thou likewise that thou hast ever served God in this holy Order many years? Moreover, rememberest thou not that God's mercy exceedeth all the sins of this world, and that Christ, our blessed Saviour, paid an infinite price to redeem us? Therefore be of good hope, for of a surety thou art saved;" and with these words, forasmuch as the term of his purgation was accomplished, temptation vanished and consolation came. And with great gladness Friar John said to Friar Matthew, " Because thou art weary and the hour is late, I pray thee, go to rest." And Friar Matthew would not leave him; but at last, at his urgent prayers, he departed from him and went to rest: and Friar John remained alone with the friar that tended him. And lo, Christ the blessed came, in great splendour and in fragrance of exceeding sweetness, even as He had promised to appear to him again when he should have greater need, and healed him perfectly from all his infirmities. Then Friar John, with clasped hands giving thanks to God that he had accomplished the great journey of this present miserable life with so good an end, commended his soul to the hands of Christ and rendered it up to God, passing from this mortal life to life eternal with Christ the blessed, that he so long a time had desired and waited to behold. And the said Friar John is laid to rest in the friary of La Penna di San Giovanni.

CHAPTER XLVI

HOW FRIAR PACIFICO, BEING AT PRAYER, BEHELD THE SOUL OF FRIAR UMILE, HIS BROTHER, ASCENDING TO HEAVEN

In the said province of the Marches there lived two brothers in the Order, after the death of St. Francis, the one called Friar Umile, the other Friar Pacifico, and they were men of the greatest holiness and perfection. And one, to wit, Friar Umile, was in the friary of Soffiano, and there died; the other belonged to the community of another friary in a far country. It pleased God, that as Friar Pacifico was at prayer one day, in a solitary place, he was rapt in ecstasy and saw the soul of his brother, Friar Umile, which but then had left his body, ascending straight to heaven without any let or hindrance. It befell that after many years this Friar Pacifico, who was left on earth, went to the community of the said friary of Soffiano, where his brother had died; and in those days the friars, at the petition of the lords of Bruforte, moved from the said friary to another; and among other things, they translated the relics of the holy friars that had died there. And Friar Pacifico, coming to the sepulchre of Friar Umile, took away his bones and washed them with good wine and then wrapped them in a white napkin, and with great reverence and devotion kissed them, weeping. Whereat the other friars marvelled and held it no good example, for he, being a man of great holiness, did seem, out of carnal and worldly affection, to weep for his brother, and show forth more devotion for his relics than for those of the other friars that had been of no less sanctity than Friar Umile, and were as much worthy of reverence as his. And Friar Pacifico, knowing the friars to be thinking badly of him, satisfied them humbly, and said to them, "My brethren, most dear, marvel not if I have done this to the bones of my brother and have done it not to the others, because, blessed be God, carnal affection hath not urged me to this, as ye believe, for when my brother passed from this life, I was at prayer in a desert place far away from him, and I beheld his soul ascend by a straight way into heaven: therefore am I sure that his bones are holy and ought to be in paradise. And if God had vouchsafed to me such certainty of the other friars, that selfsame reverence would I have shown to their bones." Wherefore the friars, seeing his holy and devout intent, were much edified by him, and praised God that worketh such wondrous things for His holy friars.

CHAPTER XLVII

TOUCHING THAT HOLY FRIAR TO WHOM THE MOTHER OF CHRIST APPEARED WHEN HE LAY SICK AND BROUGHT HIM THREE BOXES OF ELECTUARY

In the aforesaid friary of Soffiano there was of old a friar minor of such great holiness and grace that he seemed wholly divine, and ofttimes was rapt in God. This friar, being on a time wholly lifted up and ravished in God, for he had notably the grace of contemplation, certain birds of divers kinds came to him and settled themselves tamely upon his shoulders, upon his head, and in his arms, and in his hands, and sang wondrously. Now this friar loved solitude and spake but seldom; yet, when aught was asked of him, he answered so graciously and so wisely that he seemed an angel rather than a man; and he excelled in prayer and in contemplation, and the friars held him in great reverence. The friar, having run the course of his virtuous life, according to divine disposition, fell sick unto death, so that he could take naught; and withal he would receive no carnal medicine, but all his trust was in the heavenly physician, Jesus Christ the blessed, and in his blessed Mother, by whom, through divine clemency, he was held worthy to be mercifully visited and healed. Wherefore, lying on a time in his bed, and preparing for death with all his heart, the glorious Virgin Mary, Mother of Christ, appeared to him in wondrous splendour, with a great multitude of angels and holy virgins, and drew nigh to his bed; and he, gazing at her, took great comfort and joy, both of soul and body; and he began to make humble supplication that she would pray her beloved Son to deliver him, through His merits, from the prison of this miserable flesh. And persevering in this supplication, with many tears, the Virgin Mary answered him, calling him by name, and said, "Fear not, my son, for thy prayer is heard, and I am come to comfort thee a while ere thou depart from this life." Beside the Virgin Mary were three holy virgins that bore three boxes in their hands of an electuary of surpassing fragrance and sweetness. Then the glorious Virgin took one of these boxes and opened it, and the whole house was filled with fragrance; then, taking of that electuary with a spoon, she gave it to the sick friar. And no sooner had the sick man savoured it than he felt such comfort and such sweetness that it seemed as though his soul could not remain in his body. Wherefore he began to say, "No more, O most holy and blessed Virgin Mother; O blessed physician and saviour of human kind, no more, for I cannot endure such sweetness." But the compassionate Mother and kind, again and again offering of that electuary to the sick man and making him partake thereof, emptied the whole box. Then the first box being void, the blessed Virgin takes the second and puts the spoon therein to give him thereof, whereat he, complaining, saith, "O most blessed Mother of God, if my soul is well-nigh all melted with the ardour and sweetness of the first electuary, how shall I endure the second? I pray thee, O thou blessed above all the other saints and above all the angels, that thou wilt give me no more." The glorious Virgin Mary makes answer, "Taste, my son, taste yet a little of this second box," and giving him a little thereof, she said to him, "This day, son, thou hast enough to satisfy thee; be of good cheer, for soon will I come for thee and lead thee to the kingdom of my Son, that thou hast ever sought after and desired." This said, and taking leave of him, she departed, and he remained so comforted and consoled, through the sweetness of this confection, that for many days he lived on, sated and strong, without any corporeal food. And some days thereafter, while blithely speaking with the friars, he passed from this miserable life in great jubilation and gladness.

CHAPTER XLVIII

HOW FRIAR JAMES OF LA MASSA SAW IN A VISION ALL THE FRIARS MINOR IN THE WORLD IN THE SIMILITUDE OF A TREE, AND KNEW THE VIRTUES AND THE MERITS AND THE SINS OF EACH ONE OF THEM

Friar James of La Massa, to whom God opened the door of His mysteries and gave perfect knowledge and understanding of the divine scripture and of future things, was of such sanctity that Friar Giles of Assisi, and Friar Mark of Montino, and Friar Juniper and Friar Lucido, said of him, that they knew no one in the world greater in the sight of God than this Friar James. I had great desire to behold him; for on praying Friar John, the companion of the said Friar Giles, to expound to me certain spiritual things, he answered, " If thou wouldst be well informed in matters of the spiritual life, strive to speak with Friar James of La Massa (for Friar Giles was fain to be instructed by him), and to his words naught can be added nor taken away; for his mind hath penetrated the mysteries of heaven, and his words are words of the Holy Ghost, and there is no man on earth that I have so great a desire to see." This Friar James, when Friar John of Parma took up his office as minister of the Order, was rapt in God while at prayer, and remained thus rapt in ecstasy three days, bereft of all bodily senses, and was so insensible that the friars doubted lest he were truly dead: and in this ecstasy it was revealed to him by God what things were to come to pass in our Order. Wherefore, when Friar Giles said those words, my desire to hear him and to speak with him increased within me. And when it pleased God that I should have opportunity to speak with him, I besought him thus, " If this that I have heard tell of thee be true, prithee keep it not hidden from me. I have heard that when thou remained well-nigh dead for three days, God revealed to thee, among other things, what should come to pass in this our Order; for this was related to me by Friar Matthew, minister of the Marches, to whom thou didst reveal it by obedience." Then Friar James confessed to him, with great humility, that what Friar Matthew said was true. And his words, to wit, the words of Friar Matthew, minister of the Marches, were these, " I know a friar to whom God hath revealed what shall hereafter come to pass in our Order; for Friar James of La Massa hath made known to me and said, that after many things God revealed to him touching the state of the Church Militant, he beheld in a vision a tree, fair and very great, whose roots were of gold, and whose fruits were men, and all they were friars minor; and the chief branches thereof were marked out according to the number of the provinces of the Order, and each branch had as many friars as there were in the province marked on that branch. And so he knew the numbers of all the friars in the Order, and of each province, and likewise their names, and the ages and the conditions and the high offices and the dignities and the graces of all, and their sins. And he beheld Friar John of Parma in the highest place on the midmost branch of this tree; and on the top of the branches that were round about this branch were the ministers of all the provinces. And thereafter he beheld Christ seated on a pure white throne exceeding great, whereunto Christ called St. Francis and gave him a cup, full of the spirit of life, and sent him forth, saying, "Go and visit thy friars and give them to drink of this cup of the spirit of life; for the spirit of Satan shall rise up against them and shall smite them, and many of them shall fall and not rise again." And Christ gave two angels to St. Francis to bear him company. And then St. Francis came and held forth the cup of life to his friars: and he began to hold it forth first to Friar John of Parma, who, taking it, drank it all devoutly and in great haste; and forthwith he became all bright and shining as the sun. And after him St. Francis held it forth to all the others in due order, and few were they among these that took it and drank it all with meet reverence and devotion. They that took it devoutly and drank it all became straightway bright and shining as the sun; and they that poured it away, and took it not with devotion, became black or dark and misshapen and horrible to behold: and they that drank a part and threw a part away became in part bright and shining, in part dark and shadowy, more or less, according to the measure of their drinking or pouring away the cup. But, resplendent above all the others, was the aforesaid Friar John, that most completely had drunk of the cup of life, whereby he had most deeply fathomed the abyss of the infinite light divine; and therein he had foreseen the adversity and storms that were to rise up against the said tree, and buffet it and make the branches thereof to shake. Wherefore the said Friar John descended from the top of the branch whereon he was, and climbed down all the branches and hid himself beneath them against the knotted bole of the tree, and there remained deep in thought. And a friar that had drunken part of the cup and part had poured away, climbed up that branch and to that place whence Friar John had descended. And while he stood in that place the nails of his fingers became of steel, sharp and cutting as razors; whereat he came down from that place whither he had climbed, and with rage and fury would have flung himself against Friar John to do him hurt. But Friar John, beholding this, cried aloud and commended himself to Christ that was seated on the throne: and Christ, at his cries, called St. Francis to him and gave him a sharp flintstone, and said to him, "Go, and with this stone cut the nails of that friar, wherewith he would fain rend Friar John, so that they may do him no hurt." Then St. Francis came and did as Christ had commanded him. This done, there arose a storm of wind and smote against the tree so mightily that the friars fell to the ground; and first fell they that had poured out all the cup of the spirit of life, and were carried away by devils into places of darkness and torment. But Friar John, together with those others that had drunk all the cup, were translated by angels into a place of eternal life and light and beatific splendour. And the aforesaid Friar James, that beheld the vision, discerned and understood particularly and distinctly all he saw touching the names and conditions and state of each one, and that clearly. And so mightily did that storm prevail against the tree that it fell: and the wind bore it away. And then, no sooner had the storm ceased, than from the root of this tree, which was all of gold, another tree sprung up all of gold, that put forth golden leaves and flowers and fruit. Touching which tree and the growth and the deep roots thereof, the beauty and fragrance and virtue, 'twere fitter to keep silence than to tell thereof at this season.

CHAPTER XLIX

HOW CHRIST APPEARED TO FRIAR JOHN OF LA VERNA

Among the other wise and holy friars and sons of St. Francis who, according as Solomon saith, are the glory of their father, there lived in our time in the province of the Marches the venerable and holy Friar John of Fermo; and he, for that he sojourned a long time in the holy place of La Verna and there passed from this life, was likewise called Friar John of La Verna; and he was a man of great and singular holiness of life. This Friar John, while yet a boy in the world, desired with all his heart to follow the ways of penance, that ever preserveth the purity of the body and of the soul. Wherefore, when he was quite a little child, he began to wear a breastplate of mail [1] and iron rings on his naked flesh, and to practise great abstinence; and above all, when he abode with the canons of St. Peter's at Fermo, who fared sumptuously, he eschewed all carnal delights, and mortified his body with great and severe fastings; but his companions, being much set against these things, took from him his breastplate and thwarted his abstinence in divers ways; wherefore he purposed, being inspired of God, to forsake the world and those that loved worldly things and cast himself wholly into the arms of the Crucified with the habit of the crucified St. Francis; and this he did. And being thus received

[1] *See* note, p. 34.

into the Order while yet a boy, and committed to the care of the master of the novices, he became so spiritual and devout, that hearing the master once discoursing of God, his heart was melted as wax before a fire; and with such exceeding sweetness of grace was he kindled by divine love, that unable to remain still and endure such great sweetness, he arose, and as one inebriated with spiritual things, ran hither and thither, now in the garden, now in the wood, now in the church, according as the fire and spur of the spirit drave him. Then in process of time this angelic man, by divine grace, so continually increased from virtue to virtue, and in celestial gifts and divine exaltation and rapture, that at one time his soul was lifted up to the splendours of the cherubim, at another to the flaming seraphim, yet another to the joys of the blessed; yea, even to the loving and ineffable embraces of Christ. And notably, on a time, his heart was so mightily kindled by the flames of love divine, that this flame endured full three years, in which time he received wondrous consolations and divine visitations, and ofttimes was he rapt in God; and for a brief space, in the said time, he seemed all aflame and burning with the love of Christ; and this was on the holy mount of La Verna. But forasmuch as God hath singular care of His children, and giveth them according to divers seasons, now consolation, now tribulation, now prosperity, now adversity, even as He seeth their need, either to strengthen them in humility, or to kindle within them greater desire for celestial things; now it pleased divine goodness to withdraw, after three years, from the said Friar John this ray and this flame of divine love, and to deprive him of all spiritual consolation. Whereat Friar John remained bereft of the light and the love of God, and all disconsolate and afflicted and sorrowing. Wherefore, in this anguish of heart, he wandered about the wood, running to and fro, calling with a loud voice and with tears and sighs on the beloved spouse of his soul, who had withdrawn and departed from him, and without whose presence his soul found neither peace nor rest. But in no place nor in any wise could he find the sweet Jesus again, nor taste again, as he was wont to do, of those sweetest spiritual savours of the love of Christ. And the like tribulation he endured many days, wherein he persevered continually in tears and sighs, and in supplication to God, that of His pity He would restore to him the beloved spouse of his soul. At the last, when it had pleased God to prove his patience enough and fan the flame of his desire, one day, as Friar John was wandering about the said wood, thus afflicted and tormented, he sat him down a-wearied and leaned against a beech tree, and with his face all bathed in tears gazed towards heaven; and behold, Jesus Christ appeared suddenly nigh to him, in the path whereby this Friar John had come, but spake no word. And Friar John, beholding Him and knowing full well that it was the Christ, straightway flung himself at His feet, and with piteous tears entreated Him most humbly and said, "Help me, my Lord, for without Thee, O my sweetest Saviour, I wander in darkness and in tears; without Thee, most gentle Lamb, I dwell in anguish and in torments and in fear; without Thee, Son of God, most high, I remain in shame and confusion; without Thee I am stripped of all good, and blind, for Thou art Christ Jesus, true light of souls; without Thee I am lost and damned, for Thou art the Life of souls and Life of life; without Thee I am barren and withered, for Thou art the fountain of every good gift and of every grace; without Thee I am wholly disconsolate, for Thou art Jesus our Redeemer, our love and our desire, the Bread of consolation and the Wine that rejoiceth the hearts of the angels and of all the saints. Let Thy light shine upon me, most gracious Master, and most compassionate Shepherd, for I am Thy little sheep, unworthy tho' I be." But because the desires of holy men, which God delayeth to grant, kindle them to yet greater love and merit, the blessed Christ departed without hearing him, without uttering one word, and went away by the said path. Then Friar John rose up and ran after Him, and again fell at His feet, and with holy importunity held Him back and entreated Him, with devoutest tears, saying, "O Jesus Christ, most sweet, have mercy on me in my tribulation; hear me by the multitude of Thy mercies, and by the truth of Thy salvation restore to me the joy of Thy countenance and of Thy pitying eye, for all the earth is full of Thy mercy." And again Christ departed and spake him no word, nor gave aught of consolation, and did after the way of a mother with her child, when she maketh him to yearn for the breast, and causeth him to follow after her weeping, that he may take it the more willingly. Whereupon Friar John, yet again, with greater fervour and desire, followed Christ, and no sooner had he come up to Him than the blessed Christ turned round to him, and looked upon him with joyful and gracious countenance; then, opening His most holy and most merciful arms, He embraced him very sweetly, and as He thus opened His arms, Friar John beheld rays of shining light coming from the Saviour's most holy breast, that illumined all the wood, and himself likewise, in soul and body. Then Friar John kneeled down at the feet of Christ; and the blessed Jesus, even as He did to the Magdalen, graciously held forth His foot that he might kiss it; and Friar John, taking it with highest reverence, bathed it with so many tears that he verily seemed to be a second Magdalen, and devoutly said, "I pray Thee, my Lord, that Thou regard not my sins, but by Thy most holy Passion, and by the shedding of Thy most holy and precious blood, Thou mayst make my soul to live again in the grace of Thy love, forasmuch as this is Thy commandment: that we love Thee with all our hearts and all our affections, which commandment none can keep without Thy aid. Help me, then, most beloved Son of God, that I may love Thee with all my heart and with all my might." And Friar John, standing as he thus spake at the feet of Christ, was heard of Him, and he regained the former state of grace, to wit, the flame of divine love, and he felt himself all consoled and renewed; and when he knew that the gift of divine grace was restored to him, he began to give thanks to Christ the blessed and to kiss His feet devoutly. And then, rising up to gaze on the face of Christ, Jesus Christ stretched forth and offered him His most holy hands to kiss. And when Friar John had kissed them, he drew nigh and leaned on Christ's bosom and embraced Him and kissed Him, and Christ likewise embraced and kissed him. And in these embraces and kisses Friar John perceived such divine fragrance, that if all the sweet-smelling graces and all the most fragrant things in the world had been gathered together, they would have seemed but a stink compared with that fragrance; and thereby was Friar John ravished and consoled and illumined; and that fragrance endured in his soul many months. And thenceforward there issued from his mouth, that had drunk at the fountain of divine wisdom in the sacred breast of the Saviour, words so wondrous and so heavenly, that they changed all hearts and brought forth great fruit in the souls of those that heard him. And in the pathway of the wood, whereon the blessed feet of Christ had trod, and for a good space round about, Friar John perceived that same fragrance and beheld that splendour for a long time thereafter, whensoever he went thither. And Friar John, coming to himself after that rapture and after the bodily presence of Christ had vanished, remained so illumined in his soul and in the abyss of the divine nature, that albeit he was not a learned man, by reason of human study, nevertheless, he solved wondrously and made plain the most subtle and lofty questions touching the divine Trinity and the profound mysteries of the Holy Scriptures. And many times thereafter, when speaking before the pope and the cardinals and the king, and barons and masters and doctors, he set them all in great amaze at the lofty words and most profound judgments he uttered.

CHAPTER L

HOW FRIAR JOHN OF LA VERNA, WHILE SAYING MASS ON ALL SOULS' DAY, BEHELD MANY SOULS SET FREE FROM PURGATORY

On a time when Friar John was saying mass, the day after All Saints, for the souls of all the dead, according as the church hath ordained, he offered up with such great affection and charity and with such pitying compassion that most high sacrament (which, by reason of its efficacy, the souls of the dead desire above all other benefits we can bestow upon them), that he seemed all melted with the sweetness of pity and of brotherly love. Wherefore, as he devoutly elevated the body of Christ in that mass and offered it up to God the Father, and prayed that, for love of His beloved Son, Jesus Christ, who was nailed on the cross to redeem souls, He would be pleased to deliver from the pains of purgatory the souls of the dead by Him created and redeemed, he straightway beheld a multitude of souls, well-nigh infinite, come forth from purgatory, after the manner of countless sparks issuing from a fiery furnace; and he beheld them ascend to heaven through the merits of Christ's Passion, that each day is offered up for the living and the dead in that most sacred Host which is worthy to be worshipped world without end.

CHAPTER LI

OF THE HOLY FRIAR JAMES OF FALTERONE, AND HOW AFTER HIS DEATH HE APPEARED TO FRIAR JOHN OF LA VERNA

At the time when Friar James of Falterone, a man of great holiness, lay grievously sick at the friary of Moliano in the custody of Fermo, Friar John of La Verna, who then abode in the friary of La Massa, heard of his sickness; and, for that he loved him as a dear father, he betook himself to pray for him, devoutly beseeching God with all his heart that if it were good for his soul He would restore him to health of body. And while thus devoutly praying he was rapt in ecstasy, and beheld in the air, above his cell in the wood, a great host of angels and saints, of such dazzling splendour that the whole country round about was illumined thereby; and in the midst of these angels he beheld this sick Friar James, for whom he was praying, all resplendent in pure white robes. He saw likewise among them the blessed father, St. Francis, adorned with the sacred stigmas of Christ and with much glory. And he beheld also and knew the saintly Friar Lucido, and the aged Friar Matthew of Monte Rubbiano, and many other friars that in this life he had never seen nor known. And as Friar John was thus gazing, with great delight, on that blessed company of saints, it was revealed to him that of a surety the soul of that sick friar was saved, and that he was to die of that sickness; but that he was not to ascend straightway after his death to paradise, for that it behoved him to purge himself a while in purgatory. At this revelation Friar John felt such exceeding joy because of the salvation of his soul, that he grieved not for the death of the body, but with great sweetness of spirit called him within himself, saying, "Friar James, sweet father mine; Friar James, sweet brother; Friar James, faithfullest servant and friend of God; Friar James, companion of the angels and consort of the blessed!" and in this certitude and joy he came to himself again. And anon he departed from that place and went to visit the said Friar James at Moliano, and finding the sickness so heavily upon him that scarce could he speak, he announced to him the death of the body and the salvation and glory of his soul, according to the certitude he had had by divine revelation. Whereat Friar James rejoiced gladly in spirit and in countenance, and received him with great gladness, and with jocund mien gave thanks to him for the good tidings he had brought, commending himself devoutly to him. Then Friar John besought him dearly that he would return to him after his death and speak to him of his state: and Friar James promised this, if God so pleased. These words said, the hour of his passing away drew nigh, and Friar James began to recite devoutly that verse from the Psalms: *In pace in idipsum dormiam et requiescam,* which is to say, "I will both lay me down in peace and sleep." This verse said, he passed from this life with glad and joyful countenance. And after he was buried, Friar John returned to the friary of La Massa and waited for the promise of Friar James, that he would return to him on the day he had said. But while he was at prayer on that day, Christ appeared to him with a great company of angels and saints, and among them Friar James was not: whereupon Friar John, marvelling greatly, commended him devoutly to Christ. Then on the day following, as Friar John was praying in the wood, Friar James appeared to him accompanied by the angels, all glorious and all glad; and Friar John said to him, "O dearest father, wherefore hast thou not returned to me the day that thou didst promise?" Friar James answered, "Because I had need of some purgation; but in that same hour when Christ appeared to thee, and thou didst commend me to Him, Christ heard thee and delivered me from all pain. And then I appeared to the holy lay Friar James of La Massa, that was serving mass, and saw the consecrated Host, when the priest elevated it, converted and changed into the form of a living child most fair; and I said to him, 'This day do I go with that child to the realm of life eternal, whither none can go without him.'" These words said, Friar James vanished and went to heaven with all that blessed company of angels; and Friar John remained much comforted. And the said Friar James of Falterone died on the vigil of St. James the Apostle, in the month of July, in the aforesaid friary of Moliano, wherein, through his merits, divine goodness wrought many miracles after his death.

CHAPTER LII

OF THE VISION OF FRIAR JOHN OF LA VERNA WHEREIN HE KNEW ALL THE ORDER OF THE HOLY TRINITY

THE aforesaid Friar John of La Verna, for that he had wholly smothered all worldly and temporal joys and consolations, and in God had placed all his joys and all his hopes, the divine goodness gave him wondrous consolations and revelations, and, above all, in the solemn festivals of Christ; wherefore on a time when the feast of the Nativity was drawing nigh, whereon he had the expectancy of certain consolation from God in the sweet humanity of Christ, the Holy Spirit set in his mind such exceeding great love and fervour for the charity of Christ whereby He had abased Himself to take our humanity upon Him, that it verily seemed to him as were his soul ravished from his body, and that it burned like a furnace. And being unable to endure this burning, and being in sore distress of soul, he cried out with a loud voice; for by the power of the Holy Spirit and by the exceeding fervour of his love he could not withhold his cry. And at the hour when that consuming fervour came upon him, there came withal so strong and sure a hope of his salvation, that in no wise could he believe that, had he then died, he would need to pass through the pains of purgatory; and this love endured within him full six months, albeit that excessive fervour possessed him not continuously, but came upon him only at certain hours of the day, and then in these times he received wondrous visitations and consolations from God. And ofttimes was he rapt in ecstasy, even as that friar saw who first wrote down these things; among which, one night, he was so lifted up and rapt in God that he beheld in Him, the Creator, all created things in heaven and on earth, and all their perfections and degrees and their several orders. And then he perceived clearly how every created thing was related to its Creator, and how God is above, is within, is without, is beside all created things. Thereafter he perceived one God in three Persons, and three Persons in one God, and the infinite love that made the Son of God become flesh in obedience to the Father. And at the last he perceived, in that vision, how that no other way was there whereby the soul might ascend to God and have eternal life save through the blessed Christ, that is the Way, the Truth, and the Life of the soul.

CHAPTER LIII

HOW FRIAR JOHN OF LA VERNA, WHILE SAYING MASS, FELL DOWN AS ONE DEAD

On a time, as the friars that were present were wont to tell, a wondrous case befell the said Friar John in the aforesaid friary of Moliano; for, on the first night after the octave of St. Lawrence, and within the octave of the Assumption of Our Lady, having said matins in church with the other friars, and the unction of divine grace falling upon him, he went forth into the garden to meditate on the Passion of Christ and to prepare himself, with all devotion, to celebrate the mass that it was his turn to sing that morning. And while he was meditating on the words of the consecration of the body of Christ, to wit, while he was considering the infinite love of Christ, and that He had been willing to redeem us, not only with His precious blood, but likewise to leave us His most worthy body and blood for food of souls, the love of sweet Jesus began so to wax within him, and with such great fervour and tenderness, that his soul could no longer endure such sweetness; and he cried out with a loud voice, and as one inebriate in spirit, ceased not to repeat to himself, *Hoc est corpus meum:* for as he spake these words he seemed to behold the blessed Christ, with the Virgin Mother and a multitude of angels; and he was illumined by the Holy Spirit in all the deep and lofty mysteries of that most high sacrament. And when the dawn was come, he went into the church, with that same fervour of spirit, and with that same absorption, and believing he was neither heard nor seen of men, went on repeating those words; but there was a certain friar at prayer in the choir that saw and heard all. And, unable to contain himself in that fervour of spirit by reason of the abundance of grace divine, he cried out with a loud voice, and so continued until the hour of mass was come. Wherefore he went to vest himself for the altar. And when he began the mass, the farther he proceeded the more the love of Christ and that fervour of devotion increased within him, whereby an ineffable sense of God's presence was given to him, which he could neither comprehend nor thereafter express with his lips. Wherefore, fearing lest that fervour and sense of God's presence should so wax within him that he must needs leave the altar, he fell into great perplexity, and knew not what he should do—

whether to go on with the mass, or stay and wait. But, forasmuch as at other times a like case had befallen him, and the Lord had so far tempered that fervour that he had needed not to leave the altar, he trusted He might do the like this time; so he set himself with fear and trembling to go forward with the mass: and when he came as far as the preface of Our Lady, the divine illumination of the gracious sweetness of the love of God began so to increase within him, that coming to the *Qui pridie*, scarce could he endure such ravishing sweetness. At last, when he came to the act of consecration, and had said the first half of the words over the Host, to wit, *Hoc est*, in no wise could he go farther, but only repeated those selfsame words, to wit, *Hoc est enim*. And the cause wherefore he could go no farther was, that he felt and beheld the presence of Christ, with a multitude of angels, whose majesty he could not endure. And he saw that Christ entered not into the Host, or, in sooth, that the Host would not become changed into the body of Christ, except he uttered the other half of the words, to wit, *corpus meum*. Whereupon, while he stood thus perplexed and could proceed no farther, the warden and the other friars, and many lay folk likewise that were in the church hearing mass, drew nigh to the altar, and were filled with awe when they beheld and considered the acts of Friar John: and many of them wept through devotion. At the length, after a great space, to wit, when it pleased God, Friar John uttered, with a loud voice, *corpus meum;* and straightway the form of the bread vanished, and Jesus Christ the blessed appeared, incarnate and glorified, in the Host, and showed forth to him the humility and charity that made Him become incarnate of the Virgin Mary, and that every day maketh Him to come into the hands of the priest, when he consecrateth the Host: for which thing he was the more exalted in sweetness and contemplation. And no sooner had he elevated the consecrated Host and cup than he was ravished out of himself, and his soul, being lifted up above all bodily senses, his body fell backwards; and had he not been held up by the warden that stood behind him, he had fallen supine on the ground. Whereat the friars hastened towards him, and the lay folk that were in the church, both men and women; and he was carried into the sacristy as one dead; for his body had grown cold, and the fingers of his hands were so tightly clenched that scarce could they be opened or moved. And in this manner he lay between life and death, or ravished, until the hour of tierce; for it was summer time. And since I, that was present at all these things, desired much to know what God had wrought in him, I went straightway to him when his senses had returned to him, and besought him, for love of God, that he would tell me all things. Wherefore, because he had great trust in me, he related all to me in order; and, among other things, he told me that while meditating on the body and blood of Jesus Christ before him, his heart was melted like heated wax, and his flesh seemed to be without bones, in such wise that scarce could he lift up arm or hand to make the sign of the cross over the Host, or over the cup. He likewise told me that before he was made a priest, God had revealed to him that he was to swoon away in the mass; but seeing that he had since said many masses, and this thing had not befallen him, he believed the revelation was not of God. And nevertheless, about fifty days before the Assumption of Our Lady, whereon the aforesaid case befell him, God had again revealed to him that this thing was to come to pass about the feast of the Assumption; but that thereafter he no longer remembered the said vision, or revelation, made to him by our Lord.

Here endeth the first part of the book of the venerable St. Francis, and of many of the holy friars his companions. Here followeth the second part concerning the sacred stigmas.

Touching the Sacred and Holy Stigmas of St. Francis and some Considerations thereon

In this part we will treat, with devout consideration, of the glorious, sacred, and hallowed stigmas of our blessed father, St. Francis, that he received from Christ on the holy mount of La Verna. And forasmuch as the said stigmas were five, according to the five wounds of our Lord Jesus Christ, this treatise shall be divided into five considerations.

The first consideration shall be touching the manner of the coming of St. Francis to the holy mount of La Verna.

The second consideration shall be touching the life he lived, and the discourse he held with his companions on the said holy mountain.

The third consideration shall be touching the seraphic vision and the impression of the most holy stigmas.

The fourth consideration shall be, how that St. Francis came down from the mount of La Verna after he had received the sacred stigmas and returned to St. Mary of the Angels.

The fifth consideration shall be touching certain divers visions and revelations of the said sacred and hallowed stigmas to holy friars and other devout persons after the death of St. Francis.

I. *Touching the first consideration of the sacred, hallowed stigmas.*

Be it known, touching the first consideration, that when St. Francis was forty-three years of age, in the year one thousand two hundred and twenty-four, he was inspired by God to set forth from the vale of Spoleto and journey into Romagna, with Friar Leo his companion; and as they went they passed by the foot of the town of Montefeltro, wherein a great banquet and a great procession were made by reason of the knighting of one of those counts of Montefeltro. And St. Francis, hearing of this solemn festival and that many noblemen of divers countries were assembled together there, said to Friar Leo, "Let us go up thither to this festival, for with God's help we shall gather some good spiritual fruit." Now among the other nobles that were come to that festival from the country round about was a certain rich and mighty nobleman of Tuscany, called Roland of Chiusi di Casentino, who, because of the wondrous things he had heard of the holiness and of the miracles of St. Francis, held him in great devotion, and had a very great desire to behold him and to hear him preach. And St. Francis came up to that town and entered within, and went to the market-place, where all the host of those nobles was gathered together, and in fervour of spirit climbed on to a low wall and began to preach, taking for the text of his sermon these words in the vulgar tongue—

"A joy to me is every pain,
For I await a greater gain."

And upon this text he preached so devoutly and so profoundly by inspiration of the Holy Spirit, proving it by divers pains and martyrdoms of the holy apostles and the holy martyrs, and by the hard penances of the holy confessors, and the many tribulations and temptations of the holy virgins and other saints, that all the people stood with eyes and minds lifted up towards him, and hearkened as if an angel of God were speaking. And among them was the said Roland, who, touched to the heart by God through the wondrous preaching of St. Francis, was minded to confer and take counsel with him, after the sermon, touching the state of his soul. Wherefore, the sermon ended, he drew St. Francis aside and said to him, "O father, fain would I take counsel with thee touching the salvation of my soul." St.

Francis answered, "It pleaseth me well; but go this morning, honour thy friends that have bidden thee to this feast, and dine with them, and after thou hast dined, we will speak together as long as it shall please thee." Roland therefore went away to dine, and after he had dined, returned to St. Francis and thus conferred and discoursed with him fully, touching the state of his soul. And at last this Roland said to St. Francis, "I have a mountain in Tuscany most proper for devout contemplation that is called the mount of La Verna, and is very solitary and meet for those that desire to do penance in a place far away from the world, or to lead a solitary life; and if it so please thee, fain would I give it to thee and to thy companions for the salvation of my soul." St. Francis, hearing this bounteous offer of a thing he so much desired, rejoiced with exceeding great joy, and praising and giving thanks, first to God and then to Roland, spake to him thus, "Roland, when you are returned to your house I will send some of my companions to you, and you will show this mountain to them; and if it seem to them a proper place for prayer and penance, from this time forth I accept your charitable offer." This said, St. Francis departed, and when he had made an end of his journey he returned to St. Mary of the Angels; and Roland likewise, when he had celebrated the end of that festival, returned to his castle that was called Chiusi, and was distant a mile from La Verna. And St. Francis, being returned to St. Mary of the Angels, sent forth two of his companions to the said Roland, who, when they were come to him, received them with the greatest joy and charity. And being fain to show them the mount of La Verna, he sent with them full fifty men-at-arms to be their defence against the wild beasts; and these friars, thus escorted, ascended to the top of the mountain and sought diligently about, and at the last they came to a part of the mountain that was meet for a holy place and most proper for contemplation, in which place was an open plain: this spot they chose for the habitation of them and of St. Francis, and there, with the help of the men-at-arms that were in their escort, they made some little cells of the branches of trees. And thus in the name of God they accepted and took possession of the mount of La Verna, and of the friary on that mountain, and departed and returned to St. Francis. And when they were come to St. Francis they related to him how and in what manner they had taken a place on the mount of La Verna most meet for prayer and contemplation. Hearing these tidings, St. Francis rejoiced greatly, and praising and giving thanks to God, spake to these friars with a glad countenance, and said, "My sons, we are drawing nigh to our lent of St. Michael the Archangel, and I steadfastly believe that it is God's will we should keep this fast on the mount of La Verna, that by divine providence hath been prepared for us, in order that we may merit from Christ the joy of consecrating that blessed mount to the honour and glory of God and of His Mother, the glorious Virgin Mary, and the holy angels." This said, St. Francis took with him Friar Masseo of Marignano d'Assisi, that was a man of great wisdom and great eloquence; and Friar Angelo Tancredi of Rieti, that was a very noble gentleman, and in the world had been a knight; and Friar Leo, that was a man of great simplicity and purity, and therefore much beloved of St. Francis. And St. Francis with these three friars set himself to pray, and commended himself and the aforesaid companions to the prayers of the friars that were left behind; and then set forth, in the name of Jesus Christ crucified, with those three to go to the mount of La Verna. And as St. Francis went forth, he called one of those three companions, and he was Friar Masseo, and spake to him thus, "Thou, Friar Masseo, shalt be our warden and our superior on this journey, I say, while we go and remain together; and thus we will observe our Rule, for whether we say the office, or discourse of God, or keep silence, we will take no thought for the morrow, neither what we shall eat, nor what we shall drink, nor where we shall sleep; but when the hour of rest cometh we will beg a little bread, and then will stay our steps and rest ourselves in the place that God shall prepare for us." Then did these three companions bow their heads, and making the sign of the cross, journeyed on; and the first evening they came to a friary and there lodged. The second evening, by reason of the bad weather and of being so weary they were not able to come to a friary, nor to any town, nor to any hamlet, and night falling after the bad weather, they took refuge in a deserted and ruined church and there lay down to rest. And while his companions were sleeping, St. Francis betook himself to prayer, and lo, at the first watch of the night there came a great host of fiercest devils with a great noise and tumult and began to attack and annoy him mightily: for one plucked him here, another there; one pulled him down, another up; one threatened him with one thing, and one rebuked for another; and thus in divers ways they strove to disturb his prayers; but they could not, for God was with him. And when St. Francis had endured these assaults of the devils a long space, he began to cry with a loud voice, "O ye damned spirits, naught can ye avail except in so far as the hand of God suffereth you: therefore in the name of the omnipotent God I say unto you, do ye unto my body whatsoever is permitted you by God, for I suffer all willingly, since no greater enemy have I than my body; therefore, if ye avenge me of mine enemy, ye do me too great a service." Then the devils seized him and with great violence and fury began to drag him about the church and to wreak on him more grievous hurt and annoy than before. Whereat St. Francis began to cry aloud and say, "My Lord Jesus Christ, I thank Thee for the great love and charity Thou hast shown toward me; for 'tis a token of great love when the Lord well punisheth His servant for all his faults in this world, in order that he be not punished in the next. And I am prepared to endure joyfully every pain and every adversity that Thou, my God, art willing to send for my sins." Then the devils, confounded and vanquished by his constancy and patience, departed, and St. Francis came forth from the church in fervour of spirit and entered into a wood that was nigh and betook him to prayer, and with prayers and with tears, and with smitings of the breast, sought Jesus Christ, the beloved spouse of his soul.

And at last, finding Him in the secret places of his soul, now he spake with Him reverently as his Lord; now he gave answer to Him as his Judge; again he besought Him as a father, and yet again he reasoned with Him as a friend. On that night, and in that wood, his companions, after they awoke, stood hearkening and considering what he was doing, and they beheld and heard him with tears and cries devoutly entreat God's mercy for sinners. Then was he heard and seen to bewail, with a loud voice, the Passion of Christ, even as if he beheld it with corporeal eyes. And in that selfsame night they saw him praying with his arms held in the form of a cross, and lifted up from the ground and suspended for a great space, and surrounded by a bright and shining cloud. And thus he passed all that night in these holy exercises, without sleep; and in the morning his companions, knowing that St. Francis, by reason of the fatigues of that night passed without sleep, was very feeble in body, and would have ill borne to go afoot, went to a poor peasant of that country-side, and, for love of God, craved the loan of his ass for St. Francis, their father, that could not go afoot. This man, hearing the name of Friar Francis, asked of them, "Are ye of those friars of that friar of Assisi whereof so much good is told?" The friars answered, "Yea," and that in fact it was for him that they craved the animal. Then this honest fellow saddled the ass with great devotion and solicitude, and led him to St. Francis, and with great reverence bade him mount thereon; and so they went their way, the peasant with them, behind his ass. And after they had journeyed on a while, the peasant said to St. Francis, "Tell me, art thou that Friar Francis of Assisi?" And St. Francis answered, "Yea." "Now strive, then," said the peasant, "to be as good as thou art held to be by all folk, for many have great faith in thee; therefore I admonish thee that thou betray not the hopes men cherish of thee." St. Francis, hearing these words, disdained not to be admonished by a peasant, nor said within himself, "What beast is this that doth admonish me?" as many proud fellows that wear the cowl would say nowadays, but straightway flung himself off the ass and alighted on the ground and knelt down before him, and kissed his feet, and humbly thanked him for that he had deigned to admonish him thus charitably. Then the peasant, together with the companions of St. Francis, raised him up from the ground, with great devotion, and set him again on the ass and journeyed on. And when they had climbed about half-way up the mountain, a great thirst came upon this peasant, for the heat was very great, and toilsome the ascent; whereat he began to cry behind St. Francis, saying, "Ah me! I die of thirst, for if I have not water to drink I shall forthwith choke." Wherefore St. Francis got down from the ass and fell to prayer, and so long he knelt, with hands lifted up to heaven, until he knew by revelation that his prayer was heard of God. Then said St. Francis to the peasant, "Haste; hie thee quickly to that rock, there shalt thou find running water that Jesus Christ in this hour hath, in His mercy, made to issue from that rock." Now runs he to the place that St. Francis had shown to him, and there finds a fair spring which St. Francis, by virtue of his prayers, had made to gush forth from that hard rock; and he drank thereof abundantly, and was comforted. And well it appeareth that that spring was made to flow by God miraculously, at the prayers of St. Francis, for neither before nor after was ever a spring of water seen in that place, nor running water near that place for a great distance. This done, St. Francis, with his companions, and with the peasant, gave thanks to God for the miracle He had shown them, and then journeyed on. And when they were come nigh to the foot of the very rock of La Verna, it pleased St. Francis to rest a while under the oak tree that stood by the way, and there standeth to this day; and resting beneath it, St. Francis began to consider the lay of the place and of the country round about. And lo, while he was thus pondering there came a great multitude of birds from divers parts that, with singing and fluttering of their wings, showed forth great joy and gladness, and surrounded St. Francis, in such wise that some settled on his head, some on his shoulders, and some on his arms, some on his bosom, and some around his feet. His companions and the peasant, beholding this, marvelled greatly, and St. Francis rejoiced in spirit, and spake thus, "I do believe, dearest brothers, that it is pleasing to our Lord Jesus Christ that we abide on this solitary mountain, since our sisters and brothers, the birds, show forth such great joy at our coming." These words said, they rose up and journeyed on; and at last they came to the place that his companions had taken at first. And this is all that concerns the first consideration, to wit, how St. Francis came to the holy mount of La Verna.

II. *Touching the second consideration of the sacred, hallowed stigmas.*

The second consideration is touching the discourse of St. Francis with his companions on the said mount of La Verna. And as for this, be it known that when Roland heard that St. Francis, with his three companions, had gone up to dwell on the mount of La Verna, he rejoiced exceedingly, and the day following set forth with many of his friends, and came to visit St. Francis; and they brought with them bread and wine, and other necessaries of life for him and his companions. And when they came to the top of the mountain they found them at prayer, and drawing nigh, gave them salutation. Then St. Francis rose up and received Roland and his company with great joy and love; and this done, they began to discourse together. And after they had discoursed a while, and St. Francis had thanked Roland for the holy mountain he had given them, and for his coming, he besought him to have a poor little cell built at the foot of a very fair beech tree that stood about a stone's-throw from the friary; for that seemed to him a place most solemn and meet for prayer. And anon Roland had it made; and this done St. Francis, seeing that the evening was drawing nigh, and it was time to depart, preached to them a little ere they took leave; and after he had preached and had given them his blessing, it behoved Roland to depart; wherefore he called St. Francis and his companions aside, and said to them, "My dearest friars, I am not minded that ye should endure any bodily want on this wild mountain top, and so be less able to give heed to spiritual things. Therefore I desire, and this I say once for all, that ye send confidently to my house for all things needful to you, and if ye did not so I should take it very ill of you." This said, he set forth with his company and returned to his castle. Then St. Francis made his companions sit down, and instructed them touching the manner of the life that they, and whoso would desire to live like religious, in hermitages, should lead. And, among other things, he laid upon them the single-minded observance of holy poverty, saying, "Heed not overmuch Roland's charitable offer, lest ye in any way offend our lady, madonna holy Poverty Be ye sure that the more we despise poverty, the more the world will despise us, and the greater need we shall suffer; but if we embrace holy poverty, immediately the world will follow after us and feed us abundantly. God hath called us to this holy Rule of life for the salvation of the world, and hath made this covenant between us and the world, that we give good example to the world and the world provide for our needs. Let us persevere, then, in holy poverty, because that is the way of perfection, and the earnest and pledge of everlasting riches." And after many fair and devout words, and admonitions of this sort, he made an end, saying, "This is the manner of life that I lay on myself and on you; and for that I see me drawing nigh unto death, I purpose to withdraw to a solitary place and make my peace with God, and weep for my sins before Him; and let Friar Leo, when it shall seem good to him, bring me a little bread and water, and on no account to suffer any lay folk to come to me: do ye answer them for me." These words said, he gave them his blessing, and went to the cell under the beech tree, and his companions remained in their habitation with the steadfast purpose to obey the commands of St. Francis. A few days thereafter, as St. Francis was standing beside the said cell, considering the form of the mountain, and marvelling at the exceeding great clefts and caverns in the mighty rocks, he betook himself to prayer; and then it was revealed to him by God that these clefts, so marvellous, had been miraculously made at the hour of the Passion of Christ, when, according to the gospel, the rocks were rent asunder. And this, God willed, should manifestly appear on the mount of La Verna, because there the Passion of our Lord Jesus Christ was to be renewed, through love and pity, in the soul of St. Francis, and in his body by the imprinting of the sacred, hallowed stigmas. No sooner had St. Francis received that revelation than he forthwith locked himself in his cell, and retired wholly into himself, and made him ready for the mystery of this revelation, and from that hour St. Francis, through his unceasing prayers, began to taste more often of the sweetness of divine contemplation; wherefore many times was he so rapt in God that he was seen of his companions to be lifted up bodily from the ground and ravished out of himself. And in these contemplative ecstasies, not only were things present and future revealed to him, but likewise the secret thoughts and longings of the friars, even as Friar Leo, his companion, made proof of that day. Now to this Friar Leo, while enduring a mighty temptation of the devil, and not a carnal one, but a spiritual one, there came a great desire to have some pious words written by the hand of St. Francis; for he thought within himself, that if he had them, that temptation would leave him, either wholly or in part; yet, through shame or reverence, he had not the heart to tell of this desire to St. Francis. But the desire that Friar Leo spake not of, was revealed by the Holy Spirit to St. Francis: whereat he called Friar Leo to him, and made him bring pen and ink and paper, and with his own very hand did write a praise of Christ, according to the friar's desire. And at the end thereof he made the letter *Tau*,[1] and he gave the writing to him, saying, "Dearest friar, take this paper and keep it diligently until thy death. God bless thee and keep thee from all temptation. Be not afraid that thou art tempted, for the more thou art assailed by temptations the greater friend and servant of God do I hold thee, and the greater love do I bear thee. Verily I say unto thee, let no man deem himself the perfect friend of God until he have passed through many temptations and tribulations." When Friar Leo received this writing, with exceeding devotion and faith, straightway every temptation departed, and returning to the friars, he related to them, with great joy, what grace God had bestowed upon him when he received that writing from St. Francis; and putting it away and keeping it diligently, the friars wrought many miracles by means thereof.[2] And from that hour the said Friar Leo began to watch closely and meditate with great purity and good intent

[1] See Ezekiel ix. 4 (in the Vulgate). According to St. Jerome, Tau (T), which is the last letter of the Hebrew alphabet, was used in the Samaritan language to represent the cross, of which it had the form.

[2] This precious relic of St. Francis is still preserved in the sacristy of the great church of S. Francesco at Assisi.

on the life of St. Francis; and because of his purity it was vouchsafed to him many times and oft, to behold St. Francis rapt in God and lifted up from the earth: sometimes to the height of three cubits, sometimes four, sometimes as high as the top of the beech tree; and sometimes he saw him lifted up in the air so high, and surrounded by such dazzling splendour, that scarce could the eye behold him. Now what was this simple friar wont to do when St. Francis was lifted up but a little space from the earth so that he could reach him? He went softly and embraced his feet and kissed them, and said, in tears, "My God, have mercy on me, a sinner, and through the merits of this holy man give me to find grace with Thee." And one time, among others, while thus standing beneath the feet of St. Francis, when he was so far lifted up from the earth that he could not touch him, he saw a scroll descend from heaven, writ with letters of gold, and rest on the head of St. Francis; and on this scroll these words were writ, *Behold the Grace of God*. And after he had read it he saw it return to heaven. Through this gift of God's grace within him, St. Francis was not only rapt in God by ecstatic contemplation, but many times was likewise comforted by visits of angels. Wherefore, as St. Francis one day was meditating on his death, and on the state of his Order after his death, and saying, "Lord God, what will become of Thy poor little household, that Thou of Thy goodness hast committed to me, a sinner? Who shall comfort them? Who shall correct them? Who shall pray to Thee for them?" And while he was uttering such words, the angel sent of God appeared to him, and comforted him with these words, "I say unto thee, in God's name, that the profession of thy Order shall not fail until the Judgment Day; and none shall be so great a sinner, but that if he love thy Order in his heart, the same shall find mercy in God's sight; and none that evilly persecuteth thy Order shall have length of life. Moreover, no wicked member of thy Order shall long continue therein, except he amend his life. Therefore be not cast down if thou seest some that are not good friars in thy Order, and that observe not the Rule as they ought; think not that for this thy Order shall perish; for ever shall there be of them—and they shall be many and many—that will observe perfectly the life of the gospel of Christ, and the purity of the Rule; and such as these shall go straightway to life everlasting after the death of the body, without passing through any purgatory. And some shall observe the Rule, but not perfectly; and they, ere they go to paradise, shall pass through purgatory, but the time of their purgation shall be committed to thee by God. But touching those that observe not the Rule at all—have no care of them, saith God, because He careth not." These words said, the angel departed, and St. Francis remained comforted and consoled. As the feast of the Assumption of Our Lady was now drawing nigh, St. Francis seeketh the opportunity of a more solitary and more secret place, wherein he may keep the fast of St. Michael the Archangel, that beginneth with the said feast of the Assumption. Wherefore he calls Friar Leo, and speaks to him thus, "Go and stand at the doorway of the oratory of the friary, and when I call thee do thou return to me." Friar Leo goes and stands at the doorway, and St. Francis withdrew a space and called loudly. Hearing himself called, Friar Leo returns to him, and St. Francis saith, "Son, let us seek a more secret place, whence thou canst not hear me when I call." And, in their search, they caught sight of a secret place on that side of the mountain that looketh to the south, and only too meet for his purpose; but they could not get there, because in front thereof was a horrible and fearful and very great chasm in the rock; wherefore, with great labour, they laid some logs across this chasm, after the manner of a bridge, and passed over. Then St. Francis sent for the other friars, and tells them how that he purposed to keep the lent of St. Michael in that solitary place, and therefore prays them to make a little cell there, so that no call of his might be heard by them. And the little cell of St. Francis being made, he saith to them, "Go ye to your dwelling, and leave me here alone, for with God's help I purpose to keep the fast here, with mind undistraught or unperturbed: therefore let none of you come to me, nor suffer any worldly folk to come to me. But thou only, Friar Leo, shalt come to me, once a day, with a little bread and water, and once again, by night, at the hour of matins: then shalt thou come to me in silence, and when thou art at the foot of the bridge thou shalt say to me, *Domine labia mea aperies*, and if I answer 'Come,' pass thou on to the cell, and we will say matins together; but if I answer not, return thou straightway." And St. Francis said this because sometimes he was so rapt in God that he neither heard nor perceived aught with his bodily senses. This said, St. Francis gave them his blessing, and they returned to the friary. And the feast of the Assumption being come, St. Francis began the holy fast with great abstinence and severity, mortifying his body and comforting his spirit with fervent prayers, watchings, and scourgings; and ever waxing from virtue to virtue in these prayers, he made ready his soul to receive the divine mysteries and divine splendours, and his body to endure the cruel assaults of the devils, wherewith he was ofttimes smitten corporeally; and among other times, on a day during that fast, as St. Francis issued from his cell in fervour of spirit, and went to pray hard by in a hollow cave in the rock, at a great height from the ground and looking on a horrible and fearful abyss, suddenly the devil cometh in a terrible form, with tempest and mighty ruin, and smiteth him to thrust him down the abyss. Whereat St. Francis, having no whither to flee, and being unable to suffer the cruel aspect of the devil, anon turned with hands and face and all his body close to the rock, commending himself to God, and groping about with his hands, if haply he might find aught to cling to. But, as it pleased God, who never letteth His servants be tempted beyond what they can endure, straightway the rock, whereto he clung, was hollowed out by a miracle to the form of his body, and received him into itself, in such wise that the said rock was imprinted with the form of the face and the hands of St. Francis, as if he had pressed his hands and face against melted wax; and thus, with God's help, he escaped from the devil. But what the devil was unable to do then to St. Francis, to wit, thrust him down thence, was done a long time after the death of St. Francis to one, a dear and devoted friar, who was at that place, laying down some planks of wood, in order that he might go thither without peril, out of devotion to St. Francis, and in memory of the holy miracle there wrought; for on a day, as he was carrying a big log of wood on his head to lay across the chasm, he was pushed by the devil and thrust down and made to fall with that log on his head. But God, who had saved and preserved St. Francis from falling, saved and preserved that devout friar by his merits from the peril of his fall; for as the friar was falling he commended himself with a loud voice and with great devotion to St. Francis; and he straightway appeared to him, and grasping him, placed him down on the rocks, so that he felt neither shock nor wound. But the other friars, having heard the cry of this friar as he fell, and deeming him dead, and all dashed to pieces on the sharp rocks, by the great depth of his fall, took up the bier, and with great grief and many tears went to the other side of the mountain to seek the fragments of his body and bury them. And when they were come down to the foot of the rock, lo, that friar who had fallen met them, carrying the log on his head and singing *Te Deum laudamus* with a loud voice. And seeing the friars marvel greatly, he related to them, in order, all the manner of his fall, and how St. Francis had delivered him from all peril. Then all the friars came with him together to that place, singing most devoutly the aforesaid psalm, *Te Deum laudamus*, praising and giving thanks to God, and to St. Francis, for the miracle he had wrought for one of his friars.

St. Francis then, as hath been told, persevered in that fast, and albeit he endured many assaults of the devil, none the less did he receive many consolations from God, not only by visits of angels, but likewise of wild birds; for all the time of that lent, a falcon that had built her nest hard by his cell awoke him every night, a little before matins, by her singing and by beating her wings against his cell, and she departed not until he had risen up to say matins. And when St. Francis was more weary at one time than another, or more sick, or more feeble, this falcon, after the manner of a discreet and compassionate person, sang later. And so St. Francis had great pleasure of this clock; for the great solicitude of this falcon drove all sloth away from him and urged him to prayer, and beyond this, she ofttimes by day dwelt familiarly with him. Finally, as to this second consideration, St. Francis, being much weakened in body, in part by his great abstinence, and in part by the assaults of the devil, and being fain to comfort his body with the spiritual food of the soul, began to meditate on the ineffable glory and joy of the blessed in the life eternal; and he began to beseech God to grant him the grace of some foretaste of that joy. And while he remained thus meditating, anon an angel appeared to him with exceeding great splendour, that held a viol in his left hand and a bow in his right; and as St. Francis stood all dazed at this vision, the angel drew his bow once upwards across the viol; and straightway St. Francis heard such sweet melody that it ravished his soul and lifted him beyond all bodily sense, so that, as he afterwards related to his companions, he doubted lest his soul had wholly parted from his body, by reason of the unbearable sweetness, if the angel had drawn the bow downwards again. And this is all that concerneth the second consideration.

III. *Touching the third consideration of the sacred, hallowed stigmas.*

Coming to the third consideration, to wit, of the seraphic vision, and of the imprinting of the sacred, hallowed stigmas, be it known that the feast of the Most Holy Cross in the month of

September drawing nigh, Friar Leo went one night at the wonted hour to the wonted place, in order to say matins with St. Francis, and having cried from the foot of the bridge, *Domine labia mia aperies,* as he was used to do, St. Francis did not answer. And Friar Leo turned not back, as St. Francis had bidden him, but passed over the bridge, with good and holy intent, and entered softly into his cell, and finding him not, thought he might be somewhere in the wood at prayer. Whereat he comes forth and goes about the wood in search of him by the light of the moon. And at last he heard the voice of St. Francis, and drawing nigh, beheld him on his knees in prayer with face and hands lifted up to heaven, saying in fervour of spirit, "Who art Thou, my God most sweet? What am I, Thy unprofitable servant and vilest of worms?" And these self-same words he again repeated and said naught besides. Whereat Friar Leo, marvelling greatly, lifted up his eyes and looked heavenward; and as he looked, he beheld a flaming torch coming down from heaven, most beautiful and resplendent, which descended and rested on the head of St. Francis; and from the said flame he heard a voice come forth which spake with St. Francis, but the words thereof this Friar Leo understood not. Hearing this, and deeming himself unworthy to remain so near the holy place where that wondrous vision was seen, and fearing likewise to offend St. Francis, or disturb him in his meditation if he were heard of him, he stole softly back, and standing afar off, waited to see the end. And as he gazed steadfastly, he beheld St. Francis stretch forth his hands thrice towards the flame; and at last, after a great space of time, he saw the flaming torch return to heaven. Whereupon he bestirred himself and returned secretly to his cell, glad in heart at the vision. And as he was going confidently away, St. Francis heard him by the rustling of the leaves under his feet, and bade him stay his steps and await him. Then Friar Leo, obedient, stood still and awaited him, with such great fear that, as he afterwards told his companions, at that moment he would rather the earth had swallowed him up than await St. Francis, who he thought would be displeased with him; for he guarded himself with the greatest diligence against offending his father, lest through his own fault St. Francis should deprive him of his companionship. Then St. Francis, as he came up to him, asked, "Who art thou?" And Friar Leo, all trembling, answered, "I am Friar Leo, my father." And St. Francis said to him, "Wherefore camest thou hither, friar, little sheep? Have I not told thee not to go spying on me? Tell me, by holy obedience, if thou didst see or hear aught?" Friar Leo answered, "Father, I heard thee speak and say many times, 'Who art Thou, my God most sweet? What am I, thy unprofitable servant and vilest of worms?'" And then Friar Leo knelt down before St. Francis and confessed his sin of disobedience, for that he had done contrary to his commands, craving forgiveness of him with many tears. And thereafter he entreated him devoutly to interpret to him those words he had heard, and tell him those he had not understood. Then St. Francis, seeing that God had revealed to this lowly Friar Leo, because of his purity and simplicity, or in sooth had suffered him to hear and behold certain things, deigned to reveal to him and interpret to him all those things he asked of him. And he spake thus, "Know thou, friar, little sheep of Jesus Christ, that when I was saying those words that thou didst hear, two lights were shown to me within my soul—one, the knowledge and understanding of myself; the other, the knowledge and understanding of the Creator. When I said, 'Who art Thou, my God most sweet?' then was I illumined by the light of contemplation, whereby I beheld the depths of the infinite goodness and wisdom and power of God. And when I said, 'What am I, etc.?' I was in the light of contemplation, whereby I beheld the deplorable depths of my own vileness and misery; and therefore I said, 'Who art Thou, Lord, infinite in goodness and wisdom, that deignest to visit me that am a vile and abominable worm?' And God was in that flame thou sawest, who spake to me in that vision even as of old He had spoken to Moses. And among other things He said, He asked of me to make Him three gifts; and I answered, 'My Lord, I am wholly Thine; well Thou knowest I have naught save tunic, cord, and breeches, and even these three things are Thine; what, then, can I offer or give unto Thy Majesty?' Then God said, 'Search in thy bosom and offer Me what thou findest there.' I sought there and found a ball of gold, and this I offered to God; and thus did I thrice, according as God had thrice bidden me. And then thrice knelt I down, and blessed and gave thanks to God that had given me wherewithal to offer to Him. And straightway it was given me to know that those three offers signified holy obedience, most exalted poverty, and most resplendent chastity, which God had vouchsafed to me by His grace to observe so perfectly that my conscience reproved me of naught. And even as thou sawest me place my hands in my bosom and offer to God those three virtues signified by the three balls of gold that God had placed in my bosom, even so hath God given me this virtue in my soul—that for all the good and for all the grace He hath bestowed upon me by His most holy goodness, I ever in my heart and with my lips do praise and magnify Him. These are the words thou didst hear when thou sawest me lift up my hands thrice. But beware, friar, little sheep; go thou not spying upon me, but return to thy cell with God's blessing, and have diligent care of me: for yet a few days and God shall work such great and wondrous things on this mountain that all the world shall marvel thereat; for He shall do things, new and strange, such as never hath He done to any creature in this world." These things said, St. Francis had the book of the gospels brought to him, for God had put it into his soul that by opening the book of the gospels thrice, those things that God was pleased to do with him should be shown forth. And when the book was brought, St. Francis betook himself to prayer, and the prayer ended, he had the book opened thrice by the hand of Friar Leo, and in the name of the most holy Trinity; and even as it pleased the divine providence, ever in those three openings the Passion of Christ was displayed to him. Through which thing it was given him to understand that even as he had followed Christ in the acts of his life, so was he to follow Him and conform himself unto Him in the afflictions and sorrows of the Passion, ere he passed from this life. And from that time forth St. Francis began to taste and feel more bounteously the sweetness of divine contemplation and of divine visitations. Among which, he had one, immediate and preparatory to the imprinting of the divine stigmas, in this form. The day that goeth before the feast of the Most Holy Cross in the month of September, as St. Francis was praying in secret in his cell, the angel of God appeared to him and spake thus to him in God's name, "I am come to comfort and admonish thee that thou humbly prepare thee and make thee ready, with all patience, to receive that which God willeth to give thee and to work in thee." St. Francis answered, "I am ready to endure patiently all things that my Lord would do with me." This said, the angel departed. The day following, to wit, the day of the Most Holy Cross, St. Francis, on the morn before daybreak, knelt down betimes in prayer before the door of his cell; and turning his face eastwards, prayed in this wise, "O my Lord Jesus Christ, two graces do I pray Thee to grant unto me ere I die: the first, that while I live I may feel in my body and in my soul, so far as is possible, that sorrow, sweet Lord, that Thou didst suffer in the hour of Thy bitterest Passion; the second is, that I may feel in my heart, so far as may be possible, that exceeding love wherewith, O Son of God, Thou wast enkindled to endure willingly for us sinners agony so great." And remaining a long time thus praying, he knew that God would hear him; and that, so far as might be possible to a mere creature, thus far would it be vouchsafed to him to suffer the aforesaid things. St. Francis, having this promise, began to contemplate most devoutly the Passion of Christ and His infinite love; and the fervour of devotion waxed so within him that through love and through compassion he was wholly changed into Jesus. And being thus inflamed by this contemplation, he beheld, that same morning, a seraph with six resplendent and flaming wings come down from heaven; which seraph, with swift flight, drew nigh to St. Francis so that he could discern him, and he knew clearly that he had the form of a man crucified; and thus were his wings disposed: two wings were extended over his head; two were spread out in flight; and the other two covered the whole of the body. St. Francis, beholding this, was sore afraid, and yet was he filled with sweetness and sorrow mingled with wonder. Joy had he, exceeding great, at the gracious aspect of Christ that appeared to him thus familiarly and looked on him so graciously; but, on the other hand, seeing him nailed upon the cross, he suffered unspeakable grief and compassion. Thereafter, he marvelled greatly at so stupendous and unwonted a vision, well knowing that the infirmity of the Passion doth not accord with the immortality of the seraphic spirit. And being in this wonderment, it was revealed by the seraph who appeared to him, that that vision had been shown to him in such form, by divine providence, in order that he might understand he was to be changed into the express similitude of the crucified Christ in this wondrous vision, not by bodily martyrdom but by spiritual fire. Then the whole mount of La Verna seemed to flame forth with dazzling splendour, that shone and illumined all the mountains and the valleys round about, as were the sun shining on the earth. Wherefore when the shepherds that were watching in that country saw the mountain aflame and so much brightness round about, they were sore afraid, according as they afterwards told the friars, and affirmed that that flame had endured over the mount of La Verna for the space of an hour and more. Likewise, certain muleteers that were going to Romagna, arose up at the brightness of this light which shone through the windows of the inns of that country, and thinking the sun had risen, saddled and loaded their beasts. And as they went their way, they saw the said light wane and the real sun rise. Now Christ appeared in that same seraphic vision, and revealed to St. Francis certain secret and high things that St. Francis would never, during his life, disclose to any man; but, after his death, he revealed them, according as is set forth hereafter. And the words were these, "Knowest thou," said Christ, "what I have done to thee? I have given thee the stigmas that are the marks of my Passion, in order that thou be My standard-bearer. And even as I, on the day of my death, descended into limbo and delivered all the souls I found there by virtue of these My stigmas, so do I grant to thee that every year, on the day of thy death, thou mayst go to purgatory and deliver all the souls thou shalt find there of thy three orders—Minors, Sisters, and Penitents—and others likewise that shall have had great devotion to thee, and thou shalt lead them up to the glory of paradise in order that thou be conformed to Me in thy death, even as thou art in thy life." This wondrous vision having vanished, after a great space, this secret converse left in the heart of St. Francis a burning flame of divine love, exceeding great, and in his flesh, a marvellous image and imprint of the Passion of Christ. For the marks of the nails began anon to be seen on the hands and on the feet of St. Francis, in the same manner as he had then seen them in the body of Jesus Christ crucified that had appeared to him in the form of a seraph: and thus his hands and feet seemed nailed through the middle with nails, the heads whereof were in the palms of his hands and in the soles of his feet, outside the flesh; and the points came out through the backs of the hands and the feet, so far, that they were bent back and clinched in such wise that one might easily have put a finger of the hand through the bent and clinched ends outside the flesh, even as through a ring: and the heads of the nails were round and black. In like fashion, the image of a lance-wound, unhealed, inflamed, and bleeding, was seen in his right side, whence thereafter blood came out many times from the holy breast of St. Francis and stained his tunic and his under garments with blood. Wherefore his companions, before they learned these things from him, perceiving nevertheless that he never uncovered his hands or his feet, and that he could not put the soles of his feet to the ground, and finding thereafter that his tunic and under garments were all bloody when they washed them, knew of a surety that he had the image and similitude of our Lord Jesus Christ crucified, expressly imprinted on his hands and feet, and likewise on his side. And albeit he strove much to conceal and to hide those glorious, sacred, and hallowed stigmas, thus clearly marked on his flesh; yet on the other hand, seeing that he could ill conceal them from his familiar companions, and fearing to publish abroad the secrets of God, he remained in great doubt whether he ought to reveal the seraphic vision and the imprint of the sacred, hallowed stigmas. At last, pricked by conscience, he called to him certain of his most familiar friars and propounded his doubts to them in general terms, without giving expression to the fact and asked counsel of them. Now among these friars was one of great holiness called Friar Illuminatus, and he, verily illumined by God, understood that St. Francis must have beheld wondrous things, and answered him thus, "Friar Francis, know that not for thee alone, but also for others, God showeth to thee at divers times his holy mysteries; therefore hast thou reason to fear lest thou be worthy of reproof if thou keep this thing hidden that God hath shown to thee for profit of others." Then St. Francis, moved by these words, laid before them, with exceeding great fear, all the manner and form of the aforesaid vision, and added that Christ when He appeared to him, had said certain things that he would never tell while he lived. And albeit those most holy wounds, in so far as they were imprinted by Christ, gave him great joy in his heart, nevertheless to his flesh and to his bodily senses they gave unbearable pain. Wherefore, being constrained by necessity, he chose Friar Leo, simplest and purest among the friars, and to him revealed all things; and he suffered him to see and touch those holy wounds and bind them with bandages to ease the pain and staunch the blood that issued and ran therefrom: which dressings, at the time of his sickness, he suffered often to be changed, yea, even every day, save from Thursday evening to Saturday morning; for he would not that the pains of the Passion of Christ, that he bore in his body, should be eased in any way by human remedies and medicines during the time our Saviour Jesus Christ had been taken and, for our sakes, crucified and slain and buried. It befell on a time when Friar Leo was changing the swathings of the wound in his side, that St. Francis, by reason of the pain he felt in the loosing of the blood-stained bandage, laid his hand on Friar Leo's breast; and at the touch of those holy hands, Friar Leo felt such great sweetness of devotion in his heart that, a little more, and he had fallen swooning on the ground. And finally, as to this third consideration: St. Francis having completed the forty days' fast of St. Michael the Archangel, made ready by divine revelation to return to St. Mary of the Angels. Wherefore he called Friar Masseo and Friar Angelo to him, and after many words and many holy admonitions, commended the holy mountain to them with all the zeal in his power, saying that it behoved him, together with Friar Leo, to return to St. Mary of the Angels. This said, he took leave of them and blessed them in the name of the crucified Jesus; and deigned, in answer to their prayers, to stretch forth to them his most holy hands, adorned with those glorious and sacred and hallowed stigmas, that they might see them and touch them and kiss them, and leaving the friars thus comforted he departed from them and descended the holy mountain.

IV. *Touching the fourth consideration of the sacred, hallowed stigmas.*

Touching the fourth consideration, be it known, that after the true love of Christ had perfectly transformed St. Francis into God and into the true image of Christ crucified, that angelic man, having completed the fast of forty days in honour of St. Michael the Archangel on the holy mount of La Verna, came down from the mountain with Friar Leo and a devout peasant on whose ass he rode, because, by reason of the nails in his feet, he could not well go a-foot. And when he was come down from the mountain, forasmuch as the fame of his sanctity was noised abroad throughout the land (because the shepherds that had seen the mount of La Verna all aflame had said it was a sign of some great miracle God had wrought on St. Francis), the folk of that country-side all flocked to behold him as he passed by: men and women, small and great, all with great devotion and desire, strove to touch him and to kiss his hands. And St. Francis, being unable to deny his hands to the devotion of the people, albeit he had bound up the palms, nevertheless bound them over again, and covered them with his sleeves, and only held forth his uncovered fingers for them to kiss. But albeit he sought to conceal and hide the sacred mystery of the holy stigmas, that he might flee all occasion of worldly glory, it pleased God to show forth many miracles for His own glory, by virtue of the said sacred, hallowed stigmas, and notably on that journey from La Verna to St. Mary of the Angels. And very many other miracles thereafter were wrought in divers parts of the world, both during his life and after his glorious death; and this to the end that their hidden and wondrous virtue, and the exceeding love and mercy of Christ, so wondrously vouchsafed to him, might be made manifest to the world through clear and evident miracles, whereof we here set down a few.

When St. Francis was drawing nigh to a village which was on the confines of the district of Arezzo, a woman came before him, weeping greatly, and bearing her son in her arms, that was eight years of age; and this child for four years had been sick of the dropsy; and his belly was so swollen and so deformed that when he stood up he could not see his feet; and placing this child before him, this woman besought St. Francis to pray to God for him. And St. Francis first betook himself to prayer, and then, the prayer ended, laid his holy hands on the child's belly, and straightway all the swelling was down, and he was wholly healed; and St. Francis gave him back to his mother, who received him with the greatest joy, and led him home, giving thanks to God and to St. Francis; and willingly she showed her son healed to all those of the country-side that came to her house to behold him. The same day, St. Francis passed by Borgo di San Sepolcro, and before he came nigh to the town, the crowds therefrom and from the villages made towards him; and many of them went before him, bearing olive branches in their hands, crying with a loud voice, "Behold the saint! Behold the saint!" And by reason of the devotion and desire that the folk had to touch him, they made a great throng and press about him; but he went on with mind uplifted and rapt in God, through contemplation; and albeit he was touched and held and dragged about, yet as one insensible he felt naught that was done or said to him; nay, he perceived not even that he was passing by that town or through that land. Wherefore, having passed through the town, and the crowds being gone to their homes, he came to a leper house, a good mile beyond, and this celestial contemplative then returned to himself, as if he were come back from another world; and he asked his companions, "When shall we be nigh the town?" For of a truth his soul, fixed and rapt in contemplation of celestial things, had been sensible of no earthly thing; neither variety of place, nor change of time, nor of persons he passed. And this befell many other times, even as his companions proved by clear experience. On that evening, St. Francis came to the friary of Monte Casale, wherein a friar lay so cruelly sick and so horribly tormented by his sickness that his ill seemed rather a tribulation and torment of the devil than a natural sickness; for sometimes he flung himself on the ground in a mighty trembling and foaming at the mouth; now he contracted all the limbs of his body, now he thrust them forth; now he bent his body, now he writhed; now bending back his heels to the nape of his neck, he sprang high up into the air, and straightway fell again on his back. And St. Francis, hearing from the other friars, as he sat at table, of this miserably sick and incurable friar, had compassion on him; and taking a slice of the bread he was eating, he made thereon the sign of the most holy cross with his holy wounded hands, and sent it to the sick friar; and no sooner had he eaten thereof than he was perfectly healed, and never more felt that sickness. The next morning being come, St. Francis sent two of the friars that were in that house to dwell at La Verna, and sent back with them the peasant that had followed behind the ass he had lent him, desiring that he should return home with them. St. Francis, after he had sojourned some days in that friary, departed and went to Città di Castello. And behold, many of the townsfolk brought before him a woman that for a long time had been possessed by a devil, and besought him humbly to deliver her, for that she, now with grievous howlings, now with cruel shrieks, now with barks like a dog, disturbed the whole country-side. Then St. Francis, having first prayed and made the sign of the most holy cross over her, commanded the devil to depart from her, and straightway he departed, leaving her whole in body and mind. And this miracle being noised abroad among the people, another woman, with great faith, brought to him her child, that was grievously sick of a cruel wound, and devoutly besought him that he would be pleased to make the sign over him with his hands. Then St. Francis, granting her prayer, takes this child and unbinds the wound and blesses him, making thrice the sign of the most holy cross over the wound; then with his own hand he binds the wound up again, and restores him to his mother. And because it was evening, she straightway laid him in his bed to sleep. In the morning she goes to take her child from the bed and finds the wound unbound, and looks and finds him perfectly healed, as if he had never had any ill, save that the flesh had grown over the place where the wound was, in the form of a red rose; and this was to bear witness to the miracle rather than in token of the wound; for the said rose remaining there all the days of his life, did oft move him to a special devotion for St. Francis, who had made him whole. In that same city

St. Francis, at the prayers of the devout townsfolk, abode a month, in which time he wrought very many other miracles, and departed thence, to go to St. Mary of the Angels with Friar Leo and an honest fellow that lent him his ass whereon he rode. Now it befell, that what with the bad roads and what with the great cold, they could not, even by journeying the whole day, come to any place where they might lodge. Wherefore, constrained by the darkness and by the bad weather, they took shelter under the hollow cliff of a rock, to escape the snow and the darkness that had overtaken them. And being thus in sorry plight, and but ill sheltered, the man that had lent the ass was unable to sleep, and having no means of kindling a fire, he began to complain softly within himself and to weep, murmuring at St. Francis that had brought him to such a pass. Then St. Francis, hearing this, had compassion on him, and in fervour of spirit, stretched forth his hand and laid it upon him and touched him. Marvellous to tell! no sooner had he touched him with his hand, pierced and enkindled by the fire of the seraph, than all the cold vanished, and so much heat warmed him from within and without, that himseemed to be nigh to a fiery furnace; wherefore, comforted in body and soul, anon he fell asleep; and, according as he was wont to say, he slept all that night till morn, amid rocks and snow, better than he had ever slept in his own bed. On the morrow, they journeyed on and came to St. Mary of the Angels; and when they were nigh thereto Friar Leo lifted up his eyes and looked towards the said friary of St. Mary of the Angels; and he beheld a cross, exceeding beautiful, whereon was the figure of the Crucified, going before St. Francis, who was riding in front of him; and so closely did that cross conform to the movements of St. Francis, that when he stopped, it stopped; and when he went on, it went on: and that cross shone with such exceeding brightness that not only did the face of St. Francis shine resplendent, but likewise the whole way around him was illumined. And that brightness endured even up to the time that St. Francis entered the friary of St. Mary of the Angels. St. Francis then being come with Friar Leo, they were received with the greatest joy and charity, and from that hour St. Francis abode the most of his time in the friary of St. Mary of the Angels, even until his death. And ever more the fame of his holiness and of his miracles was spread abroad throughout the Order and throughout the world, albeit he, of his deep humility, concealed, so far as he could, the gifts and the graces of God, and called himself the greatest of sinners. Whereat Friar Leo marvelled, and on a time thought within himself thus foolishly, "Lo, this man calleth himself in public places the greatest of sinners; he is grown great in the Order, and is much honoured of God; nevertheless, in secret he never confessed any carnal sin: could he be a virgin?" And a very great desire came upon him to know the truth of this thing; but he had not dared to ask St. Francis. Wherefore, having recourse to God, and beseeching with great insistence that He would certify to him, through the many prayers and the merits of St. Francis, that which he desired to know, his prayer was heard, and he was certified by a vision that St. Francis was verily a virgin in body: for in a dream he beheld St. Francis standing on a high and exalted place, whereunto none could go nor attain; and it was revealed to him in spirit that that place, so high and exalted, betokened in St. Francis the high excellence of virginal chastity, that rightly was in accord with the flesh that was to be adorned with the sacred, hallowed stigmas of Christ. Now St. Francis, seeing that by reason of the stigmas of Christ his bodily strength was little by little ebbing away, and that he could no longer have care for the government of the Order, hastened to summon the Chapter-General; and when all were assembled he humbly excused himself to the friars for his waning strength, whereby he was no longer able to give heed to the cares of the Order, nor fill the office of General; albeit he might not lay down the generalship, for he could not, since he was made general by the pope; therefore, he could not leave the office nor appoint another in his place without the express licence of the pope; but he instituted Friar Peter of Catana his vicar, and commended the Order to him and to the ministers of the provinces with all the affection he could. This done, St. Francis was comforted in spirit, and lifting up his eyes and hands to heaven, spake thus, "To Thee, my Lord God, to Thee I commend Thy household, that until this hour Thou hast committed to my charge, and now, because of my infirmities, whereof Thou knowest, my sweetest Lord, no more can I have the care thereof. Likewise I commend it to the ministers of the provinces; let them answer to Thee for it, on the Day of Judgment, if any friar perish through their negligence, or through their evil example, or through their too harsh correction." And with these words, as it pleased God, all the friars at the Chapter understood that he spake of the sacred, hallowed stigmas, in that he excused himself because of his infirmities; and of their devotion none could henceforth keep back his tears. And, from that time forth, he left the care and government of the Order in the hands of his vicar and of the ministers of the provinces, and then he said, "Now since I have laid aside the cares of the Order, because of my infirmities, I am henceforth held to naught save to pray to God for our Order, and to give a good example to the friars. And well I know, and truly, that if my sickness left me, the greatest aid I could give to the Order would be to pray unceasingly to God for it, and that He would defend it and guide it and preserve it." Now, as hath been said above, albeit St. Francis strove with all his might to conceal the sacred, hallowed stigmas, and, after he had received them, ever went about or remained with his hands swathed and his feet shod, it availed not but that many friars, in divers ways, saw and felt them; and especially the wound in his side, that he strove to conceal with the greatest diligence. Wherefore, a friar that served him, craftily contrived on a time to induce him to take off his tunic, that the dust might be shaken therefrom; and it being taken off in his presence, that friar saw clearly the wound in the side; and, putting forth his hand quickly, he touched his breast with three fingers, and felt the width and depth thereof; and in like manner his vicar saw it at that time. But Friar Ruffino, a man of very great contemplation, was most clearly certified thereof—he of whom St. Francis said on a time that there was no saintlier man in the world, and whom, for his holiness, he loved tenderly and granted to him all he desired. This Friar Ruffino certified himself and others in three ways of the sacred, hallowed stigmas, and especially of the wound in the side. The first way was this: The said Friar Ruffino, when he was about to wash the hose (which St. Francis wore so large that by drawing them well up he could cover the wound in his right side), was wont to look at them and consider them diligently; and every time he did so he found them stained with blood on the right side; wherefore he perceived, of a surety, that blood issued from the said wound: and St. Francis chid him, when he saw him unfold the clothes he took away from him, in order to see the said stains. The second way was, that the said Friar Ruffino on a time purposely put his fingers in the wound in the side, whereat St. Francis, for the pain he felt, cried out loudly, "God forgive thee, O Friar Ruffino, for that thou hast done this thing." The third way was, that on a time he craved with great earnestness that St. Francis would give him his cloak, as an exceeding great favour, and take his in exchange, for love of charity; which petition the charitable father deigned to grant, albeit unwillingly, and took off his cloak and gave it to him, receiving his in return: and then, as he took it off and put on the other, Friar Ruffino clearly saw the wound. Friar Leo, likewise, and many other friars, saw the sacred, hallowed stigmas of St. Francis while he yet lived: which friars, albeit they were by their holiness worthy of faith, and to be believed on their simple word, nevertheless, to remove all doubt from men's hearts, did swear upon the sacred Book that they had clearly seen them. Certain cardinals likewise saw them that were very familiar with him, and composed and made fair and devout hymns and antiphones and rhymes[1] out of reverence for the said sacred and hallowed stigmas of St. Francis. The high pontiff, Pope Alexander, preaching to the people in the presence of the cardinals, and among them the saintly Friar Bonaventure, that was a cardinal, said and affirmed that he had seen with his own eyes the sacred and hallowed stigmas of St. Francis while he was alive. And the lady Jacqueline of Settesoli, that in her day was the greatest lady in Rome, and had a very great devotion to St. Francis, beheld them and kissed them many times with great reverence, both before he died and after his death; for she came from Rome to Assisi, by divine revelation, at the death of St. Francis, and it was in this wise: St. Francis, some days before his death, lay sick in the bishop's palace at Assisi with some of his companions; and notwithstanding his sickness, he ofttimes sang certain lauds of Christ. On a day, one of his companions said to him, "Father, thou knowest the men of this city have great faith in thee, and deem thee a holy man; and therefore they may think, that if thou art such as they believe thee to be, thou oughtest in this thy sickness to meditate on thy death, and weep rather than sing, since thou art so grievously sick; and know that this singing of thine, and ours that thou biddest, is heard of many, both within and without, since this palace is guarded by many men-at-arms by reason of thy presence, who haply may have evil example thereof. Wherefore," said this friar, "methinks thou wouldst do well to depart hence and all we return to St. Mary of the Angels, because it is not well with us here among worldly men." St. Francis answered, "Dearest brother, thou

[1] *Prose*. See Purg. xxvi. 118. The *Anonimo fiorentino*, commenting on this passage, says *far prosa di romanzi* means to compose in rhyme. The interpretation is, however, disputed.

knowest that two years now agone, when we were at Foligno, God revealed to thee the term of my life; and even so hath He revealed again to me that, yet a few days and the said term shall end during this sickness; and in this revelation God hath certified me that all my sins are remitted, and that I shall go to paradise. Until that revelation I bewailed my death and my sins; but since I had that revelation I am so filled with joy that I can weep no more; therefore do I sing, and will sing, to God, that hath given me the joy of His grace, and hath made me certain of the joys of the glory of paradise. Touching our departure hence, it pleaseth me well, and I consent thereto; but find ye some means to carry me, for by reason of my sickness I cannot walk." Then the friars took him in their arms, and so carried him, accompanied by many citizens. And when they came to an hospice that was on the way, St. Francis said to them that bore him, "Lay me down on the ground, and turn me towards the city." And when he was laid with his face towards Assisi, he blessed the city with many blessings, saying, "Blessed be thou of God, holy city, for many souls shall be saved because of thee, and in thee shall dwell many of God's servants; and from thee many shall be chosen to the kingdom of life everlasting." These words said, he had himself borne towards St. Mary of the Angels. And when they were come to St. Mary of the Angels they carried him to the infirmary, and there laid him down to rest. Then St. Francis called one of his companions to him, and spake to him thus, "Dearest friar, God hath revealed to me that on such a day in this sickness I shall pass from this life: and thou knowest that if the Lady Jacqueline of Settesoli, the dearest friend of our Order, came to hear of my death, and were not present, she would sorrow overmuch; therefore signify to her that she must straightway come hither, if she would see me alive." The friar answered, "Thou sayst but too true, father, for verily of the great devotion she hath for thee, it would be most unseemly if she were not present at thy death." "Go then," said St. Francis, "and fetch me ink and paper and pen, and write what I shall tell thee." And when he had brought them, St. Francis dictated the letter in this wise, "To the Lady Jacqueline, servant of God, greeting and fellowship of the Holy Ghost in our Lord Jesus Christ, from Friar Francis, Christ's poor little one. Know, dearest lady, that the blessed Christ hath revealed to me by His grace that the end of my life is at hand. Therefore, if thou wouldst find me yet alive, set forth when thou hast seen this letter, and come to St. Mary of the Angels; for if by such a day thou art not come, thou shalt not find me alive; and bring sackcloth, wherein my body may be shrouded, and wax needful for my burial. Prithee, also, bring me of those meats to eat that thou wast wont to give me when I lay sick at Rome." And while this letter was writing, it was revealed by God to St. Francis that the lady Jacqueline was coming to him, and was near by, and had brought with her all those things he was sending to ask for in the letter. Whereupon, having had this revelation, St. Francis told the friar that was writing the letter to write no further, since there was no need, but to lay the letter aside: whereat the friars marvelled greatly, because the letter was not finished, nor would he have it despatched. Then a little while, and a loud knocking was heard at the door, and St. Francis sent the doorkeeper to open it; and the door being opened, there was the Lady Jacqueline, the noblest lady of Rome, with her two sons, that were Roman senators, and with a great company of horsemen, and they entered in; and the Lady Jacqueline goes straight to the infirmary and comes to St. Francis. And at her coming St. Francis had great joy and consolation, and she likewise, when she beheld him living, and was able to speak with him. Then she recounted how that God had revealed to her at Rome, while she was at prayer, that the term of his life was at hand, and that he was to send for her and to ask of her all those things she had brought; and she bade them be carried in to St. Francis, and gave him to eat thereof. And when he had eaten, and was much comforted, the Lady Jacqueline knelt at the feet of St. Francis, and took those most holy feet, marked and adorned with the wounds of Christ, and kissed them, and bathed his feet with her tears, and this with such exceeding great devotion that the friars that stood around seemed to behold the Magdalen herself at the feet of Jesus Christ, and in no wise could they draw her away. Finally, after a great space, they led her thence and drew her aside; and they asked her how she had come thus in due time and provided with all those things that were necessary for the comfort and burial of St. Francis. The Lady Jacqueline answered, that one night, when she was praying at Rome, she heard a voice from heaven, saying, "If thou wouldst find St. Francis living, delay not, but haste to Assisi, and bear with thee those things thou art wont to give him when he is sick, and the things needful for his burial;" "And," said she, "thus have I done." The said Lady Jacqueline abode there until such time as St. Francis passed from this life and was buried, and she and all her company did very great honour to his burial, and paid the cost of all that was needed. And then, being returned to Rome, this noble lady, in a short time, died a holy death; and, through devotion to St. Francis, she appointed St. Mary of the Angels to be her burial-place: thither was she borne, and even there was buried.

V. *How Jerome, that believed not therein, touched and saw the sacred and hallowed stigmas.*

Not only did the said Lady Jacqueline and her sons and her company see and kiss the glorious and sacred stigmas of St. Francis at his death, but likewise many men of the city of Assisi; and among them a knight of much renown and a mighty man, called Jerome, that was incredulous and doubted much, even as St. Thomas the Apostle doubted of the wounds of Christ; and to certify himself and others thereof, he boldly moved the nails in the hands and feet, and openly felt the wound in the side in the presence of the friars and of lay folk. Wherefore he was ever after a constant witness of the truth, and sware on the gospel that thus it was and thus he had seen and touched. St. Clare also, with her nuns that were present at the burial, saw and kissed the glorious and hallowed stigmas of St. Francis.

VI. *Touching the day and the year of the death of St. Francis.*

St. Francis, glorious confessor of Christ, passed from this life in the year of our Lord one thousand two hundred and twenty-six, on Saturday, the fourth day of October, and was buried on the Sunday. And that year was the twentieth year of his conversion, to wit, when he had begun to do penance; and it was the second year after the imprinting of the sacred and hallowed stigmas, and the forty-fifth year of his life.

VII. *Of the canonisation of St. Francis.*

St. Francis was thereafter canonised by Pope Gregory IX., in the year one thousand two hundred and twenty-eight, and he came in person to Assisi to canonise him. And let this suffice for the fourth consideration.

VIII. *Touching the fifth and last consideration of the sacred and hallowed stigmas.*

The fifth and last consideration is of certain visions and revelations and miracles that God wrought and showed forth after the death of St. Francis, in confirmation of his sacred and hallowed stigmas, and in certification of the day and the hour when Christ gave them to him. And touching this be it remembered that in the year of our Lord one thousand two hundred and eighty-two, on the . . . day of October, Friar Philip, minister of Tuscany, by command of Friar John Buonagrazia, the minister-general, bade by holy obedience Friar Matthew of Castiglione Aretino, a man of great devotion and sanctity, tell him what he knew touching the day and the hour whereon the sacred and hallowed stigmas were imprinted by Christ on the body of St. Francis: for he had heard that of this he had a divine revelation. This Friar Matthew, constrained by holy obedience, answered him thus, "When I was sojourning at La Verna, this past year, in the month of May, I betook me one day to prayer in my cell, which is on the spot where it is believed that the vision of the seraph was seen. And in my prayers I besought God, most devoutly, that it would please Him to reveal to some person the day and the hour whereon the sacred and hallowed stigmas were imprinted on the body of St. Francis. And I, persevering in prayer and in this petition beyond the first sleep, St. Francis appeared to me in a great light and spake to me thus, 'Son, wherefore prayest thou to God?' And I said to him, 'Father, I pray for such a thing.' And he to me, 'I am thy father, Francis, knowest thou me well?' 'Father,' said I, 'yea!' Then he showed to me the sacred and hallowed stigmas in his hands and feet and in his side, and said, 'The time is come when God willeth that to His glory those things shall be made manifest that the friars in the past have not cared to know. Know that He who appeared to me was no angel, but Jesus Christ in the form of a seraph, that with His hands imprinted these wounds on my body, even as He received them in His body on the cross; and it was in this manner—the day before the exaltation of the holy cross, an angel came to me and in God's name bade me make ready to suffer and receive that which God willed to send me. And I answered that I was ready to receive and endure all things at God's pleasure. Then on the morrow, to wit, the morning of Holy Cross day, which in that year fell on a Friday, I came forth from my cell at the dawn in exceeding great fervour of spirit, and I went to pray in this place where thou now art, in which place I was ofttimes wont to pray. And while I was at prayer, lo, there came down through the air from heaven a youth crucified, in the form of a seraph, with six wings; and he came with great swiftness; at whose wondrous aspect I knelt me down humbly and began to meditate devoutly on the ineffable love of Jesus Christ crucified, and on the unspeakable pain of His

Passion. And His aspect begat in me compassion so great that meseemed verily to feel this passion in mine own body; and at His presence all the mountain shone, bright as the sun: and thus descending from heaven He came nigh to me. And standing before me He spake to me certain secret words that I have not yet revealed to any man; but the time is at hand when they shall be revealed. Then after some space Christ departed and went back to heaven, and I found me thus marked with these wounds. 'Go then,' said St. Francis, 'and tell these things confidently to thy minister, for this is the work of God and not of man.' These words said, St. Francis blessed me and returned to heaven with a great multitude of youths in shining raiment." All these things Friar Matthew said he had seen and heard, not sleeping, but waking. And even so he sware that he had said really and truly to the minister in his cell at Florence when he required him thereof by obedience.

IX. *How a holy friar was reading in the legend about the secret words that the seraph said when he appeared to St. Francis as set forth in the chapter touching the sacred and hallowed stigmas, and how the said friar prayed to God so fervently that St. Francis revealed them to him.*

Another time, when a devout and holy friar was reading the chapter of the sacred and hallowed stigmas in the Legend of St. Francis, he began to think with great anxiety of mind what those words, so secret, might have been that St. Francis said he would reveal to no man while he lived, and that the seraph had spoken when he appeared to him. And this friar said within himself, " St. Francis would never tell those words to any man while he lived, but now after his bodily death haply he might tell them if he were devoutly entreated." And thenceforth the devout friar began to pray to God and to St. Francis that they would be pleased to reveal those words; and this friar, persevering for eight years in this prayer, on the eighth year, by his merits, his prayer was answered in this wise: One day after he had eaten and had returned thanks in church, he was at prayer in another part of the church, beseeching God and St. Francis to grant his prayer more devoutly than he was wont to do, and with many tears, when he was called by another friar and bidden by order of the warden to bear him company to the city on the business of the Order. Wherefore, doubting not that obedience was more meritorious than prayer, on hearing the command of the prelate, he forthwith ceased to pray and humbly went forth with that friar who had called him. And, as it pleased God, in that act of ready obedience he merited what by long years of prayer he had failed to merit. Wherefore no sooner were they outside the friary door than they encountered two stranger friars that seemed to have come from a far country; and one of them seemed young in years, the other aged and lean; and by reason of the bad weather, they were all bemired and wet. And this obedient friar, having great compassion on them, said to the companion with whom he went, "O my dearest brother, if the business wherefore we go may be delayed a while, forasmuch as these stranger friars have great need of being charitably received, prithee let me first go and wash their feet, and especially the feet of that aged friar that hath the greater need thereof, and you can wash the feet of this younger one: and then we will go our way on the affairs of the Order." This friar then consenting to the charity of his companion, they returned within, and receiving these stranger friars very charitably, they led them to the kitchen fire to warm and dry themselves; and at this fire eight other friars were warming themselves. And after they had stood a while at the fire, they drew them aside to wash their feet, according as they had agreed together. And as that obedient and devout friar was washing the feet of the aged stranger, and cleansing them from the mire, he looked, and beheld his feet marked with the sacred and hallowed stigmas; and straightway embracing them tenderly, for very joy and amazement, he began to cry, "Either thou art Christ, or thou art St. Francis." At this cry and at these words the friars that were by the fire rose up and with great trembling and reverence drew nigh to behold those glorious stigmas. And at their entreaties this aged friar suffered them to see them clearly and to touch them and kiss them. And as they marvelled yet more for very joy, he said to them, "Doubt not, nor fear, dearest friars, my children; I am your father, Friar Francis, who, according to God's will, established three Orders. And forasmuch as I have been entreated, these eight years past, by this friar that washeth my feet, and this day more fervently than ever, that I would reveal to him those secret words the seraph said to me, when he gave me the stigmas, which words I would never reveal during my life, this day, by commandment of God, and because of his perseverance and his ready obedience, when he renounced the sweetness of contemplation, I am sent by God to reveal to him, in your sight, what he asked of me." And St. Francis, turning towards that friar, spake thus, "Know, dearest friar, that when I was on the mount of La Verna, all rapt in the contemplation of the Passion of Christ, in this seraphic vision I was by Christ thus stigmatised in my body; and then Christ said to me, 'Knowest thou what I have done to thee? I have given thee the marks of my Passion in order that thou mayst be My standard-bearer. And even as I, on the day of My death, descended into limbo and drew thence all the souls I found therein, by virtue of my stigmas, and led them up to paradise, so do I grant to thee from this hour (that thou mayst be conformed to Me in thy death as thou hast been in thy life) that after thou hast passed from this life thou shalt go every year, on the day of thy death, to purgatory, and shalt deliver all the souls thou shalt find there of thy three Orders, to wit, Minors, Sisters, and Penitents, and likewise the souls of thy devoted followers, and this, in virtue of thy stigmas that I have given thee; and thou shalt lead them to paradise.' And those words I told not while I lived in the world." This said, St. Francis and his companion vanished; and many friars thereafter heard this from those eight friars that were present at the vision and heard the words of St. Francis.

X. *How St. Francis appeared after his death to Friar John of La Verna while he was at prayer.*

On the mount of La Verna, St. Francis appeared on a time to Friar John of La Verna, a man of great sanctity, while he was at prayer, and remained and held converse with him a very long space; and at last being willed to depart, he spake thus, "Ask of me what thou wilt." Said Friar John, "Father, I pray thee, tell me that which for a long time I have desired to know, to wit, what you [1] were doing, and where you were, when the seraph appeared to you." St. Francis answers, "I was praying in that place where the chapel of Count Simon of Battifolle now stands, and I was craving two graces of my Lord Jesus Christ. The first was, that he would vouchsafe to me, during my life, to feel in my soul and in my body, so far as might be, all that pain He had felt in Himself at the time of His bitterest Passion. The second grace I asked of Him was that I should likewise feel in my heart that exceeding love wherewith he was enkindled to endure that Passion so great, for us sinners. And then God put in my heart that He would grant me to feel the one and the other, so far as might be possible to a mere creature: which thing was well fulfilled in me by the imprinting of the stigmas." Then Friar John asks of him if those secret words that the seraph said to him were after the manner that the aforesaid holy

[1] *See* note, p. 3.

friar had recited, who had affirmed he had heard them from St. Francis in the presence of eight friars. St. Francis answered that the truth was even as that friar had said. Then Friar John takes heart from the freedom of his condescension and says thus, " O father, thee I pray most earnestly, suffer me to behold and kiss thy sacred and glorious stigmas; not because I doubt aught thereof, but only for my consolation, for this have I ever desired." And St. Francis, freely showing them and holding them forth to him, Friar John beheld them clearly, and touched them, and kissed them. And finally he asked of him, " Father, what consolation did your soul feel on beholding the blessed Christ coming to give you the signs of His most holy Passion? Would to God that I now might feel a little of that sweetness!" Then St. Francis answers, " Seest thou these nails?" Saith Friar John, " Yea, father." " Touch yet again," saith St. Francis, " this nail in my hand." Then Friar John with great reverence and fear touched that nail, and anon, as he touched it, a great fragrance issued forth like to a column of incense, and, entering the nostrils of Friar John, filled his soul and his body with such sweetness that straightway he was rapt in God and became senseless in ecstasy, and he remained thus ravished from that hour, which was the hour of tierce, until vespers. And this vision and familiar converse with St. Francis, Friar John told to no man save to his confessor, until he came to die; but, being nigh unto death, he revealed it to many friars.

XI. *Of a holy friar who beheld a wondrous vision of one of his companions that was dead.*

A most devout and holy friar saw this wondrous vision in the province of Rome. A very dear friar, his companion, having died one night, was buried on the morrow before the entrance to the chapter-room; and on that same day this friar withdrew, after dinner, into a corner of the chapter-room to pray devoutly to God and to St. Francis for the soul of the dead friar, his companion. And as he persevered in prayer with supplication and tears, lo, at noon, when all the other friars were gone to sleep, he heard a great moving about in the cloister. Whereat, greatly afeard, anon he turned his eyes towards the grave of this his companion, and beheld St. Francis at the entrance of the chapter, and behind him a great multitude of friars all standing round the said grave; and he saw a fire with great tongues of flame in the middle of the cloister, and in the midst of the flames stood the soul of his dead companion. He looks around the cloister and sees Jesus Christ going around the cloister with a great company of angels and saints. And gazing at these things with great amaze he sees that when Christ passes before the chapter, St. Francis and all those friars kneel down; and St. Francis saith these words, "I pray Thee, my dearest Father and Lord, by that inestimable love Thou didst show forth to the generations of men when Thou didst die on the wood of the cross, have mercy on the soul of this my friar that burneth in this fire." And Christ answered naught but passed on. And He returns a second time, and passing before the chapter-room, St. Francis again kneels down with his friars as before and entreats Him in this wise, "I pray Thee, pitying Father and Lord, by the ineffable love Thou didst show to the generations of men when Thou didst die on the wood of the cross, have mercy on the soul of this my friar." And Christ, in like manner, passed on and heard him not. And going round the cloister He returned a third time and passed before the chapter-room; and then St. Francis, kneeling down as before, showed Him his hands and feet and breast, and spake thus, "I pray Thee, pitying Father and Lord, by that great pain and great consolation I felt when Thou didst imprint these stigmas on my flesh, have mercy on the soul of this my friar that is in this purgatorial fire." Marvellous to tell! Christ, being entreated this third time by St. Francis, in the name of his stigmas, straightway stays His steps and looks on the stigmas and answers his prayer and saith these words, "To thee, Francis, I grant the soul of thy friar." And thereby of a surety He willed to confirm and honour the glorious stigmas of St. Francis and openly signify that the souls of his friars that go to purgatory are delivered from their pains in no other way more readily than by virtue of his stigmas, and led to the glories of paradise; according to the words that Christ said to St. Francis when He imprinted them upon him. Wherefore, these words said, straightway that fire in the cloister vanished, and the dead friar came to St. Francis, and all that company of the blessed ascended to heaven with him, and with Christ their glorious King. Whereat this friar, his companion, that had prayed for him, had exceeding great joy when he beheld him delivered from the pains of purgatory and taken up to heaven; and thereafter he related this vision in due order to the other friars, and together with them gave praise and thanks to God.

XII. *How a noble knight, that had devotion to St. Francis, was certified of his death and of the sacred and hallowed stigmas.*

A noble knight of Massa di San Pietro, named Rudolph, that

had a great devotion to St. Francis, and who at length had received the habit of the third Order at his hands, was thuswise certified of the death of St. Francis and of his sacred and hallowed stigmas: When St. Francis was nigh unto death, the devil at that time entered into a woman of the said town and tormented her cruelly, and withal made her speak with such subtle learning that she overcame all the wise men and learned doctors that came to dispute with her. And it fell out that the devil departed from her and left her free two days: and the third day he returned to her and afflicted her more cruelly than before. Rudolph, hearing this, goes to this woman, and asks of the devil that possessed her, for what cause he had departed from her two days, and then returned and tormented her more harshly than before. The devil answers, "When I left her, it was because I, with all my companions that are in these parts, assembled together and went in mighty force to the death-bed of the beggar Francis, to dispute with him and capture his soul; but his soul being surrounded and defended by a multitude of angels, greater than we were, was carried by them straight to heaven, and we went away confounded; so I restore and make up to this miserable woman what I let pass by during those two days." Then Rudolph conjured him in God's name to tell the whole truth of the holiness of St. Francis, who he said was dead, and of St. Clare that was alive. The devil answers, "Willy-nilly, I will tell thee what there is of truth in this. God the Father was so wroth against the sinners of this world that it seemed He would, in brief time, give His last judgment against men and women, and, if they did not amend, destroy them from the face of the earth. But Christ, His Son, praying for sinners, promised to renew His life and His Passion in a man, to wit, in Francis, the poor little one and a beggar, through whose life and teaching He would bring back many from all over the world to the way of truth, and many also to repentance. And now, to show forth to the world what He had wrought in St. Francis, He hath willed that the stigmas of His Passion that He had imprinted on St. Francis's body during his life, might, at his death, be seen and touched by many. Likewise, the Mother of Christ promised to renew her virginal purity and her humility in a woman, to wit, in Sister Clare, in such wise that by her example she would deliver many thousands of women from our hands. And thus God the Father, being softened, did delay His final sentence." Then Rudolph, desiring to know of a surety if the devil, that is the abode and father of lies, spake truth in these things, and especially as to the death of St. Francis, sent one, his trusty squire, to St. Mary of the Angels at Assisi, to learn if St. Francis were alive or dead; which squire, coming thither, found of a surety it was so, and returning to his lord, reported that on the very day and at the very hour that the devil had said, St. Francis had passed from this life.

XIII. *How Pope Gregory IX., doubting of the stigmas of St. Francis, was certified thereof.*

Setting aside all the miracles of the sacred and hallowed stigmas of St. Francis, which may be read in his legend, be it known, in conclusion of this fifth consideration, that St. Francis appeared one night to Pope Gregory IX., as he afterwards told, when he was in some doubt touching the wound in the side of St. Francis, and lifting up a little his right arm, discovered the wound in his side, and asked for a vase, and he had it brought to him; and St. Francis had it held under the wound in his side, and verily it seemed to the pope that he saw the vase filled to the brim with blood mingled with water, that issued from the wound: and thenceforth all doubt departed from him. Then, in council with all the cardinals, he approved the sacred and hallowed stigmas of St. Francis, and thereof gave special privilege to the friars by a sealed Bull; and this he did at Viterbo, in the eleventh year of his pontificate; and then, in the twelfth year, he issued another Bull yet more fully indited. Pope Nicholas III. likewise, and Pope Alexander, gave abundant privileges whereby whosoever denied the sacred and hallowed stigmas of St. Francis should be proceeded against as a heretic. And let this suffice as to the fifth consideration of the glorious, sacred, and hallowed stigmas of St. Francis our father. And may God give us the grace to follow after his life, in this world, so that, through the virtue of his glorious stigmas, we may merit salvation, and be with him in paradise. To the praise of Jesus Christ and of the poor little one, St. Francis. Amen.

Here beginneth the Life of Friar Juniper

I. *How Friar Juniper cut the foot off a pig only to give it to a sick man.*

Friar Juniper was one of the most chosen disciples and first companions of St. Francis. He was a man of deep humility and of great zeal and charity; and of him St. Francis said, speaking on a time with those holy companions of his, " He were a good friar that had so overcome himself and the world as Friar Juniper hath." One day, as he was visiting a sick friar at St. Mary of the Angels, all aflame with charity, he asked with great compassion, "Can I serve thee in aught?" The sick man answers, "Much comfort and great solace would it be to me if I might have a pig's foot." And Friar Juniper said, "Trust to me, for I will get one forthwith." And off he goes and snatches up a knife (I believe 'twas a kitchen knife) and goes in fervour of spirit about the wood, where certain pigs were feeding, and falling on one of them, cuts off a foot and runs away with it, leaving the pig maimed; he returns, washes and dresses and cooks this foot, and having well dished it up, carries the said foot to the sick man with much charity. And the sick friar ate thereof greedily, to the great consolation and joy of Friar Juniper, who told the story of the assaults he had made on the pig with great glee, to rejoice the heart of the sick man. Meanwhile the swineherd, that saw this friar cut the foot off, told over the whole story with much bitterness to his master. And he, being informed of this deed, comes to the friary and calls the friars hypocrites, thieves, false knaves, and wicked rogues, exclaiming, "Wherefore have ye cut off my pig's foot?" Hearing the great uproar he made, St. Francis and all the friars hurried along, and St. Francis made excuse for his friars, saying, with all humility, that they knew naught of the deed; and to pacify the man, promised to make amends for every wrong done to him. But for all this he was not to be appeased, but departed from the friary in great wrath, uttering many insults and threats, repeating over and over again how that they had wickedly cut off his pig's foot, and accepting neither excuses nor promises, he hastened away greatly scandalised. But St. Francis, full of prudence, bethought him the while the other friars stood all stupefied, and said in his heart, "Can Friar Juniper have done this thing out of indiscreet zeal?" So he bade call Friar Juniper secretly to him, and asked him, saying, "Hast thou cut off that pig's foot in the wood?" To whom Friar Juniper answered, right gleefully, and not as one having committed a fault, but as one that believed he had done a deed of great charity, and spake thus, "My sweet father, true it is I have cut off a foot from that said pig; and the cause thereof, my father, hear, if thou wilt, compassionately. I went out of charity to visit a certain friar that was sick;" and then he related the whole story in order, and added, "I tell thee this much, that considering the consolation this friar of ours felt, and the comfort he took from the said foot, had I cut off the feet of a hundred pigs as I did this one, I believe of a surety God would have looked on it as a good deed." Whereupon St. Francis, with righteous zeal, and with great bitterness, said, "O Friar Juniper, wherefore hast thou wrought this great scandal? Not without cause doth that man grieve, and thus rail against us; and perchance even now, as I speak, he is going about the city defaming us of evil, and good cause hath he. Wherefore I command thee, by holy obedience, run after him until thou overtake him, and cast thyself on the ground prostrate before him and confess thy fault, and promise to make him such full amends as that he shall have no cause to complain of us: for of a surety this hath been too monstrous an offence." Friar Juniper marvelled much at the aforesaid words, and was filled with amaze, being astonished that there should be any disturbance over such an act of charity; for these temporal things seemed to him naught, save in so far as they were charitably shared with one's neighbour. And Friar Juniper answered, "Fear not, father mine, for anon will I repay him and make him content. And wherefore should he be so troubled, seeing that this pig, whose foot I have cut off, was God's rather than his own, and a very charitable use hath been made thereof?" And so he sets forth at a run, and cometh up with this man that was raging beyond all measure and past all patience; and he told him how, and for what cause, he had cut off the said pig's foot, and withal in such great fervour and exultation and joy, even as one that had done him a great service for which he ought to be well rewarded. But the man, boiling with anger, and overcome with fury, heaped many insults on Friar Juniper, calling him a mad fellow and a fool, a big thief, and the worst of scoundrels. But Friar Juniper cared naught for these abusive words, and marvelled within himself, for he rejoiced in being reviled, and believed that he had not heard aright; for it seemed to him matter for rejoicing, and not for spite: and he told the story anew, and fell on the man's neck and embraced him and kissed him, and told him how that this thing had been done for charity's sake alone, inviting him and entreating him to give likewise what was left of the pig; and all with such charity and simplicity and humility that the man, being come to himself, fell on the ground before him, not without many tears; and asking pardon for the wrong he had said and done to these friars, he goes and takes this pig and kills it, and having cooked it, he carries it, with much devotion and many tears, to

St. Mary of the Angels, and gives it to these holy friars to eat, out of compassion for the said wrong he had done them. And St. Francis, considering the simplicity and the patience under adversity of this said holy friar, said to his companions and to the others that stood by, "Would to God, my brethren, that I had a whole forest of such junipers!"

II. *An example of Friar Juniper's great power against the devil.*

That the devil was unable to endure the purity of the innocence of Friar Juniper and his deep humility appeareth in this. On a time, a man possessed with a devil, flung out of the way he was going, and, beyond his wont and with much fury, all of a sudden fled full seven miles by divers paths. And being overtaken and questioned by his kinsfolk who followed after him with bitter grief, wherefore in his flight he had taken such devious ways, he answered, "The reason is this: forasmuch as that fool Juniper was passing by that way, being unable to endure his presence, nor to encounter him, I fled through these woods." And certifying themselves of this truth, they found that Friar Juniper had passed along at that hour even as the devil had said. Wherefore St. Francis, when the possessed were brought to him that they might be healed, was wont to say, if the devils departed not straightway at his command, "If thou depart not forthwith from this creature I will bring Friar Juniper up against thee." And then the devil, fearing the presence of Friar Juniper and unable to endure the virtue and humility of St. Francis, would straightway depart.

III. *How at the instigation of the devil Friar Juniper was condemned to the gallows.*

On a time, the devil, desiring to affright Friar Juniper and to vex and trouble him, went to a most cruel tyrant named Nicholas that was then at war with the city of Viterbo, and said, "My lord, guard this your castle well, for anon a false traitor is to come hither, sent by the men of Viterbo, that he may slay you and set fire to your castle. And, in token of the truth of this, I give you these signs. He goeth about after the fashion of a poor simpleton, with garments tattered and patched, and with a ragged cowl falling on his shoulders; and with him he beareth an awl wherewith he is to kill you, and he hath a flint and steel with him to set fire to this castle. And if you find I speak not sooth, deal with me as you will." At these words Nicholas was filled with amaze and grew sore afraid, because he that spake these words seemed an honest fellow. And he commanded diligent watch and ward to be kept, and that if this man, with the aforesaid tokens came, he should be straightway brought into his presence. Meanwhile Friar Juniper comes alone, for because of his perfection he had licence to go forth and stay alone, even as it pleased him. Now Friar Juniper happened on certain evil youths that began to mock and abuse him shamefully; and at all these things he was not troubled, but rather led them to deride him the more. And when he came up to the door of the castle, the guards seeing him thus ill favoured and in a scant habit all in rags (for he had given part thereof to the poor by the way), and seeing he had no semblance of a friar minor, and that the tokens given them were manifestly apparent, dragged him, with great fury, before this tyrant Nicholas. And being searched by his servants for hidden weapons, they found an awl in his sleeve wherewith he was wont to mend his sandals; likewise they found a flint and steel, which he carried with him to kindle fire; for his time was his own, and oft he abode in woods and desert places. Nicholas, beholding these signs on him, in accord with the testimony of the accusing devil, commanded his servants to bind a rope about his neck, and this they did, with such great cruelty that the rope entered into his flesh; and then they put him on the rack and stretched his arms and racked his whole body without any mercy. And being asked who he was, he answered, "I am the greatest of sinners." And when asked if he had purposed to betray the castle and give it over to the men of Viterbo, he answered, "I am the greatest of traitors, and unworthy of any good thing." And asked if he purposed to kill Nicholas the tyrant with that awl and set fire to the castle, he answered that he would do even worse things and more monstrous, if God permitted. This Nicholas, maddened with rage, would suffer no more questioning of him, but, without any term or delay, condemned Friar Juniper, in his fury, as a traitor and manslayer, to be tied to the tail of a horse and dragged along the ground to the gallows and there straightway hanged by the neck. And Friar Juniper made no defence, but, as one that was content to suffer tribulation for love of God, was all joyous and glad. And the sentence of the tyrant being put in execution, Friar Juniper was bound by his feet to the tail of a horse and dragged along the ground; and he complained not, nor lamented, but as a gentle lamb led to the slaughter, went with all humility. At this spectacle and swift justice all the people ran to behold him executed thus hastily and thus cruelly: and they knew him not. But, as God willed, a good man that had seen Friar Juniper taken and thus quickly dragged to execution, runs to the house of the friars minor, and saith, "For love of God, I pray you, come quickly, for a poor wretch hath been taken and straightway condemned and led forth to die: come that at least he may give his soul into your hands; for he seemeth to me an honest fellow, and hath had no time wherein he may confess; lo, he is led forth to the gallows and seemeth to have no care for death, nor for the salvation of his soul: ah! I beseech you, deign to come quickly." The warden, that was a compassionate man, goes forthwith to provide for the salvation of his soul, and coming up to the place of execution, finds that the multitudes who had come to see were so increased that he could not pass through: and he stood and watched for an opening. And as he waited, he heard a voice in the midst of the crowd that cried, "Don't, don't, ye bad men; ye hurt my legs." At this voice a suspicion took the warden that this might be Friar Juniper, and in fervour of spirit he flung himself among them and tore aside the wrappings from the face of him; and there truly was Friar Juniper. Wherefore the compassionate warden was minded to take off his cloak to clothe Friar Juniper withal; but he, with joyous countenance and half laughing, said, "O warden, thou art fat, and it were an ill sight to see thy nakedness. I will not have it." Then the warden, with many tears, besought the hangmen and all the people for pity's sake to wait a while until he should go and entreat the tyrant for Friar Juniper, that he might grant him pardon. The hangmen and certain bystanders consenting thereto (for they truly believed he was a kinsman), the devout and compassionate warden goes to Nicholas the tyrant, and with bitter tears saith, "My lord, I am in such great bitterness and wonderment of soul that tongue cannot tell thereof, for it seems that the greatest sin and the greatest wickedness ever wrought in the days of our forefathers is this day being done in this city: and I believe it is done in ignorance." Nicholas hears the warden patiently, and asks of him, "What is the great wrong and evil deed committed this day in our city?" The warden answers, "My lord, you have condemned one of the holiest friars in the Order of St. Francis, for whom you have singular devotion, to a cruel death, and, as I verily believe, without cause." Saith Nicholas, "Now tell me, warden, who is this? for perchance knowing him not I have committed a great wrong." Saith the warden, "He that you have doomed to death is Friar Juniper, the companion of

St. Francis." Nicholas the tyrant, stupefied, for he had heard of the fame and of the holy life of Friar Juniper, runs, astonished and all pale, together with the warden, and coming up to Friar Juniper looseth him from the tail of the horse and sets him free; then, in the presence of all the people, flings himself prostrate on the ground before Friar Juniper, and with many tears confesses his guilt, and bewails the wrong and the villainy he had done to this holy friar, and cried, "Verily I believe that the days of my evil life are numbered, since I have thus tortured the holiest of men without cause. God will appoint an end to my wicked life, and in brief time I shall die an evil death, albeit I have done this thing in ignorance." Friar Juniper freely forgave Nicholas the tyrant; but God suffered, ere a few days were passed, that this Nicholas the tyrant should end his life and die a very cruel death. And Friar Juniper departed, leaving all the people edified.

IV. *How Friar Juniper gave to the poor all he could lay hands on for love of God.*

So much pity and compassion had Friar Juniper for the poor that when he saw any one ill clad or naked, anon he would take off his tunic, and the cowl from his cloak, and give them to poor souls such as these. Therefore the warden commanded him, by obedience, not to give away the whole of his tunic, nor any part of his habit. Now it fell out that Friar Juniper, ere a few days had passed, happened on a poor creature, well-nigh naked, who asked alms of him for love of God, to whom he said with great compassion, "Naught have I, save my tunic, to give thee; and this my superior hath laid on me, by obedience, to give to no one; nay, nor even part of my habit; but if thou wilt take it off my back, I will not gainsay thee." He spake not to deaf ears, for straightway this poor man stripped him of his tunic and went his way with it, leaving Friar Juniper naked. And when he was back at the friary, he was asked where his tunic was, and he answered, "An honest fellow took it from my back and made off with it." And the virtue of pity increasing within him, he was not content with giving away his tunic, but likewise gave books and church ornaments and cloaks, or anything he could lay hands on, to the poor. And for this reason the friars never left things lying about the friary, because Friar Juniper gave all away for love of God and in praise of Him.

V. *How Friar Juniper stripped certain little bells from the altar, and gave them away for love of God.*

Friar Juniper, being on a time in Assisi, at the Nativity of

Christ, engaged in deep meditation at the altar of the friary, which was richly decked and adorned, was asked by the sacristan to guard the said altar while he went to eat. And while he was in devout meditation, a poor little woman begged alms of him for love of God: to whom Friar Juniper thus answered, "Tarry a while and I will see if I can give thee aught from this altar so rich." Now there was on that altar a hanging of gold, richly and sumptuously adorned with little silver bells of great worth. Saith Friar Juniper, "These bells are a superfluity." So he takes a knife and cuts them all from the hanging, and gives them, out of compassion, to this poor little woman. No sooner had the sacristan eaten three or four mouthfuls than he remembered the ways of Friar Juniper, and was sore afeard lest out of his zealous charity he might work some mischief to the rich altar he had left in his charge. And straightway he rose from the table, in much dread, and went to the church and looked to see if any of the ornaments of the altar had been removed or taken away; and lo, he beheld the hanging hacked about and the bells cut off: whereat he was beyond all measure perturbed and scandalised. And Friar Juniper, beholding him thus agitated, saith, "Be not troubled about those bells, for I have given them to a poor woman that had very great need of them, and here they were of no use, save that they made a show of worldly pomp." Hearing this, the sacristan ran straightway through the church and about the whole city, in great affliction, to see if haply he might find her. But so far from finding her, he could not even find any one that had seen her. Returning to the friary, he took the hanging from the altar, in a great rage, and carried it to the general that was at Assisi, and said, "Father-general, I demand of you justice on Friar Juniper, who hath spoiled this hanging for me, that was the most precious thing in our sacristy; look now how he hath destroyed it and stripped off all the little silver bells, and he saith he hath given them away to a poor woman." The general answered, "Friar Juniper hath not done this, rather hath thy folly done it, for thou oughtest by this time to know his ways well; and I say unto thee, I marvel that he hath not given away all the rest; but none the less will I correct him for this fault." And having called all the friars together in Chapter, he bade call Friar Juniper, and in the presence of the whole house rebuked him very harshly because of the aforesaid little bells; and he waxed so furious in his wrath, that by raising his voice so high he grew quite hoarse. Friar Juniper heeded those words little or naught, for he rejoiced in contumely and when he was well abased; but returning good for evil, he began to think only how he might find a remedy for his general's hoarseness. So having endured the general's scolding, Friar Juniper goes to the city and orders a good dish of porridge and butter; and a good part of the night being spent, he goes and lights a candle and comes back with this mess of porridge and takes it to the general's cell and knocks. The general opens to him, and, beholding him with a lighted candle in one hand and the dish of porridge in the other, asks softly, "What is this?" Friar Juniper answered, "My father, to-day, when you chid me for my faults, I perceived that your voice was growing hoarse, and, as I ween, from over-fatigue; therefore I bethought me of a remedy, and I had this porridge made for thee; pray eat thereof, for I tell thee it will ease thy chest and throat." Said the general, "What hour is this for thee to go disturbing folk?" Friar Juniper answered, "Look now, for thee 'tis made; prithee make no more ado, but eat thereof, for 'twill do thee much good." And the general, angry at the late hour and at his importunity, bade him begone, for at such an hour he had no desire to eat, and called him a base fellow and a rogue. Friar Juniper, seeing that neither prayer nor coaxing was of any avail, spake thus, "My father, since thou wilt not eat of this porridge that was made for thee, at least do me this favour: hold the candle for me, and I will eat it." And the pious and devout general, bearing in mind Friar Juniper's compassion and simplicity, and knowing that all this was done by him out of devotion, answered, "Look now, since thou wilt have it so, let us eat, thou and I, together." And both ate of this dish of porridge, because of his importunate charity. And much more were they refreshed by their devotion than by the food.

VI. *How Friar Juniper kept silence for six months.*

Friar Juniper, on a time, made a vow to keep silence for six months, in this manner. The first day, for love of the Heavenly Father. The second day, for love of His Son, Jesus Christ. The third day, for love of the Holy Ghost. The fourth day, for reverence of the most holy Virgin Mary; and so in this order, every day, for six months, he observed silence for love of some saint.

VII. *How to resist temptations of the flesh.*

Friar Giles and Friar Simon of Assisi, and Friar Ruffino and Friar Juniper, being on a time gathered together to discourse of God and of the salvation of the soul, Friar Giles said to the others, "How do ye with temptations to carnal sin?" Said Friar Simon, "I consider the baseness and turpitude of the sin, and then ariseth within me a great horror thereof, and thus I escape." Saith Friar Ruffino, "I cast me prostrate on the ground, and so fervently do I continue in prayer, beseeching God's mercy and the Mother of Jesus Christ, until I feel me wholly delivered therefrom." Friar Juniper answers, "When I feel the tumult of this devilish suggestion, straightway I run and close the door of my heart, and for defence of the fortress of my heart I occupy me in holy meditations and in holy desires; so that when the temptation cometh and knocketh at the door of my heart, I, as it were from within, answer, 'Begone! for the hostel is already full, and herein no more guests can enter'; and thus I suffer no thought to enter within my heart: whereat the devil, seeing himself vanquished, departeth as one discomfited, not only from me, but from the whole country." Friar Giles answers, "Friar Juniper, I hold with thee: against the enemy of the flesh one cannot fight, but only flee; for within, through the traitorous appetite, and without, through the senses of the body, the enemy feeleth himself so mighty that one cannot overcome him save by flight. And, therefore, he that would fight otherwise seldom hath the victory after the toil of battle. Flee, then, from vice, and thou shalt be victorious."

VIII. *How Friar Juniper abased himself to the glory of God.*

On a time Friar Juniper, desiring truly to abase himself, stripped him of all save his breeches; and having made a bundle of his habit, placed his clothes on his head, and entering Viterbo, went to the market-place to be derided. And standing there, the children and youths of the city, deeming him bereft of his senses, reviled him sorely, casting much mire at him, and pelting him with stones. Hither and thither they rushed him, with many mocking words; and thus persecuted and scorned, he remained for the greater part of the day: then he went to the friary. And when the friars beheld him they were full of wrath, most of all for that he had come through the whole city with his bundle on his head; and they rebuked him very severely, uttering great threats. And one said, "Let us cast him into prison." And another said, "Let us hang him." And the others said, "We cannot inflict too great a punishment for so evil an example as this friar hath made of himself this day and of all the Order." And Friar Juniper, right glad, answered with great humility, "Ye say well, for I am worthy of all these pains and many more."

IX. *How Friar Juniper, to abase himself, played at see-saw.*

On a time as Friar Juniper was journeying to Rome, where the fame of his holiness was already noised abroad, many Romans, of their great devotion, went out to meet him; and Friar Juniper, beholding so many people coming, imagined how he might turn their devotion into sport and mockery. Now there were two children playing at see-saw, to wit, they had placed one log of wood across another, and each of them sat at his end of the log and see-sawed up and down. Away goes Friar Juniper and takes off one of these children from the log, and mounting thereon begins to play see-saw. Meanwhile the people came up and marvelled to see Friar Juniper see-sawing, yet, with great devotion, they greeted him and waited for him to end the game of see-saw, in order to accompany him honourably as far as the friary. And Friar Juniper heeded little their greetings, their reverence, and their waiting, but held very diligently to his see-sawing. And waiting thus a long space, certain of them began to weary thereof, and said, "What a blockhead!" Others, knowing his ways, waxed in greater devotion. Nevertheless all departed and left Friar Juniper on his see-saw. And when they were all gone, Friar Juniper was left wholly comforted, because he saw that certain of them had mocked at him. He then set forth and entered Rome, and with all meekness and humility came to the house of the friars minor.

X. *How Friar Juniper once cooked enough food to last the friars a fortnight.*

Friar Juniper, being on a time left alone in a small friary, inasmuch as all the friars, for a certain reasonable cause, had to go out from the friary, the warden saith to him, "Friar Juniper, all we have to go abroad; look to it, therefore, that when we return thou have some dish ready cooked for the refreshment of the friars." Friar Juniper answers, "Right gladly, leave it to me!" And all the friars being gone forth, as hath been told, Friar Juniper saith, "What unprofitable care is this, for one friar to be lost in the kitchen and far away from all prayer! Truly, if I am left here to cook, this time will I cook so much that all the friars, and even more, shall have enough to eat for a fortnight." And so he goes very diligently to the city and begs several great cooking pots and pans, and procures fresh meat and salt, fowls and eggs and pot herbs, and begs much firewood, and puts everything on the fire, to wit, the fowls with their feathers on, and eggs in their shells, and all the other things one after the other. When the friars came home, one that was ware of Friar Juniper's simplicity entered the kitchen and beheld many great pots and pans on a raging fire. And he sat him down and looked on with wonderment and said no word, but watched with what great diligence Friar Juniper went about his cooking. Now the fire was very fierce, and since he could not get very close to his pots to skim them, he took a wooden board and bound it closely to his body with his cord, and then leapt from one pot to another, so that it was a joy to behold. Thinking over these things, with great delight, this friar comes from the kitchen and seeks the other friars, and saith, "Friar Juniper is making a wedding feast, I can tell you!" But the friars took this for a jest. And Friar Juniper lifted his pots from the fire and bade ring the bell for supper. And the friars, having taken their places at table, Friar Juniper comes into the refectory, all ruddy with his toil and the heat of the fire, with that meal of his, and saith to the friars, "Eat well, and then let us all to prayers; and let no one have any care about cooking for days to come, because I have cooked so much to-day that I shall have enough for more than a fortnight." And he served up this hotch-potch to the friars at table, and there is no hog in the whole of Rome hungry enough to have eaten thereof. Friar Juniper, to push his wares, cries up his cooking, but seeing that the other friars eat naught thereof, saith, "Now look you, fowls such as these are comforting to the brain, and this mess will keep the body moist, for 'tis right good." And while the friars were lost in wonderment and devotion at the simplicity and devotion of Friar Juniper, lo, the warden, angry at such folly and at the waste of so much good food, rebuked Friar Juniper very harshly. Then Friar Juniper dropped straightway on his knees before the warden and humbly confessed his fault to him and to all the friars, saying, "I am the worst of men: such a one committed such a crime, and therefore his eyes were plucked out, but I was more worthy thereof than he: such a one was hanged for his sins, but I deserve it far more for my wicked deeds: and now have I wasted so much of God's bounty and of the good things of the Order." And thus he departed, all sorrowing, and all that day was not seen of any friar. And then the warden said, "My dearest friars, I would that every day this friar should spoil, even as he hath now, as many more of our good things, if we had them, solely for our edification; for he hath done this thing out of his great simplicity and charity."

XI. *How Friar Juniper went on a time to Assisi for his confusion.*

On a time, when Friar Juniper was dwelling in the vale of Spoleto, seeing that there was a solemn festival at Assisi, and that much people were going thither with great devotion, a desire took him to go to that festival: and hear how he went. Friar Juniper stripped himself to his breeches, and thus fared forth, passing through the midst of the city of Spoleto and comes to the friary. The friars, much perturbed and scandalised, rebuked him very harshly, calling him a mad fellow and a fool that brought confusion to the Order of St. Francis; and they would have put him in chains as a madman. And the general, that was then in the house, bade call Friar Juniper and all the friars, and in the presence of the whole community gave him a hard and bitter reproof. And after many words of vigorous condemnation, he spake thus to Friar Juniper, "Thy fault is such, and so heavy, that I know not what penance to lay upon thee." Friar Juniper answers, even as one that rejoiced in his own confusion, "Father, I will tell thee: for penance bid me return, in the same guise as I came hither, to the place whence I set forth to come to this festival."

XII. *How Friar Juniper was rapt in God as he was attending mass.*

Friar Juniper, on a time, while hearing mass with great devotion, was rapt in God through the elevation of his mind, and for a long space. And being left in the room, far away from the other friars, he began, when he came to himself, to say with great devotion, "O my brethren, who is there in this life so noble that would not fain carry a bushel of dung through the whole earth, if a house filled with gold were given to him?" And he said, "Ah me! wherefore are we not willing to endure a little shame, in order that we may win the blessed life?"

XIII. *Of the grief that Friar Juniper felt at the death of his companion, Friar Amazialbene.*

Friar Juniper had a companion friar that he dearly loved, whose name was Amazialbene. And truly had this friar the virtue of highest patience and obedience; for if he were beaten the whole day long never did he utter one single word of lamentation or complaint. Often was he sent to friaries where the whole community was ill to get on with, and from whom he suffered much persecution; and this he endured very patiently and without murmuring. He, at the bidding of Friar Juniper, was wont to laugh and to weep. Now, as it pleased God, this Friar Amazialbene died in the highest repute; and Friar Juniper, hearing of his death, felt such great sadness of spirit as he never in his life had felt for the loss of any material thing. And he showed forth outwardly the great bitterness that was within him, and said, "Woe is me! poor wretch! now no good thing is left to me, and all the world is out of joint at the death of my sweet and most beloved brother Amazialbene. Were it not that I should have no peace with the other friars, I would go to his grave and take away his head, and with the skull I would make me two bowls: and from one I would ever eat for devout memory of him; and from the other would I drink whenever I were athirst or had desire to drink."

XIV. *Of the hand that Friar Juniper saw in the air.*

Friar Juniper, being on a time at prayer, and haply thinking on the great works he would do, himseemed to behold a hand in the air, and he heard with his bodily ears a voice that spake to him thus, "O Friar Juniper, without this hand thou canst do naught." Whereat he straightway arose and lifted up his eyes to heaven and ran through the friary crying with a loud voice, "True indeed! True indeed!" And this he repeated for a good space.

XV. *How St. Francis bade Friar Leo wash the stone.*

When St. Francis was speaking with Friar Leo on the mount of La Verna, St. Francis said, "Friar, little sheep, wash this stone with water." And Friar Leo was quick to wash the stone with water. Saith St. Francis with great joy and gladness, "Wash it with wine." And 'twas done. Saith St. Francis, "Wash it with oil." And this was done. Saith St. Francis, "Friar, little sheep, wash that stone with balm." Friar Leo answers, "O sweet father, how shall I obtain balm in this wilderness?" St. Francis answered, "Know, friar, thou little sheep of Christ, that this is the stone whereon Christ sat when He appeared to me here: therefore have I bidden thee four times; wash it, and hold thy peace, for Christ hath promised me four singular graces for my Order. The first is, that all those who shall love my Order with all their hearts, and all steadfast friars, shall, by grace divine, make a good end. The second is, that the persecutors of this holy Order shall be notably punished. The third is, that no evil-doer who remaineth in his perversity can endure long in this Order. The fourth is, that this Order shall endure until the last judgment."

HERE BEGINNETH THE LIFE OF THE BLESSED FRIAR GILES, THE COMPANION OF ST. FRANCIS

I. *How Friar Giles and three companions were received into the Order of the friars minor.*

Forasmuch as the example of holy men on the minds of devout hearers, is to make them despise fleeting pleasures and to beget a desire for eternal salvation, I will recite, to the honour of God and of His most reverend Mother, Madonna St. Mary, and for the profit of all hearers, certain words touching the work that the Holy Ghost wrought in our holy Friar Giles, who, while yet wearing the secular habit, was touched by the Holy Ghost, and began to ponder in his heart how in all his works he might please God alone. In those days St. Francis, a new herald of God, sent as an exemplar of the life of humility and of holy penitence, drew and led, two years after his conversion, Master Bernard, a man adorned with wondrous prudence and very rich in worldly goods, and likewise Peter Cattani,[1] to the observance of the gospel and of holy poverty. And they, by the counsel of St. Francis, gave away all their worldly treasures to the poor, for love of God, and put on the glory of meekness and of gospel perfection with the habit of the friars minor; and they, with the greatest fervour, promised to keep their vows all the days of their life: and even so did they with great perfection. A week after their conversion and the distribution of their goods, Friar Giles, while yet in the secular habit, beholding such contempt of earthly things in these two noble knights of Assisi that the whole city was in amaze thereat, went betimes on the day following (that was the feast of St. George in the year one thousand two hundred and nine) to the church of St. Gregory, where the convent of St. Clare was, all enkindled with divine love and careful for his salvation. And having prayed, he had a great desire to behold St. Francis, and went towards the lazar-house, where he was dwelling apart in a hovel, in great humility, with Friar Bernard and Friar Cattani. And being come to a crossway, and knowing not whither to turn, he directed his prayer to Christ, our precious Guide, who led him to the said hovel by the straight way. And while he was pondering on the reason of this his coming, St. Francis met him as he was returning from the wood wherein he had gone to pray; whereupon, anon, he fell on his knees on the ground before St. Francis, and humbly besought him to receive him into his

[1] Elsewhere called Peter of Catana.

company, for love of God. St. Francis, gazing on the devout aspect of Friar Giles, answered and said, "Dearest brother, God hath wrought in thee a very great grace. If the emperor came to Assisi, and would make one of the men of this city his knight, or private chamberlain, ought he not to rejoice greatly? How much greater joy oughtest thou to receive in that God hath chosen thee for His knight and most beloved servant, to observe the perfect way of the holy gospel? Therefore, be steadfast and constant in the vocation whereto God hath called thee." And he takes him by the hand and raises him up, and leads him into the aforesaid hovel; and he calls Friar Bernard and saith, "Our Lord and Master hath sent us a good friar, wherefore rejoice we all in the Lord and eat together in charity." And after they had eaten, St. Francis went with this Giles to Assisi, to get cloth to make Friar Giles's habit. And they found a poor woman by the way, that begged alms of them for love of God; and knowing not how to minister to the poor little woman's needs, St. Francis turned to Friar Giles with an angelic countenance and said, "For love of God, dearest brother, let us give this cloak to the poor creature." And Friar Giles obeyed the holy father with so ready a heart, that himseemed to behold that alms fly forthwith to heaven; and Friar Giles flew with it straightway to heaven, whereat he felt unspeakable joy, and a renewed heart within him. And St. Francis, having procured the cloth and made the habit, received Friar Giles into the Order; and he was one of the most glorious religious in the contemplative life the world had ever seen in those days. After the reception of Friar Giles, anon St. Francis went with him into the Marches of Ancona, singing with him and magnifying with praise the Lord of heaven and earth; and he said to Friar Giles, "Son, our Order shall be like unto the fisher that casteth his net into the water and taketh a multitude of fishes: and the big fish he holds, and puts the little ones back into the waters." Friar Giles marvelled at this prophecy, because there were not yet in the Order more than St. Francis and three friars; and albeit St. Francis had not preached to the people in public places, yet as he went by the way he admonished and corrected both men and women, saying, with loving simplicity, "Love and fear God, and do fitting penance for your sins." And Friar Giles said, "Do that which my spiritual father telleth you, for he speaketh excellently well."

II. *How Friar Giles went to St. James the Great.*

Once in the course of time, Friar Giles went, by leave of St. Francis, to St. James the Great in Galicia; and in the whole of that way only once did he satisfy his hunger, by reason of the great poverty of all that land. Wherefore, asking alms and finding none that would give him charity, he happened by chance that evening on a threshing floor, where some few grains of beans were left: these he gathered up, and these were his supper. And here he slept that night, for he was ever fain to abide in solitary places, far from the haunts of men, that he might the better give himself up to prayer and to vigils. And in that supper he was so greatly comforted by God, that if he had eaten of divers viands he deemed he would not have eaten so full a meal. And journeying on, he finds by the way a poor man that craves alms, for love of God; and Friar Giles, most charitable of men, having naught save his habit to cover his body, cut off the cowl from his cloak, and gave it to that poor man for love of God; and thus, sans cowl, he journeyed for twenty days together. And returning by way of Lombardy, he was hailed by a man, to whom he went right gladly, thinking to receive some alms of him: and stretching forth his hand, this man put a pair of dice therein, and invited him to play a game. Friar Giles answered, very humbly, "God forgive thee this, my son." And so journeying through the world, he was much mocked at, and endured all these things meekly.

III. *Of Friar Giles's way of life when he went to the Holy Sepulchre.*

Friar Giles went, by leave of St. Francis, to visit the Holy Sepulchre of Christ, and came to the port of Brindisi, and there stayed over many days, for there was no ship ready. And Friar Giles, desiring to live by his labour, begged a pitcher, and filling it with water, went about the city crying, "Who lacks water?" And for his toil he received bread and things needful for the life of the body, both for himself and for his companion. And then he crossed the seas, and visited the Holy Sepulchre of Christ, and the other holy places, with great devotion. And journeying back, he abode many days in the city of Ancona; and forasmuch as he was wont to live by the labour of his hands, he made baskets of rushes and sold them, not for money, but for bread for himself and for his companion; and he carried the dead to burial for the aforesaid price. And when these things failed him, he returned to the table of Jesus Christ, asking alms from door to door. And thus, with much toil and poverty, he came back to St. Mary of the Angels.

IV. *How Friar Giles praised obedience more than prayer.*

A friar on a time was at prayer in his cell, and his warden

bade tell him, by obedience, to go questing for alms. Whereupon he straightway went to Friar Giles and said, "Father mine, I was at prayer, and the warden hath bidden me go for bread, and meseems 'twere better to remain at prayer." Friar Giles answered, "My son, hast thou not yet learned or known what prayer is? True prayer is to do the will of our superior; and it is a token of great pride in him who, having put his neck under the yoke of holy obedience, refuseth it for any cause, in order to work his own will, even though it may seem to him that he is working more perfectly. The perfectly obedient religious is like unto a knight mounted on a mighty steed, by whose power he passeth fearlessly through the midst of the fray; and contrariwise, the disobedient and complaining and unwilling religious is like unto one that is mounted on a lean and infirm and vicious horse, because with a little striving he is slain or taken by the enemy. I say unto thee, were there a man of such devotion and exaltation of mind that he spake with angels, and while thus speaking he were called by his superior, straightway he ought to leave his converse with the angels and obey his superior."

V. *How Friar Giles lived by the labour of his hands.*

Friar Giles, being on a time in the friary at Rome, was minded to live by bodily toil, even as he was ever wont to do since he entered the Order, and he wrought in this wise: Betimes, in the morning, he heard mass with much devotion, then he went to the wood that was eight miles distant from Rome and carried a faggot of wood back on his shoulders, and sold it for bread, or aught else to eat. One time, among others, when he was returning with a load of wood, a woman asked to buy it; and being agreed on the price, he carried it to her house. The woman, notwithstanding the bargain, gave him much more than she had promised, for she saw he was a religious. Saith Friar Giles, "Good woman, I would not that the sin of avarice overcame me, therefore I will not take a greater price than I bargained with thee." And not only would he take no more, but he took only the half of the price agreed upon, and went his way; wherefore that woman conceived a very great devotion for him. Friar Giles did any honest work for hire, and always gave heed to holy honesty; he gave a hand to gather olives and to tread the wine-press for the peasants. Standing on a day in the market-place, a certain man sought hands to beat down his walnuts, and begged one to beat them down for him, at a price; but he made excuse, saying it was very far away, and the trees were very hard to climb. Saith Friar Giles, "Friend, if thou wilt give me part of the walnuts I will come with thee and beat them down." The bargain made, he went his way, and, first making the sign of the holy cross, he climbed up to beat a tall walnut tree with great fear. And after he had beaten the branches thereof so many walnuts were due to him for his share that he could not carry them away in his lap. Wherefore he took off his habit and bound up the sleeves and the cowl, and made a sack thereof, and having filled this his habit with walnuts, he lifted it on to his shoulder and carried the walnuts to Rome; and he gave all to the poor, with great joy, for love of God. When the corn was cut, Friar Giles went with the other poor folk to glean some ears; and if any one offered him a handful of corn he answered, "Brother, I have no granary wherein to store it." And the ears of wheat he gleaned he gave away, more often than not, for love of God. Seldom did Friar Giles work the whole day through, for he always bargained to have some space of time to say the canonical hours and not fail in his mental prayers. Once on a time Friar Giles went to the fountain of San Sisto to draw water for the monks, and a man asked him for a drink. Friar Giles answers, "And how shall I carry this vessel half filled to the monks?" And this man angrily spake many words of contumely and abuse to Friar Giles: and Friar Giles returned to the monks grieving much. Begging a large vessel anon he returned to the said fountain for water, and finding that man again, said to him, "My friend, take and drink as much as thy soul desireth, and be not angry, for methinks 'tis a base thing to take water that hath been drunk of, to those holy monks." He, pricked and constrained by the charity and humility of Friar Giles, confessed his fault, and from that hour forth held him in great veneration.

VI. *How Friar Giles was miraculously provided for in a dire need when, because of the heavy snow, he could not quest for alms.*

Friar Giles, when dwelling with a cardinal at Rome, forasmuch as he had not the peace of mind he desired, said to the cardinal, as the time of the greater lent drew nigh, "My father, with your leave I would go, for my peace, with this my companion, to keep this lent in some solitary place." The cardinal answers, "Prithee, my dearest friar, whither wouldst thou go? There is a sore famine in these parts, and ye are strangers. Ah! be pleased to remain at my court, for to me 'twill be a singular grace to have you given whatsoever ye may need for love of

God." But Friar Giles was minded to go forth, and he went out of Rome to the top of a high mountain where in days of old stood a town, and he found there a deserted church that was called St. Lawrence, and therein he and his companion entered, and remained in prayer and in many meditations; and for that they were not known, small reverence or devotion was shown to them. Wherefore they suffered great want; and moreover there fell a great snowstorm that endured many days. They could not issue from the church, and naught was sent them to live upon, and of themselves they had no store; and so they remained, shut in for three mortal days. Friar Giles, seeing he could not live by his labour, and for alms could not go forth, said to his companion, "My dearest brother, let us call on our Lord Jesus Christ with a loud voice, that of His pity He may provide for us in this sore extremity and need; for certain monks, being in dire need, have called on God, and divine providence did provide for them in their needs." And after the example of these, they betook them to prayer, and besought God, with all affection, that He would provide a remedy in so sore a need. God, that is all-pitiful, had regard to their faith and devotion and simplicity and fervour in this wise: A certain man was looking towards the church where Friar Giles and his companion were, and being inspired by God, said within himself, "Haply in that church there be some good souls doing penance and, in this season of heavy snows, have naught for their needs, and by reason thereof may die of hunger." And urged by the Holy Ghost he said, "Certes, I will go and learn if my foreboding be true or not." And he took some loaves and a vessel of wine and set forth on his journey, and with very great difficulty he won his way to the aforesaid church, where he found Friar Giles and his companion devoutly engaged in prayer; and they were so ravaged by hunger that in their aspect they had the semblance of dead rather than of living men. He had great compassion on them, and having refreshed and comforted them, he returned and told his neighbours of the extreme poverty and need of these friars, and besought them, for love of God, to provide for them; whereupon many, after the example of this man, brought them bread and wine and other necessaries to eat, for love of God; and through all that lent they ordered among themselves that the needs of these friars should be provided for. And Friar Giles, considering the great mercy of God and the charity of these folk, said to his companion, "My dearest brother, but now have we prayed to God to provide for us in our need, and we have been heard; therefore it is meet that we return thanks and glory to Him and pray for those that have fed us with their alms, and for all Christian folk." And by his great fervour and devotion, so much grace was given by God to Friar Giles that many, by his example, forsook this blind world, and many others that were not called to take up the religious life did very great penance in their homes.

VII. *Touching the day of the holy Friar Giles's death.*

On St. George's eve, at the hour of matins, these fifty-two years past, the soul of Friar Giles, for that he had received the habit of St. Francis in the first days of the month, was received by God into the glory of paradise, to wit, on the feast of St. George.

VIII. *How a holy man being at prayer saw the soul of Friar Giles go to life everlasting.*

A good man being at prayer when Friar Giles passed from this life, saw his soul, together with a multitude of souls, come out of purgatory and ascend to heaven; and he beheld Jesus Christ come forth to meet the soul of Friar Giles, and with a multitude of angels, and with all those souls ascend with sweet melody into the glory of paradise.

IX. *How the soul of a friar preacher's friend was delivered from the pains of purgatory through the merits of Friar Giles.*

When Friar Giles lay sick so that in a few days he died, a Dominican friar fell sick unto death. And he had a friend that was also a friar, who, seeing him draw nigh unto death, said to the sick man, "My brother, I desire, if it be God's will, that after thy death thou return to me and tell me in what state thou mayst be." The sick friar promised to return whensoever it might be possible. The sick man died on the self-same day as Friar Giles, and after his death he appeared to the living friar preacher, and said, "'Twas God's will that I should keep my promise to thee." Saith the living friar to the dead, "How fares it with thee?" The dead friar answered, "'Tis well with me, for I died on a day whereon a holy friar minor passed from this life whose name was Friar Giles, and to him for his great holiness Christ granted that he should lead all the souls that were in purgatory to holy paradise, among which souls was I, in great torments; and through the merits of the holy Friar Giles I am delivered therefrom." This said, he forthwith vanished; and the friar revealed that vision to no man. This said friar fell sick; and anon deeming that God had smitten him because he had not revealed the virtue and the glory of Friar Giles, he sent for the friars minor, and there came to him five couples of them; and having called them, together with the preaching friars, he declared the aforesaid vision to them with great devotion, and seeking very diligently they found that on that selfsame day these twain had passed from this life.

X. *How God had given certain graces to Friar Giles and of the day of his death.*

Friar Bonaventure of Bagnoreggio was wont to say of Friar Giles that God had given and vouchsafed singular grace to him for all those that commended themselves to him, with devout intent, in the things that appertained to the soul. He wrought many miracles during his life and after his death, as appeareth from his legend; and he passed from this life to supernal glory, in the year of our Lord one thousand two hundred and fifty-two, on the day of the feast of St. George; and he is buried at Perugia in the house of the friars minor.

Here beginneth the Chapters of Certain Doctrines and Notable Sayings of Friar Giles

I. *Chapter of vices and virtues.*

The grace of God and the virtues are the way and the ladder whereby we ascend to heaven; but the vices and the sins are the way and the ladder whereby we descend to the depths of hell. Vices and sins are poison and deadly venom; but virtues and good works are healing treacle.[1] One grace bringeth and draweth after it another. Grace desireth not to be praised, and vice cannot endure to be despised. The mind is at peace and resteth in humility: patience is her daughter. Holy purity of heart seeth God; but true devotion savoureth him. If thou lovest, thou shalt be loved. If thou servest, thou shalt be served. If thou fearest, thou shalt be feared. If thou bearest thyself well towards others, it behoves that others bear themselves well towards thee. But blessed is he that truly loveth and desireth not to be loved. Blessed is he that serveth and desireth not to be served. Blessed is he that feareth and desireth not to be feared. Blessed is he that beareth himself well towards others, and desireth not that others bear themselves well towards him. But forasmuch as these things are exceeding high, and

[1] Compare Chaucer, "Christ which that is to every harm treacle." The Venetians were famed for their skilful preparation of this medicinal compound, which was universally regarded in the Middle Ages as an antidote against snake bites and other poisons.

of great perfection, the fool can neither know them nor attain to them. Three things are exceeding high and useful, and he that shall have attained to them shall never fall. The first is, if thou endure willingly, and with gladness, every tribulation that shall befall thee, for love of Jesus Christ. The second is, if thou humble thyself every day in all things thou doest, and in all things thou seest. The third is, if thou love steadfastly, and with all thy heart, that highest celestial and invisible good, which cannot be seen with mortal eyes. Those things that are most despised and most reviled by worldly men are verily most acceptable and pleasing to God and to His saints; and those things that are most honoured and most loved and are most pleasing to worldly men, those are most despised and scorned and most hated by God and by His saints. This foul unseemliness proceedeth from the ignorance and the wickedness of men, for the wretched man loveth most those things he should hate, and hateth those things he should love. Once on a time, Friar Giles asked another friar, saying, "Tell me, dearest, is thine a good soul?" That friar answered, "This I know not." Then said Friar Giles, "My brother, I would have thee to know that holy contrition and holy humility and holy charity and holy devotion and holy joy make the good and blessed soul."

II. *Chapter of faith.*

All things whatsoever that can be thought in the heart or told with the tongue, or seen with the eyes, or touched with the hands—all are as naught in respect of, and in comparison with, those things that cannot be thought, nor seen, nor touched. All the saints and all the sages that have passed away, and all those that are in this present life, and all that shall come after us, that spake or wrote, or that shall speak or write, of God, ne'er told nor e'er can tell of God so much as a grain of millet would be in respect of, or in comparison with, the heavens and the earth, nay, even a thousand thousandfold less. For all scripture that speaketh of God, speaketh of Him with stammering voice, as the mother doth who prattles with her child, that could not understand her words if she spoke in other fashion. Friar Giles said, on a time, to a worldly judge, "Believest thou that the gifts of God are great?" The judge answered, "Yea, I believe." Whereat Friar Giles said, "I will show thee how that thou believest not faithfully." And then he said to him, "What price is all thou possessest in this world worth?" The judge answered, "'Tis worth, perchance, a thousand pounds." Then said Friar Giles, "Wouldst thou give those thy possessions for ten thousand pounds?" The judge answered, without delay, "Verily, that would I." And Friar Giles said, "Certain it is that all the possessions of this world are as naught in respect to heavenly things; therefore, why givest thou not these thy possessions to Christ, that thou mayst buy those possessions that are celestial and eternal?" Then that judge, wise with the foolish wisdom of the world, made answer to the pure and simple Friar Giles, "God hath filled thee with wise and divine foolishness. Thinkest thou, Friar Giles, that there lives a man whose outward works accord with all he believes in his inmost heart?" Friar Giles answered, "Look now, my dearest, it is very truth that all the saints have striven to fulfil by their works those things they were able to comprehend or to know were the will of God, according to their power. And all those things they were not able to fulfil by their works, these they fulfilled by the holy desire of their will; in such wise, that what was lacking in their works by reason of their defect of power, this they fulfilled by the desire of their soul: and they were not found wanting." Yet again Friar Giles said, "If any man could be found of perfect faith, in short time he would attain to the perfect state, whereby full assurance of his salvation would be given him. What hurt or what ill could any temporal adversity in this present life do to that man who, with steadfast faith, awaiteth this eternal and supreme and highest good? And the miserable man, that awaiteth everlasting torment, what could any prosperity, or temporal possession, in this world avail him? Yet how grievous a sinner soever a man may be, let him not despair, while he yet liveth, of the infinite mercy of God; for there is no tree in this world so full of thorns, nor so knotted nor so gnarled, but that men cannot plane it and polish it and adorn it, and make it fair to look upon. Even so, there is no man in this world so sunk in iniquity, nor so great a sinner, but that God can convert him and adorn him with peculiar grace, and with many virtuous gifts."

III. *Chapter of holy humility.*

No man can attain to any knowledge or understanding of God, save by the virtue of holy humility: for the straight way upward is the straight way downward. All the perils and the great falls that have come to pass in this world have come about for no cause save the lifting up of the head, to wit, of the mind, in pride; and this is proven by the fall of the devil, that was cast out of heaven; and by the fall of our first parent, Adam, that was driven out of paradise through the exaltation of the head, to wit, through disobedience; and again by the Pharisee, whereof Christ speaketh in the gospel, and by many other examples. And so contrariwise: for all the great and good things that have e'er come to pass in this world, have come to pass through the abasement of the head, to wit, through the humility of the mind, even as is proven by the blessed and most humble Virgin Mary, and by the publican, and by the holy thief on the cross, and by many other ensamples in the scriptures. And, therefore, it were well if we could find some great and heavy weight that we might ever hang about our necks, in order that it might ever bear us down, to wit, that it might ever make us humble ourselves. A friar asked Friar Giles, "Tell me, father, how shall we flee from this sin of pride?" To whom Friar Giles answered, "My brother, be persuaded of this: never hope to be able to flee from pride, except thou first place thy mouth where thou hast set thy feet; but if thou wilt consider well the blessings of God, then shalt thou know that of thy duty thou art held to bow thy head. And, again, if thou wilt think much on thy faults and on thy manifold offences against God, most of all wilt thou have cause to humble thyself. But woe unto those that would be honoured for their wickedness! One degree in humility hath he risen that knoweth himself to be the enemy of his own good; another degree in humility is to render to others those things that are theirs, and not to appropriate them to ourselves, to wit, that every good thing and every virtue a man findeth in himself, he ought not to own it to himself, but to God alone, from whom proceedeth every grace and every virtue and every good thing; but all sin or passion of the soul, or whatsoever vice a man find in himself, this should he own to himself, since it proceedeth from himself and from his own wickedness, and not from others. Blessed is that man that knoweth himself, and deemeth himself vile in the sight of God, and even so in the sight of men. Blessed is he that ever judgeth himself and condemneth himself, and not others, for he shall not be judged at that dread and last judgment eternal. Blessed is he that shall bend diligently under the yoke of obedience and under the judgment of others, even as the holy apostles did before and after they received the Holy Spirit." Likewise said Friar Giles, "He that would gain and possess perfect peace and rest must needs account every man his superior; he must ever hold himself the subject and inferior of others. Blessed is that man who in his deeds and in his words desireth not to be seen or known, save only in that unalloyed being, and in that simple adornment which God created and adorned him with. Blessed is the man that knoweth how to treasure up and hide divine revelations and consolations, for there is nothing so hidden but that God shall reveal it, when it pleaseth Him. If a man were the most perfect and the holiest man in the world, and yet deemed and believed himself the most miserable of sinners and the vilest wretch on the earth—therein is true humility. Holy humility knoweth not how to prate, and the blessed fear of God knoweth not how to speak." Said Friar Giles, "Methinks humility is like unto a thunderbolt; for even as the bolt maketh a terrible crash, breaking, crushing, and burning all that it findeth in its path, and then naught of that bolt is found, so, in like manner, humility smiteth and scattereth and burneth and consumeth every wickedness and every vice and every sin; and yet is found to be naught in itself. The man that possesseth humility findeth grace in the sight of God, through that humility, and perfect peace with his neighbour."

IV. *Chapter of the holy fear of God.*

He that feareth naught showeth that he hath naught to lose. The holy fear of God ordaineth, governeth, and ruleth the soul and maketh it to come to a state of grace. If any man possess any grace or divine virtue, holy fear is that which preserveth it. And he that hath not yet gained virtue or grace, holy fear maketh him to gain it. The holy fear of God is the bringer of divine graces, for it maketh the soul, wheresoever she abideth, to attain quickly to holy virtue and divine graces. All creatures that have fallen into sin would never have fallen if they had had the holy fear of God. But this holy gift of fear is given only to the perfect; for the more perfect a man is, the more godfearing and humble he is. Blessed is he that knoweth he is in a dungeon in this world, and ever remembereth how grievously he hath offended his Lord. A man ought ever to fear pride with a great fear, lest it thrust against him and make him fall from the state of grace wherein he standeth; for a man can never stand secure being girt about with enemies; and our enemies are the seductions of this miserable world and our own flesh that, together with the devil, is ever the enemy of the soul. A man hath need of greater fear lest his own wickedness overcome him and beguile him than of any other of his enemies. It is impossible that a man can rise and ascend to any divine grace, or virtue, or persevere therein, without holy fear. He that feareth not God goeth in danger of perishing, and in yet greater peril of everlasting perdition. The fear of God maketh a man to obey humbly, and maketh him bow down his head under the yoke of obedience; and the greater the fear a man hath, the more fervently doth he worship. Not a little gift is prayer to whosoever it is given. The virtuous words of men, however great they may appear to me, are not therefore accounted nor rewarded according to our measure, but according to the measure and good pleasure of God; for God regardeth not the sum of our toils, but the sum of our love and humility. Therefore, the better part for us is to love always, and fear with great humility, and never put trust in ourselves for any good thing; ever having suspicion of those thoughts that are begotten in the mind under the semblance of good.

V. *Chapter of holy patience.*

He that with steadfast humility and patience suffereth and endureth tribulation, through fervent love of God, soon shall attain to great grace and virtues, and shall be lord of this world, and shall have a foretaste of the next and glorious world. Everything that a man doeth, good or evil, he doeth it unto himself; therefore, be not offended with him that doeth thee an injury, for rather oughtest thou to have humble patience with him, and only grieve within thee for his sin, taking compassion on him and praying God earnestly for him. The stronger a man is to endure and suffer patiently injuries and tribulations, for love of God, the greater is he in the sight of God, and no more; and the weaker a man is to endure pain and adversity, for love of God, the less is he in the sight of God. If any man praise thee, speaking well of thee, render thou that praise to God alone; and if any man speak evil of thee, or revile thee, aid thou him, speaking evil of thyself, and worse. If thou wilt make good thine own cause, strive ever to make it appear ill, and uphold thy fellow's cause, ever imputing guilt to thyself, and ever praising and truly excusing thy neighbour. When any man would contend or have the law of thee, if thou wouldst win, lose; and then shalt thou win; but if thou wouldst go to law to win, when thou thinkest to win, then shalt thou find thou hast lost heavily. Therefore, my brother, believe of a surety, the straight way of salvation is the way to perdition. But when we are not good bearers of tribulation, then we cannot be seekers after everlasting consolations. Much greater consolation and a more worthy thing it is to suffer injuries and revilings patiently, without murmuring, for love of God, than to feed a hundred poor folk and fast continually every day.

But how shall it profit a man, or what shall it avail him, to despise himself and afflict his body with great fastings and vigils and scourgings, if he be unable to endure a small injury from his neighbour? For which thing, a man shall receive a much greater reward and greater merit than for all the afflictions a man can give to himself of his own will; because to endure the revilings and injuries of one's neighbour, with humble patience and without murmuring, purgeth sin away much more quickly than doth a fount of many tears. Blessed is the man that ever holdeth before the eyes of the mind the memory of his sins and the good gifts of God; for he will endure with patience every tribulation and adversity, whereby he looketh for great consolations. The truly humble man looketh for no reward nor merit from God, but striveth ever only how he can give satisfaction in all things, owning himself God's debtor: and every good thing he hath, that, he knoweth he hath through the goodness of God, and not through any merit of his own; and every adversity he endureth, he knoweth it to be truly because of his sins. A certain friar asked Friar Giles, saying, "If in our time any great adversity, or tribulation, should befall, what should we do in that case?" To whom Friar Giles answered, saying, "My brother, I would have thee know that if the Lord rained down stones and arrows from heaven, they could not injure nor do any hurt to us, if we were such men as we ought to be; for if a man were verily what he ought to be, he would transmute every evil and every tribulation into good; for we know what the apostle said, that all things work together for good to them that love God: even so all things work together for ill and to the condemnation of him that hath an evil will. If thou wilt save thyself and go to celestial glory, thou shalt desire no vengeance nor punishment of any creature; for the heritage of the saints is ever to do good and ever to suffer evil. If thou knewest in very truth how grievously thou hast offended thy Creator, thou wouldst know that it is a worthy and just thing that all creatures should persecute thee and give thee pain and tribulation, in order that these creatures might take vengeance for the offences thou hast done to their Creator. A high and great virtue it is for a man to overcome himself; for he that overcometh himself shall overcome all his enemies, and attain to all good. And yet a greater virtue would it be if a man suffered himself to be overcome by all men; for he would be lord over all his enemies, to wit, his vices, the devil, the world, and his own flesh. If thou wilt save thyself, renounce and despise all consolation that the things of this world and all mortal creatures can give thee; for greater and more frequent are the falls that come through prosperity and through consolation than are those that come through adversity and tribulation." Once on a time a religious was murmuring against his superior, in the presence of Friar Giles, by reason of a harsh obedience he had laid upon him; to whom Friar Giles said, "My dearest, the more thou murmurest the heavier is the weight of thy burden, and the harder shall it be to thee to bear; and the more humbly and devoutly thou shalt place thy neck under the yoke of holy obedience, the lighter and easier will that obedience be to bear. But methinks thou wouldst not be rebuked in this world, for love of Christ, and yet wouldst be with Christ in the next world; thou wouldst not be persecuted or cursed for Christ's sake in this world, and in the next, wouldst be blessed and received by Christ; thou wouldst not labour in this world, and in the next, wouldst rest and be at peace. I tell thee, friar, friar, thou art sorely beguiled; for by the way of poverty and of shame and of reviling a man cometh to true celestial honour; and by enduring patiently mocking and cursing, for love of Christ, a man shall come to the glory of Christ. Therefore, well saith a worldly proverb,

> He whose gifts cost him no woe,
> Good gifts from others must forgoe.

How useful is the nature of the horse! for how swiftly soever the horse runneth, he yet letteth himself be ruled and guided, and leapeth hither and thither, and forward and backward, according to the will of his rider: and so, likewise, ought the servant of God to do, to wit, he should let himself be ruled, guided, turned aside, and bent, according to the will of his superior, or of any other man, for love of Christ. If thou wouldst be perfect, strive diligently to be full of grace and virtue, and fight valiantly against vice, enduring patiently every adversity for the love of thy Lord, that was mocked and afflicted and reviled and scourged and crucified and slain for love of thee, and not for His own sin, nor for His glory, nor for His profit, but only for thy salvation. And to do all this that I have told thee, above all things it is necessary that thou overcome thyself; for little shall it profit a man to lead and draw souls to God, if first he overcome not himself, and lead and draw himself to God."

VI. *Chapter of sloth.*

The slothful man loseth both this world and the next; for himself beareth no fruit and he profiteth not another. It is impossible for a man to gain virtue without diligence and great toil. When thou canst abide in a safe place stand not in a perilous place: he abideth in a safe place who striveth and suffereth and worketh and toileth through God, and for the Lord God; and not through fear of punishment, or for a price, but for love of God. The man that refuseth to suffer and labour for love of Christ, verily he refuseth the glory of Christ; and even as diligence is useful and profitable to us, so is negligence ever against us. Even as sloth is the way that leads to hell, so is holy diligence the way that leads to heaven. A man ought to be very diligent to gain and keep virtue and the grace of God, ever labouring faithfully with this grace and virtue; for many times it befalleth that the man who laboureth not faithfully loseth the fruit for the leaves, or the grain for the straw. To some God giveth of His grace good fruit with few leaves; to others He giveth fruit and leaves together; and there are others that have neither fruit nor leaves. Methinks 'tis a greater thing to know how to guard and keep well the good gifts and graces given to us by the Lord, than to know how to gain them. For albeit a man may know well how to gain, yet if he know not how to save and treasure up, he shall never be rich; but some there be that make their gains little by little, and are grown rich because they save well their gains and their treasure. Oh, how much water would the Tiber have stored up if it flowed not away to the sea! Man asketh of God an infinite gift, that is without measure and without bounds, and yet will not love God, save with measure and with bounds. He that would be loved of God and have infinite reward from Him, beyond all bounds and beyond all measure, let him love God beyond all bounds and beyond all measure, and ever serve Him infinitely. Blessed is he that loveth God with all his heart and with all his mind, and ever afflicteth his body and his mind for love of God, seeking no reward under heaven, but accounting himself only a debtor. If a man were in sore poverty and need, and another man said to him, "I will lend thee a very precious thing for the space of three days: know that if thou use well this thing within this term of three days thou shalt gain an infinite treasure, and be rich evermore," is it not a sure thing that this poor man would be very careful to use well and diligently this thing so precious, and would strive much to make it fruitful and profit him well:

so do I say likewise that this thing lent unto us by the hand of God is our body, which the good God hath lent us for three days; for all our times and years are but as three days in the sight of God. Therefore if thou wouldst be rich and enjoy the divine sweetness everlastingly, strive to labour well and make this thing, lent by the hand of God, bear good fruit; to wit, thy body, in this space of three days; to wit, in the brief time of thy life: for if thou art not careful of gain in this present life, while thou hast yet time, thou shalt not enjoy that everlasting riches nor find holy rest in that celestial peace everlastingly. But if all the possessions of the world were in the hands of one person that never turned them to account himself, nor put them out for others to use, what fruit or what profit would he have of those things? Of a surety, neither profit nor fruit would he have. But it might well be that a man, having few possessions and using them well, should have much profit and a great abundance of fruit for himself and for others. A worldly proverb saith, " Never set an empty pot on the fire hoping thy neighbour will come and fill it." And so likewise God willeth that no grace be left empty; for the good God never giveth a grace to any man that it be kept empty, rather doth he give it that a man may use it and bring forth fruit of good works; for good-will sufficeth not except a man strive to pursue it and use it to a profit of holy words. On a time a wayfarer said to Friar Giles, " Father, I pray thee give me some consolation." Whereto Friar Giles answered, " My brother, strive to stand well with God and straightway shalt thou have the consolation thou needest; for if a man make not a pure dwelling-place ready in his soul, wherein God may abide and rest, never shall he find an abiding place nor rest nor true consolation in any creature. When a man would work evil he never asketh much counsel for the doing thereof; but, ere they do good, many folk seek much counsel and make long delay." Once Friar Giles said to his companions, " My brethren, methinks, in these days, one findeth no man that would do those things that he seeth are most profitable, and not only for the soul but also for the body. Believe me, my brethren, I can swear, of a truth, that the more a man flees and shuns the burden and the yoke of Christ the more grievous he maketh it to himself and the more heavily it weigheth upon him, and the greater is the burden; but the more ardently a man taketh up his burden, ever heaping up more weight of his own will, the lighter and the more pleasant he feeleth it to bear. Would to God that men would labour to win the good things of the body, since they would win also those of the soul; forasmuch as the body and the soul, without any doubt, must ever be joined together, either to suffer or to enjoy; to wit, either ever to suffer together in hell everlasting pains and boundless torments, or, through the merits of good works, to enjoy perpetual joys and ineffable consolations with the saints and angels in paradise. Because, if a man laboured well, or forgave well, yet lacked humility, his good deeds would be turned to evil; for many have there been that have wrought many works that seemed good and praiseworthy, but since they lacked humility they were discovered and known to be done through pride; and their deeds have shown this, for things done through humility are never corrupted." A friar said to Friar Giles, "Father, methinks we know not yet how to understand our own good." To whom Friar Giles answered, "My brother, of a surety each man worketh the art he hath learned, for no man can work well except he have first learned: wherefore I would have thee know, my brother, that the noblest art in this world is the art of working well; and who could know that art except first he learn it? Blessed is that man in whom no created thing can beget evil; but yet more blessed is he that receiveth in himself good edification from all things he sees or hears."

VII. *Chapter of the contempt of temporal things.*

Many sorrows and many woes will the miserable man suffer that putteth his desire and his heart and his hope in earthly things, whereby he forsaketh and loseth heavenly things, and at last shall even lose also these earthly things. The eagle soareth very high, but if she had tied a weight to her wings she would not be able to fly very high: and even so for the weight of earthly things a man cannot fly on high, to wit, he cannot attain to perfection; but the wise man that bindeth the weight of the remembrance of death and judgment to the wings of his heart, could not for the great fear thereof go astray nor fly at the vanities nor riches of this world, which are a cause of damnation. Every day we see worldly men toil and moil much and encounter great bodily perils to gain these false riches; and after they have toiled and gained much, in a moment they die and leave behind all that they gained in their lives; therefore put not thy trust in this false world that beguileth every man that believeth therein, for it is a liar. But whoso desireth and would be great and truly rich, let him seek after and love everlasting riches, and good things that ever savour sweetly and never satiate and never grow less. If we would not go astray, let us take pattern from the beasts and the birds, for these, when they are fed, are content and seek not their living save from hour to hour when their need cometh: even so should a man be content with satisfying his needs temperately, and not seek after superfluities. Friar Giles said that the ant was not so pleasing to St. Francis as other living things because of the great diligence she hath in gathering together and storing up, in the time of summer, a treasure of grain for the winter; but he was wont to say that the birds pleased him much more, because they laid not up one day for the next. But yet the ant teacheth us that we ought not to be slothful in the summer of this present life, so that we be not found empty and barren in the winter of the last day and judgment.

VIII. *Chapter of holy chastity.*

Our miserable and frail human flesh is like unto the swine that ever rejoiceth to wallow and bemire himself in filth, choosing the mire for his own delight. Our flesh is the devil's knight-errant, for it fighteth and resisteth all those things that pertain to God and to our salvation. A friar asked Friar Giles, saying unto him, "Father, teach me in what manner we may guard ourselves from carnal sin." To whom Friar Giles answered, "My brother, he that would move any great weight or any great stone from one place to another, it behoveth him to strive to move it by skill rather than by force. And so likewise, if we will overcome carnal sin and gain the virtue of chastity, we shall rather gain it by humility and by good and discreet spiritual guidance, than by our presumptuous austerities and by the violence of penance. Every sin cloudeth and darkens holy and shining chastity, for chastity is like unto a bright mirror that is clouded and darkened, not only by the touch of foul things, but also by the breath of man. It is impossible for a man to attain to any spiritual grace so long as he findeth him inclined to carnal lust; therefore, thou mayst turn and turn again, as it please thee, and thou shalt find no other remedy, nor be able to attain to spiritual grace, except thou trample under foot every carnal sin. Therefore, fight valiantly against thy sensual and frail flesh, thy proper enemy, that ever striveth against thee. day and night; let him that overcometh this flesh, our mortal foe, know of a surety that he hath overcome and routed all his enemies, and soon shall attain to spiritual grace and to every good state of virtue and of perfection." Said Friar Giles, "Among all the other virtues I most do prize the virtue of chastity; for sweetest chastity hath in itself alone some perfection; but no other virtue can be perfect without chastity." A friar asked Friar Giles, saying, "Father, is not charity a greater and more excellent virtue than chastity?" And Friar Giles said, "Tell me, brother, what thing in this world is found more chaste than holy charity?" Many a time did Friar Giles chant this little song—

> O holy chastity,
> How great a good thou holdest!
> How precious to possess!
> For such sweet fragrance issueth forth from thee,
> The taste thereof the wise alone can know:
> Therefore the foolish never learn thy worth.

A friar asked Friar Giles, saying, "Father, thou that commendest so the virtue of chastity, prithee make plain to me what chastity is." Whereto Friar Giles answered, "My brother, I tell thee that the diligent custody and continual watching of our bodily and spiritual senses, keeping them pure and spotless before God—that is truly called chastity."

IX. *Chapter of temptations.*

The great graces that a man receiveth from God cannot be possessed in peace and quietness, for many contrary things and many tribulations and many adversities rise up against these graces, because the more acceptable a man is in the sight of God, the more mightily is he assailed and warred against by the devil. Therefore it behoveth a man never to cease from fighting, that he may pursue that grace he hath received from God; for the fiercer the battle the more precious shall be the crown, if he conquers in the fight. But we have not many battles, nor many hindrances, nor many temptations; for we are not such as we ought to be in the spiritual life. But, nevertheless, true it is that if a man walk warily and well in the way of God, he shall have neither toil nor weariness on his journey; but the man that walketh in the way of the world shall ne'er be able to flee from the many toils, the weariness, the anguish, the tribulations, and sorrows, even to the day of his death. Said a friar to Friar Giles, "My father, methinks thou sayest two things, one contrary to the other; for thou didst first say that the more acceptable and the more virtuous a man is in the sight of God, the more hindrances and the more battles he hath in the spiritual life, and then thou saidst the contrary; to wit, that the man who walked warily and well in the way of God would feel neither toil nor weariness on his journey." Whereto Friar Giles made plain the contrariness of these two sayings, and answered thus, "My brother, of a surety the devils assail men of good will with mightier temptations than they do others that have not good will, I mean, in the sight of God. But the man that walketh warily and fervently in the way of God, what toil, what weariness, and what hurt can the devils and all the adversities of the world bring on him? Doth he not know and see that he selleth his wares for a price a thousandfold higher than they are worth? But I tell thee more: of a surety he that were kindled with the fire of divine love, the more mightily he were assailed by sins, the more would he hate and abominate them. The worst devils are wont to pursue and tempt a man when he is weighed down by some infirmity or bodily weakness, or by great cold, or anguish, or when he is ahungered or athirst, or when he hath suffered some injury, or shame, or temporal or spiritual hurt; for these evil spirits know that it is in hours and moments such as these that a man is more apt to receive temptations. But I say unto thee that for every temptation and for every sin thou overcomest thou shalt gain in virture; and that if thou conquer that sin that warreth against thee, thou shalt receive therefore the greater grace and a greater crown of victory." A friar asked counsel of Friar Giles, saying, "Father, ofttimes am I tempted by a sore temptation, and oft have I prayed to God to be delivered therefrom, and yet the Lord taketh it not away from me. Give me thy counsel, father, what ought I to do?" Whereto Friar Giles answered, "My brother, the more richly a king harnesseth his knights with noble armour and strong, the more valiantly he desireth they should fight against his enemies, for love of him." A friar asked Friar Giles, saying, "Father, what remedy can I find that I may go more willingly to prayer and with a more fervent desire? for when I go to pray, I am hard, slothful, withered, and slack." Whereto Friar Giles answered, saying, "A king hath two servants, and the one is armed for battle, but the other hath no arms wherewith to fight; and both would go forth to battle and fight against the enemies of the king. He that is armed goeth forth to battle and fighteth valiantly; but the other that is unarmed saith thus to his lord, 'My lord, thou seest I am naked and without arms, but for love of thee fain would I join the battle and fight thus unarmed as I am.' And then the good king, beholding the love of his trusty servant, saith to his ministers, 'Go with this my servant, clothe him with all those arms that are needful for the fight, in order that he may hie securely forth to battle; and mark ye all his arms with my royal scutcheon, that he be known as my trusty knight.' And even so, ofttimes it befalleth a man, when he goeth forth to pray and findeth himself naked, indevout, slothful, and hardened in spirit; but, nevertheless, let him gird himself, for love of the Lord, and go forth to the battle of prayer; and then our good King and Lord, beholding the wrestling of his knight, giveth him fervent devotion and good will by the hands of his ministering angels. Some time this befalleth: a man setteth about some great work of heavy labour, as to clear and till the ground, or a vineyard, that in due season he may be able to gather the fruit thereof. And many men, because of the great labour and the many toils, grow a-weary and repent them of the work they have begun; but if a man sweat and toil till the time of harvest, then he forgetteth all his heaviness; he is consoled and glad, beholding the fruit he shall enjoy. Even so, a man that is strong under temptations shall attain to many consolations; for after tribulation, saith St. Paul, cometh consolation and the crown of eternal life: and not only in heaven shall the reward be given to them that resist temptation, but also in this life, even as the psalmist saith, 'Lord, in the multitude of my temptations and my sorrows thy comforts delight my soul;' so that the greater the temptation and the fight, the more glorious shall be the crown." A friar asked counsel of Friar Giles touching a temptation, saying, "O father, I am tempted by two sore temptations: one is, that when I do some good thing, anon I am tempted by vainglory; the other is, when I work any evil I fall into such sadness and such dejection that I well-nigh sink into despair." Whereto Friar Giles answered, "My brother, well dost thou and wisely to grieve for thy sin, but I counsel thee to grieve temperately and discreetly, and ever shouldst thou remember that God's mercy is greater than thy sin. But if, in His infinite mercy, God accepteth the repentance of a man that is a great sinner and one that sinneth wilfully, when he repents, thinkest thou this good God will forsake the good sinner that sinneth against his will, when he is contrite and repentant? I counsel thee, also, faint not in well-doing through fear of vainglory; for if a man said, when he should sow his seed, 'I will not sow, for if I were to sow, haply the birds would come and eat thereof'; and, if saying thus, he sowed not his seed, of a surety he would gather no corn that year. But if he sowed his seed, albeit the birds did eat of that seed, yet the labourer would reap the greater part; even so a man, assailed by vainglory, if he do good not for the sake of vainglory, but ever fighteth against it, I say he shall not lose the merit of the good he hath done, because he is tempted." A friar said to Friar Giles, "It is told that St. Bernard once recited the seven penitential psalms with such peace of mind and such devotion that he thought of naught save the proper meaning of the aforesaid psalms." Whereto Friar Giles thus made answer, "My brother, I deem there is much more prowess in a lord that holdeth his castle when it is besieged and assaulted by his enemies, defending it so valiantly that he letteth not one of his enemies enter therein, than there is in one that liveth in peace and hath no enemy."

X. *Chapter of holy penitence.*

A man ought ever to afflict himself much and mortify his body, and suffer willingly every injury, tribulation, anguish, sorrow, shame, contempt, reproach, adversity, and persecution, for love of our good Lord and Master, Jesus Christ, who gave us the example in Himself; for from the first day of His glorious Nativity, until His most holy Passion, He ever endured anguish, tribulation, sorrow, contempt, pain, and persecution, solely for our salvation. Therefore, if we would attain to a state of grace, above all things it is necessary that we walk, as far as lieth in us, in the paths and in the footsteps of our good Master, Jesus Christ. A secular once asked of Friar Giles, saying, "Father, in what way can we men in the world attain to a state of grace?" Whereto Friar Giles answered, "My brother, a man ought first to grieve for his sins, with great contrition of heart, and then he should confess to the priest with bitterness and sorrow of heart, accusing himself sincerely, without concealment and without excuse: then he must fulfil the penance perfectly that is given and laid upon him by his confessor. Likewise, he must guard himself against every vice and every sin, and against every occasion of sin; and also he must exercise himself in good and virtuous works before God and towards his neighbour; and, doing these things, a man shall attain to a state of grace and of virtue. Blessed is that man that hath continual sorrow for his sins, bewailing them ever, day and night, in bitterness of heart, solely for the offences he hath done to God! Blessed is the man that hath ever before the eyes of his mind the afflictions and the pains and the sorrows of Jesus Christ, and that for love of Him neither desireth nor receiveth any temporal consolation in this bitter and stormy world, until he attain to that heavenly consolation of life eternal, where all his desires shall be fully satisfied with gladness."

XI. *Chapter of holy prayer.*

Prayer is the beginning, middle, and end of all good: prayer illumines the soul, and through prayer the soul distinguishes good from evil. Every sinful man ought to make this prayer with a fervent heart, every day unceasingly; to wit, let him pray humbly to God to give him a perfect knowledge of his own misery and of his sins and of the blessings he hath received, and doth receive, from this good God. But the man that knoweth not how to pray, how shall he know God? All those that would be saved, if they are persons of true understanding, above all things it is necessary that they be at last converted to holy prayer. Friar Giles said, "If a man had a son, guilty of so many offences that he was condemned to death, or to be banished from the city, of a surety this man would be very diligent, and strive with all his might, both day and night, and at every hour, to obtain pardon for this his son, and save him from death or banishment, making earnest prayers and supplications, and giving presents or paying fines, to the uttermost of his means, both of himself or through his friends and kinsfolk. Therefore, if a man do this for his son that is mortal, how much more diligent ought a man to be in beseeching God, by his own prayers and through the prayers of good men in this world, and through His saints in the other world, for his own soul that is immortal, when she is banished from the celestial city, or doomed to everlasting death for sin and wickedness." A friar said to Friar Giles, "Father, methinks a man ought to grieve much, and be exceeding sorrowful, when he cannot have the grace of devotion in his prayers." Whereto Friar Giles answered, "My brother, I counsel thee, go very gently about thy business; for if thou hadst a little good wine in a cask, and in that cask the lees were still below this good wine, of a surety thou wouldst not shake or move that cask about, lest thou mingle the good wine with the lees. And so I say: as long as prayer is not free from all carnal and sinful lust it shall receive no divine consolation; for that prayer which is mingled with the lees of fleshly lusts is not clear in the sight of God. Therefore, a man ought to strive, with all his might, to free himself from all lees of vicious lusts, in order that his prayers be pure in the sight of God, and that he receive devotion and divine consolation therefrom." A friar asked Friar Giles, saying, "Father, wherefore doth this thing come to pass: that when a man is worshipping God he is more sorely tempted, assailed, and troubled in his mind than at any other time?" Whereto Friar Giles thus answered, "When any man hath a suit to further before a judge, and he goeth to plead his own cause, as 'twere asking counsel and aid, and his adversary heareth this, doth he not straightway appear before the judge and oppose and gainsay the petition of that man, and so give him great hindrance, as 'twere disproving all he said? Even so it befalleth when a man goeth forth to pray; forasmuch as he asketh God's help in his cause, straightway his adversary, the devil, appeareth with his temptations and maketh great resistance and opposition, and striveth, with all his might and cunning and devices, to hinder this prayer, so that it be not acceptable in God's sight, and that the man may have neither merit nor consolation from his prayers. And this we can see clearly, for when we speak of worldly things, then do we suffer no temptation nor distraction of mind, but if we go to prayer to delight and comfort the soul with God, anon we feel our soul smitten with divers arrows, to wit, divers temptations, which the devils put in our way to warp our minds, in order that the soul have neither joy nor consolation from those things that the said soul hath uttered to God." Friar Giles said that a prayerful man was like unto a good knight at battle, who, albeit he were pierced or smitten by his enemy, departeth not straightway from the battle, but rather resisteth manfully to gain the victory over his enemy, in order that the victory won, he may be comforted and rejoice in that victory; but if he departed from the battle when he was smitten or wounded, of a surety he would suffer confusion and shame and dishonour. And so should we do likewise; to wit, never depart from prayer for any temptation, but rather resist stoutly; for blessed is the man that endureth temptations, as the Apostle saith, for by overcoming them he shall receive the crown of eternal life; but if a man cease from prayer because of temptations, of a surety he shall suffer confusion, defeat, and discomfiture at the hands of his enemy, the devil." A friar said to Friar Giles, "Father, I have seen certain men that have received from God the grace of devotion and tears in their prayers, and none of these graces can I feel when I pray unto God." Whereto Friar Giles answered, "My brother, I counsel thee, labour faithfully and humbly in thy prayers, for the fruits of the earth are not to be had without much toil and labour beforehand; and even after this labour the desired fruit followeth not straightway, before the time and season are come: even so God giveth not this grace forthwith to a prayerful man until the convenient time be come, and the mind be purged from every carnal affection and sin. Therefore, my brother, labour humbly in thy prayer; for God, who is all-good and all-gracious, knoweth all things and discerneth the better way: when the time and the season are come, He, of His loving-kindness, will give much fruit of consolation." Another friar said to Friar Giles, "What art thou doing, Friar Giles? What art thou doing?" He answered, "I am doing ill." And that friar said, "What ill art thou doing?" Then Friar Giles turned to another friar and bespake him thus, "Tell me, my friar, who thinkest thou is the readier, our God to grant us His grace, or we to receive it?" And that friar answered, "Of a surety, God is more ready to give us His grace than we are to receive it." And then Friar Giles said, "Then do we well?" And that friar said, "Nay, we do ill." And then Friar Giles turned to the first friar and said, "Behold, friar, it is clearly shown that we do ill; and what I answered was true, to wit, that I am doing ill." Said Friar Giles, "Many works are commended and praised by Holy Scripture, to wit, the works of mercy and other holy works; but when the Lord spake of prayer, He spake thus, 'Your heavenly Father seeketh and desireth of men that they worship Him on earth in spirit and in truth.'" Friar Giles said likewise that the true religious are like unto wolves; for they seldom issue forth in public places save for hard necessity, and incontinently do strive to return to their hiding-place without much converse or dwelling with men. Good works adorn the soul, but, above all other works, prayer adorns and illumines the soul. A friar, the companion and familiar of Friar Giles, said, "Father, wherefore goest thou not sometimes to discourse of the things of God, and teach and win the salvation of Christian souls?" Whereto Friar Giles answered, "My brother, I desire to fulfil my duty to my neighbour with humility and without hurt to my soul, I mean by prayer." And that friar said to him, "At least if thou went sometimes to visit thy kinsfolk!" And Friar Giles answered, "Knowest thou not that Christ saith in the gospel, 'Every one that hath forsaken father or mother, or brethren or sisters, or possessions, for My name's sake, shall receive a hundredfold.'" Again he said, "A man of noble birth entered the Order, whose riches were worth perchance sixty thousand pounds: therefore, great rewards await them that forsake great riches, for love of God; since God giveth them a hundredfold more. But blind are we that when we behold any man virtuous and gracious in the sight of God, we cannot understand his perfection because of our own imperfection and blindness. But if a man were truly spiritual, hardly would he desire to behold or to hear any man save for great necessity; for the truly spiritual man desireth ever to dwell apart from men, and to be one with God through contemplation." Then said Friar Giles to another friar, "Father, fain would I know, what is contemplation?" And that friar said, "Father, that truly know not I." And then Friar Giles said, "Methinks the high grace of contemplation is a divine flame and a sweet emanation of the Holy Ghost, and a rapture and an exaltation of the mind, which is inebriated in the contemplation of that ineffable savour of divine sweetness; 'tis a sweet and peaceful and gentle delight of the soul that is lifted up and rapt in great marvel at the glory of supernal and celestial things—a burning inward sense of celestial and unspeakable glory."

XII. *Chapter of holy spiritual prudence.*

O servant of the King of heaven, thou that wouldst learn the mysteries and the profitable and virtuous lessons of holy spiritual doctrine, open well the ears of the understanding of thy soul, and receive with thy heart's desire, and carefully keep in the chamber of thy memory, the precious treasure of these doctrines and precepts and spiritual admonitions which I declare to thee: thereby shalt thou be illumined and guided on thy journey—the journey of the spiritual life—and shalt be defended from the wicked and cunning assaults of thine enemies, real and shadowy, and shalt walk securely, with humble boldness, voyaging on this stormy sea, to wit, of this present life, until thou come to the longed-for haven of salvation. Therefore, my son, hearken and mark well what I say unto thee. If thou wouldst see well, pluck out thine eyes and be blind; if thou wouldst hear well, be deaf; if thou wouldst speak well, be dumb; if thou wouldst walk well, stand still and walk with thy mind; if thou wouldst work well, cut off thy hands and work with thy heart; if thou wouldst love well, hate thyself; if thou wouldst live well, mortify thyself; if thou wouldst gain well and grow rich, lose and be poor; if thou wouldst enjoy well and take thine ease, afflict thyself and be ever sorrowful; if thou wouldst dwell secure, be ever afeard and in dread of thyself; if thou wouldst be exalted and have great honour, abase and decry thyself; if thou wouldst be held in great reverence, despise thyself and do reverence unto them that revile thee and spitefully use thee; if thou wouldst have good always, suffer ill always; if thou wouldst be blessed, desire that all men curse thee and speak evil of thee; if thou wouldst have true and everlasting peace, labour and afflict thyself, and desire every temporal affliction. O, how great is the wisdom that knoweth and doeth these things! But because these things are great and very lofty, therefore are they vouchsafed by God to few men. But, verily, whoso striveth well after all the aforesaid things, and doeth them, I say he will need to go neither to Bologna nor to Paris to learn other theology; for if a man lived a thousand years, and had naught to do with outward things and naught to say with his tongue, I say he would have enough to do with the inward discipline of his heart, labouring within him for the purgation and ruling and justification of his mind and of his soul. A man should neither desire, nor behold, nor hear, nor discourse of aught save in so far as it may be profitable to his soul. The man that knoweth not himself is not known; therefore, woe unto us that receive gifts and graces from the Lord and understand them not; but woe, and greater woe, unto those that neither receive them nor know them, nor even care to gain them or possess them! Man that is made in the image of God changeth even as he willeth, but the good God never changeth.

XIII. *Chapter of profitable and unprofitable knowledge.*

The man that would know much, should work much and humble himself much, abasing himself and bowing down his head, so that his belly goeth on the ground: then the Lord will give him much knowledge and wisdom. The highest wisdom is to be steadfast in well-doing, working virtuously and well, guarding oneself against every sin and every occasion of sin, ever meditating on the judgments of God. Friar Giles said, on a time, to one that would go to the schools to get knowledge, "My brother, wherefore wouldst thou go to the schools? I would have thee know that the sum of all knowledge is to fear and to love: let these two things suffice thee. For sufficient for a man's works shall his knowledge be, and no more. Vex thee not overmuch for the profit of others, but ever strive and further and do those things that are profitable to thyself; for ofttimes this befalleth: we would gain much knowledge to help others and little to help ourselves. I say unto thee, the word of God is not in the speaker, nor in the hearer, but in the true worker. Men there have been that knew not how to swim and entered the water to help those that were drowning; and it came to pass that they were all drowned together. If thou canst not save thine own soul, how shalt thou save the souls of thy neighbours? If thou canst not profit thyself, how shalt thou profit another? for it cannot be that thou lovest another's soul more than thine own. The preacher of God's word ought to be the standard-bearer, the torch and the mirror of the people. Blessed is the man that in such wise guideth others in the way of salvation and himself ceaseth not to walk in that way of salvation! Blessed is the man that in such wise inviteth others to run and himself ceaseth not to run! But more blessed is he that in such wise aideth others to gain and be rich, and himself ceaseth not to gain riches. I believe the good preacher admonishes and preaches more unto himself than to others. Methinks, the man that would convert and draw sinners to the paths of God should ever fear lest he be evilly perverted by them and drawn astray to the paths of sin and of the devil and of hell."

XIV. *Chapter of good and of evil speaking.*

The man that uttereth good words and profitable to souls is verily as 'twere the mouth of the Holy Spirit; and likewise the man that uttereth evil and unprofitable words is, of a surety, the mouth of the devil. Whenever good and spiritual men are assembled to discourse together they ought ever to speak of the beauty of virtue, in order that virtue be more pleasing to them, and that they may delight the more therein; for by delighting and taking more pleasure in virtue, the more they will be disciplined therein, and by exercising themselves therein they will be kindled to greater love thereof; and by that unceasing love and exercise of virtue, and by pleasure therein, they will ever rise to more fervent love of God and to a higher state of the soul; for which cause more gifts and more divine graces shall be vouchsafed to them by the Lord. The more a man is tempted the greater need hath he to discourse of the holy virtues; for even as a man ofttimes falleth lightly into sinful deeds through evil and sinful talk, so ofttimes through discoursing of virtue a man is lightly led and disposed to the holy works of virtue. But how shall we tell of the good that cometh from virtue? For it is so exceeding great that we cannot speak worthily of its marvellous and infinite excellence. And also, what shall we say of the evil and everlasting torments that proceed from sin? For it is an evil so great, and an abyss so deep, that it is impossible for us to comprehend or to fathom it, or, in sooth, to speak thereof. I deem it no lesser virtue to know how to keep silence well than to know how to speak well: therefore methinks a man hath need of a neck as long as the crane's, so that when he would speak, his words should pass through many joints before they came to his mouth, I mean that when a man would speak, it were needful that he should think and think again, and examine and discern right well, the how and the why, the time and the manner, and the condition of his hearers and the effect on his own self and his purpose and motives.

XV. *Chapter of good perseverance.*

What doth it profit a man to fast much and pray and give alms and afflict himself with the overpowering sense of heavenly things if he come not to the blessed haven of the salvation he desireth; to wit, the haven of good and steadfast perseverance? Some time this cometh to pass: a certain ship, very fair and mighty and strong and new, and filled with great riches, is seen on the seas; and it befalleth that through some tempest, or through the fault of the helmsman, this ship perisheth and is wrecked, and miserably sunk, and cometh not to the desired haven. What then availed all her beauty and goodness and riches since she perished thus miserably in the great waters of the sea? And, likewise, on a time, some little ship and old appeareth on the sea, with small merchandise; but having a good and skilful helmsman, she weathers the storm and escapeth from the deep waters of the sea and cometh to the desired haven: and so it befalleth men in this stormy sea of the world. Therefore, said Friar Giles, a man ought ever to fear; and albeit he abide in great prosperity, or in high estate, or in great dignity, or in great perfection, if he have not a good helmsman, to wit, a wise rule over himself, he may miserably perish in the deep waters of sin. Therefore, above all things, perseverance is needful for well-doing, as the Apostle saith, "Not he that beginneth, but he that persevereth to the end shall win the crown." When a tree springeth up, it doth not straightway wax great; and after it hath become great, it doth not forthwith yield fruit; and when it beareth fruit, not all that fruit cometh to the mouth of the lord of that tree; for much of that fruit falleth on the ground, or rots, or is spoiled; and such as this is eaten by the beasts: but yet, persevering until the proper season, the lord of that tree gathereth the greater part of the fruit thereof. Again, Friar Giles said, "What would it profit me if I tasted full a hundred years of the kingdom of heaven, if thereafter I came not to a good end?" And also he said, "I deem that these are the two greatest graces and gifts of God to him that can gain them in this life, to wit, to persevere with love in the service of God and ever guard himself from falling into sin."

XVI. *Of the true religious life.*

Friar Giles was wont to say, speaking of himself, "I would rather, as a religious in the Order, have a little of the grace of

God than I would, as a secular, living in the world, have many graces of God; for many more are the perils and hindrances in the world, and much less the healing and the help than in the religious life." Friar Giles also said, "Methinks the sinful man is more afraid of his good than he is of his hurt and his evil; for he fears to enter the religious life and do penance, but fears not to offend God and injure his own soul by remaining in the hard and stubborn world and in the filthy mire of his own sins, awaiting his eternal doom at last." A secular asked Friar Giles, saying, "Father, what dost thou counsel me to do? Shall I enter the religious life, or shall I remain in the world and do good works?" Whereto Friar Giles answered, "My brother, if any needy man knew that a great treasure lay hidden in the common field, of a surety he would not ask counsel of any man to know whether it were good to dig it out and carry it to his own house; how much the more ought a man to strive and make haste, with all care and diligence, to search out that heavenly treasure which is found in the holy orders of religion, and in spiritual communities, without so much asking of counsel?" And that secular, when he heard this answer, anon gave away all he possessed to the poor, and thus, stripped of everything, entered the Order. Friar Giles was wont to say that many men entered the religious life and yet put not those things into practice and into operation that pertain to the perfect state of the holy religious life; but that such as these are like unto that ploughman that armed himself with the arms of Roland, and knew not how to fight or wield them. Not every man knoweth how to ride a restive and vicious horse, and if he yet bestrode it, perchance he would know not how to save himself from falling when the horse ran or reared. Again, Friar Giles said, "I deem it no great thing that a man may know how to enter the court of the king, nor do I esteem it a great thing that a man may know how to win some of the king's graces or favours; but the great thing is, that he know how to stand well, and abide in, and frequent the king's court, while persevering in prudence according to what is meet and fitting. The state of the court of that great King of heaven, is the holy religious life, wherein is no great labour to enter and receive some gifts and graces from God; but the great thing is that a man shall know how to live well and persevere therein discreetly, even unto death." Yet again, Friar Giles said, "I would rather live in the world, and hope and desire unceasingly and devoutly to enter the religious life, than be clothed in the habit of the holy religious life without the practice of virtuous works, and continue in sloth and negligence. Therefore, the religious ought ever to strive to live well and virtuously, knowing that he cannot live in any other state than in his professed vows." Once Friar Giles said, "Methinks the Order of the friars minor was truly sent of God for the profit and the edification of the people; but woe unto us friars if we be not such men as we ought to be. Of a surety, in this life no more blessed men than we could be found; for he is holy that followeth holiness, and he is truly good that walketh in the way of the good, and he is rich that goeth the way of the rich; for the Order of the friars minor, more than any other Order, followeth the footsteps and the ways of the best, the richest, and the holiest that ever was or ever shall be, to wit, our Lord Jesus Christ.

XVII. *Chapter of holy obedience.*

The more bound under the yoke of holy obedience the religious is, for love of God, the greater fruit of himself he will yield unto God; and the more he is subject to his superior, for God's honour, the more free and more cleansed shall he be from his sins. The truly obedient religious is like unto a knight well armed and well horsed that breaks fearlessly through the ranks of his enemies and scatters them, because none of them can do him hurt. But he that obeys with murmurings, and as one driven, is like unto an unarmed and ill-horsed knight, that when he joineth battle shall be dragged to the ground by his enemies and wounded and taken by them and sometimes cast into prison and slain. The religious that would live according to the determination of his own will, showeth that he would build a perpetual habitation in the abyss of hell. When the ox putteth his neck under the yoke, then he plougheth the earth well, so that it bringeth forth good fruit in due season; but when the ox goeth wandering around, the ground is left untilled and wild, and giveth not fruit in its season. Even so the religious that bendeth his neck under the yoke of obedience yieldeth much fruit to the Lord God in its time; but he that is not obedient with a good heart to his superior, is barren and wild and without any fruit from his vows. Wise and great-hearted men bend their necks readily, without fear and without doubt, under the yoke of holy obedience; but foolish and faint-hearted men strive to wrest their necks from under the yoke of holy obedience, and then would obey no creature. I deem it a greater perfection in the servant of God to obey his superior with a pure heart, for reverence and love of God, than it would be to obey God in person if He commanded him: for he that is obedient to the Lord's vicar would surely obey sooner the Lord Himself if He commanded him. Methinks also that if any man having the grace of speaking with angels had promised obedience to another, and it befell that while he was standing and discoursing with these angels this other man to whom he had promised obedience called him, I say, that straightway he ought to leave his converse with the angels and run to do that obedience, for honour of God. He that hath put his neck under the yoke of holy obedience, and then would draw back his neck from under that obedience, that he might follow a life of greater perfection, I say, that if he be not first perfect in the state of obedience, it is a sign of great pride that lieth hidden in his soul. Obedience is the way that leadeth to every good and every virtue, and disobedience is the way to every evil and every vice.

XVIII. *Chapter of the remembrance of death.*

If a man had the remembrance of his death and of the last eternal judgment and of the pains and the torments of damned souls ever before the eyes of his mind, of a surety, nevermore would the desire come upon him to sin or to offend God. But if it were possible that any man had lived from the beginning of the world, even to the time that now is, and during all this time had endured every adversity, tribulation, pain, affliction, and sorrow, and if he were to die, and his soul should go to receive everlasting reward in heaven, what hurt would all that ill he had endured, in past times, do him? And so, likewise, if a man during all the aforesaid time had had every good thing and every joy and pleasure and consolation the world could give, and then when he died his soul should receive the everlasting pains of hell, what would all the good things he had received, during that past time, profit him? An unstable man said to Friar Giles, "I tell thee, fain would I live much time in this world and have great riches and abundance of all things, and I would be greatly honoured." Whereto Friar Giles answered, "My brother, but if thou wert lord of all the world, and shouldst live therein for a thousand years in every joy and delight and pleasure and temporal consolation, ah, tell me, what reward or what merit wouldst thou expect to have from this thy miserable flesh which thou hadst served and pleased so greatly! I say unto thee, that the man who liveth well in the sight of God, and guardeth him well from offending God, he shall surely receive from God the highest good and an infinite and everlasting reward, and great bounty and great riches, and great honour and long life eternal in that perpetual glory of heaven, whereunto may the good God, our Lord and King Jesus Christ, bring us, to the praise of Jesus Christ and of His poor little one, Francis."

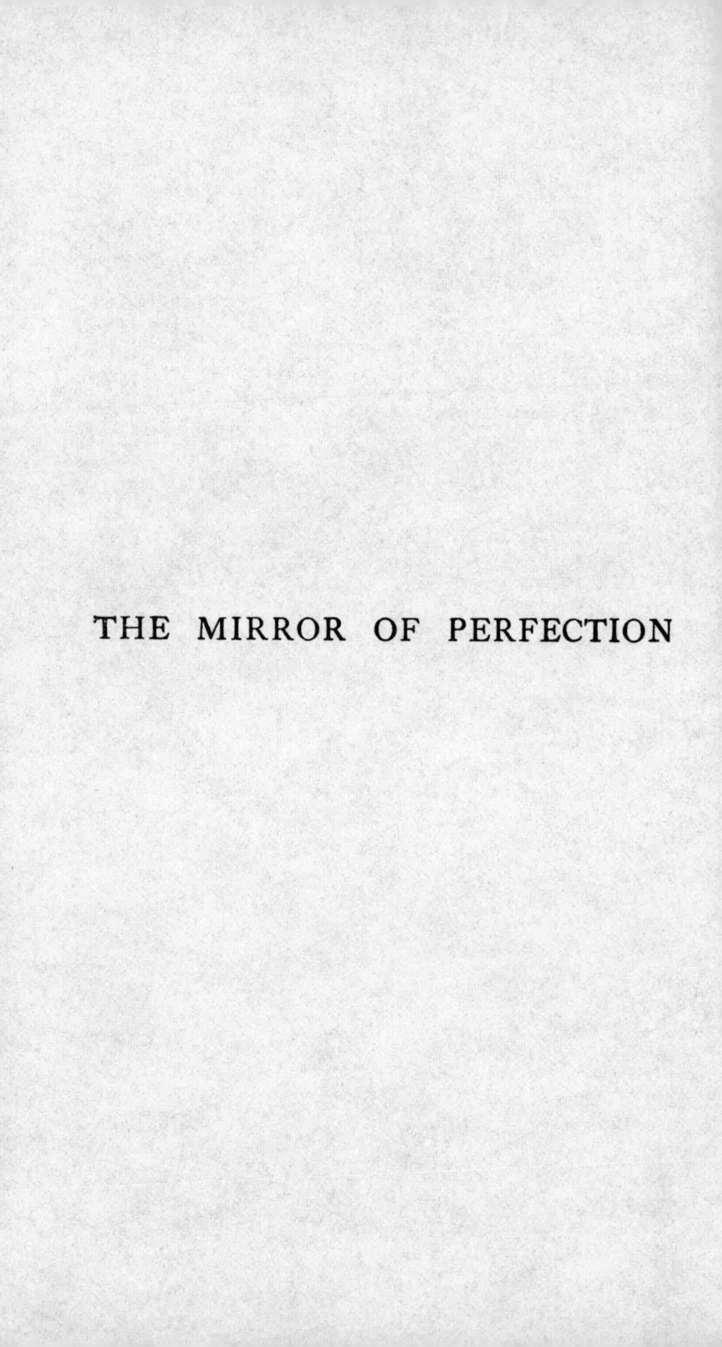

THE MIRROR OF PERFECTION

THE MIRROR OF PERFECTION

SECTION I

This book was compiled as a legend from certain ancient ones which the fellows of blessed Francis wrote and caused to be written in diverse places: and note that blessed Francis made three Rules, namely that which Pope Innocent III. confirmed without a bull. Again, he made another, shorter, namely that which he made on account of the vision revealed to him of the small host he was bidden to make from the fragments offered him and share out to those who would eat, and this Rule was lost, as is told after. Then he made another which Pope Honorius confirmed with a bull, from which Rule many things were removed by the Ministers against the will of blessed Francis as is contained hereafter

CHAPTER I

HOW ST. FRANCIS ANSWERED HIS MINISTERS WHEN THEY WOULD NOT BE BOUND TO OBSERVE THE RULE WHICH HE WAS MAKING

AFTER the second Rule which blessed Francis made had been lost, he went up into a certain mountain with Brother Leo of Assisi and Brother Bonyzo of Bologna to make another Rule, which, by the teaching of Christ, he caused to be written down. But many Ministers being gathered together to Brother Elias (who was the vicar of blessed Francis) said to him, " We have heard that this Brother Francis maketh a new Rule, but we fear lest he make it so harsh that we may not observe it. Therefore we will that thou go to him and say that we will not be bound to that Rule; let him make it for himself and not for us." To whom Brother Elias answered that he would not go without them, and then all went together. And when Brother Elias was near the place where blessed Francis was, Brother Elias called him. To whom answering, and beholding the foresaid Ministers, the blessed Father said, " What would these brethren? " And Brother Elias said, " These are Ministers, who hearing that thou art making a new Rule, and fearing lest thou shouldst make it too harsh, do say and protest that they will not be bound to it; make it for thyself and not for them." Then blessed Francis turned his face to heaven and spoke thus to Christ, " Lord, said I not well to Thee that they would not believe me? " Then all heard the voice of Christ answering in the air, " So do it, there is nought of thine in the Rule, but whatever is there is Mine, and I will that the Rule should thus be observed to the letter, without a gloss, without a gloss! " And He added, " What human weakness can, do I know, and how much I wish to help them; let those therefore who will not obey it, go out from the Order! " Then blessed Francis turned himself to those brethren and said to them, " Will you that I should cause it to be said to you again? " Then the Ministers, looking upon one another, went back confused and terrified.

SECTION II

OF THE PERFECTION OF POVERTY

CHAPTER II

FIRSTLY HOW BLESSED FRANCIS DECLARED THE WILL AND INTENTION WHICH HE HAD FROM THE BEGINNING UNTO THE END, CONCERNING THE OBSERVANCE OF POVERTY

Brother Richard of March, noble by birth and more noble by holiness, whom blessed Francis did love with great affection, on a certain day visited blessed Francis in the palace of the Bishop of Assisi, and amongst other things of which they conversed concerning the state of the Religion and the observance of the Rule, asked him specially of this matter, saying, "Tell me, Father, thy intention which thou hadst from the beginning when thou didst begin to have brethren, and the intention which thou now hast and dost think to have unto the day of thy death, that I may bear witness of thy intention and will, first and last, whether, for example, we friars who be clerks, and have many books, may have them, provided we say that they belong to the Order." Blessed Francis said to him, "I tell thee, Brother, that this was and is my first intention and last desire, if the brethren would have believed me, that no friar should have anything save a robe, as our Rule allows, with a girdle and breeches."

But if any friar should be minded to say, "Why did not blessed Francis in his own time make the Rule and Poverty to be as strictly observed by the friars as he said to Richard, nor command it should thus be observed?" we who were with him answer to this as we have heard from his own mouth, since he himself said these and many other things to the brethren, and also made many of these things to be written in the Rule which he had besought of the Lord with earnest prayer and meditation for the benefit of the Order, affirming them to be altogether according to the will of God; but after he showed these things to the brethren they seemed to them burdensome and not to be borne, not knowing then what things should come to pass in the Order after his death. And because he greatly feared scandal both towards himself and the brethren, he would not strive with them, but suffered, unwillingly, their will, and excused himself before the Lord. But that the word which the Lord had put into his mouth for the benefit of the brethren might not return unto Him empty, he wished to fulfil it in himself that from thence some reward might be obtained from the Lord, and in the end his spirit found rest herein and was consoled.

CHAPTER III

HOW HE ANSWERED A MINISTER WHO WISHED TO HAVE BOOKS WITH HIS LEAVE; AND HOW THE MINISTERS WITHOUT HIS KNOWLEDGE CAUSED THE CHAPTER OF THE PROHIBITIONS OF THE GOSPEL TO BE REMOVED FROM THE RULE

But on a time, when blessed Francis was returned from oversea, a certain Minister was speaking with him of the Chapter of Poverty, wishing to know his will and understanding thereon, and chiefly—for at that time a certain chapter of the Prohibitions of the Holy Gospel was written in the Rule, namely, "Take nothing with ye in the way." And the blessed Father answered, "I understand it thus, that friars should possess naught save a robe with a cord and breeches, as says the Rule, and if they are forced by necessity they may wear sandals." And the Minister said to him, "What shall I do, who have so many books that they be worth more than fifty pounds?" (but this he said for that he would have them with a good conscience, since against it he had owned so many books, knowing that blessed Francis understood the Chapter of Poverty so strictly). And blessed Francis said to him, "I neither will, nor ought, nor can, go against my conscience and the perfection of the Holy Gospel which we have professed." Hearing these things the Minister became sad. But the blessed one, seeing him thus troubled, with great fervour of spirit said to him in the presence of all the brethren, "You would be seen of men as Friars Minor, and be called observants of the Holy Gospel, but for your works you wish to have store-chests!"

Yet though the Ministers knew that according to the Rule friars were bound to observe the Holy Gospel, nevertheless they caused that chapter to be removed from the Rule, "Take nothing with you in the way," believing that therefor they would not be held to the observance of the perfection of the Gospel. Knowing which by the Holy Spirit, blessed Francis said therefore before certain brethren, " The brothers Ministers think to deceive God and me; though they know that all friars are bound to observe the perfection of the Holy Gospel. I will that it be written in the beginning and in the end of the Rule that friars are bound to strictly observe the Holy Gospel of our Lord Jesus Christ; and that the brethren be for ever without excuse, since I have announced and do announce to them those things which the Lord for their and my salvation placed in my mouth. I wish to show it by my works in the presence of God, and with His aid to observe it for ever." Whence he observed to the letter all the Holy Gospel from the first time when brethren began to join themselves to him unto the day of his death.

CHAPTER IV

OF THE NOVICE WHO WOULD FAIN HAVE A PSALTER WITH HIS LEAVE

On another time a certain brother novice who knew how to read the psalter, though not well, obtained from the Minister-General leave to have one; yet, because he heard that blessed Francis wished his brethren not to desire knowledge and books, he was not content to have it without the leave of blessed Francis. When therefore blessed Francis had come to the place where that novice was, the novice said, " Father, it would be a great solace to me to have a psalter, but though the General has conceded it to me, yet I wish to have it, Father, with thy knowledge." To whom the blessed Francis answered, " Charles the Emperor, Roland and Oliver, and all the Paladins and strong men, being mighty in war, chasing the infidels with much travail and sweat to the death, had over them notable victory, and at the last themselves did die in battle, holy martyrs for the faith of Christ; but now there are many who would fain receive honours and human praise for the mere telling of the things which those others did. So also amongst ourselves are many who would fain receive honours and praise by reciting and preaching only the works which the saints did." (As if he would say, " Books and science should not be esteemed, but rather virtuous labours, since knowledge puffeth up, but charity edifieth.") But after a few days, when blessed Francis was sitting at the fire, the same novice spoke to him again of the psalter. And blessed Francis said to him, "After you have a psalter, you will desire and wish to have a breviary. Then you will sit in your chair, like a great prelate, and say to your brother, 'Bring me the breviary'?" So saying, blessed Francis with great fervour of spirit took up some ashes and put them on his head, and drawing his hand over his head in a compass like one who washes the head, said, "I, a breviary, I, a breviary!" And he repeated it thus many times, drawing his hand over his head. And that brother was amazed and ashamed. Afterwards blessed Francis said to him, "Brother, I likewise was tempted to have books, but when I might not know the will of the Lord concerning this, I took up a book wherein the Gospels of the Lord were written, and I prayed the Lord that in the first opening of the book He would show me His will concerning this thing. And when the prayer was finished in the first opening of the book I lighted on that saying of the Holy Gospel: *Unto you it is given to know the mysteries of the Kingdom of God, but unto others in parables*." And he said, "There are so many who willingly rise unto knowledge, that he shall be blessed who makes himself barren for the love of God." But many months having passed, when blessed Francis was at the dwelling of St. Mary of the Porziuncula, near the cell beyond the house in the street, the aforesaid brother spoke again to him of the psalter. To whom blessed Francis said, "Go and do concerning this what thy Minister tells thee." And when he heard this, that brother began to return by the road whence he had come. And blessed Francis remaining in the street began to consider what he had said to that brother, and immediately called after him, saying, "Wait for me, brother, wait!" And he came up to him, and said to him, "Turn back with me, brother, and show me the place where I said unto thee that thou shouldst do in the matter of the psalter as thy Minister should say." When therefore they had arrived at the place, blessed Francis kneeled before that brother, and said, "*Mea culpa*, brother, *mea culpa*, for whosoever will be a Friar Minor should have nothing except a tunic, as the Rule concedes to him, and a cord and breeches, and those who are forced by manifest necessity, sandals." Whence as often as friars came to him to have his counsel on these matters, he used to answer them on this wise, because, as he often used to say, "As much knowledge hath a man as he doth work, and a Religious is as good a speaker as his works proclaim, for the worker is known by his fruit."

CHAPTER V

OF KEEPING POVERTY IN BOOKS AND BEDS AND UTENSILS

THE most blessed Father used to say that we should look for proof and not price in books, edification not ornament. He wished that few be owned and those in common, befitting the poverty and necessity of friars. In beds and bedding so great poverty abounded, that he who had half-worn-out rags over his chaff reputed them mattresses.

He taught further his friars to make their huts poor and their little cabins of wood, not of stone, and he would have them be constructed and built of mean appearance, and not only did he hate pride in dwellings, but also he did much abhor many or choice utensils. He loved that they should preserve in their tables or in their vessels nothing of worldly seeming, by which they should recall the world, so that all things should end in poverty, should sing out to them of their pilgrimage and exile.

CHAPTER VI

HOW HE MADE ALL THE FRIARS DEPART FROM A CERTAIN HOUSE WHICH WAS CALLED THE HOUSE OF THE FRIARS

WHEN he was passing through Bologna he heard that a House of Friars had been newly builded there. And immediately when he had heard that house called the House of the Friars, he turned on his steps and went out of the city, and ordered most strictly that all the friars should depart in haste, and no longer dwell therein. Therefore all the friars went out, so that even the sick did not remain there, but were turned out with the others, until Dom Hugo, Bishop of Ostia, and Legate in Lombardy, publicly announced that the said house belonged to him. And a sick friar who was turned out from that same house bears witness to these things and wrote these words.

CHAPTER VII

HOW HE WOULD FAIN DESTROY A CERTAIN HOUSE WHICH THE FOLK OF ASSISI HAD MADE AT ST. MARY OF THE PORZIUNCULA

When the Chapter-General was drawing near which took place each year at St. Mary of the Porziuncula, the people of Assisi, considering that the friars were daily multiplying, and that every year all were used to assemble together there, although they had but one small cell thatched with straw whose walls were of wattle and mud, having held their council, did in a few days with very great devotion and respect build there a great house of stone and lime, without the consent of blessed Francis, and in his absence. And when the blessed Father returned from a certain province and came thither for the Chapter, he marvelled greatly at that house constructed there, and fearing lest by occasion of that house other friars would cause to be made likewise great houses in the places in which they dwelt and should dwell, and because he wished that place to be the form and example of all other places of the Order, before the Chapter was finished he went up on the roof of that house, and ordered the friars to come up with him, and together with those friars he began to throw down on the ground the laths with which the house had been covered, being fain to destroy it even to the foundations. But certain men-at-arms of Assisi who were there to guard the place on account of the crowds of rabble who had come together to see the Chapter of the Friars, seeing that blessed Francis with other friars wished to pull the house to pieces, forthwith went to him and said, "Brother, this house belongs to the Commune of Assisi, and we be here on the part of that Commune. Whence we forbid thee to destroy our house." Hearing this, blessed Francis said to them, "Therefore if it be yours, I will not touch it." And straightway he and the friars came down from it. (For which cause the folk of the City of Assisi made a law that from that time forth their Podestà, whoever he should be, should cause that house to be repaired. And every year for a long time this law was observed.)

CHAPTER VIII

HOW HE BLAMED HIS VICAR BECAUSE HE WAS MAKING A LITTLE HOUSE TO BE BUILT FOR SAYING THE OFFICE

On another time the Vicar of blessed Francis began to have built in that place a little house where the friars might rest and say their Hours, since for the multitude of friars who came to that place they had no place wherein to say the Office. For all the brethren of the Order came together there, because no one was received into the Order save only there. And now, when the house was complete, blessed Francis returned to that place, and being in that cell heard the noises of those labouring there, and calling to him his companion he asked him what those brethren were doing. To whom his companion told all things as they were. Then forthwith he caused the Vicar to be called, and said to him, " Brother, this place is the form and example of the whole Order, and I would therefore rather that the friars of this place should bear tribulation and inconveniences for the love of the Lord God, and that other friars who come hither should carry away with them a good example of poverty to their own place, than that they should have their consolations fully, and that others should take an example of building in their own places, saying, ' In this place of Blessed Mary of the Porziuncula, which is the chief place of the Order, there are such and so great buildings; we also may well build in our own places.' "

CHAPTER IX

HOW HE WOULD NOT REMAIN IN A SPECIALLY MADE CELL OR IN ONE WHICH WAS CALLED HIS OWN

A certain brother, right spiritual and much familiar with blessed Francis, caused to be made in the hermitage wherein he was staying, a certain cell a little remote, wherein blessed Francis might stay at prayer when he should come thither. But when the holy Father came to that place that friar led him to the cell; to whom said blessed Francis, " This cell is too fair." (But it was only made of planks, rough hewn with an axe and a hatchet.) " If therefore thou wouldst that I should remain there, cause to be made for it a covering within and without, of withies and branches of trees." (For the more poverty stricken were houses and cells, so much the more gladly would he remain there.) Which when that brother had done, blessed Francis remained there for some days. But on a day, when he had gone out of that cell, a certain friar went to see it, and afterward came to the place where blessed Francis was. And when the blessed Father saw him he said to him, " Whence comest thou, brother? " And he said, " I come from thy cell." And blessed Francis said, " For that thou hast called it mine, another shall stay there henceforth, and not I." But we who were with him often heard him saying that word, *The foxes have holes, and the birds of the air have nests, but the Son of Man hath not where to lay His head.* And again he said, " The Lord, when He remained in the open air and fasted forty days and forty nights, did not cause a cell to be made for Him there or a house, but lay under the rocks of the mountains." And therefore by His example he would have neither house nor cell which could be called his own, nor ever did he cause one to be made at all. If sometimes it happened that he said to the brethren, " Go and make ready that cell," he would not afterwards abide in it, because of that saying of the Holy Gospel, *Be ye not anxious*, etc. For even at the time of his death he made it to be written in his will that all the cells and houses of the friars should be of wood and mud only; for the better safeguard of poverty and humility.

CHAPTER X

CONCERNING THE MANNER OF CHOOSING PLACES IN CITIES, AND OF BUILDING IN THEM, ACCORDING TO THE INTENTION OF BLESSED FRANCIS

On a certain time when he was at Siena for the weakness of his eyes, Dom Bonaventure, who gave the land to the brethren on which the friary was built, said to him, " What thinkest thou of this place? " And blessed Francis said to him, " Wilt thou that I tell thee how the dwellings of friars should be built? " He answered, " I do wish it, Father." And the holy Father said, " When friars go to any city where they have no dwelling, and come upon any one willing to give them a place to build a house, and have a garden and all things necessary, they should firstly consider how much land is sufficient for them, having regard always to the poverty and the good example which in all things we are bound to show." (But this he said because he was in no wise willing that friars should possess any places by right of ownership, in the houses or churches or gardens or other things which they used, but should sojourn therein as travellers and pilgrims; and therefore he wished that friars should not be gathered together in great numbers in their dwellings, because it seemed to him difficult to observe poverty in a great multitude. And his intention from the beginning of his conversion even unto the end was that poverty should be altogether observed in all things.) "Having considered therefore the land necessary for a dwelling, the friars should go to the Bishop of the city and say unto him, 'Sir, such an one would give us so much land for the love of God, and for his soul's health, that we may build therein a dwelling. Wherefore we come to you, in the first place, because you are father and lord of souls of all the flock committed unto you, and of all our brethren who shall sojourn in that place; we would fain therefore, with God's blessing and yours, build there.'" (But this he said because the harvest of souls which the friars would fain reap they do better obtain when they are in harmony with the clergy, profiting them even as the lay folk, than by causing them scandal, even though the people should be won thereby.) And he said, "The Lord hath called us to the aid of His faith, and of the clergy and prelates of the Holy Roman Church. And therefore we are bound, as much as we may, always to love and to honour and to reverence them." (For he called them Friars Minor that they should be humble like their name both in example and labour beyond other men of this age.) "And because from the beginning of my conversion He placed in the mouth of the Bishop of Assisi His words, that he should counsel me and well strengthen me in the service of Christ; on account of this and many other excellent things which I behold in prelates, I wish to love and venerate not only the bishops but also the poor priests, and to hold them for my lords."

Then, having received a blessing from the Bishop, let them go and make a great trench in the circuit of the land which they have received for building the dwelling, and let them set there a good hedge as their wall, as a sign of holy poverty and humility. Afterwards let them make poor little houses of wattle and dab, and some little cells in which from time to time the friars may pray and work, for greater seemliness, and to avoid sloth. Let them also build small churches, for they ought not to make great churches, neither to preach to the people, nor for any other reason, since their humility is greater and their example better when they go to other churches to preach. And if at any time prelates and clergy, regular or secular, come to their dwellings; the poor little houses, the little cells, and tiny churches will preach to them, and they will be more edified by these than by words." And he said, "Many times friars build great buildings, breaking our holy poverty, and cause an evil example and a murmuring and sometimes by occasion of a better and more holy dwelling, or of a greater congregation of the people, through their covetousness and avarice they leave their former dwellings or buildings and destroy them and make others great and excessive, whence those who have given their alms there, and others likewise seeing this be scandalised and troubled therefor. For which cause it is better for friars to make small and poor little buildings, observing their profession and giving a good example to their neighbours, than that they should act against their promise, giving to others an evil example. For if the friars should on a time leave a lowly place by occasion of one more fitting, the scandal would be less."

CHAPTER XI

HOW FRIARS, AND ESPECIALLY THE PRELATES AND LEARNED AMONG THEM, WERE CONTRARY TO FRANCIS IN MAKING HUMBLE DWELLINGS AND HABITATIONS

But when blessed Francis had ordered that the friars' churches should be small, and their house be builded only of wattle and dab, in token of holy poverty and humility, wishing this pattern to be set in the dwelling of St. Mary of the Porziuncula, that the houses should be constructed of wood and clay, so that it should be an everlasting memorial to all friars, present and to come, since that it was the first and principal place of the whole Order, certain friars were against him in this matter, saying that in some provinces beams were dearer than stones, so that it seemed not good to them that their houses should be made of wood and clay. But the blessed Father would not contend with them, the more because he was near death and was sore sickening. Wherefore he caused it to be written in his will, "Let friars beware of receiving churches and dwellings and all other buildings which be constructed for them save as becometh holy poverty; living there ever as guests and strangers and pilgrims." But we who were with him when he wrote the Rule and well-nigh all his other writings bear testimony that he made many things to be written in the Rule and in his other writings (wherein many of the friars were against him, notably our prelates and learned folk) which would to-day have been very useful and necessary to the whole Order: but for that he greatly feared scandal, he suffered, though not willingly, the wishes of his brethren. Yet often he was used to say these words, "Woe to those friars who are contrary to me in this matter, which I firmly know to be of the Will of God for the greater usefulness and necessity of the whole Order, though unwillingly I bend myself to their will." Whence often he used to say to us, his fellows, "Herein is my grief and my affliction; that in those things which with much labour of prayer and meditation I obtain of God through His mercy, for the benefit, present and future, of the whole Order, and which I am assured by Him are according to His will, some brethren by the authority of their knowledge and false foresight are against me and make them void, saying, 'These things are to be held and observed, and these not.'"

CHAPTER XII

HOW HE COUNTED IT A THEFT TO GET ALMS OR TO USE THEM BEYOND NEED

BLESSED Francis was used to say these words to his brethren, "I have never been a thief concerning alms, in getting them or using them beyond necessity. Always have I taken less than I needed, lest I should defraud other poor folk of their portion, for to do the contrary would have been theft."

CHAPTER XIII

HOW CHRIST SAID UNTO HIM THAT HE WOULD NOT THAT FRIARS SHOULD OWN AUGHT, NEITHER IN COMMON NOR IN SPECIAL

WHEN the Ministers would have persuaded him that he should allow something to the friars in common at the least, so that the multitude should have that to which it might have recourse, blessed Francis called upon Christ in prayer and took counsel with Him thereon. Who straightway answered him, saying, "I confer all things in general and in special; I shall always be ready to provide for this family, however much it may increase, and ever will I cherish it as long as it shall hope in Me."

CHAPTER XIV

OF HIS HORROR OF MONEY, AND HOW HE PUNISHED A FRIAR FOR TOUCHING IT

As a true friend and imitator of Christ, Francis, despising perfectly all things which are of this world, did above all things execrate money; and by word and example urged his brethren to flee it as it were the devil. For this maxim had been given by him to the friars, that they should measure with one price of love, dung and money. Now it happened on a day that a certain layman entered the church of St. Mary of the Porziuncula to pray, and put some money for an offering near the cross, which when he had departed, a certain friar taking innocently in his hand, threw into the window. But when this was told to blessed Francis, that friar seeing himself taken in a fault, sought pardon, and throwing himself on the ground, offered himself to punishment. The holy Father reproved him, and very severely blamed him for moving the money, and bade him lift the money from the window with his mouth, and convey it without the hedge of the dwelling, and put it with his own mouth on the dung of an ass. And all they that did see and hear were filled with very great fear, and from that time forth did despise money more than the dung of an ass, and daily were they animated with new examples to contemn it altogether.

CHAPTER XV

OF AVOIDING SOFTNESS AND A MULTITUDE OF TUNICS, AND OF PATIENCE IN NECESSITY

This man, being clothed with virtue from on high, was warmed more within by a divine, than without by a bodily garment. He execrated those in the Order who were clad in threefold garments, and those who used softer clothing than was needful. But he was used to say that a necessity pointed out by will only and not by reason was a sign of a dead spirit, "For with lukewarm spirit and one cooling from grace, little by little flesh and blood must seek their own." And he used to say, "For what remaineth when the wish for spiritual delight is wanting, except that the flesh should turn to its own? And when animal appetite pleadeth the article of necessity, then the sense of the flesh fashioneth the conscience. But if true necessity is on my brother, and straightway he maketh haste to satisfy it, what reward shall he receive? For an occasion of merit hath arisen, but he hath studiously proved that it displeased him. For not to bear patiently those wants is nothing other than to seek Egypt again." Never on any account would he that friars should have more than two tunics, though these he used to allow to be lined with pieces sewn together. He was accustomed to say that choice cloths were horrible, and he used to find fault very bitterly with those contrary to him, and that he might excite such by his own example, he was always used to sew rough sack upon his own tunic. Whence even in death he ordered his burial tunic to be covered with sackcloth. But to those friars whom infirmity or any other necessity compelled, he allowed another soft tunic next the skin, but yet so that outwardly roughness and vileness should always be preserved in their bearing. For he was accustomed to say with very great grief, "Now shall rigour be so much relaxed and sloth shall rule, that the sons of a beggar father shall not be ashamed to wear even scarlet cloth, its colour only being changed."

CHAPTER XVI

HOW HE WOULD NOT SATISFY HIS OWN BODY

But when blessed Francis was staying at the hermitage of St. Eleutherius, over against Rieti, on account of the great cold he lined his tunic and the tunic of his fellow Richer with some patches (because of custom he carried but one tunic), so that his body thence began to be some little cherished. And a little after when he had returned from prayer, he said with great joy to his fellow, "It behoves me to be the form and example of all the friars, and therefore though it be necessary to my body to have a lined tunic, yet must I consider my other brethren to whom the same is necessary, and who perchance have it not and cannot have it. Whence it behoves me to consider them, and bear the necessities they bear, that seeing this in me, they may be strong to suffer with great patience." But how many and how great necessities he denied his body that he might give a good example to his brethren, and that they might more patiently bear their needs, we who were with him can neither by words or by writing set forth. For after the friars began to be multiplied he set his chief and highest study in this, to teach his brethren rather by works than by words what they had to do or avoid.

CHAPTER XVII

HOW HE WAS ASHAMED TO SEE ANY ONE POORER THAN HIMSELF

ONCE when he had come on a certain poor man, considering his poverty, he said to his fellow, "The poverty of that man brings great shame upon us, and much rebukes ours. For very great shame it is to me when I find any one poorer than I am: since I have chosen holy poverty for my Lady, and for my spiritual and bodily riches: and this saying has gone out into the whole world, that I have professed poverty before God and man."

CHAPTER XVIII

HOW HE INDUCED AND TAUGHT THE FIRST FRIARS TO GO AND SEEK ALMS

WHEN blessed Francis first began to have friars he rejoiced so much at their conversion, and that God had given to him a goodly fellowship, and loved and venerated them so much, that he did not bid them go for alms, and the more because it seemed to him that they were ashamed to go, for which reason their father went alone for alms. But when he was greatly fatigued by this, especially because he was well nurtured while he was in the world, and feeble of nature, and by too great abstinence and affliction up to that time was still more weakened, and considering that he could not bear such labour alone, and that they themselves were called to it, though they were ashamed to do it, because they did not yet fully know nor were they so discreet as to say, "We also wish to go seek alms." Therefore he said to them, "Dearest brethren and my little children, be not ashamed to go, for this is our heritage which our Lord Jesus Christ acquired and left to us and to all who wish by His example to live in holy poverty. In truth I say to you, that many of the more noble and more holy of this world shall come to this congregation, and shall hold it for great honour and grace to go seek alms. Go, therefore, confident in mind and rejoicing with the benediction of God for alms; and ye ought the more willingly and rejoicingly to go for alms, than he who for one piece of money should return an hundred pence, since ye offer to them from whom you seek an alms the love of God, saying, 'For the love of God do us an alms-deed, in comparison with Whom heaven and earth are as nought.'" But because the brethren were so few, he could not send them two by two, but sent them one by one through villages and towns. And so it was that when they returned with the gifts which they had found, each of them showed to blessed Francis his alms which he had collected. And one used to say to another, "I have received more alms than thou." And at this time the blessed Father was rejoiced, seeing them so merry and jocund. And from that time forward each of them more willingly sought leave to go beg alms.

CHAPTER XIX

HOW HE WOULD NOT THAT FRIARS SHOULD TAKE THOUGHT AND BE SOLICITOUS FOR THE MORROW

AT that same time, when blessed Francis was living with the brethren whom he then had, he lived in such poverty with them, that they observed the Holy Gospel in and through all things to the letter, from that day in which the Lord revealed to him that he and his brethren should live according to the form of the Holy Gospel. Whence he forbade the brother who used to cook for the friars to put dried beans in warm water when they were to be given to the friars to eat on the following day, as the custom is, so that they might observe that saying of the Holy Gospel, *Take no thought for the morrow.* And so that brother put off setting them to soften till after Matins, because by then the day in which they were to be eaten had begun. (On account of which many friars observed this rule in many places for a long time and would neither ask nor accept more alms than were necessary to them for one day; and this especially in cities.)

CHAPTER XX

HOW BY WORD AND EXAMPLE HE REBUKED THE FRIARS WHO HAD PREPARED A SUMPTUOUS TABLE ON CHRISTMAS DAY

When a certain Minister of the friars had come to blessed Francis to celebrate the feast of Christmas with him in the friars' dwelling at Rieti, the friars, because of the Minister and the feast, laid out the table a little worshipfully and choicely on that Christmas Day, putting on fair and white napery and glass vessels. But the blessed Father coming down from his cell to eat, saw the tables placed on high, and so choicely laid out. Then forthwith he went secretly, and took the staff and wallet of a certain poor man who had come thither that day, and calling to him with a low voice one of his fellows, went out to the door of the dwelling, the brethren of the house not knowing of it. But his fellow remained inside near the door. The friars in the meantime had entered to the table. For the blessed Father had ordered that the friars should not wait for him, when he did not come straightway at meal-time. And when he had stood a little while outside, he knocked at the door, and forthwith his fellow opened to him, and coming with his wallet behind his back and his stick in his hand, he went to the door of the room in which the friars were eating like a pilgrim and a pauper, and called out, saying, "For the love of the Lord God, give an alms to this poor and infirm pilgrim." But the Minister and the other friars knew him straightway. And the Minister answered him, "Brother, we also be poor, and since we be many, the alms we have be necessary to us. But for the love of that Lord Whom thou hast named, enter the house, and we will give you of the alms which the Lord hath given to us." And when he had entered and stood before the table of the friars, the Minister gave him the platter in which he was eating, and bread likewise. And humbly accepting it he sat down next the fire in the presence of the friars sitting at the table. And sighing, he said to the friars, "When I saw the table worshipfully and sumptuously laid out, I thought within myself it was not the table of poor religious who daily go from door to door for alms. For it becomes us, dearest, more than other religious to follow the example of the humility and poverty of Christ, because we are professed and called to this before God and men. Whence it seems that I now sit as a Friar Minor, for the feasts of the Lord and of other saints are rather honoured with the want and poverty by which those saints conquered heaven for themselves, than with the elegance and superfluity by which they be made distant from heaven." But the friars were ashamed, considering he was speaking the pure truth. And some of them began to weep greatly, seeing how he was sitting on the earth, and that he would correct and instruct them in so holy and pure a wise. For he admonished the friars that they should have such humble and decent tables that by them the worldly might be edified. And if any poor man should come and be invited by the friars that he might sit as an equal beside them, and not the poor man on the earth, and the friars on high.

CHAPTER XXI

HOW MY LORD OF OSTIA WEPT AND WAS EDIFIED AT THE POVERTY OF THE FRIARS

My Lord of Ostia, who was afterwards Pope Gregory, when he had come to the chapter of the friars of St. Mary of the Porziuncula, entered the house to see the dormitory of the friars, with many knights and clerks. And seeing that the friars used to lie on the earth, and had nothing under them except a little straw and some pallets as if all broken, and no pillows, he began to weep sore before them all, saying, "Behold, here sleep the friars, but we wretched ones, how many superfluities do we use! What therefore shall happen to us?" Whence he and all others were much edified. Also he saw no table there, for that in that dwelling the friars were accustomed to eat on the earth.

CHAPTER XXII

HOW THE MEN-AT-ARMS WENT SEEKING ALMS FROM DOOR TO DOOR ACCORDING TO THE COUNSEL OF BLESSED FRANCIS

When blessed Francis was in the dwelling of Bagni, over the city of Nocera, his feet began to swell sore by reason of his ailment of dropsy; and sore sick was he there. Which, when they of Assisi had heard, certain men-at-arms came hastily to that place to bring him back to Assisi, fearing lest he should die there, and that others should have his most holy body.

But while they were bringing him home, they rested in a certain fortified place of the lordship of Assisi, to break their fast, and the blessed Father rested in the house of a certain poor man, who willingly received him. But the soldiers went through the place to buy themselves necessaries, and found none. And they returned to blessed Francis, saying to him as if making pastime, ' You, Brother, must give us of your alms, since we can get nothing to eat." And blessed Francis said to them with great fervour of spirit, " You have not found, because you confided in your fly-gods and pence, and not in God. But return now to the houses whither you went seeking to buy, and laying aside your shame, ask alms there for the love of the Lord God; and the Holy Spirit inspiring them, they shall give to you abundantly." They went therefore and sought alms as the blessed Father said to them, and those from whom they sought alms gave to them joyfully and with abundance of the things which they had. And knowing this to have happened to them as by a miracle, the soldiers praising God returned with great joy to blessed Francis.

Thus verily the blessed Father held it for great nobility and dignity before God and the world, to seek alms for the love of the Lord God; because all things which the Father of Heaven had created for the use of man on account of His beloved Son are granted freely to the worthy and the unworthy alike by charity since their sin. For he was wont to say that the servant of God ought more willingly and joyfully to seek alms for the love of the Lord God, than he who of his own bounty and courtesy should go, saying, " Whoever shall give to me a coin worth one single penny, I will give to them one thousand marks of gold." " For the servant of God when seeking an alms offers the love of God to those from whom he begs, in comparison with which reward all things which are in heaven and in earth are nothing." Whence before the friars were multiplied, and even after they were multiplied, when they went through the world preaching and were invited by any one, however noble and rich, to eat and guest with them, always at the hour of eating they were accustomed to go for alms before they would go to his house, on account of the good example of the brethren and the dignity of the Lady Poverty. And many times he who had invited him would say to him that he ought not to go, to whom he answered, " I will not put off my royal dignity and heirship, and my profession and that of my brethren, namely, to go for alms from door to door." And sometimes he who had invited him used to go with him himself, and took to him the alms which blessed Francis obtained, and on account of his devotion kept them for relics. He who has written this saw this many times, and bears testimony concerning these things.

CHAPTER XXIII

HOW HE WENT BEGGING BEFORE HE WOULD GO IN TO THE TABLE OF THE CARDINAL

On a certain time when the blessed Father had visited my Lord of Ostia (who was afterwards Pope Gregory), at the hour of meals he went as if by stealth for alms from door to door. And when he had returned, my Lord of Ostia had already gone in to table with many knights and nobles. But blessed Francis approaching placed those alms which he had received on the table beside him, for he would that the blessed Father should always sit near him. And the Cardinal was a little ashamed because he went for alms and put them on the table, but he said nothing to him then on account of his guests. And when blessed Francis had eaten a little, he took of his alms and sent a little to each of the knights and chaplains of my Lord Cardinal on behalf of the Lord God. Who all received them with great joy and devotion, stretching out to him cowls and sleeves. And some did eat while others put it aside, out of their great devotion to him. But my Lord of Ostia rejoiced greatly at their devotion, chiefly because those alms were not of wheaten bread. After the meal he entered his chamber, taking with him blessed Francis, and lifting up his arms he embraced him with great joy and exultation, saying to him, "Why, my most simple brother, hast thou done me this shame to-day, that coming to my house, which is the home of thy brethren, thou shouldst go begging alms?" The blessed Father answered him, "Nay, my Lord, I have done you great honour, for when a servant does his duty and fulfils his obedience to his lord, he does honour to his lord." And he said, "It behoves me to be a form and example to my poor ones, especially because I know that in this order of friars there will be Friars Minor in name and in deed, who for the love of the Lord God and the unction of the Holy Spirit Who shall teach them concerning all things, shall be humiliated to all humility and subjection and service of their brethren. But there are, and will be, some amongst them who, held back by shame or evil usage, disdain and will disdain to humiliate themselves and to stoop to go begging alms and to do other servile work; wherefore it behoves me by my deeds to teach those who are and will be in the Order, that they shall be without excuse in this life and the next before God. Being therefore with you, who are our lord and our apostle, and with other magnates and rich men of the world, who for the love of the Lord God not only receive me with much devotion into your houses, but also compel me to sit at your table, I will not be ashamed to beg alms, nay, I would fain have and hold this a very great nobility and royal dignity before God, and in honour of Him Who, when He was Lord of all, wished for our sakes to become servant of all, and when He was rich and glorious in His majesty became poor and despised in our humility. Whence let those who are and shall be friars know that I hold it for greater consolation of soul and body to sit at the sorry table of the friars, and see before me the wretched alms which they beg from door to door for the love of the Lord God, than to sit at your table, or that of other lords, abundantly prepared with diverse dainties. For the bread of charity is holy bread, which the praise and love of the Lord God sanctifies, since when a brother ask an alms he should first say, 'Praised and blessed be the Lord God,' afterwards he should say, 'Do to us an alms for the love of the Lord God.'" And the Cardinal was much edified at this conversation of the blessed Father, and said to him, "My son, do that which is good in thine eyes, since God is with thee, and thou with Him." For this was the oft-repeated desire of blessed Francis, that a friar ought not to remain long without going out for alms, both on account of the great merit of the act and lest he should afterwards be ashamed to go. Nay, the more noble and great in this world was the friar, so much the more was he rejoiced and edified with him, when he went to seek alms and did other servile work, as at that time the friars were wont to do.

CHAPTER XXIV

OF THE FRIAR WHO NEITHER USED TO PRAY NOR WORK, BUT WHO ATE WELL

In the first days of the Order, when the friars dwelt at Rivo Torto near Assisi, there was amongst them a certain friar who prayed little and did not work, who would not ask for alms and used to eat well. Considering these things, blessed Francis knew by the Holy Spirit that he was a carnal man, and said to him, "Go thy way, friar fly, since thou wilt eat of the labour of thy brethren and be idle in the work of God, like a lazy and sterile drone which profiteth nothing and laboureth not, but eateth the labour and profit of the good bees." And so he went his way. And because he was carnal, he sought not for mercy nor found it.

CHAPTER XXV

HOW HE WENT OUT WITH FERVOUR TO MEET A POOR MAN WHO WENT AWAY WITH HIS ALMS THANKING GOD

On another time also, when the blessed Father was at St. Mary of the Porziuncula, a certain very spiritual poor man was coming through the street returning from Assisi with alms, and went along praising God in a loud voice with much joyfulness. But when he drew near the church of blessed Mary, blessed Francis heard him, and straightway with great fervour and joy went out to him, running up to him in the way, and with great joyfulness kissing the shoulder whereon he carried the scrip with alms. And he took the wallet from his shoulder and put it on his own shoulder, and thus brought it into the house of the friars, and in their presence said, "Thus I would that a brother of mine should go and return with alms, glad and joyful and praising God."

CHAPTER XXVI

HOW IT WAS REVEALED BY THE LORD THAT THEY SHOULD BE CALLED FRIARS MINOR TO ANNOUNCE PEACE AND SALVATION

On a certain day blessed Francis said, "The order and life of the Friars Minor is a certain little flock which the Son of God in these last times asked of His Heavenly Father, saying,

'Father, I would that Thou shouldst make and give to Me a new and humble folk in these last times, unlike to all others who have gone before them, in humility and poverty, and content to possess Me alone.' And the Father said, having heard the Son, 'My Son, that which Thou hast asked is done.'" Whence the blessed Father used to say that for this reason God willed and revealed to him that they should be called Friars Minor, because this is that poor and humble folk which the Son of God demanded of His Father. Of which folk the Son Himself speaks in the Gospel, *Fear not, little flock, for it is your Father's good pleasure to give you the kingdom.* And again, *Inasmuch as ye have done it unto one of the least of these My brethren, ye have done it unto Me.* And the Lord understood this of all spiritual poor men, yet He spake it more especially of the Order of Friars Minor, which was to be in His Church. Whence, as it was revealed to blessed Francis that it should be called the Order of Friars Minor, so he made it to be written in his testament and the first Rule which he took to the Lord Pope, Innocent III., who approved and conceded it, and afterwards announced it to all in Consistory. Likewise the Lord revealed to him the salutation which the friars should use, as he caused to be written in his testament, saying, "The Lord revealed to me that I should say for a greeting: *The Lord give thee peace.*" Whence, in the first days of the Order, when he would go with a certain friar who was one of the first twelve, he saluted the men and women on the road, and those who were in the fields, saying, "The Lord give you peace." And for that men had not heard up to then such a salutation from any religious they wondered greatly. Nay, some used to say to them with great indignation, "What does this salutation of yours mean?" So that that brother began to be ashamed of it, whence he said to blessed Francis, "Let me use another greeting." And the holy Father said to him, "Let them talk, since they perceive not those things which are of God. But be not ashamed, because from henceforth the nobles and princes of this world shall show reverence to thee and other friars for this salutation. For it is no great thing if the Lord should wish to have a new and little flock, singular and unlike all those who have come before them in life and work, a folk which should be content to have Him alone most sweet."

SECTION III

OF CHARITY AND COMPASSION AND YIELDING TO ONE'S NEIGHBOUR

CHAPTER XXVII

AND FIRSTLY, HOW HE CONDESCENDED TO A BROTHER WHO WAS DYING OF HUNGER, BY EATING WITH HIM, ADMONISHING THE BRETHREN THAT THEY SHOULD DO PENANCE DISCREETLY

ON a certain time when blessed Francis began to have friars, dwelling with them at Rivo Torto near Assisi, it fell on a night, all the friars being at rest, about the middle of the night, one of them called out, saying, "I am dying! I am dying!" whereon all the friars woke up amazed and affrighted. And the holy Father, rising, said, "Rise, brothers, and kindle the light!" And when it was lit he said, "Who is he that said, 'I am dying'?" The brother answered, "It is I." And he said to him, "What is the matter, brother? How dost thou die?" And he said, "I die of hunger." Then the blessed Father caused the table to be laid straightway, and like a man full of charity and discretion, ate with him lest he should be put to shame by eating alone, and by his will, all the other friars ate likewise. For that brother and all the other friars who had newly turned to the Lord, used to inflict their bodies even beyond measure. And after the meal the holy Father said to the other friars, "Dearest, I bid you, each of you, consider his nature, because though one of you may be able to sustain himself on less food, yet I will that another who requires more food shall not be bound to imitate the first in this thing, but shall, considering his own nature, give his body what it requires, so that it may be able to serve the spirit. For as we are bound to beware of superfluity of eating, which harms body and soul, so also must we beware of too great abstinence, nay, even more, since the Lord will have mercy and not sacrifice." And he said, "Dearest brothers, this which I have done, to wit, that on account of charity towards my brother, we have eaten together with him, lest he should be ashamed to eat alone, necessity and charity rather forced me to do. But I say to you that I would not so do again, seeing it would be neither religious nor becoming. But I will and command you that each of our brethren according to our poverty satisfy his body as it shall be necessary for him." For the first friars, and the others who came after them for a long time, afflicted their bodies beyond measure with abstinence from food and drink, with vigils, with cold, with roughness of raiment, and the labour of their hands; they wore next their flesh very strong iron belts and coats, and hair shirts; on which account, seeing by occasion of this the friars might become weak, and that some were already in that short time ill, he forbade in a certain chapter any friar to wear anything next the skin except a tunic.

But we who were with him bear testimony of him, that though in the whole time of his life he was thus discreet and temperate concerning his brethren, yet it was so that they should at no time deviate from the way of poverty and the decorum of our Order. Nevertheless the most holy Father himself, from the beginning of his conversion unto the end of his life, was austere to his own body, although he was by nature feeble, and could not have lived in the world, except delicately. Whence, considering on a certain day, that the friars were exceeding the measure of poverty and of decency in their food and in other things, in a certain sermon which he made to sundry brethren, in the presence of all the friars he said, "Let not the brethren think that some allowance is necessary to my body, for because it behoves me to be the form and example of all friars, I wish to use and be content with few and very wretched meats, and to use all other things according to poverty, and utterly to turn in disgust from things rare and delicate."

CHAPTER XXVIII

HOW HE CONDESCENDED TO A SICK FRIAR BY EATING GRAPES WITH HIM

On another time when the blessed Father was at the same place, a certain friar, spiritual and old in the Order, was there infirm and very feeble. And when he saw him blessed Francis was moved with pity for him. But because then the friars, both well and ill, with great joy were using poverty for their abundance, and not using in their sickness medicines nor even asking for them, but on the other hand taking by choice those things which were contrary to the body, blessed Francis said within himself, "If that brother would eat some ripe grapes early in the morning I believe it would do him good." And as he thought so he did in its turn.

For he rose on a certain day, very early, and called to him that friar privately, and led him into a certain vineyard which was near the dwelling. And he chose a vine whereon the grapes were good to eat, and sitting near the vine with that friar, began to eat of the grapes, lest the brother himself should be ashamed to eat alone. And while they were eating, the friar was cured, and together they praised the Lord. Whence that friar for the whole time of his life, remembered this the mercy and piety which the most holy Father showed and did unto him, and often with great devotion and shedding of tears was wont to relate this among the brethren.

CHAPTER XXIX

HOW HE STRIPPED HIMSELF AND HIS FELLOW THAT HE MIGHT CLOTHE THE POOR

At Celano in the winter time, when blessed Francis had a cloth folded like a mantle which a certain friend of the friars had lent to him, there came to him an old woman seeking alms. Who forthwith loosed the cloak from his neck, and though it belonged to another, gave it to the poor old woman, saying, "Go and make a tunic for yourself, because you want it enough." The old woman laughed, and astonished, I know not whether from fear or joy, took the cloth from his hands, and lest delay should bring about a danger of his taking it back, ran very swiftly, and fell upon the cloth with her scissors. But when she found the cloth was not enough for a tunic, she came back to the first kindness of the holy Father, pointing out to him that the cloth was not large enough for a tunic. The saint turned his eyes to his fellow who wore such another cloth on his back, and said to him, "Hearest thou what this poor woman says. For the love of God let us bear the cold, and give that cloth to the poor woman that her tunic may be finished." And forthwith as he had given it so also did his fellow. Thus both of them remained bare that the poor woman might be clothed.

CHAPTER XXX

HOW HE COUNTED IT THEFT NOT TO GIVE TO ONE WHOSE NEEDS WERE GREATER

ONCE when he was returning from Siena, he came across a poo man on the way, and said to his fellow, "We ought to returı this mantle to its owner. For we received it only as a loan until we should come upon one poorer than ourselves." Bu his fellow, considering the necessity of the holy Father, main tained that he ought not to neglect himself to provide fo another. To whom the saint answered, "I will not be a thief For it would be counted to us for a theft if we should not giv to him who is more needy." And so the pious Father hande over the mantle to the poor man.

CHAPTER XXXI

HOW HE GAVE A MANTLE TO A POOR MAN ON AN AGREEMENT

AT the cell of Cortona, the blessed Father was wearing a nev mantle which the friars had been at some trouble to obtain fo him. A poor man came to the dwelling, weeping for his dea wife and his wretched orphaned family. To whom the com passionate saint said, "I give thee this mantle on conditio that you will not give it up to any one except he buy it fror you and pay you well." The friars, hearing this, ran togethe to the poor man to take away that mantle from him. But th poor man, gathering boldness from the face of the holy Fathe with clasped hands was carrying it away as his own. At las the friars redeemed the mantle, procuring that the due pric should be given to the poor man.

CHAPTER XXXII

HOW A CERTAIN POOR MAN, BY VIRTUE OF THE ALMS OF BLESSE FRANCIS, FORGAVE HIS INJURIES AND HATE TO HIS LORD

AT the hill of the lordship of Perugia, blessed Francis met certain poor man whom he had known before in the world, an said to him, "Brother, how is it with thee?" But he wit angry mind began to utter curses on his lord, saying, "By tl grace of my lord, whom may the Lord curse, I can be nothing but ill, since he has taken away from me all my goods." But blessed Francis, seeing that he persisted in mortal hatred, having pity on his soul, said to him, "Brother, forgive thy lord for the love of God, and free your own soul; it may be that he will restore what he has taken away; otherwise thou hast lost thy goods and wilt lose thy soul." And he said, "I cannot forgive him at all, unless he first return what he has taken away from me." Then the holy Father answered, "Behold, I give thee this mantle; I beg thee to forgive thy lord for the love of the Lord God." And immediately his heart was sweetened, and moved by this good deed he forgave his lord his injuries.

CHAPTER XXXIII

HOW HE SENT A MANTLE TO A POOR WOMAN WHO SUFFERED FROM HER EYES LIKE HIMSELF

A CERTAIN poor woman of Machilone came to Rieti for a disease of the eyes; and when the doctor came to blessed Francis, he said to him, "Brother, a certain woman diseased in the eyes has come to me, who is so poor that I have had to pay her charges for her." And when he had heard this, he was forthwith moved with pity for her, and calling one of the friars who was his Warden, he said to him, "Brother Warden, we must return what we borrowed." Who answered, "What is that loan, brother?" But he said, "This mantle which we have received as a loan from that poor sick woman, we should return to her." And his Warden said to him, "Brother, what seemeth best to thee to be done, so do." Then the holy Father called with glee a certain spiritual man familiar with him, and said to him, "Take this mantle, and twelve loaves with it, and go to the poor woman sick of her eyes whom the doctor shall show thee, and say to her, 'The poor man to whom you entrusted this mantle gives thanks to thee for the loan of the mantle, take that which is thine own.'" He went therefore and said to the woman all the things that blessed Francis had said to him. But she, thinking he was making game of her, said to him with fear and modesty, "Leave me in peace, for I know not what thou sayest." But he put the mantle and the twelve loaves in her hands. She then, considering that he must have spoken this in truth, accepted it with fear and reverence, rejoicing and praising the Lord. And fearing lest it should be taken away from her, she rose secretly by night and returned to her home with gladness. But blessed Francis had arranged with the Warden to give her her charges every day while she abode there. Whence we who were with him bear testimony of him that he was of so much charity and pity to the sick and the whole, not only toward his brethren but also toward other poor folk, well or ill, that he used to give to the poor those necessaries of his body which the brethren used sometimes to acquire with great solicitude and labour, first soothing us lest we should be troubled by it, with great joy inward and outward, taking away those things from himself even which were very necessary to him. And on account of this thing the Minister-General and his Warden had ordered him not to give his tunic to any friars without their leave. For the friars of their devotion used sometimes to beg a tunic of him, who immediately gave it to them, and sometimes he divided it and gave them a part, and kept a part for himself, because he only carried one tunic.

CHAPTER XXXIV

HOW HE GAVE HIS TUNIC TO FRIARS WHO BEGGED IT FOR THE LOVE OF GOD

WHENCE on a time, when he was going through a certain province preaching, two French-born friars met him. Who when they had had great consolation from him, finally begged his tunic of him for the love of God. But he, when he heard "for the love of God" forthwith took off his tunic and gave it to them, remaining bare for some hours. For when the love of God was named to him, he never denied to any one his cord, or his tunic, or anything whatever that was asked for; nay, he greatly misliked it and often reproved the friars when he heard them for anything whatever name uselessly "for the love of God." For he was wont to say, "So very high and very precious is the love of God, that it should never be named save seldom and in great necessity, and with much reverence."

But one of those friars took off his own tunic, and gave it to him. When he gave a tunic or part of it to any one he suffered thence great necessity and tribulation, since he could not very quickly have another, especially because he always wished to wear a sorry tunic patched with pieces of cloth sometimes both within and without; nay, he would never or rarely wear a tunic of new cloth, but he used to get from another friar his tunic which he had already worn for some time, and sometimes he would take from one brother a part of his tunic and from another a part. But on account of his many infirmities and chills of the stomach and the spleen, he used sometimes to patch it on the inside with new cloth. And this manner of poverty in his clothes he held and observed until the year in which he passed to the Lord; for a few days before his death, because he was dropsical, and as if all dried up, and on account of the many other infirmities which he had, the friars made for him several tunics, for that of necessity his tunic should be changed every day and night.

CHAPTER XXXV

HOW HE WISHED TO GIVE A PIECE OF CLOTH SECRETLY TO A POOR MAN

ANOTHER time a certain poor man came to the place where blessed Francis was, and begged a piece of cloth for the love of God. Hearing which, blessed Francis said to a certain friar, "Seek through the house if thou canst find some cloth or any piece, and give it to that poor man." And that friar, running through the whole of the house, said that he could not find any. Then that the poor brother should not go away empty, blessed Francis went by stealth lest his Warden should forbid him, and took a knife, and sitting in his hiding-place, began to cut off that part of his tunic which was sewed on in the inside, wishing to give that piece to the poor man by stealth. But the Warden learning this, went forthwith to him, and forbade him to give it, especially because there was then a great frost, and he was very ill and cold. Then blessed Francis said to him, "If thou wilt not that I should give that piece to him, thou must arrange that some piece be given to that poor brother." And so the friars gave to that poor man some cloth from their own clothing, for the sake of blessed Francis. When he went through the world to preach, either on his feet or on an ass (after he began to grow sick), or on a horse in the greatest and strictest necessity (because otherwise he would not ride, and this only a little before his death), if any brother used to lend him a mantle, he would not receive it unless he might give it to any poor man meeting him or coming to him, so only that the testimony of his spirit showed him that it was necessary to him.

CHAPTER XXXVI

HOW HE BADE BROTHER GILES CLOTHE A POOR MAN

In the first days of the Order, when he was staying at Rivo Torto, with the two companions whom he then had, alone, behold, a certain man, by name Giles, who was the third friar, came from the world to him, to receive his life. And after he abode there for some days clothed with the garments he had brought from the world, it happened that a certain poor man came to the place, seeking an alms from blessed Francis. Turning to Giles, blessed Francis said to him, "Give thy mantle to thy poor brother." Who forthwith with great joy took it from his back and gave it to the poor man. And then it was seen that God had put a new grace into his heart, for that he had given with joy his mantle to the poor. And so he was received by blessed Francis, and ever went forward virtuously to the greatest perfection.

CHAPTER XXXVII

OF THE PENANCE HE GAVE TO A FRIAR WHO MISJUDGED A POOR MAN

When blessed Francis had gone to preach at a certain dwelling of the friars near Rocca Brizzi, it happened that on that day on which he should preach a certain poor and infirm man came unto him. On whom having much compassion, he began to speak to his fellow of his poverty and sickness, and his fellow said to him, "Brother, it is true that he seems poor enough; but it may be that in the whole province there is no one who wishes more to be rich than he." And being immediately severely reproved by blessed Francis, he confessed his fault. And blessed Francis said, "Wilt thou for this do the penance which I shall bid thee?" Who answered, "I will do it willingly." And he said to him, "Go and put off your tunic, and throw yourself naked at the poor man's feet, and tell him how thou hast sinned against him in speaking evil in that matter, and ask him to pray for you." He went therefore and did all the things which blessed Francis had told him. Which done, he arose and put on his tunic and returned to blessed Francis. And blessed Francis said to him, "Wouldst thou know how thou hast sinned against him, nay, against Christ? When thou seest a poor man, thou oughtest to consider Him in Whose Name he cometh, namely, Christ, Who took our poverty and infirmity on Him: for the infirmity and poverty of this man, is as it were a mirror to us, wherein we may see and consider with pity, the sickness and poverty of our Lord Jesus Christ."

CHAPTER XXXVIII

HOW HE CAUSED A NEW TESTAMENT TO BE GIVEN TO THE MOTHER OF TWO FRIARS

ANOTHER time, when he was abiding at St. Mary of the Porziuncula, a certain woman, poor and old, who had two sons in the order, came to the dwelling seeking an alms from the holy Father. Immediately blessed Francis said to Friar Peter of Catana, who was then the Minister-General, "Have we aught which we can give to this our mother?" (For he was wont to say that the mother of any friar was the mother of him and of all friars.) Friar Peter answered him, "We have nothing in the house which we can give her, for she would have an alms to sustain her body. But we have in the church one only New Testament wherein we read the lessons at Matins." (For in that time the friars had no breviaries nor many psalters.) Blessed Francis said to him therefore, "Give the Testament to our mother, that she may sell it for her necessity. For I believe firmly that it will please the Lord and the Blessed Virgin more, than if we were to read in it." And so he gave it her. For that can be said and written of him, which is read of blessed Job: *For from my youth (charity) was brought up with me . . . and from my mother's womb.* Whence unto us who were with him not only what we have learned from others of his charity and pity toward friars and other poor men, but also those things which our eyes have seen would be very difficult to write or tell.

SECTION IV

OF THE PERFECTION OF HOLY HUMILITY AND OBEDIENCE IN HIMSELF AND HIS BRETHREN

CHAPTER XXXIX

AND FIRSTLY HOW HE RESIGNED THE OFFICE OF HIS PRELACY AND APPOINTED PETER OF CATANA MINISTER-GENERAL

To observe the virtue of holy humility, a few years after his conversion he resigned the office of his prelacy in a certain Chapter before the friars, saying: "From henceforth am I dead to you, but behold Brother Peter of Catana, whom both I and we all will obey." And throwing himself on the earth before him, he promised him obedience and reverence. Thereupon all the friars wept, and their exceeding great grief forced from them deep sighs, when they saw themselves in a manner become orphans of such a father. But the holy Father rising, with his eyes raised to heaven and his hands joined, said, "Lord, I commend to Thee Thy family which hitherto Thou hast committed to me; and now on account of the infirmities which Thou knowest, O most sweet Lord, being unable to have the care of it, I commend it to its Ministers, who shall be held in the day of judgment to show cause before Thee, O Lord, if any brother should perish through their negligence, or evil example, or bitter correction."

He remained therefore from that time a subject unto the day of his death, bearing himself more humbly in all things than any of the others.

CHAPTER XL

HOW HE GAVE UP HIS FELLOWS, BEING UNWILLING TO HAVE A SPECIAL FELLOW

At another time he gave up all his fellows to his Vicar, saying, "I will not seem singular in this prerogative of liberty to have a special fellow, but let friars join me from place to place as the Lord shall have inspired them." And he added, "I saw just now a blind man who had but a puppy as a guide on his way, and I will not seem better than he." But this was always his glory, that having left behind him all appearance of singularity or boasting, there should dwell in him the virtue of Christ.

CHAPTER XLI

THAT HE RESIGNED OFFICE BY REASON OF EVIL PRELATES

ONCE having been asked by a certain friar, why he had thus cast off his brethren from his care, and handed them over into strange hands, as if they did not belong to him in the smallest degree, he answered, " My son, I love the brethren as I am able, but if they would follow in my footsteps, I would love them still more, nor would I make myself strange to them. For there are certain of the prelates, who draw them to other things, proposing to them the example of the ancients, and little considering my warnings. But what and how they do shall appear more clearly in the end." And a little after, when his exceeding great infirmity weighed upon him, in the vehemence of his spirit he rose in his bed, and crying out, said, " Who are they who snatch my Order and my brethren from my hands? If I come to the General Chapter, I will show them what will they have."

CHAPTER XLII

THAT HE HUMBLY ACQUIRED MEAT FOR THE INFIRM, AND WARNED THEM TO BE PATIENT

THE blessed Father was not ashamed to obtain flesh meat for a sick friar in the public places of the cities, yet he warned them that lay sick to bear want patiently, and not to rise in scandal when they were not fully satisfied. Whence in the first Rule he caused it to be written thus, " I beseech my brethren that in their infirmities they grow not angry, nor be disturbed against God or their brethren, nor demand medicines too eagerly, nor desire too greatly to set free the flesh that so soon shall die, which is the enemy of the spirit. But let them give thanks for all things, and desire to be such as God would have them to be. For those, whom the Lord hath preordained to life eternal, He teaches with the stings of scourges and infirmities, as He Himself says, *As many as I love, I rebuke and chasten.*"

CHAPTER XLIII

OF THE HUMBLE ANSWER OF BLESSED FRANCIS AND DOMINIC WHEN THEY WERE ASKED AT THE SAME TIME BY THE CARDINALS, WHETHER THEY WOULD THAT THEIR BRETHREN SHOULD BE PRELATES OF THE CHURCH

In the city of Rome when those two renowned lights, blessed Francis and blessed Dominic, were together before my Lord of Ostia, who was afterwards Pope, and each in turn had poured forth sweet things concerning God, then my Lord of Ostia said to them, " In the primitive church the pastors and prelates were poor, and men fervent in charity, not greed. Why therefore should we not make bishops and prelates of your friars, who should prevail over all others for a document and example? " Then was there between the saints a humble and devout contention concerning their answer, not indeed a pushing forward, but each in turn turning to the other, and forcing him to answer. But at the last the humility of Francis conquered, so that he did not answer first, and Dominic conquered, who by answering first did humbly obey. Blessed Dominic therefore answering said, " My Lord, my brethren have been exalted to a good condition if they will but know it, and, as far as lies in my power, I shall never permit them to attain any form of dignity." Then blessed Francis, inclining himself before the aforesaid Lord, said, " My Lord, my brethren be called Minors for this reason, that they should not presume to become greater. For their vocation teaches them to remain lowly, and to imitate the footsteps of the humility of Christ, that hereby at last they may be exalted more than others in the sight of the saints. For if you would that they bring forth fruit in the Church of God, hold and keep them in the state of their calling, and if they strive for high things, cast them down violently to the ground, and never permit them to rise to any prelacy." These were the answers of the saints. And when they were ended, my Lord of Ostia, much edified by the responses of them both, gave exceeding great thanks to God. Both going away together, blessed Dominic asked blessed Francis to deign to give him the cord by which he was girded. And blessed Francis denied it him from humility, as he had demanded it from charity. Yet the happy devotion of him who asked did conquer, and blessed Dominic having received the cord of blessed Francis bv the violence of his charity, girded it under his tunic, and from that time forth devoutly wore it. Then either of them placed his hands between the hands of the other, and commended each to the other with the sweetest mutual commendations. And so holy Dominic said to holy Francis, "I would, brother Francis, that thine and mine should make one Order, and that we should live in like manner in the Church." Then when they were separated from one another, Dominic said to several who were standing by, "In truth I say unto you, that all religious ought to imitate this holy man Francis, so great is the perfection of his holiness."

CHAPTER XLIV

THAT AS A FOUNDATION OF HUMILITY, HE WILLED HIS FRIARS TO SERVE THE LEPERS

BLESSED Francis, from the beginning of his conversion, the Lord aiding him, founded himself like a wise builder upon the rock, that is, on the exceeding great humility and poverty of the Son of God, calling his Order that of the Friars Minor because of his great humility. Whence in the beginning of the Order he wished that the friars should abide in leper houses to serve them, and there lay a foundation of holy humility. For when gentle and simple came to the Order, amongst the other things which were announced to them, he was wont to say that it behoved them to serve lepers, and abide in their houses; as it was contained in the first Rule, "Willing to have naught under heaven except holy poverty, whereby they may be fed by the Lord in this world with bodily and spiritual food, and in the life to come attain their heavenly heritage." And thus he chose for himself and others a foundation on the greatest humility and poverty, inasmuch as when he might have been a great prelate in the Church of God, he chose and wished to be lowly, not only in the Church, but also among his brethren. For this lowliness, in his opinion and desire, was very great exaltation in the sight of God and man.

CHAPTER XLV

THAT HE WISHED THE GLORY AND HONOUR OF ALL HIS GOOD WORKS AND DEEDS TO BE GIVEN TO GOD ALONE

When he had been preaching to the people in Rieti in the market place of the city, after the preaching was finished, the bishop of that city straightway rose up, a man both discreet and spiritual, and said to the people, "The Lord, from the first day in which He planted and built up His church, has always adorned it with holy men, to nourish it by word and example. But now, in this latest hour, He has adorned it with this poor and despised and unlettered man, Francis, and therefore are we bound to love and honour the Lord, and beware of sin. For he hath not done after this manner to any nation." Having finished these words, the bishop came down from the place where he had preached, and entered the Cathedral. And blessed Francis coming to him, throwing himself at his feet, bowed down before him, and said, "In truth I say unto you, my Lord Bishop, that no man has done so much honour to me in this life, as you have done to me to-day, for those men say, 'This is a holy man,' attributing to me glory and sanctity, and not to the Creator. But you, as one discreet, have separated the precious from the vile."

For when the holy Father used to be praised and called holy, he was wont to answer to such speeches, saying, "I am not yet so secure, that I may not have sons and daughters. For at whatever hour the Lord should take away from me the treasure which He has commended to me, what else would remain to me but body and soul, which even infidels have? Nay, I ought to believe that if the Lord should have granted so many and so great gifts to a thief or an infidel as to me they would have been more faithful to their Lord than I. For, as in the picture of the Lord and the Blessed Virgin painted on wood, the Lord and the Blessed Virgin are honoured, and yet the wood and the picture take nothing of it to themselves, so the servant of God is in a manner a picture of God, wherein God is honoured on account of His goodness. But he ought to take nothing of this to himself, since in respect of God, he is less than the wood and the picture, nay, he is pure nothing. And therefore unto God alone must the glory and honour be rendered, but unto him only shame and tribulation while he lives among the miseries of this life."

CHAPTER XLVI

HOW UP TO HIS DEATH HE WOULD FAIN HAVE A WARDEN AND LIVE IN SUBJECTION

BUT wishing to remain in perfect humility and subjection unto death; some time before his death he said to the Minister-General, "I would that thou shouldst commit thy rule over me to one of my fellows, to whom I may do obedience in thy place, for on account of the merit of obedience I desire that in life and in death it should ever remain with me." And from that time forward he had one of his fellows as a Warden, whom he obeyed in the stead of the Minister-General, nay, on a time he said to his fellows, "The Lord has granted me this grace amongst others, to obey as diligently the novice who enters the Order to-day, if he were assigned to me for Warden, as he who is foremost and ancient in life and in the Order. For a subject ought to look upon his superior, not as a man, but as that God for Whose love he is subject to him." Afterwards he said, "There is no prelate in the whole world who is so much feared as the Lord would make me to be feared, if so I wished it, by my brethren. But the Lord has granted me this grace, that I wish to be content with all, as he that is least in the Order."

This also we have seen with our eyes who were with him, as also he himself testified, that when certain of the friars did not satisfy him in his necessities, or said to him some word by which a man is wont to be disturbed, straightway he went to prayer, and on his return he would remember nothing, nor ever said, "Such an one did not satisfy me," or, "Such an one said to me such a word." And thus persevering in this wise, by so much the more as he drew near to death was he solicitous to consider how he might live and die in all humility and poverty, and in all perfection of virtues.

CHAPTER XLVII

OF THE PERFECT MANNER OF OBEYING WHICH HE TAUGHT

THE most holy Father was wont to say to his brethren, "Brothers most dear, fulfil a command at the first word, nor wait till what was said to you is repeated. Do not argue or judge, for there is no impossibility in the command, for even if I were to order you aught above your strength, holy obedience will not be wanting to aid your weakness."

CHAPTER XLVIII

HOW HE LIKENED PERFECT OBEDIENCE, IN A PARABLE, TO THE BODY OF A DEAD MAN

BUT on a time before his fellows he uttered this sigh, "Hardly is there one Religious in the world who obeys his superior well." Immediately his fellows said to him, "Tell us, Father, what is the perfect and highest obedience?" But he answering, described true and perfect obedience under the figure of a dead body, thus, "Take a lifeless body and put it where it shall please thee, you will see that it will not resist moving, nor change its place, nor claim dismissal. But if it be exalted on a throne, it looks not on high things but low. If it be robed in purple, it grows doubly pale. He therefore is truly obedient who judges not why he is moved, takes no thought where he is placed, and asketh not that he should be moved; promoted to office he keeps his unwonted humility, while the more he is honoured, the more he reputes himself unworthy."

Things ordered purely and simply, not asked of him, he called holy obediences. But he believed that the highest obedience, that in which flesh and blood had no part, was when men should go by divine inspiration among the infidels, either for the good of their fellows, or for the desire of martyrdom, and he judged that to seek this was right acceptable.

CHAPTER XLIX

THAT IT IS DANGEROUS TO ORDER TOO LIGHTLY BY OBEDIENCE, OR NOT TO OBEY AN ORDER

AND so the blessed Father thought that an order should be given by virtue of obedience seldom, nor should that weapon be used first which should be the last; for said he, "The hand should not be laid readily on the sword." But he was wont to say that he who did not immediately obey the precept of obedience, neither feared God nor revered man (so long, namely, as there was no necessary cause for delay). Nor is there anything more true, for what else is the power of command in a rash governor than a sword in the hand of a wrathful man? But who more hopeless than the Religious who neglects and contemns obedience?

CHAPTER L

HOW HE ANSWERED THE FRIARS PERSUADING HIM TO SEEK THE PRIVILEGE OF PREACHING FREELY

CERTAIN friars said to blessed Francis, " Father, dost thou not see that sometimes the bishops will not permit us to preach, and make us stand idle many days in one place before we can announce the word of the Lord. It were better that thou shouldst obtain from the Lord Pope a privilege concerning this matter, as it would be for the salvation of souls." To whom he answered with sore rebuke, saying, " You, Friars Minor, know not the will of God, and do not allow me to convert the whole world as God willeth. For I wish by perfect humility and reverence first to convert the prelates; who, when they shall see our holy life and humble reverence towards them, shall beseech you to preach and convert the people, and they shall call them to the preaching better than your privileges which would lead you into pride. And if you be separated from all avarice, and persuade the people to give to the churches their due, they themselves would ask you to hear the confession of their flock, though of this you need not take heed, for if these were converted they should well find confessors. But as for me, I desire this privilege from the Lord, that never may I have any privilege from man, except to do reverence to all, and to convert the world by obedience to the holy Rule rather by example than by word."

CHAPTER LI

OF THE MANNER IN RECONCILING ONE ANOTHER WHEN ONE OFFENDED ANOTHER

HE was wont to affirm that the Friars Minor had been sent by the Lord in these last times, that they might show examples to those bound up in the darkness of sinners. He was wont to say that he was filled with the sweetest odours and anointed with the virtue of precious ointment, when he heard great things of the holy friars dispersed through the world. It fell on a day that a certain friar, in the presence of a nobleman of the Island of Cyprus, reproached another, but when he perceived that his brother was somewhat disturbed thereby, being wrathful with himself, he straightway took the dung of an ass and put it in his own mouth, breaking it small with his teeth, saying, "Eat dung, O tongue, which poured out the venom of wrath on my brother." But he who beheld these things, being astonished to stupor, went his way much edified, and from that time forth submitted himself and all he had to the will of the friars. And this custom all the friars observed that if one of them should have uttered a word of injury or trouble to another, having thrown himself prostrate upon the earth, he kissed the foot of his angered brother straightway, and humbly asked forgiveness. The holy Father was rejoiced in such things when he heard that his sons had drawn examples of holiness for themselves from him, and he loaded those friars with most worthy benedictions of all acceptation, who by word or work should lead sinners to the love of Christ. For in the zeal of souls wherewith he himself was perfectly filled, he wished his sons to resemble him with a perfect similitude.

CHAPTER LII

HOW CHRIST COMPLAINED TO BROTHER LEO, OF THE INGRATITUDE AND PRIDE OF THE FRIARS

On a certain time the Lord Jesus Christ said to Brother Leo, the fellow of blessed Francis, "Brother Leo, I lament for the friars." To Whom answered Brother Leo, "Wherefore, O Lord?" And the Lord answered, "For three things: namely, because they do not recognise My benefits which so largely and abundantly I shower on them, as thou knowest; while they sow not neither do they reap. And because the whole day they murmur, and are idle. And for that they provoke each other often to anger, and do not return to love, and do not forgive the injurv they receive."

CHAPTER LIII

HOW HE ANSWERED HUMBLY AND TRULY TO A CERTAIN DOCTOR OF THE ORDER OF PREACHERS WHO QUESTIONED HIM CONCERNING THE WORDS OF SCRIPTURE

But while he was abiding at Siena, there came to him a certain doctor of divinity of the Order of Preachers, a man both humble and right spiritual. When he had discussed with blessed Francis for some time together the words of the Lord, the said master asked of him concerning that word of Ezekiel: *If thou speakest not to warn the wicked from his wicked ways, his blood will I require at thine hand.* For he said, "I know many, however, good Father, that be in mortal sin, to whom I do not speak to warn them of their impiety, will their souls therefore be required at my hands?" To whom blessed Francis humbly said that he was a simpleton, and that therefore he should rather be taught of him than answer concerning the meaning of Scripture. Then that humble master added, "Brother, though I have heard an exposition of this text from sundry wise men, yet would I willingly learn your understanding of it." Therefore blessed Francis said, "If the text is to be understood generally, I take it thus, that the servant of God should so burn and shine forth by life and holiness in himself, that by the light of his example and by the speech of his holy conversation he should reprove all the impious. Thus, say I, his splendour and the odour of his fame will announce to all their iniquities." And so that doctor, going away much edified, said to the fellows of the blessed Father, "My brethren, the theology of this man, founded on purity and contemplation, is a flying eagle, while our science crawls on its belly on the earth."

CHAPTER LIV

OF HUMILITY AND PEACE WITH THE SECULAR CLERGY

Blessed Francis would that his sons should have peace with all men, and hold themselves lowly to all. Yet he taught them by word and showed them by example to be chiefly humble to the clergy. For he was wont to say, "We have been sent in aid of the clergy for the salvation of souls, and that whatsoever is found wanting in them may be supplied by us, but each will receive his reward, not according to his authority, but according to his labour. Learn, brethren, that the gain of souls is most pleasing to God, and this we can better obtain when in peace, than in discord with the clergy. But if these hinder the welfare of the people, revenge is of God, and He will reward them in His time. And therefore be ye subject to superiors, nor let any evil emulation arise from you. For if you shall have been sons of peace, you will gain clergy and people, and this is more acceptable to God, than to gain the people alone with a scandalised clergy. Cover," he said, " their lapses and supply their manifold defects, then when ye have done this, be the more humble."

CHAPTER LV

HOW HE HUMBLY ACQUIRED THE CHURCH OF ST. MARY OF THE ANGELS FROM THE ABBOT OF ST. BENEDICT, AND HOW HE WISHED HIS BRETHREN TO DWELL THERE AND LIVE HUMBLY

BLESSED Francis, seeing that the Lord wished to multiply the number of his friars, said to them, " Dearest brethren and my little sons, I see that the Lord wills to multiply us, whence it seems good and religious to me that we should obtain either from the canons of St. Rufinus, or from the Abbot of St. Benedict some church where the friars may say their Hours, and only have near it some small sorry hut constructed from mud and branches, where the brethren may rest and work. For this place is not fitting nor sufficient to the friars, since the Lord wishes to multiply them, and especially since we have here no church wherein the friars may say their Hours. And if any friar should die, it would not be fitting to bury him here, nor in a church of the secular clergy." And this speech pleased all the friars.

He went therefore to the Bishop of Assisi, and laid the aforesaid request before him. Unto whom said the Bishop, " Brother, I have no church which I can give you," and the canons also answered the same. Then he went to the Abbot of St. Benedict of Monte Subasio, and laid the same proposition before him. But the Abbot, moved with piety, having taken counsel with his monks, the divine grace and will operating, conceded to blessed Francis and to his friars the church of St. Mary of the Porziuncula, as the smallest and the poorest church they had. And the Abbot said to blessed Francis, " Behold, brother, we have granted what thou hast asked. But if the Lord shall multiply this congregation, we would that this place should be the chief of all your dwellings." And the speech pleased blessed Francis and his brethren, and the blessed Father rejoiced greatly concerning the place conceded to the friars, especially on account of the name of the church, of the Mother of Christ, and because it was so small and poor a church, and also because it was named the Porziuncula, in which it was prefigured that it should be the head and the mother of the poor Friars Minor. For the church was called the Porziuncula, because of that court which was formerly called " the little portion." Whence the blessed Father was wont to say, " The Lord wished that no other church should be conceded to the friars, and that the first friars should not as then build a new church nor have any other except that, since by this, through the advent of the Friars Minor, a certain prophecy was fulfilled." And though it was poor and now destroyed, yet for a great time the men of the city of Assisi and of all its lordship had had great devotion to that church, and they have a greater to-day, and daily doth it wax. Whence as the brethren went there to dwell, forthwith the Lord multiplied their number almost daily, and the odour of their fame was wonderfully scattered through all the valley of Spoleto, and many parts of the land. Yet of old it was called St. Mary of the Angels because, as it was said, the songs of Angels and of celestial spirits were there heard of those coming to the place.

(But now, because the friars are colder in prayer and virtuous works and more lax and idle, and given to uttering idle words and the news of this world, than they were used, that place itself is not held in so great reverence and devotion, as heretofore it has been of custom, and as I would wish it to be.)

When the blessed Father had said these words, forthwith with great fervour he concluded, saying, " I would that this place should always be immediately under the power of the Minister-General and servant, for the reason that he should have greater care and solicitude in providing there a good and holy family. Let clerks be chosen among the better and more holy and more fitting friars, those of the whole Order who can best say the Office, that not only lay folk but also the other friars may willingly and with great devotion see and hear them. But of the lay brothers, let holy men discreet and humble and decent be chosen, who may serve them. I will also that no woman and no friar enter that place except the Minister-General and the friars who serve them. And they shall not speak with any person, except with the friars who serve them and with the Minister who shall visit them. I will, likewise, that the lay brothers themselves who serve them, be bound never to say to them idle words or this world's news, or anything not useful to their souls. And on account of this, I especially will that no one shall enter into the dwelling, that they the better preserve its purity and sanctity, and that in that place nothing be said or done uselessly, but the whole place itself be preserved pure and holy in hymns and the praises of the Lord. And when any of those friars shall have passed away to the Lord, I will that in his place another holy friar, wherever he may be, be sent thither by the Minister-General. For if the other friars shall have fallen off somewhat from purity and honesty, I will that this place be blessed, and that it remain for ever a mirror and a good example of the whole Order, and like a candlestick before the throne of God and the blessed Virgin, always burning and shining. On account of which the Lord will have mercy on the defects and faults of all friars, and always preserve and protect this Order and this His tender plant."

CHAPTER LVI

OF THE HUMBLE REVERENCE WHICH HE SHOWED CONCERNING THE SWEEPING AND CLEANING OF CHURCHES

On a time when he was staying at St. Mary of the Porziuncula, and there were as yet but few friars, blessed Francis went by those villages and churches in the neighbourhood of Assisi announcing and preaching to men that they should do penance, and he carried a broom to sweep out unclean churches. For the holy Father grieved much when he saw any church not so clean as he wished. And therefore, when the preaching was finished, he always made all the priests who were there gather together in some remote place, lest he should be overheard by the lay folk, and preached to them of the salvation of souls, and especially that they should be careful to keep clean the churches and altars, and all things which pertained to the celebration of the divine mysteries.

CHAPTER LVII

OF THE RUSTIC WHO FOUND HIM SWEEPING A CHURCH, AND BEING CONVERTED ENTERED THE ORDER, AND WAS A SAINTLY FRIAR

But when he had gone to a certain village belonging to the city of Assisi, he began to sweep it and clean it. And immediately a rumour of him went through the whole village, for he was gladly seen of those men and more willingly heard. But when a certain rustic of strange simplicity, who was ploughing in his field, John by name, heard this he went straightway to him and found him sweeping the church humbly and devoutly. And he said to him, " Brother, give me the broom, for I wish to help thee." And taking the broom from his hands he swept out the remainder. And while they were sitting together he said to blessed Francis, " Brother, it is now a long time that I have had the will to serve God, and especially after I have heard the rumour of thee and thy brethren, but I knew not how to come to thee. Now therefore, since it has pleased the Lord that I should see thee, I have the will to do whatever shall be pleasing to thee." But the blessed Father, considering his fervour, rejoiced in the Lord, especially for that he had then few brethren, and it seemed to him that for his simplicity and purity this should be a good Religious. But he said to him, " Brother, if thou wilt be of our life and society, thou must strip thee of all that which thou mayest not own without scandal, and give it to the poor, according to the counsel of the Holy Gospel, since all my brethren that were able have done the same." When he had heard this, he went straightway to the field where he had left his cattle, and loosened them and led one of them before blessed Francis, and said to him, " Brother, so many years have I served my father and all them of my house, and though this portion of my heritage be small, I wish to take this ox for my part, and give it to the poor as may seem best to thee." But his parents and his brothers, who were still little, and all of his house, seeing that he would leave them, began to weep so sore and to utter such plaintive noises with grief, that blessed Francis was moved by it to pity, because it was a large family, and feeble. And blessed Francis said to them, " Prepare a feast for us all, and let us all eat together, and weep not, for I will make you truly joyful." So they prepared it forthwith, and all together with great joy did eat. But after meat blessed Francis said, "This, your son, wishes to serve God, and ye ought not to be saddened because of this, but rather to rejoice. For not only as regards God, but also according to this life it shall be reputed to you great honour and profit of souls and bodies, that God is honoured of your flesh, and all our brothers will be your sons and brothers. And because he is a creature of God, and wishes to serve his Creator, to serve Whom is to reign, I cannot nor ought not to return him unto you, but that ye may have consolation concerning him, I will that he give you that ox as to the poor, though he ought to give it to other poor folk according to the Gospel." And all were consoled with the words of St. Francis, and chiefly they rejoiced on account of the ox, because it was returned to them, since they were very poor. And because pure and holy simplicity in himself and in others greatly pleased blessed Francis, he clothed him with the garments of religion straightway, and led him with him humbly for his fellow. For he was of so great simplicity, that he believed himself bound to all things which blessed Francis did. Whence when the blessed Father stood in any church or in any place to pray, he also wished to see him, that he might conform himself in all his acts and gestures to him. And so if the blessed Father bent his knees, or raised his hands to heaven, or spat, or sighed, he himself did all these things in like manner. But when blessed Francis perceived this, he began with great gladness to reprove him for simplicity of this kind. To whom he answered, "Brother, I promised to do all things which thou didst, and therefore I must conform to thee in all things." And at this the blessed Father wondered and rejoiced wonderfully, beholding in him such purity and simplicity. But he afterwards began to profit so much that blessed Francis and all the other friars wondered greatly at his perfection. And after a little time he died in that holy profit of virtues. Whence afterwards blessed Francis with joy of mind and body was wont to tell amongst the friars of his conversion, naming him not Brother, but Saint, John.

CHAPTER LVIII

HOW HE PUNISHED HIMSELF BECAUSE HE HAD DONE SHAME TO A LEPER

But blessed Francis, having returned to the church of blessed Mary of the Porziuncula, found Brother James the Simple with a certain leper much ulcerated. For the blessed Father had commended that leper and all the others to him, because he was as it were their physician, and he freely touched their wounds and cleansed them and took care of them, for then the friars used to abide in the hospitals of the lepers. The holy Father therefore said to Brother James, as if reproving him, "You ought not to lead out these Christians, because it is neither decent for you nor for them." For though he wished to serve them, yet he was unwilling that he should take those who were much afflicted out of the hospital, because men are accustomed to hold such in abhorrence, and Brother James himself was so simple, that he used to go with them from the hospital up to the church of St. Mary of the Porziuncula, as he would have gone with the friars. But blessed Francis used to call the lepers themselves Christian brothers. And when he had said these things, the blessed Father immediately blamed himself, believing that the leper had been put to shame for the blame which he had thrown on Brother James. And therefore being fain to satisfy God and the leper, he told his fault to Brother Peter of Catana, who was then Minister-General. And he said, "I will that thou shouldst confirm to me the penance which I have chosen to do for this fault, and that thou shouldst in no respect contradict me." Who answered, "Brother, do that which shall please thee." For Brother Peter so much venerated and feared him that he did not presume to contradict him, though he was often thence afflicted. Then said the blessed Father, "Let this be my penance, that I eat in one dish with my Christian brother." When therefore blessed Francis sat down to table with the leper and with the other friars, one dish was placed between blessed Francis and the leper. But he was all ulcerated and loathsome, and especially he had his fingers shrivelled and bleeding with which he took up lumps from the dish, so that when he put them in the dish the blood and matter of the fingers flowed into it. And seeing this Brother Peter and the other friars were much saddened, but did not dare to say anything on account of the fear and reverence of the holy Father. He who saw this wrote it down, and bears testimony of these things.

CHAPTER LIX

HOW HE PUT THE DEMONS TO FLIGHT WITH HUMBLE WORDS

On a certain time blessed Francis went to the church of blessed Peter of Bovara near the castle of Trevi in the valley of Spoleto, and with him went Brother Pacificus, who in the world used to be called the King of Verse, a noble and courtly doctor of singers. But that church was abandoned. Therefore the blessed Father said to Brother Pacificus, "Return to the leper hospital, for I wish to remain here alone to-night, and to-morrow very early return to me." But when he had been left alone there, and had said Compline and other prayers, he wished to be quiet and to sleep, but he was not able. For his spirit began to fear and to feel diabolical suggestions, and immediately he went out of the church and crossed himself, saying, "On the part of Almighty God I say unto you, O Demons, that ye may work on my body whatever is given to you to do by the Lord Jesus Christ, since I am ready to sustain all things. For since I hold that my body is my greatest enemy, ye shall but avenge me on my adversary and worst enemy." And immediately those suggestions altogether ceased, and having returned to the place where he was lying, he slept in peace.

CHAPTER LX

OF THE VISION OF FRIAR PACIFICUS WHICH HE SAW, AND HOW HE HEARD THAT THE SEAT OF LUCIFER WAS RESERVED FOR BLESSED FRANCIS

But when it was morn Brother Pacificus returned to him. He was then standing before the altar in prayer, and Brother Pacificus waited for him without the choir praying likewise before a crucifix. And when he began to pray, he was raised up and snatched into Heaven, *whether in the body or out of the body God only knoweth.* And he saw in Heaven many seats, among which he saw one more notable than the others, and beyond all the rest glorious, shining and adorned with every precious stone. And admiring its beauty, he began to wonder in himself whose that seat should be. And immediately he heard a voice saying unto him, "This was the seat of Lucifer, and in his stead shall the humble Francis sit." And when he returned to himself, blessed Francis forthwith came out to him, at whose feet that brother fell in the shape of a cross with his arms extended. And looking upon him as if he were already in Heaven sitting in that seat, he said to him, "Father, do me this grace, and ask the Lord that He may have mercy on me, and forgive me my sins." But the blessed Father stretching out his hands raised him, and forthwith knew that he had seen something in prayer, for he seemed all transfigured, and he spoke to blessed Francis as one not living in the flesh, but as already reigning in Heaven. But after, because he was unwilling to tell the vision to the blessed man, he began to speak with himself words as if from afar, and amongst other things he said to him, "What thinkest thou of thyself, Brother?" The blessed Father answered and said unto him, "It seems to me that I am a greater sinner than any one in the whole world." And immediately it was revealed to the soul of Brother Pacificus, "By this thou mayest know that the vision which thou hast seen was true, since as Lucifer was ejected from his place on account of his pride, so Francis on account of his humility shall merit to be exalted, and to sit in it."

CHAPTER LXI

HOW HE MADE HIMSELF TO BE DRAGGED BOUND WITH A ROPE AT HIS NECK UNCLOTHED BEFORE THE PEOPLE

But on a certain time when he had got a little stronger from a certain very great infirmity of his, it seemed to him that he had had some allowance in that weakness, though he had eaten but little. And rising on a certain day, though he was not entirely freed from the quartan fever, he made the people of the city of Assisi be called together in the market place, for preaching. But when the sermon was done he warned the people that no one should go away from thence until he should return to them. And entering the cathedral of St. Rufinus with many friars and with Brother Peter of Catana who had been canon of that church and was chosen first Minister-

General by blessed Francis, he spoke to that brother Peter, ordering him by obedience, that he should without contradiction do whatever he should say to him. Brother Peter answered him, " Brother, I neither may nor ought, will or do anything concerning thee and me, except as it may please thee." Casting off therefore his tunic, blessed Francis bade him drag him unclad before the people with a cord bound round his neck to the place where he had preached. He bade another friar that he should take a dish full of ashes and should go up to the place where he had preached, and when he should have been drawn up to that place to throw the ashes over his face. Yet this last did not obey him in this on account of the great compassion by which he was moved towards him. And Brother Peter, taking the cord bound to his neck, dragged him after him as he had ordered him. But he was weeping very sore, and the other friars with him shed tears of compassion and of bitterness. When he was thus led naked in the sight of all men up to the place where he had preached, he said, " You, and all those who, after my example, leave this world and enter religion and the life of the friars, believe me to be a holy man, but I confess to God and to you that I have eaten in this my infirmity flesh and broth made with flesh." And all began to weep over him for great pity and compassion, especially because it was then winter time and a very intense frost, and he was not yet recovered from the quartan fever. And striking their breasts they accused themselves, saying, " If this saint, for just and manifest necessity, accuses himself with so much shame of body, whose life we know to be holy, whom even we know to be living in the flesh as if almost dead on account of the great abstinence and austerity which he has made to his body from the beginning of his conversion to Christ, what shall we wretched ones do, who for the whole time of our life have lived and still live according to the desires of the flesh."

CHAPTER LXII

HOW HE WISHED THAT WHATEVER OF COMFORT HIS BODY RECEIVED SHOULD BE KNOWN

LIKEWISE on a certain time when he had eaten in a certain hermitage in the Advent fast (St. Martin's Lent), cakes cooked with lard on account of his infirmities, for which oil was very unwholesome; Lent being finished, when he should preach to a great crowd, he said to them in the first word of his sermon, "You come to me with great devotion, believing me to be a holy man, but I confess to God and to you, that I have eaten in this Lent cakes cooked with lard." Nay, well-nigh always when he used to eat with any seculars, or when any bodily comfort was given him by the friars on account of his infirmities, immediately in the house and outside, before those friars who did not know of it, and the seculars, he was accustomed to say openly, "I have eaten such and such a food." For he was unwilling to hide from men what was laid open to God. Likewise also, wherever, in the presence of whatever Religious and laymen, his spirit was moved to pride or vainglory, or to any fault, he confessed it immediately in their presence openly, without any veil. Whence once he said to his companions, "Thus would I live in hermitages and in the other places where I abide, as if all men could see me. For if they think me to be a holy man, and I lead not the life which becomes a holy man, I should be a hypocrite." And thus, when on account of the weakness of the spleen and coldness of the stomach, one of his fellows who was his Warden wished to sew under his tunic a little foxskin opposite his spleen and stomach, especially as there was then a great cold, blessed Francis answered him, "If you would that I have foxskin under my tunic you must put a piece of that skin outside, so that every one may know by this that I have foxskin inside." And so he caused it to be done, but he wore it very little, though it would have been very necessary to him.

CHAPTER LXIII

HOW HE ACCUSED HIMSELF IMMEDIATELY OF VAINGLORY IN GIVING CHARITY

WHEN he went through the city of Assisi, a certain poor old woman begged an alms of him for the love of God. And he immediately gave her the mantle which he had on his back, and forthwith without delay he confessed in the presence of those who followed how he had thence vainglory. And we have seen and heard so many other examples like to these of his very great humility, we who were always in his company, that neither with words nor with letters can we narrate them.

For in this blessed Francis had his chief and highest study, that he should not be a hypocrite before God, and though on account of his infirmity an allowance would have been necessary to him, yet he took thought with himself, always to show a good example to the friars and to others, whence he sustained all poverty patiently that he might take away from all any occasion of murmuring.

CHAPTER LXIV

HOW HE DESCRIBED THE STATE OF PERFECT HUMILITY IN HIMSELF

WHEN the time of the Chapter was drawing near, the holy Father said to his fellow, "It seemeth not to me that I am a Friar Minor, unless I be in the state which I will tell thee. Behold, the friars invite me with great devotion to the Chapter, and moved by their devotion I go to the Chapter with them. But they, being gathered together, ask me to announce to them the Word of God, and to preach amongst them. And rising up, I preach to them as the Holy Spirit shall have taught me. Having finished therefore my sermon, put it that all cry out against me, 'We will not have thee to reign over us, for thou art not eloquent, as is becoming, and thou art too simple and idiotic, and we fear greatly to have so simple and despised a superior over us, whence henceforth, presume not to call thyself our prelate!' And so they cast me out with blame and reproach. It would seem to me that I was not a Friar Minor, if I did not rejoice to the same extent when they reproached me and cast me out with shame, unwilling that I should be their prelate, as when they venerate and honour me; holding their profit and usefulness to be equal in either case. For if I am glad when they exalt and honour me on account of their profit and devotion, where yet there may be a danger to my soul, much more ought I to rejoice and be glad of the profit and salvation of my soul when they blame me, where is certain gain of my soul."

CHAPTER LXV

HOW HE WISHED TO GO HUMBLY TO FOREIGN PARTS AS HE HAD SENT OTHER FRIARS, AND HOW HE TAUGHT THE FRIARS TO GO HUMBLY AND DEVOUTLY THROUGH THE WORLD

When that Chapter was finished in which many friars were sent to certain provinces over sea, blessed Francis, remaining with certain friars, said to them, "Dearest brethren, it behoves me to be the form and example of all friars. If therefore I have sent some of them to distant parts to bear labours and shame, hunger and thirst, and other privations; it is just, and holy humility requires it, that I should go likewise to some distant province, so that the friars may the more patiently sustain adversity when they shall have heard that I bear the same. Go, therefore, and pray the Lord that He may give me to choose that province which should be most to His praise and the profit of souls and the good example of our body." (For it was the manner of the most holy Father when he would go to any province, to pray first the Lord, and to set the friars to pray that the Lord would direct his heart to that same place which was most pleasing to Him.) The brethren therefore went to pray, and when it was finished they returned to him, and straightway he said to them, "In the name of Our Lord Jesus Christ, and of the glorious Virgin Mary His Mother, and of all saints, I choose the province of France in which is a Catholic folk, especially because amongst all other Catholics they show great reverence to the Body of Christ, wherefore I shall converse with them most willingly."

For the holy Father had so much reverence and devotion to the Body of Christ, that he wished it to be written in the Rule that friars should have care and solicitude in the provinces where they should stay concerning this thing; and that they should admonish clerks and priests, to keep the Body of Christ in a good and decent place, which if they neglected, the friars should do it. He wished it also to be placed in the Rule that wherever friars should find the names of the Lord, and these words by which the body of the Lord is made, not well and decently placed, that they themselves should collect them and decently put them away, honouring the Lord in His words. And though these things were not written in the Rule, because it did not seem good to the Ministers that the friars should have this in command, yet he wished to leave his will to the friars concerning these things in his testament and in his other writings. Nay on a certain time, he wished to send some friars through all the provinces carrying many fair and clean pyxes; and wherever they should find the Body of the Lord unsuitably preserved they should put it honourably in those pyxes. Also he wished to send some other friars with good and new wafer-irons to make fair and clean hosts.

When therefore the holy Father chose those brethren whom he wished to take with him, he said to them, "In the name of the Lord, go two and two on the way humbly and decently, and especially with strict silence from the dawn till past the hour of tierce, praying the Lord in your hearts, and let not idle and useless words be so much as named amongst you. For though you walk, let your conversation be as humble and seemly as if you were in a hermitage or in a cell. For wherever we are and walk, we may have always our cell with us. For Brother Body is our cell; and our soul is the hermit, who remains within his cell, to pray to God and to meditate on Him. Whence if the soul does not remain in quiet in its cell, little profits the Religious a cell made with hands?" And when he had arrived at Florence he found there Lord Hugo, the Bishop of Ostia, who was afterwards Pope Gregory. Who, when he had heard from the blessed man, that he wished to go into France, forbade him to go, saying, "Brother, I do not wish you to go beyond the mountains, because there are many prelates who would willingly hinder the good of thy fellowship in the Roman Court. But I and the other Cardinals, who love that body, will more gladly protect and aid it, if you remain in the circuit of this province." And blessed Francis said to him, "My Lord, it is great shame to me to send my other brethren to remote provinces if I remain in these provinces, and am not partaker of the tribulations which they shall suffer on the Lord's behalf." But the Bishop said to him, as if reproving him, "Why hast thou sent thy brethren so far to die with hunger and to sustain other tribulations?" Blessed Francis answered him with great fervour and with the spirit of prophecy, saying, "My Lord, think you that the Lord sent the friars on account of these provinces alone? But I say unto you in truth, that God chose out and sent the friars for the profit and welfare of the souls of all men of this world; and they shall be received, not only in the lands of the faithful, but even among the infidels, and shall gain many souls." Then the Bishop of Ostia wondered at his words, affirming that he spoke the truth. And thus he did not permit him to go into France, though blessed Francis sent thither Brother Pacificus with many other friars, but he himself returned to the valley of Spoleto.

CHAPTER LXVI

HOW HE TAUGHT CERTAIN FRIARS TO GAIN THE SOULS OF SOME THIEVES BY HUMILITY AND CHARITY

To a certain hermitage of friars above the Borgo San Sepolcro there came from time to time thieves, who used to lie in the woods and spoil the passers-by. And some of the friars used to say that it was not good to give them charity, but others gave out of compassion, that they might admonish them to penitence. In the meantime blessed Francis came to that place, whom the friars asked whether it were right to give charity to them. And the holy Father said to them, "If you will do as I will tell you, I trust in the Lord that you shall gain their souls. Go therefore and get some good bread and good wine, and carry them into the wood where they dwell, and shout, saying, 'Brother thieves, come to us, because we are friars, and we bring you good bread and good wine.' They will come forthwith, but you spread a cloth on the earth, and place on it the bread and wine, and serve them humbly and joyfully until they have eaten. But after the meal ye shall speak to them of the Word of the Lord, and finally ye shall ask of them for the love of God that they will promise you this first petition, that they shall not strike nor do evil to any one, in his body. For if ye ask all things at once, they will not hear you, but on account of your humility and charity they will immediately promise you this. Then on another day on account of their good promise, you will carry to them with the bread and wine some eggs and cheese; and ye shall serve them until they have eaten, and after the meal ye shall say to them, 'Why stay ye here all the day to die of hunger and to bear so much adversity, and do many evil things for the which ye shall lose your souls except ye be converted to the Lord? Better is it that ye should serve the Lord, Who will give you in this life the necessities of the body, and in the end will save your souls.' Then the Lord shall inspire them; so that for your humility and charity that ye have shown them they shall be converted." And so the friars did all these things as the holy Father bade them; and those robbers, through the grace and mercy of God, heard and kept letter by letter and point by point all things which the friars humbly asked of them. Nay, on account of the humility and kindliness of the friars towards them, they began to humbly serve the friars themselves, carrying on their shoulders their wood up to the hermitage. And some of them at last entered religion. But the others, confessing their faults, did penance for their sins, promising in the hands of the friars for the future that they would live by the labour of their hands, and never again do such deeds.

CHAPTER LXVII

HOW FROM THE BLOWS OF THE DEMONS HE KNEW IT WAS MORE PLEASING TO THE LORD THAT HE SHOULD STAY IN POOR AND HUMBLE DWELLINGS RATHER THAN WITH CARDINALS

On a certain time blessed Francis went to Rome to visit my Lord of Ostia. And when he had remained some days with him, he visited also my Lord Leo the Cardinal, who was very devoted to the blessed men. And because it was then winter, and altogether unfit for going on foot because of the cold and the winds and the rain, he asked him to abide with him some days, and as a beggar to receive his food from him, with the other beggars who daily used to eat in his house. But this he said, because he knew that the blessed man ever would be received like a beggar wherever he was guested, though the Cardinals and the Lord Pope would receive him with the greatest devotion and reverence, and would venerate him as a saint. And he added, " I will give thee a good house apart where thou mayest abide and where thou canst pray and eat as thou wishest." Then Friar Angelo Tancredi, who was one of the twelve first friars, who also abode with the said Cardinal, said to the blessed man, " Brother, there is near here a certain tower right spacious and apart, where thou mayest abide as if in a hermitage." And when the blessed man had seen it, it pleased him, and returning to the Lord Cardinal he said to him, " My Lord, perchance I will stay with you for some days." And my Lord Cardinal rejoiced greatly. So Brother Angelo went and prepared the place in the tower for the blessed man and his fellow. And because blessed Francis would not come down from thence as long as he should remain with the Cardinal nor wish any one to enter to him, Brother Angelo promised and took orders to daily carry food to him and his fellow. And when the blessed Father had gone there with his fellow; on the first night when he would sleep there, came demons and beat him very sore. And calling his fellow he said to him, " Brother, demons have beaten me very sore, and therefore I will that thou remain with me, for I fear to stay alone." And that night his fellow abode near him. For blessed Francis trembled as a man who suffers fever, wherefore both watched through the whole night. In the meantime the holy Father said to his fellow, " Why have the demons beaten me, and why is that power of hurting me given them by the Lord? " And he said, " The demons are the sergeants of our Lord. For as the Podestà sends his sergeants to punish him who has sinned, so the Lord by sergeants, that is, by the demons who in this world are His ministers, corrects and chastens those whom He loves. For many times he who is a perfect Religious sins ignorantly; whence since he knows not his sin, he is chastened by demons, that he may diligently see and consider, within and without, those things in which he has offended, for whom the Lord loves with a true love, nothing in them He leaves unpunished. But by the mercy and grace of God, I know not that I have offended in anything which I have not amended by confession and satisfaction, nay, by His mercy God has granted me this gift that I may receive in prayer a clear knowledge of all things in which I may please or displease Him. But it may be that He now chastises me by His sergeants for that though my Lord Cardinal willingly showed me mercy, and though it is necessary to my body to receive this rest, yet my brethren who go through the world bearing hunger and many tribulations and the other friars who live in hermitages and poor little dwellings, when they shall hear that I live with my Lord Cardinal, may have an occasion of murmuring, saying, ' We bear so many adverse things, and he has his consolations.' But I am bound always to give them a good example, because for this reason I was given unto them. For the brethren are more edified when I abide in their own poor little dwellings amongst them, than in others; and they bear their tribulations more patiently when they hear that I bear also the same." And it was, therefore, the highest and continual study of our Father, that in all things he might afford a good example, and that he might take away any occasion of murmuring concerning him from other friars. And on account of this, well or ill, he suffered so much, that whichever friars knew him as we who were with him to the day of his death did, as often as they read those things or call them to memory, cannot contain themselves from tears, and they sustain all their tribulations and necessities with greater patience and joy. Therefore blessed Francis came down very early from the tower, and went to my Lord Cardinal; telling him all things that had befallen him and what he had borne with his fellow: nay, he said to him, "Men think me to be a holy man, and behold demons have cast me out of a cell!" And my Lord Cardinal was much rejoiced with him. Yet because he knew and venerated him as a saint, he would not contradict him after he was unwilling to remain there. And so the holy man bidding him farewell, returned to the hermitage of Fonte Palumbo, near Rieti.

CHAPTER LXVIII

HOW HE BLAMED FRIARS WISHING TO GO BY THE WAY OF THEIR WISDOM AND KNOWLEDGE, AND NOT BY THE WAY OF HUMILITY; AND FORETOLD THE REFORMATION OF THE ORDER TO ITS FIRST STATE

When blessed Francis was in the Chapter-General at St. Mary of the Porziuncula (which was called the Chapter of the Mats, because there were no dwellings there except made of mats, and there were five thousand friars there), several wise and learned friars went to my Lord of Ostia who was there and said to him, "My Lord, we wish thee to persuade Brother Francis to follow the counsel of wise brethren, and to allow himself now and then to be led by them." And they quoted the Rule of St. Augustine, of St. Benedict, and of St. Bernard, who taught thus and thus to live in order. And when the Cardinal had repeated this to the holy man, by way of admonition, blessed Francis answered him nothing, but took him by the hand and led him to the friars assembled in the Chapter, and spoke thus to the friars in the fervour and power of the Holy Spirit, "My brethren, my brethren, the Lord called me by the way of simplicity and humility, and this way hath He shown me in truth for me and those who will believe and imitate me. And therefore I would that ye name not to me any rule, neither of St. Augustine, nor St. Benedict, nor of Bernard, nor any way or form of living, but that which was mercifully shown and given me by the Lord. And the Lord said to men that He wished me to be a new covenant in this world, and He would lead me by another way than by this science. But God will confound you through your wisdom and knowledge, and I trust in the sergeants of the Lord that God will punish you by them, and that you will yet return to your state with reproach, willye, nillye." Then the Cardinal was much amazed; and answered nothing, and all the friars feared greatly.

CHAPTER LXIX

HOW HE FORESAW AND PREDICTED THAT LEARNING WOULD BE THE RUIN OF THE ORDER

BLESSED Francis grieved greatly if any one, neglecting virtue, sought after the science which puffeth up, especially if any one did not persist in that vocation to which he was called from the beginning. For he was wont to say, " My brethren who are led by desire of learning shall find their hands empty in the day of tribulation. I would therefore, that they be rather strengthened in virtues, that when the time of tribulation shall come they shall have the Lord with them in their straits. For a time of tribulation is to come, when books shall be useful for nothing, and shall be thrown in windows and cupboards." (This he did not say, for that the reading of Holy Scriptures displeased him, but that he might draw back all from overmuch care of learning. For he wished them rather to be good by charity than smatterers through the desire of knowledge. For he weighed beforehand the time shortly to come, in which already he foreknew that knowledge which puffeth up should be an occasion of ruin. Whence appearing after his death to one of his fellows too intent on the study of preaching, he reproved and prohibited him, and ordered him that he should study to tread the path of humility and simplicity.)

CHAPTER LXX

HOW IN THE TIME OF THE TRIBULATION TO COME, THOSE WHO SHALL ENTER THE ORDER SHALL BE BLESSED, AND THOSE WHO SHALL BE PROVED SHALL BE BETTER THAN THEIR PREDECESSORS

BLESSED Francis used to say, " The time shall come in which this Order beloved by God shall be so defamed by the bad example of evil friars, that it will be ashamed to go forth in public. But they who in that time shall come to join the Order, shall be led only by the working of the Holy Spirit, and flesh and blood shall raise no stain on them, and they shall be blessed by the Lord. Though meritorious deeds be not found in them, since charity grows cold which made the saints work fervently, very great temptations shall come upon them; and those who in that time shall have been found worthy shall be better than their predecessors. But woe unto those, who, with the form and appearance only of religious conversation, applauding themselves in their wisdom and confident in their learning, be found idle (that is, not exercising themselves in virtuous works, in the way of penitence, and in the pure observance of the Gospel; which by their profession they are bound to observe pure and simply). For these will not resist with constancy the temptation which shall be permitted to happen for the proving of the elect; but those who have been tried and approved shall receive the crown of life, to which in the meantime the malice of the reprobate urges them on."

CHAPTER LXXI

HOW HE ANSWERED HIS FELLOW WHO ENQUIRED WHY HE DID NOT CORRECT THE EXCESSES WHICH WERE IN THE ORDER IN HIS OWN DAY

A CERTAIN companion once said to blessed Francis, " Father, forgive me that I would say unto you, which already many have thought." And he said, " Thou knowest how formerly through the grace of God, the whole Order flourished in the purity of perfection; how all friars with great fervour and solicitude observed holy poverty in everything, in small and poor buildings and furniture, in few and poor books and clothes; and as in these so in all other externals they were of one will and fervour, and in the solicitude of observing all things which pertain to our profession and vocation and the example of all; and thus they were of one mind in the love of God and their neighbour, as men truly apostolical and evangelical. But now of late this purity and affection begin to change, though many speak and excuse the friars on account of their multitude, saying that on this account the Rule cannot be observed by them. Nay, many friars have come to such blindness that they think that people will be edified and turn to devotion by this rather than by the former way, and it seems to them that they on this account live more decently, despising and counting for naught the way of holy simplicity, humility, and poverty, which was the beginning and foundation of our Order. Whence we, considering these things, believe that they are displeasing to thee; but we wonder much if they do displease thee, why thou dost allow and not correct them." The holy man answered and said to him, "May the Lord have mercy on thee, brother, since thou wilt be contrary and adversary to me, and mix me up in those things which pertain not to my office. For as long as I had the office of prelacy over the friars, and they remained in their vocation and profession, though from the beginning of my conversion I was always infirm, yet with my small solicitude I satisfied them by example and preaching. But after I saw that the Lord multiplied the number of the friars, and that they, on account of their lukewarmness and want of spirit, began to depart from the right and secure way by which they had been used to walk, and entering on the broader way which leads to death, were not following their vocation and profession and a good example, nor did they wish to abandon that dangerous and deadly journey which they had begun for my preaching and admonition and the example which I showed to them continually, therefore, I handed over the rule of the Order to the Lord and the Ministers. Whence, though at the time when I gave up the office of the prelacy of the friars, I excused myself before them in the Chapter-General, that on account of my infirmities I was not able to have the charge of them, yet if the friars wish to walk according to my will even now, for their consolation and utility, I would not that they should have any other Minister except me until the day of my death." (For from when a faithful and good subject knows and observes the will of his superior, the prelate need have little solicitude concerning him.) "Nay, so much would I rejoice at the profit and the welfare of the brethren on account of their and my gain, that if I were lying ill in bed I should not be ashamed to satisfy them, because my office (that is of prelacy) is spiritual only (namely, to keep under faults and to correct and amend them spiritually). But since I am not able to correct and amend them by preaching, admonition, and example, I will not become an executioner, punishing and flogging them, like the magistrates of this world. For I trust in the Lord that the invisible enemies, who are the sergeants of the Lord for punishment in this world and the next, will take vengeance on those who have transgressed the commands of

God and the vow of their profession, and will make them to be corrected by the men of this world to their disgrace and shame, and thus shall they return to their vocation and profession. Yet truly, until the day of my death I will not cease at once by example and the good works which the Lord has shown me to teach the brethren, and walk by that way which I have taught and shown them by word and example; that they may be inexcusable before God; and I am not bound to give account of them in the presence of God."

After this are written the words which Brother Leo, the companion and confessor of St. Francis, wrote for Brother Conrad of Offida, at Saint Damian near Assisi, saying that he had them from the mouth of the blessed man, the which holy Father was standing near Assisi behind the pulpit of the church of St. Mary of the Angels in prayer, lifting his hands on high to Christ, that He should have mercy on the people, in the great tribulation which must needs come.

And the Lord said, " Francis, if thou wouldst that I should have mercy on the Christian people, do this for Me, that thy Order may remain in that state in which it was placed, because of the whole world there will remain nothing more to Me, and I promise thee, that for the love of thee and of thine Order, I will not permit the world to suffer any tribulation. But I say unto thee, that they must needs go back from the way in which I have placed them, and they will provoke Me to such wrath, that I shall rise against them, and I shall call the demons and I shall give them the power which they have desired, and they shall place such a scandal between them and the world, that there shall be no one who may wear thy habit except in the woods. And when the world loses faith there will not remain any other light except that of thine Order, because I have placed them for a light to the world." And St. Francis said, " On what shall my brethren live who shall dwell in the woods? " And Christ said, " I will feed them as I fed the sons of Israel, with manna in the desert; because they will be like them, and then shall they return to the first state, in which thy Order was founded and begun."

CHAPTER LXXII

THAT THOSE SOULS ARE CONVERTED BY THE PRAYERS AND TEARS OF THE HUMBLE AND SIMPLE BRETHREN WHICH SEEM TO BE CONVERTED BY THE KNOWLEDGE AND PREACHING OF OTHERS

THE most holy Father was unwilling that his friars should be desirous of knowledge and books, but he willed and preached to them that they should desire to be founded on holy humility, and to imitate pure simplicity, holy prayer, and our Lady Poverty, on which the saints and first friars did build. And this, he used to say, was the only safe way to one's own salvation and the edification of others, since Christ, to Whose imitation we are called, showed and taught us this alone by word and example alike. For the blessed Father himself, looking forward to the future, knew by the Holy Spirit, and many times used to say to the brethren, that friars by occasion of teaching others, lose their own vocation, that is, holy humility, pure simplicity, prayer, and devotion, and our Lady Poverty. " And it will happen to them, that they will think themselves to be more filled with devotion and fired with love, and illuminated with the knowledge of God on account of their understanding of the Scriptures. Thence on occasion they will remain cold and empty within, and they cannot return to their first vocation, because they have wasted their time of living according to their vocation in vain and false study. And I fear that that which they seem to have will be taken away from them; because that which was given to them, that is, to hold and to imitate their vocation, they have altogether neglected." And he said, " There are many friars who place all their study and care in acquiring knowledge, leaving their holy vocation, and wandering with mind and body out of the way of humility and of holy prayer. Who, when they shall have preached to the people, and shall have learnt that some are thence edified or turned to penitence, will be puffed up or extol themselves for their work and another's profit, as for their own; when yet they have preached rather to their own condemnation and prejudice, and have done nothing more in truth, except as instruments of those by whom the Lord truly acquired this fruit. For those whom they believe to be edified and converted to penitence by their knowledge and preaching, the Lord has taught and converted by the prayers and tears of holy, poor, and humble and simple friars, though those holy friars, for the most part, know not of it. For thus it is the will of God that they know it not lest they grow proud. These are my brethren of the Table Round, who lie hidden in deserts and hidden places, that more diligently they may give place to prayer and meditation, deploring their own and others' sins, living simply and conversing humbly, whose sanctity is known of God, even when it is unknown to their brethren and to men. And when their souls are brought by the angels to the Lord, then the Lord shall show them the fruit of their labours, namely the many souls which by their example, prayers, and tears, are saved. And He shall say to them, 'My beloved sons, such and so many souls have been saved by your prayers, tears, and example; and because ye have been faithful over few things I will make you rulers over many things. Others, indeed, have preached and have laboured by the speeches of their wisdom and knowledge, and I, by your merits, have brought about the fruit of salvation. Therefore receive the reward of their labours and the fruit of your merits, which is an everlasting kingdom; which you have taken by the force of the violence of your humility and simplicity, and of your prayers and tears.' And thus these, carrying their sheaves (that is, the fruits and merits of their holy humility and simplicity), shall enter into the joy of the Lord rejoicing and exulting. But they who have taken no thought except to know and to show to others the way of salvation, doing nothing for themselves, shall stand naked and empty before the tribunal of Christ, bringing only sheaves of confusion, shame, and grief. Then shall the truth of holy humility and simplicity, and holy prayer and poverty, which is our vocation, be exalted and glorified and magnified, which truth those puffed up with the wind of science condemned with their life, and with the vain speeches of their wisdom, saying that the truth was falsehood, and like blind men, persecuting cruelly those who have walked in the truth. Then the error and falsity of their opinions by which they have walked, which they have preached for truth, by which they have thrown many into the pit of blindness, shall be ended in grief, confusion, and shame, and they themselves with their opinions shall be plunged in outer darkness with the spirits of darkness." Whence blessed Francis often used to say concerning that word: *then the barren hath born many, and she that hath many children is waxed feeble:* "the barren is a good Religious, simple, humble, poor, and despised, who by his holy prayers and virtues continually edifies others, and brings forth good fruit with dolorous sighs." This word he used to say very often before the Ministers and other friars, especially in the Chapter-General.

CHAPTER LXXIII

HOW HE WILLED AND TAUGHT THAT PRELATES AND PREACHERS SHOULD EXERCISE THEMSELVES IN PRAYER AND WORKS OF HUMILITY

THE faithful servant and perfect imitator of Christ, Francis, feeling himself to be most thoroughly transformed by the virtue of holy humility in Christ: above all other virtues desired this humility in his brethren, and that they might love, desire, acquire, and preserve this grace, he animated them incessantly both with word and example, and especially did he admonish and induce the Ministers and preachers to exercise works of humility. For he used to say that they ought not on account of the duty of their prelacy and their solicitude of preaching to neglect holy and devout prayer, or going for alms, working sometimes with their hands, and doing other works like the rest of the friars, for the sake of the good example and the profit of their own and others' souls. And he said, "For subject friars are much edified, when their Ministers and preachers spend time in prayer, and bend themselves willingly to works of utility, and lightly-esteemed duties. But otherwise they cannot without confusion, prejudice, and condemnation of themselves, admonish other friars concerning works; for it becomes us by the example of Christ rather to do than to teach, and to do and teach together."

CHAPTER LXXIV

HOW HE TAUGHT THE FRIARS TO KNOW WHEN HE WAS THE SERVANT OF GOD AND WHEN NOT

BLESSED Francis once called together many friars, and said to them, "I have asked the Lord, that He would deign to show me when I am His servant. But the most gracious Lord in His condescension answered me, 'I know that thou art truly

My servant when thou thinkest, speakest, and doest holy things.' Therefore have I called you, brethren, and have shown this to you, that I may be put to shame before you, when you shall see me wanting in any of the aforesaid things."

CHAPTER LXXV

HOW HE WILLED EXPRESSLY THAT FRIARS LABOUR NOW AND THEN WITH THEIR HANDS

HE used to say that lukewarm ones who did not apply themselves to any task busily and humbly would quickly be spewed out from the mouth of the Lord; so that no idle man could appear before him, without being at once sternly rebuked. And thus he, the example of all perfection, laboured humbly with his hands, permitting nothing of the best gift of time to flow to waste. For he said, "I wish all my friars to labour and be exercised humbly in good works, that we be the less burdensome to men, and that neither heart nor tongue may wander in ease. But let those who know nothing learn to work." For he used to say that the profit and reward of the labour should not be left to the will of the labourer, but to the judgment of the warden or the community.

SECTION V

CONCERNING HIS ZEAL FOR THE PERFECTION OF THE RULE AND THE WHOLE ORDER

CHAPTER LXXVI

AND FIRSTLY, HOW HE USED TO PRAISE THE PROFESSION OF THE RULE AND WISH THE FRIARS TO KNOW IT, AND THAT IT SHOULD BE KEPT BY ALL FRIARS

BLESSED Francis, perfectly zealous and a lover of the Observance of the Holy Gospel, was most ardently zealous for the common profession of our Rule, which is none other than the perfect Observance of the Gospel; and he endowed those who are and shall be true enthusiasts for it with his special blessing. For he used to say to his imitators that this our profession was the book of life, the hope of salvation, the foretaste of Glory, the marrow of the Gospel, the way of the cross, the state of perfection, the key of Paradise, and the pact of the eternal covenant. This he wished to be held and known of all, and he wished his brethren to confer concerning it very often in their conversation against weariness, and in memory of their first oath full often to talk of it with their inner man. He taught them also that it should always be carried before their eyes in commemoration and memory of leading the life, and of the due Observance of the Rule, and what is more, he wished and taught that the friars should die with it.

CHAPTER LXXVII

OF A HOLY LAYBROTHER WHO WAS MARTYRED HOLDING THE RULE IN HIS HAND

NOT unmindful therefore of the teaching of the most blessed Father, a certain laybrother, whom we believe undoubtedly to have been taken into the choir of martyrs, when he was amongst the infidels for the desire of martyrdom, and while he was being led to martyrdom by the Saracens, holding the Rule with great fervour in both his hands, his knees humbly bent, said to his fellow, "I confess myself guilty, dearest brother, before the eyes of the Divine Majesty and before thee, of all things which I have done against this Rule." To this short confession succeeded the sword, by which, finishing his life, he attained the crown of martyrdom. For he had entered the Order so young, that he was hardly able to bear the yoke of the Rule, and yet a youth he bore a shirt of mail next his flesh. Happy boy, who happily began, and more happily ended!

CHAPTER LXXVIII

HOW HE WISHED HIS ORDER TO BE ALWAYS SUBJECT TO THE PROTECTION AND CORRECTION OF THE ROMAN CHURCH

Blessed Francis used to say, "I will go and commend the Order of the Friars Minor to the holy Roman Church, by whose mighty rod its evil wishers may be terrified and kept in check, and the sons of God may rejoice everywhere with full liberty, to the increase of their eternal salvation. Let my sons recognise from this the sweet benefits of their mother, and ever embrace her reverend footsteps with spiritual devotion towards her. For under her protection, no evil son of Belial shall come into the Order, the impious shall pass through the vineyard of the Lord. That mother shall gather up the glory of our poverty and will not permit the joy of obedience and the reward of humility in any way to be darkened by the cloud of pride. She will preserve untouched the bonds of charity and of peace among us; striking with her strictest censure the unwilling, and the holy Observation of Evangelical purity shall continually flourish in her sight, nor will she suffer the odour of good fame and holy conversation to be lost at any time."

CHAPTER LXXIX

OF THE FOUR PREROGATIVES WHICH THE LORD GAVE TO THE ORDER REVEALING THEM TO SAINT FRANCIS

Blessed Francis said that he had obtained from the Lord these four things, announced to him by an angel: namely, that the Order and profession of Friars Minor should never fail even to the Day of Judgment. Also that no one setting himself with all his might to persecute the Order should live long. Also that no evil man, wishing to live evilly in the Order, should be able to remain in it long. Also whoever from his heart should love the Order, although he should be a sinner, yet he should at the last obtain mercy.

CHAPTER LXXX

OF WHAT SORT THE MINISTER-GENERAL SHOULD BE

SUCH was the zeal which he had for the preservation of perfection in the Order, and such seemed to him the perfection of the profession of the Rule, that he often used to consider who would be sufficient after his death for the governance of the whole Order, and to the conservation of perfection in it with the help of God; and he could come upon none fit.

Whence near the end of his life, a certain friar said to him, "Father, thou wilt pass away to the Lord, and this family which has followed thee will remain in the vale of tears. Point out any one in the Order, if thou knowest one, in whom thy mind might be at rest, on whom the burden of the Minister-General may be worthily imposed." Blessed Francis answered, pointing all his words with sighs, "My son, I behold no sufficient leader of so great and various an army, no shepherd of so wide and scattered a flock, but I will paint to you one in whom should shine out how the leader and shepherd of this family ought to be. This man (he said) ought to be of most grave life, of great discretion, of laudable report, without private affections, lest while he loves more dearly on one side, scandal may grow in the whole body. There should be in him friendly zeal for prayer, yet so that he distribute certain hours to his own soul, and certain to his flock. For early in the morning, he should put before all things the most holy sacrifice of the Mass, and there, with long devotion, most earnestly commend himself and his flock to the divine protection. But after prayer he shall place himself in the midst that he may be questioned by all, answer to all, to provide for all with charity and patience and gentleness.

"For he should be no acceptor of persons, so that he should take no less heed of the simple and foolish than of the wise and learned. To whom if the gift of learning be granted, yet let him bear in his manner the stamp of piety and simplicity, of patience and humility, and let him cherish these virtues, in himself and in others, and continually exercise himself in preaching them, inciting others more by example than by speech. Let him be a hater of money, which is the chief corruption of our profession and perfection, and as the head and example to be imitated by all, let him in no wise be wasted by many store-chests.

"Let a habit and a book be sufficient for himself, but for others his pencase with a reed and writing tablets, and a seal. Let him not be a collector of books nor much given to reading, lest haply that be taken from his office which is given to study. Let him console piously the afflicted, since he is the last resort of those in tribulation, lest if the remedies of health be wanting with him, despair of disease should prevail in the infirm. That he may bend the violent to gentleness, let him bear himself humbly, and relax something of his own rights that he may have profit of their soul. To the runaways of the Order, as to sheep who have perished, let him extend the bowels of pity, and let him never deny mercy to them; knowing those temptations to be very great which could compel to such a fall, which temptations if the Lord should permit to him, he himself might haply fall into a greater precipice.

"I will that he, as vicar of Christ, be honoured by all with devotion and reverence and that he be provided for by all and in all things with all good-will, according to his necessity and the lowliness of our condition. Yet it will behove him not to smile on honours; nor to rejoice more in favours than in injuries, so that his manners be not changed by honours except for the better. But if sometimes he may need pleasanter and better food; let him not take it privately but in a public place, that the shame may be taken from others of providing them in their infirmities and weaknesses. It behoves him chiefly to distinguish hidden knowledge, and to search out the truth from secret veins. Let him hold all accusations suspect in the beginning, until the truth begin to appear by diligent examination. Let him not lend his ear to much speakers, and let him hold them especially suspect in accusations, nor lightly believe them. He should be such as would, for the desire of retaining vile honour, never injure nor relax the form of justice and equity. Yet so, that out of too much rigour the soul of no one may be destroyed, and out of superfluous gentleness sloth be not generated, and out of lax indulgence the dissolution of discipline come not: and thus that he be feared by all, and loved of those that fear him.

Let him always think and feel the office of his prelacy rather a burden than an honour to him. I wish also that he have for fellows men well spoken of for honesty, rigid against their own wills, strong in need, pious and compassionate to delinquents, having equal affection to all, receiving nothing of their labour except the pure necessity of the body; and desiring nothing except the praise of God, the welfare of the Order, the merit of their own souls, and the perfect health of all the brethren; suitably affable to all, and receiving those coming to them with holy joy, and showing the form and Observance of the Gospel, according to the profession of the Rule, in themselves purely and simply to all. Behold, I say, such should be the Minister-General of this Order, and such the fellows he should have."

CHAPTER LXXXI

HOW THE LORD SPAKE UNTO HIM, WHEN HE WAS GREATLY AFFLICTED ON ACCOUNT OF THE FRIARS WHO WERE DEPARTING FROM PERFECTION

SINCE, according to the measure of zeal which he continually had for the perfection of the Order, he must needs be sad if he saw or heard any imperfection therein, when he began to understand that some friars were giving an evil example to the Order, and that the friars (now at the highest point of their perfection and profession) had begun to decline, touched inwardly with too great sorrow of heart, on a time he said to the Lord in prayer, "Lord, I give back to Thy charge the family which Thou hast given me!" And immediately the Lord said to him, "Tell Me, oh simple and feeble-minded mannikin, why thou art so sad when any man goes out of the Order, and when the friars do not walk by the way which I have shown thee? Also, tell Me Who has planted this order of friars? Who has made man to be converted to penitence; Who gives the virtue of perseverance? Is it not I? I have not chosen thee over My household as a learned and eloquent man, because I wish neither thee nor those that were true friars and true observers of the rule which I have given thee, to walk by the way of science and eloquence. But I have chosen thee a simple and unlearned man that thou mayest know, both thou and others, that I will watch over My flock, and I have placed thee for a sign to them, that the works which I work in thee, they may work in themselves.

For those who walk in the way I have shown thee, have Me more abundantly. But those who wish to walk by another way, even that which they seem to have shall be taken away from them. Wherefore I say unto thee, for the rest, be not so sad, but do what thou doest, work what thou workest, since I have planted in perpetual charity the Order of Friars. Whence thou art to know that because I love them so much if any friar, having returned to his vomit, should die outside the Order, I will send another into the Order, who in his place shall have his crown. And if he be not born, I will make him to be born. And that you may know how freely I love the life and Order of Friars; let it be granted that in the whole Order there should not remain except three, yet even then it shall be My Order, and I will not give it up for ever." And when he heard these words his mind remained wonderfully consoled. And though on account of the great zeal which he always had for the perfection of the Order he was not able wholly to contain himself from growing vehemently sad when he heard of any imperfection done by the friars by which evil example or scandal might arise, yet after he was thus strengthened by the Lord he recalled to memory that word of the psalm: *I have sworn and I will perform it, that I will keep thy righteous judgments:* "and to preserve the rule which the Lord Himself gave to me, and to those who would wish to imitate me."

"But all those friars have obliged themselves to this as I; and therefore since I have put off me the burden of the brethren by reason of my infirmities and other reasonable causes, I am not bound further than to pray for the Order, and to show a good example to the brethren. For this I have from the Lord and know for truth, that if infirmities did not excuse me, the greatest help which I could give the Order is, to spend the time daily in prayer for it to the Lord, because He governs, keeps, and protects it. For in this, I have bound myself to the Lord and to the brethren; that if any friar should perish by my evil example, I will be bound to render reason for him to the Lord." These words he used to speak within himself to quiet his heart, and he also used to explain it right often to the friars in his discourses and at Chapters. Whence if any friar said at any time to him, that he ought to interfere with the governance of the Order, he used to answer saying, "The friars have their Rule, and have sworn to keep it. And that they may not have any excuse on my account, after it pleased the Lord to command me to be their prelate, I swore before them likewise to observe it. Whence, since the friars know what they ought to do, and what also to avoid, there remains nothing, except that I should teach them by my works; since for this cause I am given to them, in my life and after my death."

CHAPTER LXXXII

OF THE SINGULAR ZEAL WHICH HE HAD TO THE PLACE OF BLESSED MARY AND OF THE CONSTITUTIONS WHICH HE HAD MADE AGAINST IDLE WORDS THERE

ABOVE the other dwellings of the Order, he had a singular zeal and especial desire always, while he lived, to observe all perfection of life and conversation in the holy dwelling of St. Mary of the Angels, as toward the head and mother of the whole Order; intending and willing that place to be the form and example of humility and poverty and all Evangelical Perfection for all places, and that the friars staying there should ever be, beyond other friars, circumspect and solicitous in doing and avoiding all things which tend to the perfection of the Observance of the Rule. Whence on a certain time, to avoid idleness which is the root of all evils, especially in a Religious, he ordained that each day after meals the friars should engage with him in some work lest they should lose altogether or in part, the good which they had gained in the time of prayer by useless and idle words, to which man is especially disposed after food. Also he ordered and commanded it to be firmly observed; that if any of the friars idling or working amongst the brethren, should utter any idle word, he should be bound to say one *Pater Noster*, praising God in the beginning and the end of the prayer. Yet so, that if by chance he, conscious of his fault, should have confessed that which he had done, he should say the *Pater Noster* for his own soul, together with the *Laudes Domini* as has been said. But if he were first blamed by any other friar, then he should be bound to say the *Pater Noster* as aforesaid for the soul of the brother rebuking him. But if he who was blamed excused himself, and would not say the *Pater Noster*, he should be bound in the same way to say it twice for the soul of the brother reproving him. But if, by the testimony of himself or of another, it should prove to be true that he had said that idle word, then he should say also the said *Laudes* at the beginning and end of his prayer, so loudly that he may be heard or understood by all friars standing round about. Which friars, while he is saying it, shall hold their peace and listen. But if anybody seeing and hearing a brother say an idle word shall keep silent and shall not reprove him, he shall be bound in the same way to say the *Pater Noster* with the *Laudes* for his soul. And any friar whatever entering a cell or a house, or any place, who shall find there a friar or friars, should immediate devoutly thank and praise the Lord. The most holy Father was always solicitous to repeat these *Laudes*, and he taught other friars with a most ardent will and desire and excited them to saying those *Laudes* carefully and devoutly.

CHAPTER LXXXIII

HOW HE ADMONISHED THE FRIARS THAT THEY SHOULD NEVER LEAVE THAT PLACE

THOUGH blessed Francis knew that the kingdom of Heaven was established in every place of the earth, and though he believed that in every place the divine grace could be given to the elect of God, yet he had found the dwelling of blessed Mary of the Porziuncula to be filled with richer grace, and to be frequented by the heavenly visitations of celestial spirits. For this reason he used often to say to the friars, "See, oh my sons, that ye never leave this place, if you are thrown out on one side enter by another, for this place is holy, and the habitation of Christ and of the Virgin His mother. Here, when we were few, the Most High increased us, here He enlightened the souls of His poor by the light of His wisdom, here He inflamed our wills by the fire of His love. Here he who shall pray with a devout heart shall obtain what he seeks, and an offender shall be more heavily punished. For which cause, O sons, hold this dwelling most worthy with reverence and honour as truly the dwelling of God, singularly beloved by Him and His mother, and therein with your whole heart with the speech of exultation and confession, confess to God the Father and to His Son Our Lord Jesus Christ, in the unity of the Holy Spirit."

CHAPTER LXXXIV

OF THE PREROGATIVES WHICH THE LORD WROUGHT IN THE DWELLING OF ST. MARY

Holy of holies   truly is this place of places.
Worthily held worthy   of great honours.
Happy its surname   more happy is its name.
And now its third name   arises, omen of the gift.
The Angelic presence   here casts abroad the light.
Here watches oft by night   sounding hymns with the voice.
Afterward all fell to ruin   Francis raised it up again.
Out of the three it was one   which the Father himself repaired.
This the Father chose   when with sackcloth he clothed his members.
Here he broke the body   and forced it to obey the mind.
Here by the fire of his love   he kindled our wills.
Here within the temple   was begotten the Order, of Minors.
While the Father's example   a crowd of men doth follow.
Clara, the spouse of God   was here the first time shorn.
Cast off the pomps of the world   and followed Christ.
Here the renowned birth   of brothers at once and of sisters.
The holy mother bare   by whom she brought back Christ to the world.
Here was made narrow   the broad road of the old world.
And virtue made wider   for the chosen race.
Here grew the Rule   Holy Poverty reborn.
Pride smitten down   the cross called back among us.
Thus where was troubled   Francis, and sore wearied.
Here was he rested   his death here was renewed.
Here was he shown   the truth whereof he doubted.
Nay, here was granted   whatever that Father desired.

SECTION VI

OF HIS ZEAL FOR THE PERFECTION OF THE BRETHREN

CHAPTER LXXXV

AND, FIRSTLY, HOW HE DESCRIBED TO THEM THE PERFECT FRIAR

The most blessed Father, having transformed in some sort his brethren into saints by the ardour of the love and the fervour of the zeal which he had for their perfection, often thought within himself, by what conditions and virtues a good Friar Minor should be adorned. And he used to say that he would be a good Friar Minor who should have the life and conditions of these holy friars, to wit: the faith of Brother Bernard, which he had most perfectly, with the love of poverty: the simplicity and poverty of Brother Leo, who was truly of the holiest purity: the courtesy of Brother Angelo, who was the first knight who came to the Order, and who was adorned with all courtesy and benignity: the gracious and natural sense, with the fair and devout eloquence, of Brother Masseo: the mind raised in contemplation, which Brother Giles had in the highest perfection: the virtuous and continual labour of holy Rufinus, who without intermission prayed always, for even when sleeping or doing anything, his mind was always with the Lord: the patience of Brother Juniper, who arrived at the perfect state of patience, because of the perfect truth of his own vileness which he had before his eyes: and the desire in the highest degree of imitating Christ through the bodily and spiritual strength of the cross, of Brother John of the Lauds, who in his time was strong of body above all men: the charity of Brother Roger, whose whole life and conversation was in the fervour of charity: and the solicitude of Brother Lucido, who was of the greatest solicitude, and was unwilling to stay in one place for a month, but when it pleased him to stay in any place, immediately he went away from there, and said, "We have no dwelling-place here but in Heaven."

CHAPTER LXXXVI

HOW HE DESCRIBED SHAMEFAST EYES, THAT HE MIGHT TEACH BECOMING BEHAVIOUR

AMONGST the other virtues which he loved and desired to be in the brethren, after the foundation of holy humility, he specially loved the fairness and cleanness of decency. Whence wishing to teach the friars to have shamefast eyes, he was accustomed to represent wanton eyes by this tale: A pious and powerful king sent to the queen two messengers successively. The first returns and brings back word for word, and speaks nothing of the queen. For he had held his eyes in his head wisely, nor had cast them at all upon the queen. The other returned and after a few words wove a long history of the beauty of the queen: "Truly," said he, "Lord, I have seen a most beautiful woman; happy is he who enjoys her!" And the king said to him, "Thou, wicked servant, hast cast shameless eyes on my wife; it is plain that thou hast wished subtily to obtain that thou hast seen." He ordered the first therefore to be called again, and said to him, "What thinkest thou of the queen?" "She seems," said he, "to me right good, because she listened willingly and patiently" (and he answered wisely). And the king said to him, "But what of the beauty which is in her?" He answered, "My Lord, it is thine to behold it, it was mine to carry thy words." The sentence was given by the king: "Thou," said he, "having chaste eyes, be of chaster body in my chamber, and enjoy my delights, but let this shameless one go out from my house, lest he should pollute my bed." Therefore he used to say, "Who would not fear to look upon the spouse of Christ?"

CHAPTER LXXXVII

OF THE THREE SAYINGS WHICH HE LEFT TO THE FRIARS TO PRESERVE THEIR PERFECTION

ON a certain time when on account of the weakness of his stomach he desired to vomit, on account of the great violence he did to himself, he vomited blood for the whole night until the morning. And when his companions saw him ready to die, through his great weakness and affliction, they said to him with the greatest grief and shedding of tears, "Father, what shall we do without thee? Thou wast ever our father and mother, begetting and bringing us forth in Christ. Thou wast a leader and a shepherd to us, a master and a corrector, teaching and correcting us more by example than by word. Whither therefore shall we go, sheep without a shepherd, orphans without a father, rude and simple men without a leader? Where shall we go to seek thee, O glory of poverty, praise of simplicity, and honour of our vileness? Who shall show us, blind ones, henceforth the way of truth; where will the speaking mouth be, and the tongue that counselled us? Where will be the fervent spirit, directing us in the way of the cross; and strengthening us to evangelical perfection? Where wilt thou be that we may come to thee, light of our eyes; that we may seek thee, consoler of our souls? Behold, Father, thou diest; behold, thou desertest us thus desolate, leaving us thus sad and bitter; behold, that day, the day of weeping and bitterness, the day of desolation and sadness draweth near! Behold the bitter day which we have always been fearing to see since we have been with thee; even when we were not able to think of it. Nor is it strange, truly, because thy life is a continuous light to us, and thy words were torches, burning and guiding us continually to the way of the cross and evangelical perfection, to the love and imitation of the most sweet Crucified One! And therefore, Father, forthwith bless us and thy other friars whom thou hast begotten in Christ; and leave to us some memorial of thy will; that thy brethren may have thee always in memory, and that they may say, 'These words our Father left to his brethren and his sons at his death.'" Then the most pious Father, turning his paternal eyes on his sons, said to them, "Call to me Brother Benedict of Prato." For that brother was a priest, holy and discreet, who celebrated for blessed Francis while he lay there infirm (because always when he was able, he wished to have or hear a mass as long as he was sick). And when he had come to him, he said to him, "Write how I bless my brethren who are in the Order, and who shall come, unto the end of the world. And since on account of my weakness and the pain of my infirmity I may not speak, in these three words I make plain my will and intention briefly to all my brethren, present and to come; namely, that in token of my memory and benediction and will, they should always love one another like as I have loved and do love them; that they should always love and observe our Lady Poverty, and always remain faithful subjects to the prelates and clergy of holy Mother Church."

For thus in the Chapter of the friars our Father had always been anxious at the end of the Chapter to bless and absolve all friars present and to come in the Order, and even out of Chapter he did the same many times in the fervour of his charity. But he used to warn the friars, that they should fear and guard themselves from evil example; and he cursed all those who by evil example provoked men to blaspheme the Order and life of the friars, because good and holy poor men are shamed by this and much afflicted.

CHAPTER LXXXVIII

OF THE LOVE WHICH HE SHOWED TO THE FRIARS WHEN NEAR HIS DEATH, GIVING TO EACH A MOUTHFUL OF BREAD BY THE EXAMPLE OF CHRIST

On a certain night blessed Francis was so weighed upon by the pains of his infirmities, that he could neither rest nor sleep that whole night. But in the morning, when his pains had a little ceased, he caused all the friars in the dwelling to be called. And placing his right hand on the head of each of them, he blessed them all, present and absent, and those who should come to the Order up to the end of the world; and he seemed to have compassion on himself, because he was not able to see all his brethren and his sons before his death. But wishing in his death to imitate his Lord and Master, as he had perfectly imitated Him in his life, he ordered loaves to be brought to him, and blessed them, and made them to be broken into portions; because on account of his great weakness he was not strong enough to break it. And taking it, he handed to each of the friars a portion, bidding him eat the whole of it. Whence as the Lord before His death wished in token of His love to eat with His disciples on the Thursday, so blessed Francis, His perfect imitator, wished to show the same sign of love to his brethren. And that he wished to do this in the likeness of Christ appears manifestly, because he afterwards asked if it were then Thursday. But one of those friars kept back a particle of that bread, and after the death of blessed Francis, many sick who tasted thereof were immediately liberated from their infirmities.

CHAPTER LXXXIX

HOW HE FEARED LEST THE FRIARS SHOULD COMPLAIN OF HIS INFIRMITY

When, on account of the pain of his infirmities he was not able to rest, and had seen that thereby the friars were much distracted and fatigued on his account, since he loved the souls of his brethren more than his own body, he began to fear lest from their too great labour on his account the friars should incur even the least offence before God on account of some impatience. Whence on a time he said with piety and compassion to his companions, " Dearest brethren, and my little sons, let it not weary you to labour for my infirmity; since the Lord will return to you all the fruit of your works for His humble servant in this world and in the future; and those things which ye may not do now on account of the care of my infirmity, ye shall acquire even greater profit than if you had done them for yourself, since he who aids me, aids the whole religion and life of the friars. Nay more, ye ought to say thus, ' We will make our expense over thee, and the Lord will be our debtor on your account.' " (But the holy Father said this wishing to assist and raise the cowardice of their spirits, on account of the great zeal which he had for the perfection of their souls. He feared also lest sometimes tempted by that labour they might say, " We cannot pray nor suffer such labour," and thus they should become wearied and impatient of such small labour, and lose great fruit.)

CHAPTER XC

HOW HE ADMONISHED THE SISTERS OF ST. CLARE

After blessed Francis made his " Praises to the Lord concerning His creatures," he made also certain holy words with a song for the consolation and edification of the poor ladies, knowing them to be greatly troubled concerning his infirmity; and when he could not visit them in person he sent those words to them by his companions. For he wished to make plain his will to them in those words, namely, how they should live and converse humbly, and be of one mind in charity. For he saw that their conversion and holy conversation was not only an exaltation of the Order of the friars but also a very great edification of the Church Universal. But knowing that in the beginning of their conversion they had led a very narrow and poor life, he was always moved to pity and compassion for them. Whence he asked them in those same words that as the Lord had gathered them together from many places into one, to holy charity, holy poverty, and holy obedience, so they should always live and die in them. And strictly did he warn them, that they should provide for their bodies discreetly out of the alms which the Lord should give to them, with joyfulness and giving of thanks; and especially that they should ever be patient in the labours which they sustained for their infirm sisters, and that the infirm themselves should be likewise patient in their infirmities.

SECTION VII

OF HIS CONTINUAL FERVOUR OF LOVE AND PASSION FOR THE PASSION OF CHRIST

CHAPTER XCI

AND FIRSTLY, HOW HE TOOK NO CARE OF HIS OWN INFIRMITIES ON ACCOUNT OF HIS LOVE OF THE PASSION OF CHRIST

So great was the fervour of love and compassion of blessed Francis for the pains and sufferings of Christ, and so much was he daily afflicted on account of that passion, within and without, that he took no care of his own infirmities. Whence, though for a long time, up to the day of his death, he had suffered ailments of the stomach and liver and spleen, and from the time when he returned from over-sea he had had very great pains of his eyes continually, yet he would not on that account take any pains to make himself be made whole. Whence my Lord of Ostia, seeing that he was and ever had been austere to his body, and especially as he had now begun to lose the light of his eyes; and because he would not be made whole, admonished him with great pity and compassion, saying, "Brother, thou dost not well, because thou dost not get thyself cured, though thy life and health be very useful to friars and seculars, and the whole church. For if thou hadst compassion on thy infirm brethren, and wert always pious and merciful to them, thou shouldst not be cruel to thyself in so great a necessity. For which reason I command thee to cause thyself to be cured and assisted." (For that most holy Father ever took that which was bitter for sweet, because he drew immense sweetness from the humility and footsteps of the Son of God.)

CHAPTER XCII

HOW HE WAS FOUND GOING, LAMENTING IN A LOUD VOICE THE PASSION OF CHRIST

On a certain time a little after his conversion, when he was walking alone on the road not very far from the church of St. Mary of the Porziuncula, he went with a loud voice lamenting. But a certain spiritually-minded man met him, and fearing lest he had pain of some ailment, said to him, " What is the matter, Brother? " But he answered, " Thus I go through the world without shame, lamenting the Passion of my Lord." Then they both began to weep together, and shed many tears. This man we have known, and have learnt this from him, who also showed much consolation and mercy to the blessed man and to us his fellows.

CHAPTER XCIII

HOW THE JOYS WHICH HE SOMETIMES HAD WERE TURNED INTO TEARS

DRUNKEN with the love and compassion of Christ, blessed Francis on a time did things such as these. For the most sweet melody of spirit boiling up within him frequently broke out in French speech and the veins of murmuring which he heard secretly with his ears, broke forth into French-like rejoicing. And sometimes he picked up a branch from the earth, and laying it on his left arm, he drew in his right hand another stick like a bow over it, as if on a viol or other instrument, and making fitting gestures, sang with it in French unto the Lord Jesus Christ. But all this playing ended in tears, and this joy dissolved in sorrow for the Passion of Christ. In these times he would draw sighs continually; and with deep-drawn groans, forgetful of those things which he held in his hands, he was raised to Heaven.

SECTION VIII

OF HIS ZEAL FOR THE ORDER AND THE DIVINE WORK

CHAPTER XCIV

AND FIRSTLY, OF PRAYER AND THE DIVINE OFFICE

THOUGH for many years he had been afflicted with the aforesaid infirmities, yet was he so devout and reverent at prayer and the Divine Office, that every time he was praying or repeating the canonical Hours, he would never lean on the wall or doorpost. For he generally stood erect and bareheaded, though he was sometimes on his knees; more especially because he spent the greater part of the day and the night in prayer; nay, when he went through the world afoot he always stayed his steps when he wished to say his Hours. But if he were riding, on account of his ailment, he always alighted to say the Office. On a certain time it was raining very much, and he was riding by reason of his infirmity and very great necessity, and though he was wholly soaked through, he got off the horse when he wished to say his Hours, and said his Office with as great a fervour of devotion and reverence thus, standing on the road with the rain falling on him continually, as if he had been in a church or a cell. And he said to his companion, " If the body wishes to eat its food in peace and quietness, when both are but the food of worms, with how much quiet and peace, with how great a reverence and devotion, should the mind receive that food which is God Himself."

CHAPTER XCV

HOW HE EVER LOVED SPIRITUAL GLADNESS IN HIMSELF AND OTHERS

THE blessed Father ever used to have his highest and especial study in this, that apart from prayer and the Divine Office, he should continually have spiritual gladness; and this likewise he singularly loved in his brethren, nay, he often reproved them for sadness and outward grief. For he used to say that "if the servant of God would study to preserve within and without the spiritual joy which comes of cleanness of heart and is acquired by devoutness of prayer, the demons would not be able to harm him, for they would say, 'Since this servant of God has joy in tribulation as in prosperity, we can find no way of entering to him nor of hurting him.' But the demons exult when they can quench or hinder in any way the devotion and joy which arises from prayer and other virtuous works. For if the devil may have aught of his own in the servant of God, except he be a wise man and solicitous to take away and destroy it as soon as possible by the virtue of holy prayer, contrition, confession, and satisfaction, in a short time he will make from one hair a beam to throw upon him. Since, therefore, my brethren, this spiritual joy comes of cleanness of heart and the purity of continual prayer, ye should be first and foremost desirous to acquire and conserve these two things, that ye may have, within and without, that joy which with the greatest longing I desire and wish to know and feel in you and myself, to the edification of our neighbours and the reproach of the enemy. For it pertaineth to him and to his members, to grow sad, but to you ever to rejoice and be glad in the Lord."

CHAPTER XCVI

HOW HE REPROVED HIS FELLOW WHO WAS SAD OF FACE, AND CONCERNING INTELLIGIBLE GLADNESS

THE holy Father used to say, "Although I know the demons envy me the blessings which the Lord has given me; yet I know and see that they cannot hurt me by myself, and they intend and desire to hurt me by my fellows. But if they cannot harm me by myself, or by my fellows, they retire with great confusion. Nay, if I am sometimes tempted or full of grief, when I perceive the gladness of my fellows immediately on account of their joy I return from my temptation and grief to my interior and exterior joy." On account of these things, the Father himself used often to blame those who made a show of sadness. For on a certain time he blamed one of his fellows who appeared sad of face, and said to him, "Why dost thou make an outward show of sorrow and sadness for thy offences? Keep thou this sadness between thee and thy God, and pray to Him that by His mercy He may spare thee, and restore to thy soul the gladness of His salvation, which is taken away from thee on account of sin; but before me and others, study always to have joy, for it befits not the servant of God to show before his brother or another sadness or a troubled face."

Not that it should be thought or believed that our Father, a lover of all gravity and decency, would have wished this gladness to be shown by laughing or by the least vain word; since by this not spiritual gladness but rather vanity and folly is shown; nay, he even singularly abhorred laughing and idle words in the servant of God; since not only did he wish that he should not laugh, but not even afford to others the slightest occasion for laughing. Whence in a certain admonition of his, he laid down more clearly what should be the joy of the servant of God. For he said, "Blessed is that Religious, who has no joy nor gladness except in the most holy words and works of the Lord, and with these provokes man to the love of the Lord in joy and gladness. And woe to that Religious who rejoices in idle and vain words, and with these provokes men to laughter."

By gladness of face, therefore, he understood fervour and solicitude and the disposition and preparation of mind and body to doing freely all good works, because by fervour and disposition of this kind others are more provoked sometimes than by the good deed itself; nay, if an act, however good, does not seem to be done willingly and fervently, it rather causes disgust than provokes to good. And so he did not wish to see sadness in the face, which most often represents melancholy and indisposition of mind and idleness of body to all good. But he ever loved above all things gravity and maturity in face and in all the members of the body and the senses in himself and in others, and he induced others to do this as much as he could by word and example. For he had found out that gravity and modesty of manners of this kind was like a wall and a very strong shield against the shafts of the devil; and that the soul without the protection of this wall and shield was like a naked knight amongst very strong and well-furnished enemies, continually intent on his death.

CHAPTER XCVII

HOW FRIARS SHOULD SATISFY THE NECESSITIES OF THE BODY

OUR most holy Father, considering that the body was created for the soul, and that bodily acts should be wrought on account of spiritual, used to say, "The servant of God, in eating and drinking and sleeping and satisfying the other necessities of the body, ought to satisfy his body with discretion, so that Brother Body may not be able to murmur against him, saying, 'I cannot stay erect and remain at prayer, nor rejoice in tribulations of the mind, nor work any other good works, because you do not satisfy my need.' For if the servant of God would satisfy his body with discretion and in a sufficiently good and fitting manner, and Brother Body should wish to be negligent and fat and sleepy in prayer, vigils, and good works, then he ought to punish it like a bad and fat beast for that he would eat and not be of profit, and bear a load. But if on account of want and poverty Brother Body cannot have his necessities in health and weakness, when he shall have humbly and honestly asked it from his brother or from his prelate for the love of God, and it is not given to him; let him bear it patiently for the love of God, Who should console him, Who sought it and also found it not; and this necessity with patience shall be counted to him by the Lord for martyrdom. And because he has done that which was his to do (that is, has humbly asked his need), he shall be excused, even if his body were thence made sore feeble."

SECTION IX

OF CERTAIN TEMPTATIONS WHICH THE LORD PERMITTED TO HIM

CHAPTER XCVIII

AND FIRSTLY, HOW THE DEMON ENTERED A PILLOW WHICH HE HAD UNDER HIS HEAD

WHEN blessed Francis was staying in the hermitage of Greccio for prayer in the last cell beyond the greater cell, on a certain night in his first slumber he called his fellow who was sleeping near him. And this fellow, rising, went to the door of the cell where the blessed man was sleeping. And the saint said to him, "Brother, I have not been able to sleep this night, neither to stand erect at prayer, for my head and my legs tremble very much, and it seems to me that I must have eaten some darnel bread." And when his fellow spoke to him in compassionate words, the holy man said, "But I believe that the devil is in that pillow which I have at my head." (For though he had never wished to sleep on feathers, or to have a feather pillow since he left the world; yet against his will the friars forced him to have that pillow then on account of the weakness of his eyes.) So he threw it to his fellow. His fellow, taking it, set it on his left shoulder, and when he had gone out of the porch of that cell, forthwith he lost his speech, and was not able to put down the pillow or move his arms, but stood there erect, unable to move himself from that place, and feeling nothing in him. But when for some space of time he had stood thus, by the grace of God the holy Father called him; and immediately he returned to himself, letting the pillow fall behind his back. And when he had returned to the blessed man, he told him all things that had happened to him. And the saint said, "In the evening, when I was saying Compline, I felt the devil come into the cell; whence I see that this devil is very astute, because when he could not hurt my soul, he wished to hinder the necessity of the body; so that I could not sleep nor stand erect at prayer, and that thus he would hinder the devotion and joy of my heart, and through this I should murmur at my infirmity."

CHAPTER XCIX

OF THE VERY GRAVE TEMPTATION WHICH HE HAD FOR MORE THAN TWO YEARS

WHEN he was staying in the dwelling of St. Mary, a very grave temptation of spirit was sent to him for the profit of his soul. Thereby he was so much afflicted in mind and body that many times he drew himself away from the company of the friars, because he was not able to show himself joyful to them as he was accustomed. He afflicted himself nevertheless by abstinence from food and drink and words; and he prayed more instantly and shed tears more abundantly, that the Lord would be pleased to send to him a sufficient remedy in such a tribulation. But when he had been thus afflicted for more than two years, it happened on a certain day, while he was praying in the church of St. Mary, that the word of the Gospel was spoken to him in his spirit: *If ye have faith as a grain of mustard seed ye shall say unto this mountain, Remove hence to yonder place, and it shall remove.* Immediately the holy Father answered to Him, "Lord, what is that mountain?" And it was answered, "That mountain is thy temptation." The holy Father said, "Therefore, Lord, it is done unto me as Thou hast said." And immediately he was so perfectly set free, that it seemed to him that he had never had any temptations. Likewise in the holy mountain of Alverna, at the time when he received the stigmata of the Lord in his body, he suffered such trials and temptations from the demons that he was not able to show himself joyful to his brethren as he was used, and he used to say to his fellows, "If the friars knew how many and what afflictions the demons cause me, there is not one of them who would not be moved to compassion and pity on me."

CHAPTER C

OF THE TEMPTATION WHICH HE HAD THROUGH MICE, CONCERNING WHICH THE LORD CONSOLED HIM, CERTIFYING HIM OF HIS KINGDOM

Two years before his death, while he was at St. Damian in a certain cell made of reeds, and was very greatly afflicted by the infirmity of his eyes, so that for more than sixty days he was not able to see the light of day, or even the light of the fire, it happened, by the Divine permission, that so many mice came into his cell for the increase of his affliction and of his merit, that they, running about over him in that cell by day and by night, allowed him neither to pray nor to remain quiet, nay, when he was eating they climbed up on his table, and worried him very much. Whence it appeared manifest both to himself and to his fellows, that it was a diabolical temptation. The blessed man therefore, seeing himself to be punished with so many afflictions, on a certain night, moved with compassion, said within himself, "Lord, look down on my infirmities and help me, that I may be able to bear them patiently." And immediately it was said to him in the spirit, "Tell me, my brother, if any one should give to thee for these thy infirmities and tribulations so great and precious a treasure, that if the whole earth should be compared to it, it would be nothing in respect of that great treasure; would you not rejoice greatly?" And blessed Francis answered, "O Lord, great would be that treasure and very precious, and much admirable and desirable." And he heard again One saying unto him, "Therefore, brother, rejoice and be glad in thy infirmities and tribulations; and for the rest hold thyself as secure as if thou wert now in My kingdom." And rising early, he said to his companion, "If the Emperor should give to any slave a whole kingdom; ought not that slave to rejoice greatly? If he should give his whole empire to him, ought he not much more to rejoice?" And he said to them, "Therefore I should rejoice greatly in my infirmities and tribulations, and be strong in the Lord, and always give thanks to God the Father and to His only Son our Lord Jesus Christ, and to the Holy Spirit, for such grace given me by the Lord, namely, that He has deigned to certify me His unworthy servant, yet living in the flesh, of His kingdom. Whence I wish to make to His praise and to our consolation and to the edification of our neighbour a new Praise of the Creatures of the Lord, which we daily use and without which we cannot live, and in whom the human race much offends their Creator; and we are continually ungrateful for so much grace and benefit, not praising God, the Creator and Giver of all things, as we ought. And sitting down, he began to meditate a little, and afterwards he said, "Most high, omnipotent good Lord," etc. And he sang a song over this, and taught his fellows to say and sing it. For his spirit was then in so great consolation and sweetness; that he wished to send for Brother

Pacificus, who in the world used to be called the King of Verses, and was a truly courteous teacher of singers, and he wished some friars to be given to him that they should go together with him through the world preaching and singing praises of the Lord. For he said that he wished that he who knew how to preach best among them should first preach to the people, and after the preaching they should all sing together the praises of the Lord like minstrels of the Lord. But when the praises were finished, he wished that the preacher should say to the people, "We are the minstrels of the Lord, and for these things we wish to be paid by you, that is, that you should remain in true penitence." And he said, "For what are the servants of the Lord but His minstrels, who should raise the hearts of men and move them to spiritual joy." And this he used to say specially of the Friars Minor, who were given to the people of God for their welfare.

SECTION X

OF THE SPIRIT OF PROPHECY

CHAPTER CI

AND FIRSTLY, HOW HE PREDICTED THAT PEACE WOULD BE MADE BETWEEN THE BISHOP AND PODESTÀ OF THE CITY OF ASSISI, WHEN THE CANTICLE WAS HEARD WHICH HE HAD MADE TO THE PRAISES OF THE CREATURES

AFTER blessed Francis had composed the aforesaid Praises of the Creatures, which he called the "Canticle of Brother Sun," it happened that a great discord arose between the Bishop and the Podestà of the city of Assisi, so that the Bishop excommunicated the Podestà of the city, and the Podestà warned every one that no one should buy or sell anything with him, or make any contract with him.

Blessed Francis, although he was sick when he heard this, was moved with compassion on them, especially as no one interfered to make peace between them. And he said to his fellows, "It is great shame to us, servants of God, that the Bishop and the Podestà should hate one another thus, and that no one should concern himself with their peace." And so he made immediately a verse in the aforesaid Praises on that occasion and said:

Be Thou praised, my Lord, of those who pardon for Thy love
and endure sickness and tribulations.

Blessed are they who will endure it in peace,
for by Thee, Most High, they shall be crowned.

Afterwards he called one of his fellows, and said to him, "Go to the Podestà and tell him on my part to go to the Bishop's palace with the magnates of the city and what others he may take with him." And when that brother had gone, he said to two others of his fellows, "Go and sing the Canticle of Brother Sun before the Bishop and the Podestà and the others who are with them, and I trust in the Lord that He will immediately humble their hearts, and they will return to their first love and friendship." But when they were all gathered together in the open court of the cloister of the Bishop's palace, those two friars arose, and one of them said, "Blessed Francis has made in his weakness the Praise of the Lord concerning his Creatures, to the praise of the said Lord, and the edification of his neighbour. Whence he asks of you that you should hear him with great devotion." And thus they began to speak and to sing. But the Podestà immediately rose and with joined hands and arms listened intently to those verses as to the Gospel of the Lord with very great devotion and even with many tears, for he had great faith and devotion to blessed Francis. When the Praises of the Lord were finished, the Podestà said before them all, "In truth, I say unto you, that not alone my Lord the Bishop, whom I wish and ought to have for my lord, but if any one should have slain my blood-friend or my son I will forgive him," and so saying he threw himself at the feet of the Bishop and said to him, "Behold, I am ready to make satisfaction for everything as it shall please you, for the love of Our Lord Jesus Christ, and of His servant blessed Francis." But the Bishop taking him with his hands, raised him and said to him, "My office bids me be humble, yet because I am naturally prompt to wrath, it behoves that thou shouldst pardon me." And thus with much benignity and love they embraced and kissed each other. But the friars seeing what the blessed man had predicted of their concord fulfilled to the letter, were amazed and rejoiced. And all the others who were present held this for a very great miracle, ascribing the whole to the merits of the blessed man; because the Lord had so quickly visited them, and that they had turned away without the uttering of any word from such discord and scandal to such harmony. But we who were with the blessed Father bear testimony that when he said of any one, "thus it is," or, "thus it will be," always it happened thus to the letter. And we have seen so often and so much of this that it would be long to write or to tell it.

CHAPTER CII

HOW HE FORESAW THE FALL OF A FRIAR UNWILLING TO CONFESS UNDER AN APPEARANCE OF SILENCE

There was a certain friar outwardly of honest and holy conversation, who by day and night seemed solicitous concerning prayer, and in such wise observed continual silence, that sometimes when he would confess to the priest he used to confess by signs only and not by words. For he seemed so devout and fervent in the love of God that sometimes sitting with his brethren even though he did not speak, yet he rejoiced greatly within and without on hearing such good words, so that from this he drew other friars to devotion. But when he had remained some years in this kind of life, it happened that blessed Francis came to the habitation where he was staying. Who, when he heard from the friars his conversation, said to them, "Know in truth that it is because of a diabolical temptation that he does not wish to confess." In the meantime the Minister-General came there to visit the holy man and began to commend that one to the blessed man. And the blessed one said to him, "Believe me, brother, that friar, since he is led by an evil spirit, will be deceived." The Minister-General said, "It seems strange to me, and almost incredible, that this could be of a man who has so many signs and works of holiness." And the holy man said to him, "Prove him," saying to the friar, "Brother, I wish that you should confess twice in a week." But he placed his finger over his mouth, shaking his head and showing by signs that he did not wish to do this for the love of silence. But the Minister, fearing to scandalise him, let him go. And not many days after, that friar left the Order of his own will, and returned to the world, wearing the secular dress.

But so it was, that while on a day two of the companions of the blessed man were walking by a certain road, they came upon him walking alone like a very poor pilgrim. And having compassion on him, they said, "Oh wretched one, where is thy honest and holy conversation? For thou wast unwilling to speak and to show thyself to thy brethren, and now thou goest wandering through the world, like a man ignorant of God." But he began to speak to them, swearing often "by his faith," like the men of this world. And they said to him, "Wretched man, why dost thou swear by thy faith like lay-folk, thou who was wont to be silent, not only from idle words, but from all speech?" And so they left him, and a little after he died. And we wondered greatly, seeing what blessed Francis had predicted of him in the time when the wretched one was reputed a saint by the friars to be true to the letter.

CHAPTER CIII

OF A CERTAIN MAN WHO WEPT BEFORE THE BLESSED FRANCIS THAT HE MIGHT BE RECEIVED INTO THE ORDER

At the time when no one was received into the Order except by the leave of the blessed man, the son of a noble citizen of Lucca with many others, wishing to enter the Order, came to blessed Francis, who was then sick in the palace of the Bishop of Assisi. And when they all presented themselves to the blessed man, he bowed down before him and began to weep greatly, begging him to receive him. The blessed Father looking upon him said to him, "Oh wretched and carnal man; why dost thou lie to the Holy Spirit and to me? Thou weepest carnally and not spiritually." And as these things were said, his relations came on horseback outside the palace, wishing to take him away, and carry him off by force. But he, hearing the noise of the horses, looked through a window and saw his kinsmen and straightway went down to them, and as the blessed man had foreseen, returned to the world with them.

CHAPTER CIV

OF THE VINEYARD OF THE PRIEST SPOILED ON ACCOUNT OF BLESSED FRANCIS

Blessed Francis abode a while by reason of the weakness of his eyes at the church of St. Fabian, which is near Rieti, with a poor priest. For my Lord Pope Honorius was then at that city with all his court; whence many Cardinals and other great clerks used to visit blessed Francis almost daily, on account of the devotion which they had towards him. Now that church had a little vineyard next the house in which the blessed Francis was: and in that house was a door by which well-nigh all who visited him entered the vineyard, especially as the grapes were then ripe and the place was very pleasant; so that for that reason the whole vineyard was stripped and spoiled of its grapes. On account of which that priest began to be scandalised, saying, "Though it was a small vineyard, yet I used to collect thence as much wine as was sufficient for my need, and behold I have lost it all for this year!" Hearing which blessed Francis made him to be called and said to him: "Be not any further disturbed, because we cannot do anything else now. But trust in the Lord, since He is able to make up thy loss by His servant to thee in full. Tell me, how many measures of wine thou hadst, when thou hadst most from thy vineyard?" The priest answered, "Father, thirteen measures." Blessed Francis said to him, "Be no more sad, nor say any injurious word to any one on account of this, but have faith in the Lord and in my word, and if thou hast less than twenty measures of wine I will cause it to be made up to thee." And from that time forward the priest held his tongue and was quiet, and in the time of the vintage he had from that vineyard twenty measures of wine and not less. And all those who heard this wondered greatly, saying that if the vineyard had been full of grapes it would have been impossible that there should have been twenty measures of grapes there. But we who were with him bear testimony that what he said of this and of all things was fulfilled to the letter.

CHAPTER CV

OF THE KNIGHTS OF PERUGIA WHO HINDERED HIS PREACHING

WHILE blessed Francis was preaching in the square at Perugia to a great crowd of people congregated there, behold, some knights of Perugia began to run through the place on horseback and hinder his preaching. And though they were reproved by those who were present, yet they did not cease on account of this. Therefore the holy Father, turning towards them, said to them with fervour of spirit, "Hear and understand what the Lord announces to you by me the least of His servants, nor say, 'this man is of Assisi.'" (But this he said, because there is an old hatred between them of Perugia and the men of Assisi.) And he said to them, "The Lord has exalted you over all your neighbours, on account of which ye ought rather to recognise your Creator by humiliating yourself not only to God but also to your neighbours. But your heart is lifted up in pride, and ye lay waste your neighbours and slay many of them. Wherefore I say unto you, that unless ye be quickly converted to God, satisfying those whom ye have offended, the Lord, Who leaves nothing unpunished, will cause you to rise one against the other to your shame, for your greater vengeance and punishment, and, moved by sedition and internal war, ye shall suffer greater tribulation than your neighbours could bring upon you." (For thus the holy Father never held his peace on the faults of the people, when he used to preach, but reproved them all, publicly and manfully. But the Lord gave so much grace to him, that all, of whatever state and condition they were, who saw and heard him, feared and venerated him on account of the abundant grace of God which he had; so that however often they were reproved by him they were always edified by his words, and were converted to the Lord or inwardly struck with penitence.) And so it was, by divine permission, that a few days after a dissension arose between the knights and the people, so that the people turned the knights out of the city, and the knights, with the Church which assisted them, laid waste their fields and vine-yards and trees, and did all the evil which they could do to the people. And the people likewise destroyed all the goods of the knights. And so, according to the word of the blessed man, the people and the knights were punished.

CHAPTER CVI

HOW HE FORESAW THE HIDDEN TEMPTATIONS AND TRIBULATIONS OF A CERTAIN FRIAR

A CERTAIN friar, right spiritual and familiar with the blessed man, had suffered for many days most grievous suggestions of the devil, so that he was like to fall into the depths of despair, and every day he was so tormented that he was ashamed to confess so often, and afflicted himself greatly for this reason by fasting, vigil, tears, and disciplines. And it happened, by the divine dispensation, that blessed Francis went to that place. And while on a certain day that friar was walking with the blessed man, blessed Francis knew through the Holy Spirit his tribulation and temptation, and drawing himself a little apart from the friar who was walking with him, he turned to that afflicted brother and said to him, "Dearest brother, I will that henceforth thou shalt not feel thyself bound to confess these diabolical suggestions. And fear not, for nothing shall hurt thy soul. But, with my leave, you shall say seven *Paternosters* as often as you are troubled by them." And that brother rejoiced greatly at the words which he had said to him (namely, that he should not be bound to confess these temptations), for he had been greatly afflicted by this. Nevertheless he was greatly stupefied, seeing that blessed Francis knew that which was known only by the priest to whom it had been confessed. And immediately he was set free from that tribulation by the grace of God and the merits of St. Francis; and from that time forward remained in great peace and quiet. (And it was because the saint had hoped this, that he had securely absolved him from confession.)

CHAPTER CVII

OF THOSE THINGS WHICH HE FORETOLD OF BROTHER BERNARD, WHICH WERE AFTERWARDS FULFILLED AS HE HAD PREDICTED

WHEN near his death a certain dainty dish was prepared for him, he remembered Brother Bernard who was the first friar that he had, and said to his companions, "This dish is good for Brother Bernard," and forthwith he made him be called to him. Who, when he had come, sat near the bed whereon the saint was sitting. And Brother Bernard said, "Father, I ask thee that thou shouldst bless me, and show me thy benediction; for if thou shouldst show me thy paternal benediction, I believe that God Himself and all men will love me more." But the blessed man was not able to see him, because he had lost the light of his eyes for many days before. But stretching out his right hand he placed it on the head of Brother Giles who was the third friar, believing that he had put it on the head of Brother Bernard, who was sitting next to him. And immediately knowing it by the Holy Spirit, he said, "This is not the head of my brother Bernard." Then Brother Bernard drew nearer, and the blessed Father putting his hand on his head blessed him, saying to one of his fellows, "Write what I say to thee: Bernard was the first friar, who first began and completed the most perfect perfection of the Holy Gospel, by distributing his goods to the poor: on account of which, and on account of many other prerogatives, I am bound to love him more than any other friar of the whole Order. Whence I will and command as far as I am able, that whoever shall be Minister-General should love and honour him as myself. But let the Minister and all friars of the whole Order hold him as myself." And with this Brother Bernard and the other friars were greatly consoled. For the blessed Father, considering the very great perfection of that Brother Bernard, had prophesied before certain friars, saying, "I say unto you that some of the great and most subtle demons are allotted to Brother Bernard for his warfare, who shall bring many tribulations and temptations upon him. But the merciful Lord will take away from him near his end all tribulation and temptation, and will set his spirit in such peace and consolation, that all friars who shall see these things shall wonder greatly and shall hold it for a great miracle; and in that quiet and consolation of soul and body he shall pass away to the Lord."

But all these things, not without very great wonder of all the friars who heard these things from the blessed Father, were afterwards fulfilled to the letter in that brother Bernard. For Brother Bernard in the bitterness of death was in so much peace and consolation of spirit that he was unwilling to lie down. And if he lay down, he lay as if sitting, nor even the slightest humour ascending to his head was able to hinder meditation concerning God, through sleep or any imagination. And if this in any way happened, immediately he rose up and struck himself, saying, "What was it? Why did I thus think?" He wished to take no medicine, but said to him that offered it, "Do not hinder me." And thenceforward, that he might more freely and peacefully die, he put all the duties of his body in the hands of a certain brother who was a physician, saying to him, "I wish to have no care of eating or drinking, but I commit them to thee; if thou givest I will take, if thou dost not give I will not ask." But when he began to grow weak, he wished to have near him a priest unto the hour of his death, and when anything came into his mind which burdened his conscience, he confessed it immediately. But after his death, his body became white and soft, and he seemed to smile. Whence he was fairer dead than alive; and all rejoiced more to look upon him dead than alive, for he seemed rightly "a smiling saint."

CHAPTER CVIII

HOW WHEN NEAR HIS DEATH HE PROMISED TO BLESSED CLARE THAT SHE SHOULD SEE HIM, AND HOW AFTER HIS DEATH IT WAS FULFILLED

In that week in which blessed Francis passed away, the lady Clare, the first offshoot of the poor sisters of St. Damian of Assisi, the foremost rival of the holy man in preserving Evangelical Perfection, fearing to die before him, because both were then sore sick, wept most bitterly and would not be consoled, for that she thought that she should not see before her death blessed Francis, her consoler and master and her first founder in the grace of God, and therefore she signified this by a certain friar to the blessed Father. Hearing which the saint was moved with compassion, for he loved her singularly with fatherly affection. But considering that that could not be which she wished (that is to see him), he wrote to her by letters for the consolation of her and all her sisters his benediction; and absolved her from all defect, if she had been guilty of any, against the admonition and against the mandates and counsels of the Son of God; and that she should lay aside all sadness and sorrow, he said to that friar whom she had sent, "Go and bid sister Clare put aside all sorrow and sadness on account of not being able to see me. But let her know in truth that before her death, she and her sisters shall see me, and shall be much consoled concerning me." But so it was, that when a little later blessed Francis passed away in the night, there came early the whole of the people and clergy of the town of Assisi, and bore his holy body from the place where he had died, with hymns and praises, carrying each of them branches of trees, and thus they bore him, by the will of God, to St. Damian, that the word might be performed which the Lord had said through blessed Francis to console His daughters and His handmaids. And having moved the iron grating by which they were accustomed to communicate and hear the Word of God, the friars took the holy body from the bier, and held it between their arms to the window for a great space; until lady Clare and her sisters were consoled concerning him, though they were full and stricken with many sorrows and tears, seeing themselves deprived of the consolations and admonitions of such a father.

CHAPTER CIX

HOW HE FORETOLD THAT HIS BODY WOULD BE HONOURED AFTER HIS DEATH

On a certain day when he was lying ailing in the Bishop's palace at Assisi, a certain spiritually-minded friar said to him, as if in sport, and smiling, "For how much wouldst thou sell to the Lord all thy sackcloths? Many baldachinos and silken palls shall be placed over this little body of thine, which now is clothed with sackcloth." For then he was bandaged with sackcloth, and had a garment also of sackcloth. And blessed Francis answered (but not he but the Holy Spirit through him) and said, with great fervour and joy of spirit, "Thou sayest truth, since so it will be for the praise and grace of my God."

SECTION XI

OF THE DIVINE PROVIDENCE CONCERNING HIM

CHAPTER CX

AND FIRSTLY, HOW THE LORD PROVIDED FOR THE FRIARS SITTING AT A POOR TABLE WITH THE PHYSICIAN

WHEN blessed Francis was at the hermitage of Fonte Palumbo near Rieti, on account of the weakness of his eyes there visited him on a certain day an eye-doctor. When he had stayed with him for some time and now wished to depart, the blessed Father said to one of his companions, "Go and give the doctor something of the best to eat." And his fellow answered him, saying, "Father, we say it with shame, we are so poor that we should be ashamed to invite him now to eat." Blessed Francis said to his companion, "O ye of little faith, say no more to me of it." And the doctor said to blessed Francis, "Brother, for that the friars are poor, I will the more willingly eat with them." For that physician was very rich. And though the blessed Father and his fellows had often invited him, yet he had never wished to eat there. Therefore the friars went and prepared the table; and with shame set thereon a little bread and wine, and some cabbage which they had got ready for themselves. And sitting down to that poor table they had begun to eat, when behold there was a knock at the door of the dwelling. So one of the friars, rising, went to open the door. And behold, there was a certain woman there, carrying a great vessel full of good bread and fishes, and crayfish patties, and honey, and grapes; which the lady of a castle about seven miles off had sent to blessed Francis. Having seen which, the friars and the doctor rejoiced greatly, considering the sanctity of the holy Father, and ascribing all to his merits. And the doctor said to the friars, "My brethren, neither you nor we know as we ought the holiness of this man!"

CHAPTER CXI

OF THE FISH WHICH HE DESIRED IN HIS INFIRMITY

On another time when he was grievously sick in the palace of the Bishop of Assisi, the friars besought him to eat. And he answered, "I have no will to eat; but if I could have some of the fish called squail, perhaps I could eat it." And as he said this, behold, some one came carrying a wicker basket in which there were three great squails well prepared, and some crayfish, which the holy Father did willingly eat. And this, Brother Gerard, the Minister of Rieti, had sent to him. And they praised God for the divine providence, Who had provided for His servant those things which were impossible to be had then at Assisi, since it was winter.

CHAPTER CXII

OF THE FOOD AND CLOTH WHICH HE DESIRED AT HIS DEATH

When he was ailing in the habitation of St. Mary of the Angels with the last sickness by which he died, on a certain day he called his fellow to him, saying, "You know how the lady Jacqueline of Settesoli was and is very faithful and devoted to our Order. And therefore I believe that she will hold it for a great grace and consolation if you would signify my state to her, and send specially to her to send me some religious garments in colour like to ashes, and that with the cloth she should send also some of that sweetmeat which she has often made for me in the City." But the Romans call that sweetmeat *mostaccioli*, which is made of almonds and sugar and other things. For that lady was truly spiritual, and one of the richest and best-born widows of all Rome; who, by the merits and preaching of blessed Francis, had received so much grace from the Lord, that she seemed like another Magdalene, ever full of tears and devotion for the love and sweetness of Christ. They wrote therefore a letter as the holy man said, and a certain friar went seeking some brother to carry the letter to the aforesaid lady. And immediately there was a knock at the door of the habitation. And when the door was opened by a friar, behold the lady

Jacqueline was there, who had come in great haste to visit blessed Francis; and with great pleasure he told him how lady Jacqueline had come from Rome, with her son, and many others, to visit him. And he said, "What shall we do, Father? Shall we allow her to enter and come to thee?" (But this he said, because it had been ordered that at that place, with the will of St. Francis, no woman should enter, on account of the great seemliness and devotion of it.) And the holy Father said, "This rule is not to be observed with that Lady, seeing that her great faith and devotion has made her come hither from distant parts." The dame entered therefore to the blessed man, shedding many tears before him. And behold a wonder! She brought a shroud cloth (that is, of ashen colour) for a tunic, and all the things which were contained in the letter she had fetched with her, as if she had received it. And the dame said to the friars, "My brethren, it was said unto me in the spirit when I was praying, "Go and visit thy Father, blessed Francis, and delay not, for if thou delayest much, thou wilt not find him alive; and carry with thee such a cloth for a tunic, and such and such things; and thou shalt make him that sweetmeat. Take with thee likewise a great quantity of wax for lights, and also of incense." (But this was not contained in the letter that should have been sent.) And thus it was that He Who inspired kings to go with gifts to honour His Son in the time of His nativity, inspired also that noble and holy lady to go with gifts to honour His most beloved servant in the day of his death, nay, of his true birth. That lady, therefore, prepared the dish of which the holy Father had desired to eat. But he ate little thereof, because he grew continually weaker, and drew nearer to death. She caused also many candles to be made which should burn after his death before his most holy body. But of the cloth, the friars made for him a tunic, in which he was buried. But he himself ordered the friars to sew a sack over him, in token and in example of humility and Lady Poverty. And in that week in which dame Jacqueline came, our most holy Father passed away to the Lord.

SECTION XII

OF HIS LOVE FOR CREATURES AND OF CREATURES FOR HIM

CHAPTER CXIII

AND FIRSTLY, OF THE LOVE WHICH HE ESPECIALLY HAD FOR THE BIRDS WHICH ARE CALLED LARKS

BLESSED Francis, wholly wrapped up in the love of God, discerned perfectly the goodness of God not only in his own soul, now adorned with the perfection of virtue, but in every creature. On account of which he had a singular and intimate love of creatures, especially of those in which was figured anything pertaining to God or the Order. Whence above all other birds he loved a certain little bird which is called the lark, or by the people, the cowled lark. And he used to say of it, "Sister Lark hath a cowl like a Religious; and she is a humble bird, because she goes willingly by the road to find there any food. And if she comes upon it in foulness, she draws it out and eats it. But flying she praises God very sweetly like a good Religious, despising earthly things, whose conversation is always in the heavens, and whose intent is always to the praise of God. Her clothes are like to the earth (that is her feathers), and she gives an example to Religious that they should not have delicate and coloured garments, but vile in price and colour, as earth is viler than the other elements." And because he perceived this in them, he looked on them most willingly. Therefore it pleased the Lord, that these most holy little birds should show some sign of affection towards him in the hour of his death. For late on the Saturday, after vespers, before the night in which he passed away to the Lord, a great multitude of that kind of birds called larks came on the roof of the house where he was lying; and flying about, made a wheel like a circle round the roof, and sweetly singing, seemed likewise to praise the Lord.

CHAPTER CXIV

HOW HE WISHED TO PERSUADE THE EMPEROR TO MAKE A LAW THAT MEN SHOULD MAKE A GOOD PROVISION FOR BIRDS AND OXEN AND ASSES AND THE POOR AT CHRISTMAS-TIME

WE, who were with blessed Francis, and have written these things, bear testimony that many times we have heard him say, "If I were to speak to the Emperor, I would, supplicating and persuading him, tell him for the love of God and me to make a special law that no man should take or kill sister Larks, nor do them any harm. Likewise, that all the Podestas of the towns, and the Lords of castles and villages, should be bound every year on Christmas day to compel men to throw wheat and other grains outside the cities and castles, that our sister Larks may have something to eat, and also the other birds, on a day of such solemnity. And that for the reverence of the Son of God, Who rested on that night with the most blessed Virgin Mary between an Ox and an Ass in the manger, whoever shall have an Ox and an Ass shall be bound to provide for them on that night the best of good fodder. Likewise on that day, all poor men should be satisfied by the rich with good food." For the blessed Father had a greater reverence for Christmas day than for any other festival, saying, "Since the Lord had been born for us, it behoves us to be saved," and on account of which he wished that on that day every Christian should rejoice in the Lord; and for His love who gave Himself for us, that all should provide largely not only for the poor, but also for the animals and birds.

CHAPTER CXV

OF THE OBEDIENCE OF THE FIRE TO HIM, WHEN HE WAS CAUTERISED

WHEN he came to the hermitage of Fonte Palumbo near Rieti, for the cure of his ailment of the eyes, to which cure he had been forced by obedience to my Lord of Ostia, and by Brother Elias, the Minister-General, on a certain day the physician came to him, who, considering the disease, said to blessed Francis that he would make a cautery over the jaw up to the eyebrow of that eye which was weaker than the other. But blessed Francis was unwilling to begin the cure unless Brother Elias was there; because he had said that he wished to be present when the physician began that operation, and because he himself feared, and it was grave to him, to have so much solicitude for himself; and so he wished that the Minister-General should cause all to be done. When therefore they had waited for him, and he did not come, on account of the many impediments which he had, at last he permitted the physician to do what he would. And having placed the iron in the fire to make the cautery, blessed Francis, wishing to strengthen his spirit, lest he should faint, spoke thus to the fire, "My Brother Fire, noble and useful among all other creatures, be kindly to me in this hour, because formerly I have loved thee for the love of Him Who created thee. But I pray our Creator Who created us, that He will so temper thy heat that I may be able to sustain it." And the prayer finished, he signed the fire with the sign of the cross. But we who were with him then did all flee, out of pity and compassion for him, and the physician alone remained with him. But when the cautery was made we returned to him, who said to us, "O cowards, and of little faith, why did you fly? In truth I say unto you, that I have felt neither any pain nor the heat of the fire; nay, if it be not well burnt now, let him burn it better." And the physician marvelled greatly, saying, "My brethren, I say unto you that I should fear not only for him who is so weak and ailing, but for even the strongest man, lest he should not be able to suffer so great a cautery. But this man neither moved nor showed the least sign of pain." For all the veins from the ear to the eyebrow had to be cut open, and it did him no good. Likewise another physician bored through both his ears with a red-hot iron, and it benefited him nothing. Nor is it strange, if the fire and the other creatures were obedient to him and venerated him, for, as we who were with him have very often seen, he was so much drawn to them, and rejoiced in them so much, and his spirit was moved with so much pity and compassion for them, that he would not see them badly treated, and he used to speak with them with inward gladness, as if they had reason, whence by their occasion, he was ofttimes wrapt up to God.

CHAPTER CXVI

THAT HE WOULD NOT QUENCH THE FIRE THAT HAD BURNT HIS BREECHES

AMONGST all the lower and insensible creatures he was singularly drawn to fire on account of its beauty and use, wherefore he never wished to hinder its office. For on a time, when he was sitting next the fire, without his knowledge it caught hold of his linen clothes or breeches near the knee. When he felt the heat of the fire he did not wish to put it out. But his fellow seeing his clothes burn, ran to him wishing to quench the fire. But he forbade him, saying, "Nay, dearest brother, harm not the fire," and thus he would by no means let him quench it.

Then he hurriedly went to the friar who was his Warden, and led him to blessed Francis, and straightway, against the will of the blessed Father, put out the fire. For whatever necessity urged him, he would never extinguish a fire or a lamp or a candle, with so much pity was he moved towards it. Also he would not that a friar should throw out fire or smoking wood from place to place, as is wont to be done; but they should simply set it on the ground, on account of the reverence for Him of Whom it is the creature.

CHAPTER CXVII

HOW HE WOULD NOT WEAR A SKIN BECAUSE HE HAD NOT PERMITTED IT TO BE BURNT WITH FIRE

WHEN he was keeping Lent in Mount Alverna, on a certain day his fellow at the hour of eating prepared a fire in the cell where he was used to eat. And when the fire was alight he went to another cell for the blessed man, where he was praying, carrying with him the Missal that he might read the Gospel for that day to him, for he always wished to hear the Gospel which was read for the Mass of that day before he ate, when he was not able to hear Mass. And when he came to that cell where the fire was alight, behold, the flame of the fire had ascended to the roof and was burning it. But his fellow as he was able began to put out the fire, but could not do it alone. However, holy Francis was unwilling to help him; yet he took up a certain skin which he wore over him at night and went away with it to the wood. But the friars of the place, who dwelt far from that cell, when they learnt that it was being burnt, immediately came and extinguished the fire. Afterwards blessed Francis returned to meat, and when he had eaten he said to his fellow, "I will not have that skin over me again, since by reason of my avarice I would not that Brother Fire should eat it."

CHAPTER CXVIII

OF HIS LOVE FOR WATER AND STONES AND WOOD AND FLOWERS

After fire, he most singularly loved water, by which is figured holy penitence and tribulation, whereby the filth of the soul is washed away, and because the first ablution of the soul is by the water of baptism. Whence, when he washed his hands, he used to choose such a place that the water which fell should not be trodden by his feet; when he would walk over stones, moreover, he used to walk with great fear and reverence, for the love of Him Who is called "The Rock." Whence when he used to say that verse of the Psalm, *Thou didst exalt me on a rock*, he used to say, out of his great reverence and devotion, "Under the foot of the rock hast thou exalted me." He used also to say to the friar who made ready the wood for the fire, that he should never cut down a whole tree; but so that always some part of a tree should remain whole for the love of Him Who did work out our salvation on the wood of the cross. Likewise he used to say to the friar who did the garden, not to till the whole ground for pot-herbs; but to leave some part of it to produce green herbs, which in their time should produce flowers for the friars, for the love of Him Who is called the "flower of the field" and "the lily of the valley." Nay, he used to say to that brother gardener that he ought always to make a fair flower-bed in some part of the garden; setting and planting there all sweet-smelling herbs and all herbs which bring forth fair flowers, that in their time they might call them that looked upon those herbs and flowers to the praise of God. For every creature cries aloud, "God made me for thee, O man!" Whence we who were with him used to see him rejoice, within and without, as it were, in all things created; so that touching or seeing them his spirit seemed to be not on earth but in heaven.

And by reason of the many consolations which he used to have in things created, a little before his death he composed certain Praises of the Lord for His creatures, to incite the hearts of those who should hear them to the praise of God, and that the Lord Himself might be praised by men in His creatures.

CHAPTER CXIX

HOW HE USED TO COMMEND THE SUN AND FIRE ABOVE ALL OTHER CREATED THINGS

Above all other creatures wanting reason, he loved the sun and fire with most affection. For he was wont to say, "In the morning when the sun rises, every man ought to praise God, Who created it for our use, because through it our eyes are enlightened by day. Then in the even when it becomes night, every man ought to give praise on account of Brother Fire, by which our eyes are enlightened by night; for we be all as it were blind, and the Lord by these two, our brothers, doth enlighten our eyes. And therefore we ought specially to praise the Creator Himself for these and the other creatures which we daily use." The which he himself always did to the day of his death, nay, when he was struck down with great infirmity he begun to sing the Praises of the Lord which he had made concerning created things, and afterwards he made his fellows sing, so that in considering the praise of the Lord, he might forget the bitterness of his pains and infirmities. And because he deemed and said that the sun is fairer than other created things, and is more often likened to our Lord, and that in Scripture the Lord Himself is called "the Sun of Righteousness," therefore giving that name to those Praises which he had made of the creatures of the Lord, what time the Lord did certify him of His kingdom, he called them "The Song of Brother Sun."

CHAPTER CXX

THIS IS THE PRAISE OF CREATED THINGS, WHICH HE MADE WHEN THE LORD CERTIFIED HIM OF HIS KINGDOM

Most High, Omnipotent, Good Lord.
Thine be the praise, the glory, the honour, and all benediction.
To Thee alone, Most High, they are due,
  and no man is worthy to mention Thee.

Be Thou praised, my Lord, with all Thy creatures,
above all Brother Sun,
who gives the day and lightens us therewith.

And he is beautiful and radiant with great splendour,
of Thee, Most High, he bears similitude.

Be Thou praised, my Lord, of Sister Moon and the stars,
in the heaven hast Thou formed them, clear and precious and comely.

Be Thou praised, my Lord, of Brother Wind,
and of the air, and the cloud, and of fair and of all weather,
by the which Thou givest to Thy creatures sustenance.

Be Thou praised, my Lord, of Sister Water,
which is much useful and humble and precious and pure.

Be Thou praised, my Lord, of Brother Fire,
by which Thou hast lightened the night,
and he is beautiful and joyful and robust and strong.

Be Thou praised, my Lord, of our Sister Mother Earth,
which sustains and hath us in rule,
and produces divers fruits with coloured flowers and herbs.

Be Thou praised, my Lord, of those who pardon for Thy love
and endure sickness and tribulations.

Blessed are they who will endure it in peace,
for by Thee, Most High, they shall be crowned.

Be Thou praised, my Lord, of our Sister Bodily Death,
from whom no man living may escape.
woe to those who die in mortal sin:

Blessed are they who are found in Thy most holy will,
for the second death shall not work them ill.

Praise ye and bless my Lord, and give Him thanks,
and serve Him with great humility.

SECTION XIII

OF HIS DEATH, AND OF THE GLADNESS WHICH HE SHOWED WHEN HE FIRST KNEW FOR CERTAIN THAT HE WAS NEAR DEATH

CHAPTER CXXI

AND FIRSTLY, HOW HE ANSWERED BROTHER ELIAS WHEN HE REBUKED HIM FOR THIS

WHEN he was lying sick in the palace of the Bishop of Assisi and the hand of the Lord did seem to be more than of wont heavy upon him, the people of Assisi, fearing lest if he should die by night the friars would bear away his holy body to another city, ordered that every night ward should be diligently kept in the circuit outside the wall of the palace. But the most holy Father himself, that he might comfort his spirit lest it should at any time give way by reason of the violence of the pain by which he was daily and continually afflicted, made the Praises of the Lord to be sung by his companions often in the day, and thus he did also in the night, for the edification and consolation of the lay-folk who were keeping watch in the palace. But Brother Elias, considering that blessed Francis thus comforted himself in the Lord and rejoiced in the midst of such sickness, said to him, "Dearest brother, I am greatly consoled and edified by all the gladness which thou showest, for thee and thy fellows in thine ailments. But though the men of this city venerate thee as a holy man, yet for that they believe firmly that thou art nigh unto death because of thine incurable sickness, hearing these Praises sung by day and night, they may say within themselves, 'Why doth this man show such light-heartedness, who is near death? He ought to be thinking of death.'" Blessed Francis said to him, "Dost thou remember when thou didst see the vision at Foligno, and didst tell me that a certain man had said unto thee that I should not live more than two years; before that vision thou sawest how, by the grace of God Who suggests all good things to the heart and puts it in the mouth of His faithful, I used often to consider my end, both by day and by night; but from that hour in which thou hadst seen the vision, I was more solicitous to daily consider the day of my death." And straightway he said with great fervour of spirit, " Suffer me, brother, to rejoice in the Lord, both in His praises and in my infirmities; since by the grace of the Holy Spirit helping me, I am so united and joined to my Lord, that by His mercy may I well rejoice in the Most High."

CHAPTER CXXII

HOW HE INDUCED THE PHYSICIAN TO TELL HIM HOW LONG HE SHOULD LIVE

In those days there visited him in the same palace a certain physician of Arezzo, by name Good John, who was very familiar with blessed Francis. And blessed Francis questioned him, saying, " What thinkest thou, Bembenignate, of this my infirmity of dropsy? " For he would not call him by his name; for that he would never name anybody who was called " Good," out of reverence to the Lord, Who said, *There is none good but one, that is God.* Likewise he would never call any one " father " or " master," nor write it in his letters, out of reverence to the Lord, Who said, *And call no one man father on earth nor be ye called masters*, etc. And the physician said to him, " Brother, it shall be well with thee, by the grace of God." And blessed Francis said again, " Tell me the truth; what do you think? Fear not, since by the grace of God I am no faint-heart that I should fear death. For by the grace of the Holy Spirit, I am so made one with my Lord, that I am equally content with death as with life." Then the physician said to him openly, " Father, according to our medicine-craft thine infirmity is incurable, and I believe that either in the end of September or on the fourth of the Nones of October, thou wilt die." Then blessed Francis, lying on his bed, spread his hands out to the Lord with very great devotion and reverence, and said with great joy of mind and body, " Welcome, my Sister Death."

CHAPTER CXXIII

THAT STRAIGHTWAY, WHEN HE HEARD THAT HE SHOULD DIE SO SOON, HE CAUSED THE PRAISES WHICH HE HAD MADE TO BE SUNG TO HIM

AFTER these things a certain friar said to him, "Father, thy life and conversation was and is a light and a mirror, not only to thy brethren, but also to the whole Church, and thy death shall be the same. And though thy death will be a matter of sadness and grief to thy brethren, and to many others, yet it will be to thee consolation and infinite joy. For thou shalt pass from great labour to the greatest rest, from many pains and temptations to eternal peace, from the earthly poverty which thou hast ever loved and perfectly observed to endless true riches, and so from temporal death to perpetual life, where thou shalt see thy Lord God face to face, Whom thou hast loved in this life with so much fervour and desire." And having said these things, he said openly to him, "Father, thou knowest in truth except the Lord should send thee His medicine from heaven thine infirmity is incurable, and thou hast little longer to live, as the physicians but now foretold thee. Now I have said this to thee, that thy spirit may be made strong, and that thou mayst rejoice in the Lord within and without, so that thy brethren and the others who visit thee may find thee always rejoicing in the Lord, and that to those who see, and to others who hear it after thy death, thy death may be a perpetual memorial, as thy life and conversation was and ever shall be." Then blessed Francis, even though his infirmities were more than usually heavy upon him, was seen from these words to derive a new joy to his mind, hearing that Sister Death threatened him so nearly, and with great fervour of spirit he praised the Lord, saying to him, "Therefore, if it pleases my Lord that I must quickly die, call to me Brother Angelo and Brother Leo, that they may sing to me of Sister Death." And when those two brethren had come to him, they sang, with many tears, the "Song of Brother Sun," and of the other created things of the Lord, which the saint himself had made. And then before the last verse of the Canticle he added some verses of Sister Death, saying:

Be Thou praised, my Lord, of our Sister Bodily Death,
from whom no man living can escape.
woe to those who die in mortal sin:

Blessed are they who are found in Thy most holy will,
for the second death shall not work them ill.

Praise ye, and bless my Lord, and give Him thanks,
and serve Him with great humility.

CHAPTER CXXIV

HOW HE BLESSED THE CITY OF ASSISI WHEN HE WAS BEING CARRIED TO ST. MARY'S THEREAT TO DIE

Now when the most holy Father was made certain, as much by the Holy Spirit, as by the sentence of the physician, that his death was near, seeing that up to then he had been in the palace, and feeling that he grew continually worse, and that the forces of his body were leaving him, he made himself be carried in his bed to St. Mary of the Porziuncula, that there he might finish the life of his body, where he had begun to find the light and life of his soul. But when those who were carrying him had come to the Hospice which is in the midst of the way by which one goes from Assisi to St. Mary's, he bade his bearers lay down the bed on the ground. And though on account of his long and very great disease of the eyes, he was not able to see it, he made his bed be turned so that he should hold his face towards Assisi. And raising himself a little in his bed, he blessed the city, saying, "Lord, like as this city of old was, as I believe, a place and a habitation of wicked men, so I see that on account of the abundance of Thy mercy, in the time which hath pleased Thee, Thou hast singularly shown it the multitude of Thy mercies. On account of Thy goodness alone, Thou hast chosen it to Thyself, that it might be the place and habitation of those who should know Thee in truth, and should give glory to Thy Holy Name, and should show forth the odour of good fame, of holy life, of most true doctrine, and of Evangelical Perfection to all Christian People. I ask of Thee therefore, O Lord Jesus Christ, Father of mercies, that Thou shouldst not consider our ingratitude, but be ever mindful of Thy most abundant pity which Thou hast shown towards it, that it may be ever the place and habitation of those who know Thee truly, and glorify Thy most blessed and glorious Name, for ever and ever, Amen."

And having said this he was carried to St. Mary of the Angels, where, having completed forty years of his age and twenty years of perfect penitence, he, in the year of Our Lord 1227, on the fourth of the Nones of October, passed away to the Lord Jesus Christ, Whom he loved with his whole heart, with his whole mind, his whole soul, his whole strength, his most ardent desire, and fullest affection, following Him most perfectly, running after Him most swiftly, and at the last reaching Him most gloriously, Who with the Father and the Holy Spirit lives and reigns, for ever and ever, Amen.

Here endeth the Mirror of perfection of the state of the Friar Minor, in which one can sufficiently behold the perfection of his vocation and profession. All praise, all glory be to God the Father, to the Son, and to the Holy Spirit. Alleluia! Alleluia! Alleluia!

ST. BONAVENTURE'S
LIFE OF ST. FRANCIS

LIFE OF ST. FRANCIS

PROLOGUE

1. THE grace of God our Saviour hath in these latter days appeared in His servant Francis unto all such as be truly humble, and lovers of Holy Poverty, who, adoring the overflowing mercy of God seen in him, are taught by his example to utterly deny ungodliness and worldly desires and to live after the manner of Christ, thirsting with the unwearied desire of blessed hope. For God Most High regarded him, as one that truly was poor and of a contrite spirit, with so great condescension of His favour as that not only did He raise him up in his need from the dust of his worldly way of life, but also made him a true professor, leader, and herald of Gospel perfection. Thus He gave him for a light unto believers, that by bearing witness of the light he might prepare for the Lord the way of light and peace in the hearts of the faithful. For Francis, even as the morning star in the midst of a cloud, shining with the bright beams of his life and teaching, by his dazzling radiance led into the light them that sat in darkness and in the shadow of death, and, like unto the rainbow giving light in the bright clouds, set forth in himself the seal of the Lord's covenant. He preached the gospel of peace and salvation unto men, himself an Angel of the true peace, ordained of God to follow in the likeness of the Forerunner, that, preparing in the desert the way of sublimest Poverty, he might preach repentance by his example and words alike. For, firstly, he was endowed with the gifts of heavenly grace; next, enriched by the merits of triumphant virtue; filled with the spirit of prophecy and appointed unto angelic ministries; thereafter, wholly set on fire by the kindling of the Seraph, and, like the prophet, borne aloft in a chariot of fire; wherefore it is reasonably proven, and clearly apparent from the witness of his whole life, that he came in the spirit and power of Elias.

In like wise, he is thought to be not unmeetly set forth in the true prophecy of that other friend of the Bridegroom, the Apostle and Evangelist John, under the similitude of the Angel ascending from the sunrising and bearing the seal of the Living God. For at the opening of the sixth seal, I saw, saith John in the Apocalypse, another Angel ascending from the sun-rising and bearing the seal of the Living God.

2. Now that this Angel was indeed that messenger of God, beloved of Christ, our example and the world's wonder, Francis, the servant of God, we may with full assurance conclude, when we consider the heights of lofty saintliness whereunto he attained, and whereby, living among men, he was an imitator of the purity of the Angels, and was also set as an example unto them that do perfectly follow after Christ. That this belief should be faithfully and devoutly held we are convinced by the vocation that he showed to call to weeping and to mourning, and to baldness, and to girding with sackcloth, and to set a mark upon the foreheads of the men that sigh and that cry, by the sign of his penitent's Cross and habit fashioned like unto a Cross. Moreover, it is further confirmed, with unanswerable witness unto its truth, by the seal of the likeness of the Living God, to wit, of Christ Crucified, the which was imprinted on his body, not by the power of nature or the skill of art, but rather by the marvellous might of the Spirit of the Living God.

3. Feeling myself unworthy and insufficient to relate the life most worthy of all imitation of this most venerable man, I should have in no wise attempted it, had not the glowing love of the Brethren moved me thereunto, and the unanimous importunity of the Chapter-General incited me, and that devotion compelled me, which I am bound to feel for our holy Father. For I, who remember as though it happened but yesterday how I was snatched from the jaws of death, while yet a child, by his invocation and merits, should fear to be convicted of the sin of ingratitude did I refrain from publishing his praises. And this was with me the chief motive for undertaking this task, to wit, that I, who own my life of body and mind to have been preserved unto me by God through his means, and have proved his power in mine own person, and knew the virtues of his life, might collect as best I could, albeit I could not fully, his deeds and words—fragments, as it were, overlooked in part, in part scattered—that they might not be utterly lost on the death of those that lived with the servant of God.

4. Accordingly, that the true story of his life might be handed down unto posterity by me the more assuredly and clearly, I betook me unto the place of his birth, and there did hold diligent converse with his familiar friends that were yet living, touching the manner of life of the holy man and his passing away; and with those in especial that were well acquainted with his holiness,

and were his chief followers, who may be implicitly believed by reason of their well-known truthfulness and approved uprightness. But in relating the things that through His servant God vouchsafed to work, I deemed it best to shun all fantastic ornaments of style, forasmuch as that the devotion of the reader increaseth more by a simple than by an ornate speech. Nor have I always woven together the history according unto chronology, that I might avoid confusion, but I rather endeavoured to preserve a more coherent order, setting down sometimes facts of divers kinds that belong unto the same period, sometimes facts of the same kind that belong unto divers periods, as they seemed best to fit in together.

5. Now the beginning of the life of Francis, its course, and its consummation, are divided into fifteen chapters, as set down below, and thuswise described.

The first treateth of his manner of life in the secular state.

The second, of his perfect conversion unto God, and of the repairing of the three churches.

The third, of the founding of his Religion, and sanction of the Rule.

The fourth, of the advancement of the Order under his hand, and of the confirmation of the Rule already sanctioned.

The fifth, of the austerity of his life, and of how all created things afforded him comfort.

The sixth, of his humility and obedience, and of the divine condescensions shown unto him at will.

The seventh, of his love for Poverty, and of the wondrous supplying of his needs.

The eighth, of the kindly impulses of his piety, and of how the creatures lacking understanding seemed to be made subject unto him.

The ninth, of his ardent love, and yearning for martyrdom.

The tenth, of his zeal and efficacy in prayer.

The eleventh, of his understanding of the Scriptures, and of his spirit of prophecy.

The twelfth, of the efficacy of his preaching, and of his gift of healing.

The thirteenth, of the sacred stigmata.

The fourteenth, of his sufferings and death.

The fifteenth, of his canonisation, and the translation of his body.

Thereafter is added some account of the miracles shown after his blessed departure.[1]

[1] Omitted in the present volume.

HERE BEGINNETH THE LIFE OF THE BLESSED FRANCIS

CHAPTER I

OF HIS MANNER OF LIFE IN THE SECULAR STATE

1. THERE was a man in the city of Assisi, by name Francis, whose memory is blessed, for that God, graciously preventing him with the blessings of goodness, delivered him in His mercy from the perils of this present life, and abundantly filled him with the gifts of heavenly grace. For, albeit in his youth he was reared in vanity amid the vain sons of men, and, after gaining some knowledge of letters, was appointed unto a profitable business of merchandise, nevertheless, by the aid of the divine protection, he went not astray among the wanton youths after the lusts of the flesh, albeit given up unto pleasures; nor among the covetous merchants, albeit intent on his gains, did he put his trust in money and treasure. For there was divinely implanted in the heart of the young Francis a certain generous compassion toward the poor, the which, growing up with him from infancy, had so filled his heart with kindliness that, when he came to be no deaf hearer of the Gospel, he was minded to give unto all that asked of him, in especial if they pleaded the love of God. But once on a time, when he had been busied with the cares of his trading, and, contrary unto his wont, had sent empty away a certain beggar who besought an alms for the love of God, he forthwith, returning unto his pitiful mind, ran after him, and bestowed alms in merciful wise upon him; promising unto the Lord God that thenceforward he would never, while he could, refuse any that asked of him, pleading the love of God. And this promise with unwearied goodness he did observe until his death, thereby winning abundant increase of the love and grace of God. For he was wont to say in after time, when he had perfectly put on Christ, that, even while he was in the secular state, he could scarce ever hear words telling of the love of God, and remain unmoved in heart. Assuredly the charm of his gentleness and his courtly bearing, his submissiveness and docility surpassing men's wont, his open-handed

largesse even beyond his means, were all clear tokens of the fair disposition of the youth, and seemed to be a presage of the abundance of divine blessing that should thereafter be poured out more richly upon him.

A certain citizen of Assisi, a simpleton as was believed, yet one taught of God, whensoever he met Francis going through the city, would doff his cloak and spread the garment before his feet, declaring that Francis was worthy of all honour, as one that should ere long do mighty deeds, and was on this account to be splendidly honoured by all the faithful.

2. But as yet Francis knew not the intent of God concerning him, forasmuch as he was both drawn away unto external things by his father's calling, and weighed down toward earthly things by the corruption inborn in our nature, and had not yet learned to contemplate heavenly things, nor accustomed himself to taste of divine. And, because the infliction of tribulation giveth understanding unto the spirit, the hand of the Lord was upon him and the changes of the right hand of the Most High, afflicting his body with protracted sickness, that so He might prepare his soul for the anointing of the Holy Spirit. Now when he had regained his bodily strength, and had made ready for himself in his wonted fashion meet apparel, he met a certain soldier, of noble birth, but poor and ill-clad; whereupon, compassionating his poverty, with a kindly impulse he forthwith took off his garments and put them on him, thus in one act fulfilling a two-fold ministry of kindliness, insomuch as he both covered the shame of a noble knight, and relieved the destitution of a poor man.

3. Now on the night following, when he had yielded himself unto sleep, the divine mercy showed him a fair and great palace, together with military accoutrements adorned with the sign of the Cross of Christ, thus setting forth unto him that the mercy he had shown unto the poor soldier for the love of the King Most High was to be recompensed by this peerless reward. Accordingly, when he enquired whose were these things, answer was made him by a divine declaration that they all were his own and his soldiers'. Then, waking at early morn—since he had not yet practised his mind in examining the divine mysteries, and knew not how to pass through the appearance of things seen unto the beholding of the truth of things unseen—he accounted this strange vision a token of great good fortune. Wherefore he purposed, being as yet ignorant of the divine counsel, to betake himself into Apulia, unto a certain munificent Count, hoping in

his service to win glory in arms, as the vision shown unto him had betokened. With but little delay, he set forth on his journey and had gone as far as the neighbouring city; there he heard the Lord speaking unto him by night as with the voice of a friend, and saying, " Francis, who can do better for thee, the lord or the servant, the rich man or the poor? " And when Francis had made reply that alike the lord and the rich man could do the best, the Voice answered forthwith, " Why, then, dost thou leave the Lord for the servant, the rich God for a poor mortal? " And Francis said, " Lord, what wilt Thou have me to do? " And the Lord said unto him, " Return unto thy country, for the vision that thou hast seen betokeneth that which shall be spiritually wrought, and is to be fulfilled in thee not by mortal counsel, but by divine." So, when it was morning, he returned in haste toward Assisi, confident and rejoicing, awaiting the will of the Lord.

4. Thenceforward he withdrew him from the stir of public business, devoutly praying the heavenly mercy that it would deign to show him that which he ought to do. And so by the constant practice of prayer the flame of heavenly yearning was mightily kindled within him, and for the love of his heavenly fatherland he now contemned all earthly things as naught; for he felt that he had found the hid treasure and, like a wise merchant man, meditated selling all that he had to buy the pearl that he had found. But he knew not yet how to compass this, except that it was whispered unto his spirit that spiritual merchandise hath its beginning in the contempt of the world, and that the warfare of Christ is to be begun by victory over self.

5. Now on a day while he was riding over the plain that lieth beneath the city of Assisi, he met a certain leper, and this unforeseen meeting filled him with loathing. But when he recalled the purpose of perfection that he had even then conceived in mind, and remembered that it behoved him first of all to conquer self, if he were fain to become the soldier of Christ, he leapt from his horse and ran to embrace him. When the leper stretched forth his hand as though to receive an alms, he kissed it, and then put money therein. Then forthwith mounting his horse, he looked round him on all sides, and the plain was spread before him unbroken, and no trace of that leper might he see. Then, filled with wonder and joy, he began devoutly to chant praises unto the Lord, purposing from this to rise ever unto greater heights.

From that time forth, he would seek lonely places, dear unto mourners, and there he devoted himself without ceasing unto groanings which cannot be uttered, and, after long importunity in prayer, won an answer from the Lord. For while one day he was thus praying in seclusion, and in his exceeding fervour was wholly absorbed in God, there appeared unto him Christ Jesus in the likeness of One Crucified. Beholding Him, his soul was melted within him, and so deeply was the remembrance of Christ's Passion imprinted inwardly on his heart that from that hour, whensoever he recalled the Crucifixion of Christ, he could scarce refrain from tears and from groaning aloud; even as he himself in after time told his friends, when he was drawing nigh his end. For in sooth by this vision the man of God understood that Gospel saying to be addressed unto him, "If thou wilt come after Me, deny thyself, and take up thy cross, and follow Me."

6. From that time forth, he put on the spirit of poverty, the feeling of humility, and the love of inward godliness. For whereas aforetime not only the company, but even the distant sight, of lepers had inspired him with violent loathing, now, for the sake of Christ Crucified—Who, saith the prophet, appeared despised, and marred as a leper—and that he might fully vanquish self, he would render unto the lepers humble and kindly services in his benevolent goodness. For he would often visit their dwellings, and bestow alms upon them with a bountiful hand, and with a deep impulse of pity would kiss their hands and faces. Unto poor folk that begged of him, he was fain to give not his goods alone, but his very self, at times stripping off his garments, at times tearing or cutting them, to bestow upon them, when he had naught else at hand. Poor priests, moreover, he would succour reverently and piously, more especially with ornaments for the altar, whereby he both became a sharer in the divine worship, and supplied the needs of the worshippers.

Now about this time he was visiting, with devout reverence, the shrine of the Apostle Peter, and beheld a host of beggars before the doors of the church; thereupon, constrained in part by gentle piety, in part led by the love of poverty, he bestowed his own garments on one of the neediest, and, clad in his rags, passed that day in the midst of the beggars, with unwonted gladness of spirit; that so, despising worldly repute, he might attain by gradual steps unto Gospel perfection. He kept right strict watch over the mortification of the flesh, that he might bear the Cross of Christ, the which he bore inwardly in his heart, outwardly also in his body. So all these things were wrought by the man of God, Francis, ere yet he had separated himself from the world in habit or way of life.

CHAPTER II

OF HIS PERFECT CONVERSION UNTO GOD, AND OF THE REPAIRING OF THE THREE CHURCHES

1. FORASMUCH as the servant of the Most High had none to instruct him in this way except Christ, His mercy was now further vouchsafed unto him in visitations of His sweet grace. For on a certain day, when he had gone forth to meditate in the fields, he was walking nigh the church of Saint Damian, which from its exceeding great age was threatening to fall, and, at the prompting of the Spirit, went within to pray. Prostrating himself before an image of the Crucified, he was filled with no small consolation of spirit as he prayed. And as with eyes full of tears he gazed upon the Lord's Cross, he heard with his bodily ears a Voice proceeding from that Cross, saying thrice, "Francis, go and repair My House, which, as thou seest, is falling utterly into ruin." Francis trembled, being alone in the church, and was astonished at the sound of such a wondrous Voice, and, perceiving in his heart the might of the divine speech, was carried out of himself in ecstasy. When at length he came unto himself again, he prepared to obey, and devoted himself wholly unto the behest to repair the material church; howbeit, the principal intent of the message had regard unto that Church which Christ had purchased with His own blood, even as the Holy Spirit taught him, and as he himself afterward revealed unto the Brethren.

Accordingly he rose up, and, fortifying himself with the sign of the Cross, he put together cloth stuffs for sale, and hastened unto the city that is called Foligno, and there sold the goods that he had brought and the horse whereon he had ridden. Then this joyful merchant, putting together his gains, departed on his return for Assisi, and there did reverently enter the church concerning whose repair he had received the command. Finding there a poor priest, he showed him due reverence, and proffered him the money for the repair of the church, and the use of the poor, humbly petitioning that he would permit him to sojourn with him for a time. The priest granted him to sojourn there, but, for fear of his parents, refused the money, whereupon that true despiser of monies threw it on a window-ledge, valuing it no more than dust that is trodden under foot.

2. But when his father learnt that the servant of God was tarrying with the priest aforesaid, he was sore vexed in spirit, and ran unto the place. And Francis, being yet but a newly-recruited soldier of Christ, when he heard the threats of them that pursued him, and knew beforehand of their coming, was fain to give place unto wrath, and hid himself in a certain secret pit; therein for some days he lay concealed, beseeching the Lord without ceasing, and with floods of tears, that He would deliver his soul from the hands of them that pursued him, and would by His gracious favour fulfil the holy purposes wherewith He had inspired him. Then, filled with an overflowing joy, he began to blame himself for his craven sloth, and, leaving his hiding-place, and casting aside his fear, he took his way toward the city of Assisi. But when the townsfolk beheld him unkempt in appearance, and changed in mind, and on this account deemed him to have lost his senses, they rushed upon him with mud of the streets and stones, and mocked him with loud shouts as a fool and madman. But the servant of the Lord, not moved or overborne by any insults, passed through all as one deaf unto them. When his father heard these outcries, he ran out at once, not to deliver him, but rather to destroy him; laying aside all compunction, he dragged him into the house, and there afflicted him first with words, then with stripes and bonds. But Francis was thereby rendered but the more eager and valiant to carry out that which he had begun, remembering that saying of the Gospel, "Blessed are they which are persecuted for righteousness' sake: for theirs is the kingdom of heaven."

3. After a little space, on his father's departure from the country, his mother—who misliked her husband's dealings, and deemed it hopeless to soften the unyielding constancy of her son—freed him from his bonds, and let him go forth. Then he, giving thanks unto the Lord Almighty, returned unto the place where he had been afore. When his father returned, and found him not in the house, heaping reproaches on his wife, he ran in fury unto that place, intending, if he could not bring him back, at least to drive him from the province. But Francis, strengthened of God, of his own accord came forth to meet his raging father, crying aloud that he cared naught for his bonds and stripes, yea more, protesting that he would gladly endure all hardships for the sake of Christ. Accordingly, when his father saw that he could

not bring him back, he turned his thoughts unto the recovery of the money, the which, when he had at length found it on the window-ledge, somewhat soothed his rage, the thirst of avarice being relieved, as it were, by a draught of money.

4. Then this father according unto the flesh was fain to take this son of grace, now stripped of his wealth, before the Bishop of the city, that into his hands he might resign his claim unto his father's inheritance, and render up all that had been his. This that true lover of poverty showed himself right ready to do, and coming into the Bishop's presence, he brooked no delays, he was kept back of none, tarried for no speech, nor spake himself, but at once took off all his garments, and restored them unto his father. Then was the man of God seen to have a hair-shirt next his skin under his rich apparel. Yea more, as one drunk with wondrous fervour of spirit, he threw aside even his breeches, and stood up naked in the presence of all, saying unto his father, "Hitherto I have called thee my father on earth, but henceforth I can confidently say 'Our Father, Who art in heaven,' with Whom I have laid up my whole treasure, and on Whom I have set my whole trust and hope." The Bishop, seeing this, and marvelling at such exceeding fervour in the man of God, rose forthwith, and, weeping, put his arms round him; then, devout and kindly man as he was, covered him with the cloak wherewith he himself was clad, bidding his servants give him something to clothe his limbs withal, and there was brought unto him a mean and rough tunic of a farm-servant of the Bishop. This Francis gladly received, and with his own hand marked it with the sign of the Cross, with a piece of chalk that he chanced upon, thus making it a garment meet for a man crucified, poor, and half naked. Thus, then, the servant of the Most High King was left despoiled, that he might follow the Lord Whom he loved, Who had been despoiled and crucified; thus he was fortified with the Cross, that he might entrust his soul unto that wood of salvation, that should bring him forth unscathed from the shipwreck of the world.

5. Thereafter, this despiser of the world, loosed from the bonds of worldly desires, left the city, and, glad and free, sought an hidden solitude where he might hearken in loneliness and silence unto the hid treasures of the divine converse. And while the man of God, Francis, was making his way through a certain wood, chanting praises unto the Lord in the French tongue, and rejoicing, it chanced that some robbers rushed out on him from their hiding-places. With fierce mien they asked

the man of God who he was, and he, full of confidence, gave a prophetic answer, saying, "I am a herald of the great King." Then they fell upon him, and cast him into a ditch full of snow, crying, "Lie there, lout, thou herald of God!" But he, on their departure, climbed out of the ditch, and, uplifted with exceeding gladness, with yet louder voice began to make the woods echo with praises unto the Creator of all.

6. When he came unto a neighbouring monastery, he asked an alms as a beggar, and received it as one unrecognised and despised. Departing thence, he came unto Gubbio, where he was recognised and entertained by a friend of former days, and was clad by him with a poor tunic, such as became the little poor one of Christ.

Thence that lover of utterest humility betook himself unto the lepers, and abode among them, with all diligence serving them all for the love of God. He would bathe their feet, and bind up their sores, drawing forth the corrupt matter from their wounds, and wiping away the blood; yea, in his marvellous devotion, he would even kiss their ulcerated wounds, he that was soon to be a Gospel physician. Wherefore he obtained from the Lord such power as that he received a marvellous efficacy in marvellously cleansing both soul and body from disease. I will relate one instance out of many, whereby the fame of the man of God was afterward bruited abroad.

A man in the county of Spoleto had his mouth and jaw eaten away by the ravages of a loathsome disease, and received no succour from any remedy of the physicians. It chanced that, after visiting the shrines of the holy Apostles to implore their merits, he was returning from his pilgrimage, and met the servant of God. When out of devotion he was fain to kiss his footprints, Francis in his humility would not brook it, but kissed on the mouth him that had been fain to kiss his feet. Lo, as in his wondrous goodness the servant of the lepers, Francis, touched that loathsome sore with his holy lips, the disease utterly vanished, and the sick man at once regained his longed-for health. I know not which of these twain is the more rightly to be marvelled at, the depth of humility in such a gracious embrace, or the excellence of power in such an astounding miracle.

7. Francis, now stablished in the humility of Christ, recalled unto mind the obedience laid upon him by the Crucifix as to the repairing of the church of Saint Damian, and like one truly obedient returned unto Assisi, that he might, if even by begging,

obtain means to accomplish the divine behest. Laying aside all shamefastness for the love of the Poor Man Crucified, he went about begging from those who had known him in his affluence, bearing the loads of stones on his frail body, worn with fasting. When the church aforesaid had been repaired, the Lord helping him, and the devotion of the citizens coming unto his aid—that his body after its toil might not relax in sloth, he turned to repair the church of Saint Peter, at some distance from the city, by reason of the especial devotion that in the purity of his candid faith he had for the Prince of the Apostles.

8. When this church too was at length finished, he came unto the place that is called the Porziuncula, wherein a church had been reared in days of old in honour of the most Blessed Virgin, Mother of God, but which was then deserted and cared for by none. When the man of God beheld it thus abandoned, by reason of the ardent devotion that he had toward the Sovereign Lady of the world, he took up his abode there, that he might diligently labour to repair it. Perceiving that Angels ofttimes visited it—according unto the name of that church, that from old time was called Saint Mary of the Angels—he abode there by reason of his reverence for the Angels, and his especial love for the Mother of Christ. This place the holy man loved before all other places in the world; for here he began in humility, here he made progress in virtue, here he ended in happiness, and, dying, commended it unto the Brethren as a place most beloved of the Virgin. Concerning this place a certain devout Brother, before his conversion, beheld a vision right worthy to be recounted. He beheld a countless host of men stricken with blindness, with their faces uplifted unto heaven, on bended knees, encircling this church, and they all, stretching out their hands on high, cried unto God with tears, beseeching His mercy and light. And lo, there came a great radiance from heaven, illumining all, and this gave light unto each one of them, and granted the longed-for salvation. This is the place wherein the Order of Friars Minor was begun by Saint Francis according unto the impulse of the divine revelation. For at the bidding of the divine providence, by the which the servant of Christ was guided in all things, he built three material churches before that, instituting the Order, he preached the Gospel; thus not only did he make progress in ordered course from things perceived by the senses unto things perceived by the understanding, and from lesser things unto greater, but he did also prefigure in mystic wise by his

material labours the work that should be wrought thereafter. For, like the thrice-repeated repairing of the material fabric, the Church, under the guidance of the holy man, was to be renewed in threefold wise, according unto the pattern given by him, and the Rule, and teaching of Christ; and a triple army of such as should be saved was to be triumphant, even as we now perceive to be fulfilled.

CHAPTER III

OF THE FOUNDING OF HIS RELIGION, AND SANCTION OF THE RULE

1. Now Francis, the servant of God, abiding at the church of the Virgin Mother of God, with continuous sighing besought her that had conceived the Word full of grace and truth that she would deign to become his advocate; and, by the merits of the Mother of Mercy, he did himself conceive and give birth unto the spirit of Gospel truth. For while on a day he was devoutly hearing the Mass of the Apostles, that Gospel was read aloud wherein Christ gave unto His disciples that were sent forth to preach the Gospel pattern for their life, to wit, that they should possess neither gold, nor silver, nor money in their purses, nor scrip for their journey, neither two coats, neither shoes, nor yet staves. Hearing this, and understanding it, and committing it unto memory, the lover of Apostolic poverty was at once filled with joy unspeakable. "This," saith he, "is what I desire, yea, this is what I long for with my whole heart." Forthwith he loosed his shoes from off his feet, laid down his staff, cast aside his purse and his money, contented him with one scanty tunic, and, throwing aside his belt, took a rope for girdle, applying all the care of his heart to discover how best he might fulfil that which he had heard, and conform himself in all things unto the rule of Apostolic godliness.

2. From this time forward, the man of God began, by divine impulse, to become a jealous imitator of Gospel poverty, and to invite others unto penitence. His words were not empty, nor meet for laughter, but full of the might of the Holy Spirit, penetrating the heart's core, and smiting all that heard them with great wonder. In all his preaching, he would bring tidings of peace, saying, "The Lord give you peace," and thus

he would greet the folk at the beginning of his discourses. This greeting he had learnt by revelation from the Lord, even as he himself did afterward testify. Whence it befell, according unto the prophet's words, that he—himself inspired by the spirit of the prophets—brought tidings of peace, and preached salvation, and by salutary admonitions allied many unto the true peace who aforetime were at enmity with Christ, far from salvation.

3. Accordingly, as many remarked in the man of God alike the truth of his simple teaching and of his life, certain of them began by his example to turn their thoughts unto penitence, and, renouncing all, to join themselves unto him in habit and life. The first of these was that honour-worthy man, Bernard, who, being made a partaker in the divine calling, earned the title of the firstborn son of the blessed Father, both by being first in time, and by being of an especial holiness. For he, having proved the saintliness of the servant of Christ, was minded after his example to utterly despise the world, and sought counsel from him how he might accomplish this. Hearing this, the servant of God was filled with consolation by reason of his first offspring conceived of the Holy Spirit. "From God," saith he, "it behoveth us seek this counsel." Forthwith, when it was morning, they entered into the church of Saint Nicholas, and, having first prayed, Francis, the worshipper of the Trinity, did thrice open the book of the Gospels, seeking by a threefold witness from God to strengthen the holy purpose of Bernard. In the first opening of the book was discovered that saying, "If thou wilt be perfect, go and sell that thou hast, and give to the poor." In the second, "Take nothing for your journey." And in the third, "If any man will come after Me, let him deny himself, and take up his cross, and follow Me." "This," saith the holy man, "is our life and Rule, and that of all that shall be minded to join our fellowship. Do thou go, then, if thou wilt be perfect, and fulfil that which thou hast heard."

4. Not long after, five men were called by the same Spirit, and thus the sons of Francis numbered six; the third place among them fell unto the holy Father Giles, a man verily filled with God and worthy to be famed in remembrance. For he became afterward noted for the practice of lofty virtues, even as the servant of the Lord had foretold concerning him, and, albeit he was ignorant and simple, he was exalted unto the peak of sublime contemplation. For while for a long space of time he was continuously absorbed in uplifting of the heart unto God, he was so often snatched up unto Him in ecstasies—even

as I myself beheld with the witness of mine own eyes—as that he might be deemed to live among men an angelic rather than a mortal life.

5. Moreover, about that same time, a certain priest of the city of Assisi, Silvester by name, a man of honourable life, received of the Lord a vision not to be passed over in silence. For since, in his finite judgment, he had looked askance at the manner of life of Francis and his Brethren, he was visited—lest he should be imperilled by his rash verdict—by the regard of the heavenly grace. For in a dream he beheld the whole city of Assisi beset by a great dragon, whose huge bulk seemed to threaten all the countryside with destruction. Then he saw a Cross of gold proceeding out of the mouth of Francis, the top whereof touched heaven, and its arms outstretched at the side seemed to reach unto the ends of the world, and at its glittering aspect that foul and loathly dragon was utterly put to flight. When this had been thrice shown unto him, he deemed it a divine portent, and related it in order unto the man of God and his Brethren; and no long time thereafter he left the world, and clung so constantly unto the footsteps of Christ as that his life in the Order rendered true the vision that he had received while yet in the world.

6. When this vision was related unto him, the man of God was not puffed up with the glorying of men, but, recognising the goodness of God in the favours shown unto him, he was the more keenly incited to repel the craft of the ancient enemy, and to preach the glory of the Cross of Christ. Now on a day, while in a certain lonely place he was bitterly bewailing the remembrance of past years, the joy of the Holy Spirit came upon him, and he was assured of the full remission of all his offences. Then, carried out of himself, and wholly wrapt into a marvellous light, the horizons of his mind were enlarged, and he clearly beheld the future story of himself and of his sons. Returning after this unto the Brethren, "Be consoled," saith he, "my dearest, and rejoice in the Lord, and be not sad for that ye be few in number, nor let my simpleness nor your own make you afeared, for the Lord hath verily shown me that God will cause us to wax into a great host, and will enlarge us in manifold wise with the grace of His blessing."

7. Whereas about this time another good man did enter the Religion, the blessed family of the man of God reached the number of seven. Then the holy Father called all his sons unto him and told them many things concerning the Kingdom of

God, the contempt of the world, the sacrifice of their own wills and the chastisement of the body, and did lay before them his intent of sending them forth into the four quarters of the world. For now the barren and poor humble simpleness of the holy Father had brought forth seven sons, and he was fain to give birth unto the whole company of the faithful in the Lord Christ, calling them unto the mourning of penitence. "Go ye," saith the sweet Father unto his sons, "bringing tidings of peace unto men, and preach repentance for the remission of sins. Be ye patient in tribulation, watchful unto prayer, zealous in toil, humble in speech, sober in manner, and thankful for kindnesses, seeing that for all these an everlasting kingdom is prepared for you." Then they, humbly prostrating themselves on the ground before the servant of God, received with gladness of spirit the behest of holy obedience. And Francis said unto each one singly, "Cast thy burden upon the Lord, and He shall sustain thee." He was wont to say these words whensoever he was guiding any Brother unto obedience. Then he himself, knowing that he was set as an example unto the rest, that he might first do that which he had taught, set forth with one companion toward one quarter of the world, the remaining six being apportioned, after the fashion of a Cross, unto the other three parts. After some little time had passed, the kindly Father, longing for the presence of his beloved family—since he could not of himself call them together into one place—prayed that this might be accomplished by Him Who gathereth together the outcasts of Israel. And this came to pass. For, with no mortal summoning, and all unexpectedly, within a short time all came together according as he had desired, by the effectual working of the divine goodness, and to their no small marvel. Moreover, as four other honourable men joined them about that time, their number increased unto twelve.

8. Now when the servant of Christ perceived that the number of the Brethren was gradually increasing, he wrote for himself and for his Brethren a Rule for their life, in simple words. Herein the observance of the Holy Gospel was set as the inseparable foundation, and some few other points were added that seemed necessary for a consistent manner of life. But he desired that what he had written should be approved by the Supreme Pontiff, wherefore he purposed to approached the Apostolic See with that his company of simple men, relying only on the divine guidance. God from on high had regard unto

his desire, and fortified the minds of his companions, that were afeared at the thought of his simpleness, by a vision shown unto the man of God after this wise. It seemed unto him that he was walking along a certain road, near by which stood a very lofty tree. When he had drawn nigh unto it, and was standing beneath it, wondering at its height, on a sudden he was so raised on high by the divine might so that he touched the top of the tree, and bent down its highest branches unto its roots right easily. The portent of this vision Francis, filled with the Spirit of God, understood to refer unto the stooping of the Apostolic See unto his desire; wherefore he was gladdened in spirit, and his Brethren were strengthened in the Lord, and thus he set forth with them on the journey.

9. Now when he had come unto the Roman Curia,[1] and had been introduced into the presence of the Supreme Pontiff, he expounded unto him his intent, humbly and earnestly beseeching him to sanction the Rule aforesaid for their life. And the Vicar of Christ, the lord Innocent the Third, a man exceeding renowned for wisdom, beholding in the man of God the wondrous purity of a simple soul, constancy unto his purpose, and the enkindled fervour of a holy will, was disposed to give unto the suppliant his fatherly sanction. Howbeit, he delayed to perform that which the little poor one of Christ asked, by reason that unto some of the Cardinals this seemed a thing untried, and too hard for human strength. But there was present among the Cardinals an honour-worthy man, the lord John of Saint Paul, Bishop of Sabina, a lover of all holiness, and an helper of the poor men of Christ. He, inflamed by the Divine Spirit, said unto the Supreme Pontiff, and unto his colleagues, "If we refuse the request of this poor man as a thing too hard, and untried, when his petition is that the pattern of Gospel life may be sanctioned for him, let us beware lest we make the Gospel of Christ a stumbling-block. For if any man saith that in the observance of Gospel perfection, and the vowing thereof, there is contained aught that is untried, or contrary unto reason, or impossible to observe, he is clearly seen to blaspheme against Christ, the author of the Gospel." When these arguments had been set forth, the successor of the Apostle Peter, turning unto the poor man of Christ, said, "Pray unto Christ, my son, that He may show us His will through thee, and when

[1] A paragraph inserted here in some editions, relating how the Pope at first repulsed Francis, but was converted by a vision, is not from Bonaventure's pen, but from that of the Minister-General who succeeded him (*vide* Quaracchi text, p. 29, note).

we know it more surely, we will more confidently assent unto thy holy desires."

10. Then the servant of God Almighty, betaking himself wholly unto prayer, gained by devout intercession that which he might set forth outwardly, and the Pope feel inwardly. For when he had narrated a parable of a rich King that had of free will espoused a fair woman that was poor, and how the children she bare showed the likeness of the King that begat them, and so were brought up at his table, even as he had learnt this of the Lord—he added, as an interpretation thereof, "It is not to be feared that the sons and heirs of the everlasting King will perish of hunger, even they that have been born of a poor mother in the likeness of the King, Christ, by the power of the Holy Spirit, and that shall themselves beget sons through the spirit of Poverty in a little poor Religion. For if the King of heaven hath promised an everlasting kingdom unto them that follow Him, how much more shall He provide for them those things that He bestoweth alike on the good and on the evil?" When the Vicar of Christ had diligently hearkened unto this parable, and the interpretation thereof, he marvelled greatly, and perceived that Christ had of a truth spoken through a man. Moreover, he maintained, by the inspiration of the Divine Spirit, that a vision that at that time was shown unto him from heaven would be fulfilled in Francis. For in a dream he saw, as he recounted, the Lateran Basilica about to fall, when a little poor man, of mean stature and humble aspect, propped it with his own back, and thus saved it from falling. "Verily," saith he, "he it is that by his work and teaching shall sustain the Church of Christ." From this vision, he was filled with an especial devotion unto him, and in all ways disposed himself unto his supplication, and ever loved the servant of Christ with an especial affection. Then and there he granted his request, and promised at a later day to bestow yet more upon him. He sanctioned the Rule, and gave him a command to preach repentance, and made all the lay Brethren that had accompanied the servant of God wear narrow tonsures, that they might preach the word of God without hindrance.

CHAPTER IV

OF THE ADVANCEMENT OF THE ORDER UNDER HIS HAND, AND OF THE CONFIRMATION OF THE RULE ALREADY SANCTIONED

1. THENCEFORWARD Francis, relying on the favour of heaven and on the Papal authority, took his way with all confidence toward the valley of Spoleto, that he might both live and teach the Gospel of Christ. While he was holding converse with his companions on the road, as to how they might observe in sincerity the Rule that they had professed, and how in all holiness and righteousness they might walk before God, how they might progress among themselves, and be an example unto others, their discussion was prolonged, and the hours slipped by. And at last they found themselves, wearied with the length of their toilsome way, and an hungered, in a certain lonely place. Then verily, when there was no means whereby they might provide them with the needful food, the providence of God came speedily unto their aid. For, on a sudden, there appeared a man carrying bread in his hand, the which he gave unto the little poor ones of Christ, and, also on a sudden, vanished, without any man knowing whence he came or whither he went. Hereby the Brethren in their poverty perceived that the guardian care of heaven was about the company of the man of God, and were refreshed more by the gift of the divine bounty than by the food of the body; moreover, they were filled with heavenly comfort, and firmly resolved, and strengthened themselves in the irrevocable determination, never to retreat from their vow of Holy Poverty for any goad of necessity or affliction.

2. Thus they returned in their holy intent unto the valley of Spoleto, and began to discuss whether they ought to live among men, or to betake them unto lonely places. But Francis, the servant of Christ, trusting not in his own efforts or those of his Brethren, with importunate prayer enquired the pleasure of the divine will concerning this. Then he was illumined by a divinely revealed oracle, and understood that he had been sent of the Lord unto this end, that he might win for Christ the souls that the devil was striving to carry off. Wherefore he chose to live rather for all men than for his single self, inspired by the example of Him Who willed to die, One Man for all.

3. Accordingly, the man of God returned with the rest of his companions unto a certain deserted hut nigh the city of Assisi,

wherein, after the pattern of Holy Poverty, they lived in much toil and necessity, seeking to be refreshed rather with the bread of tears than of luxury. For they gave themselves up continuously unto divine prayers, being earnest in the practice of devout intercession—of the heart rather than of the lips—for they had not yet any ecclesiastical books wherein they might chant the Canonical Hours. Howbeit, in the place of such, they meditated day and night on the book of the Cross of Christ, continuously looking thereupon, by the example of their Father, and taught by his discourse, for he continually spake unto them concerning the Cross of Christ. When the Brethren besought him to teach them to pray, he said, "When ye pray, say 'Our Father,' and, 'We adore Thee, O Christ, in all Thy churches that be in the whole world, and we bless Thee because by Thy holy Cross Thou hast redeemed the world.'" Moreover, he taught them to praise God in all things and through all His creatures, to reverence priests with an especial honour, to firmly hold and simply confess the true faith, according as the Holy Roman Church doth both hold and teach it. The Brethren observed the instructions of the holy Father in all things, and, using the form of prayer that he had given unto them, would humbly prostrate themselves before all churches and crosses that they beheld, were it even from a distance.

4. Now while the Brethren were abiding in the place aforesaid, the holy man one Saturday entered the city of Assisi, to preach early on the Sunday, as was his wont, in the Cathedral Church. While the man devoted unto God was passing the night, after his wonted manner, in a hut within the Canon's garden, praying unto God, and absent in the body from his sons—lo, about midnight, while some of the Brethren were taking rest, others keeping vigil in prayer, a chariot of fire of marvellous brightness, entering by the door of the house, turned thrice hither and thither through the dwelling, and over the chariot a shining ball of fire rested, in appearance like unto the sun, making the night radiant. The watchful Brethren were astounded, they that slept were awakened and alarmed at the same moment, and felt the light no less in their hearts than with their bodies, while by the power of that marvellous brightness the conscience of each was laid bare unto his fellow. For they all understood alike—all seeing in turn the hearts of each—that their holy Father was absent from them in body, but present in spirit, and that, transformed into such a likeness, illumined with heavenly rays, and flaming with ardent heat, he was shown unto them by the Lord with

supernatural might in a shining chariot of fire; so that they, as Israelites indeed, might follow after him who, like another Elias, had been made by God the chariot and the horseman of spiritual men. We must verily believe that He opened the eyes of those simple men at the prayers of Francis, that they might see the mighty deeds of God, Who aforetime opened the eyes of the young man that he might see the mountain full of horses and chariots of fire round about Elisha. When the holy man returned unto the Brethren, he began to scrutinise the secret things of their consciences, to console them with that marvellous vision, and to foretell many things that should come to pass concerning the progress of the Order. And as he revealed many things surpassing mortal sense, the Brethren perceived of a truth that the Spirit of the Lord had rested upon His servant Francis in such fulness as that they would walk most securely in following his teaching and life.

5. After this, Francis, shepherd of a little flock, led his band of twelve Brethren unto Saint Mary of the Porziuncula—the favour of heaven going before him—that in the place wherein, by the merits of the Mother of God, the Order of Minors had taken its beginning, it might by her aid gain an increase. There too he became an herald of the Gospel, going round among cities and fortified places, proclaiming the Kingdom of God, not in the words which man's wisdom teacheth, but which the Holy Ghost teacheth. He seemed unto them that beheld him a man of another world, one, to wit, that had his heart ever set on heaven, and his face turned toward it, and that endeavoured to draw all men upwards. From this time, the vine of Christ began to bring forth pleasant savour of the Lord, and the flowers produced therefrom became the rich fruit of sweetness, honour, and righteousness.

6. For, enkindled by the fervour of his preaching, very many folk bound themselves by new rules of penitence, after the pattern received from the man of God, and that same servant of Christ ordained that their manner of living should be called the Order of the Brethren of Penitence. Of a truth, even as the way of penitence is known to be common unto all that strive after heaven, so it is noted of how much worth in the sight of God was this Order, embracing clerks and laymen, virgins, and married folk of either sex, by the many miracles wrought by some of its members. And there were maidens converted unto lifelong virginity, among whom that virgin dearest unto God, Clare, the first plant among them, like a snowy spring blossom,

breathed fragrance, and shone like a star exceeding bright. She is now glorified in heaven, and rightly honoured by the Church on earth, she that was the daughter in Christ of the holy Father Francis, the little poor one, and herself the Mother of the Poor Ladies.

7. Now many were not only smitten with devotion, but also kindled by yearning after the perfection of Christ, and, despising all the vanity of worldly things, followed in the footsteps of Francis; and these, increasing by daily additions, speedily reached unto the ends of the earth. For Holy Poverty, whom alone they took with them for their charges, made them swift unto all obedience, strong to labour, and speedy in journeying. And since they possessed no earthly things they set their affections on naught, and had naught that they feared to lose; they were everywhere at ease, weighed down by no fear, harassed by no care; they lived like men who were removed from vexations of the mind, and, taking no thought for it, awaited the morrow, and their night's lodging. Many reproaches were hurled upon them in divers regions of the world, as on men contemptible and unknown; howbeit, their love for the Gospel of Christ rendered them so longsuffering as that they sought rather to be in places where they would endure persecution in the body, than in those where their saintliness was recognised, and where they might be puffed up by the applause of the world. Their very destitution of possessions seemed unto them overflowing wealth, while, according unto the counsel of the Wise King, they were better pleased with little than with much.

On a time when some of the Brethren had come unto the regions of the infidels, it chanced that a certain Saracen, moved by kindly feeling, offered them money for their needful food. And when they refused to take it, the man marvelled, perceiving that they were penniless. But when at last he understood that they had become poor for the love of God, and were resolved not to own money, he associated himself with them in such affection as that he offered to supply all their needs, so long as he should have aught in his possession. O priceless value of poverty, by whose marvellous power the mind of a fierce barbarian was changed into such compassionate gentleness! How appalling and scandalous a crime it is, that any Christian should trample on this rare pearl, that a Saracen exalted with such honour!

8. About that time, a certain Religious of the Order of Crossbearers, Morico by name, was lying in an hospital hard by Assisi

suffering from an infirmity so serious and so protracted as that he was given up unto death by the physicians; he became a suppliant of the man of God, beseeching him earnestly through a messenger that he would deign to intercede with the Lord on his behalf. The blessed Father graciously acceded thereunto, and, having first prayed, took some crumbs of bread, and mixed with them some oil taken from the lamp that burned before the altar of the Virgin, and sent it by the hand of the Brethren unto the sick man, as though it were an electuary, saying, "Carry this medicament unto our brother Morico, by the which the power of Christ shall not only restore him unto full health, but shall also render him a hardy warrior, who shall cleave with constancy unto our ranks." Forthwith, so soon as the sick man tasted of that remedy made by inspiration of the Holy Spirit, he rose up healed, and gained from God such strength of mind and body as that shortly thereafter he entered the Religion of the holy man, and, clothing himself with one tunic alone—beneath the which he wore for a long space of time a shirt of mail—and satisfied with but uncooked fare—herbs to wit, and vegetables and fruits—he thus for many years tasted neither bread nor wine, and yet remained strong and sound.

9. As the merits of the virtues of these little ones of Christ waxed greater, the fragrance of their good repute was spread on all sides, and drew much folk from divers parts of the world to see the holy Father in person. Among whom was a certain skilled composer of secular songs, who by reason of this gift had been crowned by the Emperor, and thence called "King of Verse," and he now was minded to seek the man of God, the despiser of worldly things. And when he had found him preaching in a Monastery at Borgo San Severino, the hand of the Lord was upon him, and he beheld that same preacher of the Cross of Christ, Francis, marked after the likeness of a Cross with two exceeding shining swords set crosswise, whereof the one reached from his head unto his feet, the other across his breast from hand to hand. He had not known the servant of Christ by face, but speedily recognised him when signalled out by so great a portent. Forthwith, all astonished at this sight, he began to resolve on better things, and, at length, pricked by the power of his words, and pierced as though by the sword of the Spirit proceeding out of his mouth, he did utterly despise worldly glories, and followed the blessed Father, professing his vows. Wherefore the holy man, seeing that he had utterly

turned from the disquiet of the world unto the peace of Christ, called him Brother Pacificus. He afterward made progress in all holiness, and, before that he became Minister in France—being the first who held the office of Minister there—he merited to behold once more a great T on the forehead of Francis, the which, marked out by a diversity of colours, adorned his face with its marvellous beauty. This sign, in sooth, the holy man revered with deep affection, praised it often in his discourse, and, in the letters that he dictated, signed it with his own hand at the end, as though all his care was, in the prophet's words, to set a mark [1] upon the foreheads of the men that sigh and that cry, and that be truly converted unto Christ Jesus.

10. Now as time went by, and the Brethren were multiplied, their watchful shepherd began to call them together unto Chapters-General in the place of Saint Mary of the Porziuncula, so that, God dividing them an inheritance by line in the land of poverty, he might allot unto each his portion of obedience. Here, albeit there was destitution of all things needful, a company of more than 5000 Brethren came together at one time, and, the divine mercy succouring them, there was both a sufficiency of victual, and bodily health together with it, while gladness of spirit abounded. In the provincial Chapters, albeit Francis could not there show himself present in the body, yet in spirit—by his zealous care for their ruling, by his urgency in prayer, and the efficacy of his blessing—he was present there; yea, and once, by the operation of God's marvellous power, he did visibly appear. For while that glorious preacher, who is now a noted Confessor of Christ, Anthony, was preaching unto the Chapter of the Brethren at Arles on the title inscribed on the Cross, "Jesus of Nazareth, the King of the Jews," a certain Brother of proved uprightness, Monaldo by name, looking, by a divine impulse, toward the door of the Chapter-house, beheld with his bodily eyes the Blessed Francis uplifted in the air, his hands outstretched after the manner of a Cross, blessing the Brethren. All the Brethren felt that they had been filled with a consolation of spirit so great and so new as that the Spirit bore indubitable witness within them of the true presence of the holy Father, albeit this was further assured, not alone by manifest tokens, but also by external testimony through the words of that same holy Father. We must verily believe that the almighty power of God—that vouchsafed unto the

[1] Vulg. Ezek. ix. 4. *Signa tau* (T) *super frontes* etc., the letter T being in form like a Cross.

holy Bishop Ambrose to be present at the burial of the glorious Martin, that he might honour the holy prelate with his holy ministry—did also make His servant Francis to appear at the preaching of His true herald Antony, that he might sanction his preaching of the truth, and in especial his preaching of the Cross of Christ, whereof he was a supporter and servant.

11. Now as the Order was spreading abroad, Francis was minded to make the Rule of their life, that the lord Innocent had sanctioned, be confirmed in perpetuity by his successor Honorius, and he was admonished by a revelation from God on this wise. He seemed unto himself to have gathered from the ground some very small crumbs of bread, and to have to part them among many famished Brethren that stood round about him. While he hesitated, fearing to part among them such minute crumbs, lest haply they might slip between his hands, a Voice from above said unto him, "Francis, make one Host out of all the crumbs, and give it unto these that would fain eat." This he did, and such as did not receive it devoutly, or despised the gift as they received it, were speedily stricken with leprosy, and so marked out from the rest. At morn, the holy man narrated all these things unto his companions, grieving that he could not interpret the mystic meaning of the vision. But on the day following, as he kept prayerful vigil, he heard a Voice speaking unto him from heaven on this wise, "Francis, the crumbs of the night past are the words of the Gospel, the Host is the Rule, the leprosy is sin." Being fain, therefore, to reduce unto more convenient form the Rule that was to be confirmed—it having been somewhat diffusely compiled by putting together the words of the Gospel—and being directed thereunto by the vision that had been shown him, he went up into a certain mountain with two companions, the Holy Spirit leading him. There, fasting, or living on bread and water alone, he made the Rule to be compiled, according unto what the divine Spirit had taught him in prayer. When he came down from the mountain, he entrusted this Rule unto the keeping of his Vicar, who, when a few days had gone by, affirmed that he had lost it through negligence. Then the holy man returned unto the lonely place, and there drew up the Rule again, like the former one, as though he had received the very words from the mouth of God; and he obtained its confirmation, as he had desired, from the lord Pope Honorius aforesaid, in the eighth year of his pontificate. When persuading the Brethren with ardour to observe this Rule, he would say that he had set naught

therein of his own devising, but that he had made all things be written according as they had been divinely revealed unto him. And that this might be more assuredly confirmed by the witness of God, it was but a few days thereafter that the stigmata of the Lord Jesus were imprinted upon him by the finger of the Living God—the seal, as it were, of the Chief Pontiff, Christ, to sanction in all ways the Rule, and to approve its author, even as is described in its own place below, after the recital of his virtues.

CHAPTER V

OF THE AUSTERITY OF HIS LIFE, AND OF HOW ALL CREATED THINGS AFFORDED HIM COMFORT

1. When therefore the man of God, Francis, perceived that by his example many were incited to bear the Cross of Christ with fervour of soul, he himself was incited, like a good leader of the army of Christ, to reach unto the palm of victory by the heights of unconquered valour. For, considering that saying of the Apostle, "They that are Christ's have crucified the flesh with the affections and lusts," and being fain to wear the armour of the Cross upon his body, he restrained his sensual appetites with such strict discipline as that he would barely take what was necessary to support life. For he was wont to say that it was difficult to satisfy the needs of the body without yielding unto the inclinations of the senses. Wherefore he would hardly, and but seldom, allow himself cooked food when in health, and, when he did allow it, he would either sprinkle it with ashes, or by pouring water thereupon would as far as possible destroy its savour and taste. Of his drinking of wine what shall I say, when even of water he would scarce drink what he needed, while parched with burning thirst? He was alway discovering methods of more rigorous abstinence, and would daily make progress in their use, and albeit he had already attained the summit of perfection, yet, like a novice, he was ever making trial of some new method, chastising the lusts of the flesh by afflicting it. Howbeit, when he went forth abroad, he adapted himself—as the Gospel biddeth—unto them that entertained him, in the quality of their meats, yet only so as that, on his return unto his own abode, he strictly observed the sparing frugality of abstinence. In this wise he showed himself harsh toward his

own self, gracious toward his neighbour, and in all things subject unto the Gospel of Christ, and did thus set an example of edification, not alone by his abstinence, but even in what he ate. The bare ground for the most part served as a couch unto his wearied body, and he would often sleep sitting, with a log or a stone placed under his head, and, clad in one poor tunic, he served the Lord in cold and nakedness.

2. Once when he was asked how in such scant clothing he could protect him from the bitterness of the winter's cold, he made answer in fervour of spirit, "If through our yearning for the heavenly fatherland we have been inwardly kindled by its flame, we can easily endure this bodily cold." He abhorred softness in clothing, and loved harshness, declaring that for this John the Baptist had been praised by the divine lips. In sooth, if ever he perceived smoothness in a tunic that was given him, he had it lined with small cords, for he would say that, according unto the Word of Truth, it was not in poor men's huts, but in Kings' houses, that softness of raiment was to be sought. And he had learnt by sure experience that the devils be afeared of hardness, but that by luxury and softness they be the more keenly incited to tempt men.

Accordingly, one night when by reason of an infirmity in his head and eyes he had, contrary unto his wont, a pillow of feathers placed beneath his head, the devil entered thereinto, and vexed him until the morning hour, distracting him in divers ways from his exercise of holy prayer; until, calling his companion, he made the pillow and the devil withal be carried afar from the cell. But as the Brother was leaving the cell, carrying the pillow, he lost the power and use of all his limbs, until, at the voice of the holy Father, who perceived this in spirit, his former powers of mind and body were fully restored unto him.

3. Stern in discipline, Francis stood continually upon the watch-tower, having especial care unto that purity that should be maintained in both the inner and the outer man. Wherefore, in the early days of his conversion, he was wont in the winter season to plunge into a ditch full of snow, that he might both utterly subdue the foe within him, and might preserve his white robe of chastity from the fire of lust. He would maintain that it was beyond compare more tolerable for a spiritual man to bear intense cold in his body, than to feel the heat of carnal lust, were it but a little, in his mind.

4. When he was at the hermitage of Sartiano, and had one night devoted himself unto prayer in his cell, the ancient enemy

called him, saying thrice, "Francis, Francis, Francis." When he had enquired of him what he sought, that other made reply to deceive him, "There is no sinner in the world whom God would not spare, should he turn unto Him. But whoso killeth himself by harsh penance, shall find no mercy throughout eternity." Forthwith the man of God perceived by revelation the deceits of the enemy, and how he had striven to render him once more lukewarm. And this the following event proved. For but a little after this, at the instigation of him whose breath kindleth coals, a grievous temptation of the flesh laid hold on him. When the lover of chastity felt its oncoming, he laid aside his habit, and began to scourge himself severely with a cord, saying, "Ah, brother ass, thus must thou be led, thus must thou submit unto the lash. The habit is the servant of Religion, it is a token of holiness, the sensual man may not steal it; if thou art fain to go forth anywhere, go!" Then, impelled by a marvellous fervour of spirit, he threw open the door of his cell, and went out into the garden, where, plunging his now naked body into a great snow-heap, he began to pile up therefrom with full hands seven mounds, the which he set before him, and thus addressed his outer man, "Behold (saith he), this larger heap is thy wife, these four be two sons and two daughters, the other twain be a serving man and maid, that thou must needs have to serve thee. Now bestir thee and clothe them, for they be perishing with cold. But if manifold cares on their behalf trouble thee, do thou be careful to serve the one Lord." Then the tempter departed, routed, and the holy man returned unto his cell victorious, in that, by enduring the external cold in right penitent fashion, he had so extinguished the fire of lust within that thereafter he felt it no whit. Now a Brother, who at the time was devoting himself unto prayer, beheld all these things by the light of a clear shining moon. When the man of God discovered that he had seen these things on that night, he revealed unto him how that temptation had befallen him, and bade him tell no man, so long as he himself lived, the thing that he had seen.

5. And not only did he teach that the appetites of the body must be mortified, and its impulses bridled, but also that the outer senses, through the which death entereth into the soul, must be guarded with the utmost watchfulness. He bade that intimate intercourse with women, holding converse with them, and looking upon them—the which be unto many an occasion of falling—should be zealously shunned, declaring that by

such things a weak spirit is broken, and a strong one ofttimes weakened. He said that one who held converse with women —unless he were of an especial uprightness—could as little avoid contamination therefrom as he could, in the words of Scripture, go upon hot coals and his feet not be burned. He himself so turned away his eyes that they might not behold vanity after this sort that he knew the features of scarce any woman—thus he once told a companion. For he thought it was not safe to dwell on the appearance of their persons, that might either rekindle a spark of the vanquished flesh, or spot the radiance of a chaste mind. For he maintained that converse with women was a vain toy, except only for confession or the briefest instruction, such as made for salvation, and was in accord with decorum. "What dealings," saith he, "should a Religious have with a woman, except when she seeketh, with devout supplication, after holy penitence, or counsel about a better life? In overweening confidence, the enemy is less dreaded, and the devil, if so be that he can have a hair of his own in a man, soon maketh it wax into a beam."

6. He taught the Brothers zealously to shun sloth, as the sink of all evil thoughts, showing by his example that the rebellious and idle body must be subdued by unceasing discipline and profitable toil. Wherefore he would call his body "brother ass," as though it were meet to be loaded with toilsome burdens, beaten with many stripes, and nourished on mean fare. If he beheld any man wandering about in idleness, and fain to feed on the toil of others, he thought he ought to be called "brother fly," for that, doing no good himself, and spoiling the good done by others, he made himself an hateful pest unto all. Wherefore he ofttimes said, "I would that my Brethren should labour and employ themselves, lest, being given up unto sloth, they should stray into sins of heart or tongue." He was minded that a Gospel silence should be observed by the Brethren, such as, to wit, that they should at all times diligently refrain from every idle word, as those that shall give account thereof in the Day of Judgment. But if he found any Brother prone unto vain words, he would sharply chide him, declaring a shamefast sparingness of speech to be the guard of a pure heart, and no small virtue, seeing that death and life are in the power of the tongue, not so much with regard unto taste as with regard unto speech.

7. But albeit he sought with all his might to lead the Brethren unto the austere life, yet the utmost rigour of severity pleased

him not—such rigour as hath no bowels of compassion, nor is flavoured with the salt of discretion. Thus, on a certain night, when one of the Brethren by reason of his excessive abstinence was so tormented by hunger that he could take no repose, the kindly shepherd, perceiving the danger that threatened his sheep, called the Brother, set bread before him, and, that he might remove any cause for his confusion of face, began first to eat himself, then gently bade him partake. The Brother, laying aside his shamefastness, took the food, rejoicing exceedingly that, through the wise kindliness of his shepherd, he had both escaped that bodily peril, and had received no small example of edification withal. When morning came, and the Brethren had been called together, the man of God related that which had befallen in the night, adding the sage exhortation, "Be the act of love, not the food, an example unto you, my Brethren." Moreover, he taught them to follow discretion, as the charioteer of the virtues—not that discretion unto which the flesh persuadeth, but that which Christ taught, Whose most holy life is acknowledged to be the express image of perfection.

8. And since it is not possible for a man beset with the infirmity of the flesh so perfectly to follow the Crucified Lamb without spot as to escape contracting some defilement, by his own firm example he made declaration that they who keep watch over the perfection of their life ought to cleanse themselves daily with floods of tears. For, albeit he had already attained a wondrous purity of heart and body, yet would he not abstain from continual floods of tears whereby to cleanse the mental vision, not weighing the detriment unto his bodily sight. For when by incessant weeping he had sustained a very grievous injury unto the eyes, and the physician would fain have persuaded him to refrain from tears, if he wished to escape blindness of his bodily sight, the holy man made answer, "It is not meet, brother physician, that for the love of that light that we have in common with the flies, the visitation of the eternal light should be impaired, be it but by little. For the spirit did not receive the blessing of light for the sake of the flesh, but the flesh for the sake of the spirit." He preferred rather to lose the light of his bodily vision than, by thwarting the devotion of the spirit, to check the tears whereby the inner eye is cleansed, that it may avail to see God.

9. Now on a time when he was counselled by the physicians, and urgently importuned by the Brethren, to permit himself to be succoured by the remedy of a cautery, the man of God did

humbly assent thereunto, forasmuch as he perceived it to be alike salutary and arduous. The surgeon, then, was summoned, and, having come, laid his iron instrument in the fire to prepare for the cautery. Then the servant of Christ—consoling his body that at the sight shuddered in fear—began to address the fire as a friend, saying, "My brother fire, the Most High hath created thee beyond all other creatures mighty in thine enviable glory, fair, and useful. Be thou clement unto me in this hour, and courteous. I beseech the great Lord, Who created thee, that He temper thy heat unto me, so that I may be able to bear thy gentle burning." His prayer ended, he made the sign of the Cross over the iron instrument, that was glowing at white heat from the fire, and then waited fearlessly. The hissing iron was impressed on the tender flesh, and the cautery drawn from the ear unto the eyebrow. How much suffering the fire caused him, the holy man himself told: "Praise the Most High," saith he unto the Brethren, "for that of a truth I say unto you, I felt neither the heat of the fire, nor any pain in my flesh." And, turning unto the surgeon, "If," saith he, "the cautery be not well made, impress it again." The surgeon, finding such mighty valour of spirit in his frail body, marvelled, and exalted this divine miracle, saying, "I tell ye, Brethren, I have seen strange things to-day." For, by reason that Francis had attained unto such purity that his flesh was in harmony with his spirit, and his spirit with God, in marvellous agreement, it was ordained by the divine ruling that the creature that serveth its Maker should be wondrously subject unto his will and command.

10. At another time, when the servant of God was afflicted by a very grievous sickness, at the hermitage of Saint Urban, and, feeling his strength failing, had asked for a draught of wine, answer was made him that there was no wine there that could be brought unto him; whereupon he bade that water should be brought, and, when brought, he blessed it, making the sign of the Cross over it. At once that which had been pure water became excellent wine, and that which the poverty of the lonely place could not provide was obtained by the purity of the holy man. Tasting thereof, he forthwith so easily recovered his strength as that the new flavour and the renewed health, by the sense of taste and by the miracle renewing him that tasted, attested, with twofold witness, his perfect laying aside of the old man and putting on of the new.

11. Nor did created things alone obey the servant of God at

his beck, but everywhere the very providence of the Creator stooped unto his good pleasure. Thus, on a time when his body was weighed down by the suffering of many infirmities together, he had a yearning for some tuneful sound that might incite him unto gladness of spirit, yet discreet decorum would not allow this to be rendered by human agency—then the Angels gave their services to fulfil the good pleasure of the holy man. For one night while he was wakeful, and meditating on the Lord, on a sudden was heard the sound of a lyre of wondrous harmony and sweetest tune. No one was to be seen, but the coming and going of a lyrist was betokened by the volume of sound, now here, now there. With his mind uplifted unto God, he enjoyed such sweetness from that melodious strain as that he thought him to have exchanged this world for another. This was not hidden from the Brethren that were his close companions, who ofttimes perceived, by assured tokens, that he was visited of the Lord with such exceeding and continual consolations as that he could not utterly hide them.

12. On another time, while the man of God, with a Brother for companion, was making his way to preach between Lombardy and the March of Treviso, and was nigh the Po, the shadowy darkness of night surprised them. And since their way was beset by many and great dangers by reason of the darkness, the river, and the marshes, his companion said unto the holy man, "Pray, Father, that we be delivered from instant peril." Unto whom the man of God made answer with great confidence, "God is able, if it be His sweet will, to put to flight the thick darkness, and to grant us the blessing of light." Scarce had he ended his speech ere, lo! such a great light began to shine around them with heavenly radiance that, while for others it was dark night, they could see in the clear light not their road only, but many things round about. By the leading of this light they were guided in body and consoled in spirit, until they arrived safely, singing divine hymns and lauds, at their place of lodging that was some long way distant. Consider how wondrous was the purity of this man, how great his merits, that at his beck the fire should temper its heat, water should change its flavour, angelic music should afford him solace, and light from heaven leading; thus it was evident that the whole frame of the world was obedient unto the consecrated senses of the holy man.

CHAPTER VI

OF HIS HUMILITY AND OBEDIENCE, AND OF THE DIVINE CONDESCENSIONS SHOWN UNTO HIM AT WILL

1. HUMILITY, the guardian and glory of all virtues, abounded in rich fulness in the man of God. In his own estimation, he was naught but a sinner, whereas in very truth he was the mirror and brightness of all saintliness. In humility he strove to build himself up, as a wise masterbuilder laying the foundation that he had learnt of Christ. He would say that for this end the Son of God had come down from the heights, and from His Father's bosom, unto our mean estate, to wit, that both by example and precept our Lord and Master might teach humility. Wherefore Francis, as a disciple of Christ, strove ever to make himself of no esteem in his own and other men's eyes, mindful of that saying of the greatest Teacher, "That which is highly esteemed among men is abomination in the sight of God." This too he was wont to say, "A man's worth is what he is in the sight of God, and no more." Accordingly, he deemed it a fool's part to be uplifted by the applause of the world, but he rejoiced in railings, and was saddened by praise. He would rather hear himself reviled than praised, knowing that reviling leadeth unto amendment, while praise impelleth toward a fall. Wherefore ofttimes when folk exalted the merits of his saintliness, he would bid one of the Brethren offer him a contrast, by pouring contemptuous words into his ears. And when that Brother, albeit against his will, called him a lout and an hireling, one unskilled and unprofitable, he would rejoice in spirit and in countenance alike, and would make answer, "The Lord bless thee, dearest son, for thou hast spoken words most true, and such as it becometh the son of Peter Bernardone to hear."

2. Now that he might make himself contemned of others, he spared not his shamefastness, but in preaching before the whole folk laid bare his failings. It befell once that, while weighed down by sickness, he had some little relaxed the strictness of his abstinence, with the intent of regaining his health. But when that he had recovered his bodily strength, this true despiser of self was inspired to rebuke his own flesh. "It is not fitting," saith he, "that the folk should believe me to observe abstinence while that I, on the contrary, do refresh my

body in secret." Accordingly, he arose, kindled with the spirit of holy humility, and, calling the folk together in an open space of the city of Assisi, he, together with many Brethren that he had brought with him, made a solemn entrance into the Cathedral Church, and then, with a rope tied round his neck, and naked save for his breeches, bade them drag him in the sight of all unto the stone whereupon criminals were wont to be set for punishment. Mounting it, albeit he was suffering from quartan fever and weakness, and the season was bitterly cold, he preached with much power of spirit, and, while all gave ear, declared that he ought not to be honoured as a spiritual man, but that rather he ought to be despised of all as a fleshly glutton. Then they that were present and beheld this amazing sight, marvelled, and, for that they had long known his austerities, were devoutly pricked to the heart, exclaiming that humility after this sort were easier admired than imitated. Yet, albeit this seemed rather like unto the prodigy foretold of the prophet than an example, it set forth a pattern of perfect humility, whereby the follower of Christ was taught that he ought to despise the vaunting of a transient praise, and restrain the pomp of swelling pride, and refute the lies of a deceitful semblance.

3. Many things after this sort he ofttimes did, that outwardly he might become as it were a vessel that perisheth, while inwardly he possessed the spirit of sanctification. He sought to hide in the secret places of his heart the favours of his Lord, loth to reveal them and so gain praise, that might be an occasion of falling. Ofttimes, when he was glorified of many, he would speak after this wise, "I may yet have sons and daughters; praise me not as one that is safe. No man should be praised before that his end be known." This unto them that praised him; unto himself this, "Had the Most High shown such favours unto a robber, he would have been better pleasing than thou, Francis." Ofttimes he would say unto the Brethren, "Concerning all that a sinner can do, none aught to flatter himself with undeserved praise. A sinner (he saith) can fast, pray, lament, and mortify his own body—this one thing he cannot do, to wit, be faithful unto his Lord. In this, then, we may glory, if we render unto the Lord the glory that is His due, and if, while serving Him faithfully, we ascribe unto Him whatsoever He giveth."

4. Now this Gospel merchant—that he might in many ways make profit, and make the whole time that now is be turned into merit—preferred not so much to be set in authority as to

be set under authority, not so much to command as to obey. Wherefore, giving up his office unto the Minister-General, he sought a Warden, unto whose will he might submit him in all things. For he maintained that the fruit of holy obedience was so rich as that they who placed their necks under her yoke spent no portion of their time without profit; wherefore he was ever wont to promise and to render obedience unto the Brother that was his companion. He said once unto his companions, "Among other gifts that the divine goodness hath deigned to bestow upon me, it hath conferred this grace, that I would as heedfully obey the novice of an hour, were he appointed unto me for Warden, as I would the eldest and wisest Brother. The subordinate (saith he) ought to regard him that is set in authority over him not as a man, but as Him for love of Whom he doth make himself subject. And the more despicable is he that commandeth, the more acceptable is the humility of him that obeyeth."

When once it was enquired of him what man should be esteemed truly obedient, he set before them as an example the similitude of a dead body. "Lift up," saith he, "a dead body, and place it where thou wilt. Thou shalt see it will not murmur at being moved, it will not complain of where it is set, it will not cry out if left there. If it be set in a lofty seat, it will look not up, but down. If it be clad in purple, it but redoubleth its pallor. This (saith he) is the truly obedient man, who reasoneth not why he is moved, who careth not where he be placed, who urgeth not that he should be transferred; who, when set in authority, preserveth his wonted humility, and the more he is honoured, considereth himself the more unworthy."

5. He said once unto his companion, "I esteem not myself to be a Friar Minor unless I be in the state that I shall describe unto thee. Lo now, I suppose me to be one set in authority over the Brethren; I go unto the Chapter, I preach unto the Brethren and exhort them, and at the end they speak against me, saying, 'Thou offendest us, for that thou art unlettered, slow of speech, a fool, and simple,' and thus I am cast forth with reviling, little esteemed of all. I tell thee—unless I can hear such words with unchanged countenance, with unchanged gladness of spirit and unchanged holy intent—I am vainly called a Friar Minor." And he added, "In exalted place there is the fear of all, in praises a precipice, in the humility of a submissive spirit there is profit. Why, then,

do we look for perils rather than profits, when we have had time bestowed on us that we may make profit therein?"

From this same reason of humility, Francis was minded that his Brethren should be called by the name of *Minors*, and that the rulers of his Order should be called Ministers, that thus he might employ the very words of the Gospel that he had vowed to observe, and that his followers might learn from their very name that they had come to learn humility in the school of the humble Christ. For that Teacher of humility, Christ Jesus, when He would teach His disciples what was perfect humility, said, "Whosoever will be great among you, let him be your minister; and whosoever will be chief among you, let him be your servant."

When therefore the lord Bishop of Ostia, the protector and chief helper of the Order of Friars Minor (he that afterward, as the holy man had foretold, was raised unto the dignity of the Supreme Pontificate, under the name of Gregory the Ninth), enquired of him whether it would be his will for his Brethren to be promoted unto high places in the Church, he made answer, "Lord, my Brethren be called Minors with this very intent, that they may not arrogate unto themselves to be called greater. If thou desirest (saith he) that they should bear fruit in the Church of God, maintain and keep them in the state of their calling, and in no wise suffer them to rise unto authority in the Church."

6. Now since in himself as well as in them that obey he set humility before all honours, God, Who loveth the humble, deemed him worthy of loftier heights, as a vision sent from heaven made evident unto a Brother that was of an especial holiness and devoutness. For he had been in the company of the man of God, and, together with him, had been praying with fervour of spirit in a certain deserted church, when, falling into an ecstasy, he beheld among many seats in heaven one that was more honourable than the rest, adorned with precious stones, and shining with utmost splendour. Marvelling within himself at the splendour of this exalted throne, he began to consider with anxious thought who should be deemed worthy to sit thereon. Then, as he considered, he heard a voice saying unto him, "This seat pertained unto one of the fallen Angels, and is now kept for the humble Francis." At length, when the Brother had come back unto himself from that trance of prayer, he followed the holy man as he went forth, as was his wont. And as they walked by the way, conversing of God

each in turn, that Brother, not unmindful of his vision, enquired of him discreetly what he thought of himself. And the humble servant of Christ answered him, " I think myself the chief of sinners." When the Brother said in opposition that he could not, with a sound conscience, say or feel this, Francis added, " If any man, howsoever guilty, had received such mercy from Christ as I, I verily think he would have been far more acceptable unto God than I." Then, by the hearing of such marvellous humility, the Brother was assured of the truth of the vision that had been shown him, knowing by the witness of the Holy Gospel that the truly humble shall be exalted unto that excellent glory wherefrom the proud is cast down.

7. On another time, when that he was praying in a deserted church in the province of Massa, nigh Monte Casale, he learnt through the Spirit that certain holy relics had been deposited there. Perceiving with sorrow that for a long time past they had been deprived of the reverence due unto them, he bade the Brethren bring them unto the place, with all honour. But when, need arising, he had departed from them, his sons were forgetful of their Father's behest, and neglected the merit of obedience. Then on a day, when they were fain to celebrate the holy mysteries, and the upper covering of the altar was removed, they found, not without amazement, some bones right fair and fragrant, beholding the relics that the power of God, not men's hands, had brought thither. Returning shortly after, the man devoted unto God began to make diligent enquiry whether his behest concerning the relics had been carried out. The Brethren humbly confessed their sin of neglected obedience, and gained pardon, with an award of penance. And the holy man said, " Blessed be the Lord my God, Who Himself hath fulfilled that which ye ought to have done." Consider heedfully the care of the divine providence for our dust, and weigh the goodness of the humble Francis, that did excel in the sight of God. For when man obeyed not his bidding, God fulfilled his desires.

8. Coming on a time unto Imola, he approached the Bishop of the city, and humbly besought him that, with his sanction, he might call the people together to preach unto them. The Bishop answered him harshly, saying, " It sufficeth, Brother, that I myself preach unto my people." Francis, in his true humility, bowed his head, and went forth; howbeit, after a short space, he returned into the house. When the Bishop, as one in wrath, asked of him what he meant by coming again, he

replied, with humility alike of heart and voice, "Lord, if a father drive his son forth by one door, he must enter again by another." Vanquished by his humility, the Bishop embraced him eagerly, saying, "Thou and all thy Brethren shall from henceforward have a general licence to preach throughout my diocese, for this thy holy humility hath earned."

9. It befell once that he came unto Arezzo at a time when the whole city was shaken by a civil war that threatened its speedy ruin. As he was lodging in the outskirts of the city, he beheld the demons exulting above it, and inflaming the angry citizens unto mutual slaughter. Then, that he might put to flight those powers of the air that were stirring up the strife, he sent forward as his herald Brother Silvester, a man of dovelike simplicity, saying, "Go out before the city gate, and, on behalf of God Almighty, command the demons in the power of obedience to depart with all speed." The Brother, in his true obedience, hastened to perform his Father's behests, and, coming before the presence of the Lord with thanksgiving, began to cry with a loud voice before the city gate, "On behalf of God Almighty, and at the bidding of His servant Francis, depart far from hence, all ye demons!" At once the city was restored unto a state of peace, and all the citizens peacefully and quietly began to fashion anew their civil laws. Thus when the raging arrogance of the demons had been driven out, that had held the city as it were in a state of siege, the wisdom of the poor, to wit, the humility of Francis, came unto its aid, and restored peace, and saved the city. For by the merit of the difficult virtue of humble obedience, he obtained so powerful an authority over those rebellious and insolent spirits as that he could restrain their fierce arrogance, and put to flight their lawless molestation.

10. The proud demons flee before the lofty virtues of the humble, save when at times the divine mercy permitteth them to buffet them that humility may be preserved, even as the Apostle Paul writeth concerning himself, and as Francis learnt by experience. For when the lord Cardinal of Sta. Croce, Leo, did invite him to tarry for a while with him in Rome, he humbly agreed thereunto, for the reverence and love that he bore him. When on the first night, his prayers ended, he was fain to sleep, the demons rose up against the soldier of Christ, cruelly attacking him, and, when they had beaten him long and sorely, at the last left him as it were half dead. On their departure, the man of God called his companion, and when he came, related unto him the whole affair, adding, "I believe, Brother, that the

demons, who can avail naught save in so far as the divine providence permitteth them, have now assailed me thus furiously because that my lodging in the palaces of the great affordeth no good example. My Brethren that sojourn in poor little abodes, when they hear that I lodge with Cardinals, will perchance surmise that I am being entangled in worldly affairs, that I am carried away by honours paid me, and that I am abounding in luxuries. Wherefore I deem it better that he who is set for an example should shun palaces, and should walk humbly among the humble in humble abodes, that he may make those that bear poverty strong, by himself bearing the like." At morn, then, they came and, humbly excusing themselves, took farewell of the Cardinal.

11. The holy man did in truth loathe pride—the root of all evils—and disobedience, its most evil offspring, yet none the less he would alway receive the humility of the penitent. It befell once that a certain Brother was brought unto him who had transgressed against the rule of obedience, and deserved correction by a just discipline. But the man of God, perceiving by manifest tokens that that Brother was truly contrite, was moved by his love of humility to spare him. Howbeit, that the easiness of gaining pardon should not be a pretext unto others for wrong-doing, he bade that his hood should be taken from that Brother, and cast into the midst of the flames, that all might take note by what grave punishment sins of disobedience were to be chastised. When the hood had lain for some time in the midst of the fire, he bade that it should be withdrawn from the flames, and restored unto the Brother that was humbly penitent. Marvellous to relate, the hood, when withdrawn from the midst of the flames, showed no trace of burning. Thus it came to pass that, through this one miracle, God commended both the virtue of the holy man, and the humility of penitence.

Thus the humility of Francis is meet to be imitated, that even on earth gained such wondrous honour as that God condescended unto his desires, and changed the feelings of men, drove forth the arrogance of demons at his bidding, and by a mere gesture bridled the ravenous flames. Verily, this humility it is that exalteth them that possess it, and that, while paying respect unto all, from all gaineth honour.

CHAPTER VII

OF HIS LOVE FOR POVERTY, AND OF THE WONDROUS SUPPLYING OF HIS NEEDS

1. AMONG other gifts of graces that Francis had received from the bounteous Giver, he merited to abound, as by an especial prerogative all his own, in the riches of simplicity, through his love of sublimest Poverty. The holy man regarded Poverty as the familiar friend of the Son of God, and as one now rejected by the whole world, and was zealous to espouse her with such a constant affection as that not only did he leave father and mother for her sake, but he did even part with all that might have been his. For none was ever so greedy of gold as he of poverty, nor did any man ever guard treasure more anxiously than he this Gospel pearl. One thing more than aught else was displeasing in his eyes, to wit, if he beheld aught in the Brethren that was not wholly in accord with poverty. He himself, verily, from his entrance into Religion until his death was content with, and counted himself rich with, a tunic, a cord, and breeches. Ofttimes with tears he would recall unto mind the poverty of Christ Jesus, and of His Mother, declaring Poverty to be the queen of virtues inasmuch as she shone forth thus excellently in the King of Kings and in the Queen His Mother. And when the Brethren in council asked of him which virtue would render a man most pleasing unto Christ, he answered, as though laying bare the secret thought of his heart, "Ye know, Brethren, that poverty is an especial way of salvation, being as it were the food of humility, and the root of perfection, and her fruits are manifold, albeit hidden. For poverty is that treasure hid in a field of the Gospel, to buy which a man would sell all that he hath, and the things that cannot be sold are to be despised in comparison therewith."

2. He also said, "He that would attain this height must needs in all ways renounce, not alone the wisdom of the world, but even knowledge of letters, so that, dispossessed of such an inheritance, he may go in the strength of the Lord, and give himself up naked into the arms of the Crucified. For in vain doth he utterly renounce the world who keepeth in the secret places of his heart a shrine for his own senses." Ofttimes indeed would he discourse of poverty, impressing on the Brethren that saying of the Gospel, "The foxes have holes, and the birds of the air have

nests, but the Son of Man hath not where to lay His Head." Wherefore he would teach the Brethren that, after the fashion of the poor, they should build poor little houses, wherein they should dwell, not as their owners, but as pilgrims and strangers dwell in other men's houses. For he said that the rules of pilgrims were to abide under a strange roof, to thirst for their fatherland, and to pass on their way in peace. More than once, he bade houses that had been built be pulled down, or the Brethren removed thence, if he saw in them aught that by reason of ownership or of magnificence was opposed unto Gospel poverty. Poverty he declared to be the foundation of his Order, and, with this first laid as a basis, he said the whole edifice of the Religion would so rest upon it as that, while it stood firm, the Religion stood firm; were it overthrown, that other likewise would be overthrown from the foundations.

3. Furthermore, he taught, as he had learnt by revelation, that the entrance into holy Religion must be made through that saying of the Gospel, "If thou wilt be perfect, go and sell that thou hast, and give to the poor;" and accordingly he would admit none into the Order that had not dispossessed themselves, keeping absolutely naught back, both because of the saying of the Holy Gospel, and that there might be no treasure-chests laid up to cause scandal. Thus, when a certain man, in the March of Ancona, sought to be received into the Order, the true patriarch of the poor made answer, "If thou art fain to be joined unto the poor of Christ, part thy goods among the poor of this world." Hearing this, the man arose, and, led by carnal affection, bequeathed his goods unto his own kin, and naught unto the poor. But when the holy man heard of this from his own mouth, he chid him with stern reproofs, saying, "Go thy way, brother fly, for thou hast not yet gotten thee out from thy kindred and from thy father's house. Thou hast given thy goods unto thy kin, and hast cheated the poor, thou art not meet for the holy poor. Thou hast begun in the flesh, and hast laid but a shaking foundation for a spiritual edifice." Then that carnal man returned unto his kin, and sought again his goods, the which he was not minded to bequeath unto the poor; thus quickly he abandoned his virtuous intent.

4. At another time, there was in the place of Saint Mary of the Porziuncula such scarcity as that they could not provide for the guest Brethren as their needs demanded. Accordingly, his Vicar went unto the man of God, pleading the destitution of the Brethren, and begging that he would permit some portion

of the novices' goods to be retained on their entrance, so that the Brethren might resort thereunto for their expenditure in times of need. Unto whom Francis, instructed in the heavenly counsels, made reply, " Far be it from us, dearest Brother, to act wickedly against the Rule for the sake of any man whomsoever. I had rather that thou shouldst strip the altar of the glorious Virgin, when our need demandeth it, than that thou shouldst attempt aught, be it but a little thing, against our vow of poverty and the observance of the Gospel. For the Blessed Virgin would be better pleased that her altar should be despoiled, and the counsel of the Holy Gospel perfectly fulfilled, than that her altar should be adorned, and the counsel given by her Son set aside."

5. When on a time the man of God was passing, with a companion, through Apulia, and was nigh unto Bari, he found in the road a great purse, swelling as though full of coins, such as in the common speech is called *funda*. The poor man of Christ was exhorted, and earnestly besought, by his companion, to lift the purse from the ground, and distribute the money among the poor. But the man of God refused, declaring that there was some devilish contrivance in the purse that they had found, and that what the Brother was proposing was no good deed but a sin, to wit, taking goods not their own and giving them away. They left the spot, and hastened to complete the journey on which they had entered. Howbeit, that Brother would not hold his peace, deceived by an empty piety, but still vexed the man of God, as though he were one who cared naught for relieving the destitution of the poor. At length the gentle Francis consented to return unto the spot, not to fulfil the desire of the Brother, but to unmask the wiles of the devil. Accordingly, returning where the purse lay, with the Brother and with a youth who was on the road, he first prayed, and then bade his companion take it up. The Brother trembled and was adread, now presaging some devilish portent; nevertheless, by reason of the command of holy obedience, he conquered the doubts of his heart, and stretched forth his hand unto the purse. Lo! a serpent of no mean size leapt forth from the purse, and at once vanished together with it, showing that it had been a snare of the devil. The wiles of the enemy's cunning being thus apparent, the holy man said unto his companion, " Money, O my brother, is unto the servants of God naught else than the devil and a poisonous serpent."

6. After this, a wondrous thing befell the holy man while that,

at the call of a pressing need, he was betaking him unto the city of Siena. Three poor women, alike in all respects as to height, age, and countenance, met him on the wide plain between Campiglio and San Quirico, proffering a new greeting by way of gift: "Welcome," said they, "Lady Poverty!" At these words, that true lover of poverty was filled with joy unspeakable, inasmuch as there was naught in him that he would rather have saluted by men than that whereof they had made mention. On a sudden the women vanished, whereupon the Brethren that were his companions pondered on their wondrous resemblance each unto the other, and on the newness of their greeting, their appearing, and their vanishing, and deemed, not without reason, that some mystery was thereby signified concerning the holy man. Verily, by those three poor women—for such they seemed—with such resemblance in countenance, that met him, that gave him such unwonted greeting, and that so suddenly vanished, it was fittingly shown that the beauty of Gospel perfection—touching chastity, to wit, and obedience, and poverty—shone forth perfectly in kindred form in the man of God; howbeit, he had chosen to make his chief boast in the privilege of Poverty, whom he was wont to name now his mother, now his bride, now his lady. In this, he was greedy to surpass others, he who thereby had learnt to think himself of less account than all others. Accordingly, if ever he saw any man who, judging by his outward appearance, was poorer than himself, he would forthwith blame himself, and stir himself up unto the like, as though, striving jealously after poverty, he feared to be outdone by that other.

It chanced once that he met a poor man on the road, and, beholding his nakedness, was stricken to the heart, and said with a sighing voice unto his companion, "This man's destitution hath brought on us great reproach, for we have chosen Poverty as our great riches, and lo! she shineth forth more clearly in him."

7. By reason of his love for holy Poverty, the servant of Almighty God had far rather partake of alms begged from door to door than of food set before him. Thus, if ever he was invited by great folk, who would fain honour him by a well-spread board, he would first beg crusts of bread from the neighbouring houses, and then, thus enriched in his poverty, sit down at the board. Once he did thus when he had been invited by the lord Bishop of Ostia, who loved the poor man of Christ with an especial affection, and when the Bishop complained that it brought shame upon

him that a guest at his table should go forth for alms, the servant of God made answer, " My lord, I have done you a great honour, while honouring a greater Lord. For poverty is well-pleasing unto the Lord, and that before all which is a free-will beggary for the sake of Christ. This royal dignity—that the Lord Jesus took upon Him when for our sakes He became poor, that we through His poverty might be rich, and that He might make them that be truly poor in spirit kings and heirs of the Kingdom of Heaven—I am not minded to abandon for a fee of deceptive riches lent unto you for an hour."

8. Ofttimes when he was exhorting the Brethren to go forth for alms, he would speak on this wise, " Go forth," saith he, " since at this eleventh hour the Friars Minor have been lent unto the world, that the number of the elect may be in them fulfilled; wherefore they shall be praised by the Judge, and shall hear those most delectable words, ' Inasmuch as ye have done it unto one of the least of these My brethren, ye have done it unto Me.' " Accordingly, he would say it was a delightsome thing to beg under the name of Friars Minor, since the Master of Gospel truth had with His own mouth thus spoken of that name—" the least "—in the rewarding of the just.

Moreover, on the chief Feasts, when opportunity offered, he was wont to go begging, saying that in the holy poor was fulfilled that prophecy, " Man did eat Angels' food." For he said that bread was truly Angels' food that was begged for the love of God, and with the aid of the blessed Angels, and that holy Poverty gathered from door to door, where it was bestowed for love of her.

9. Accordingly, when he was once sojourning on the holy Easter Day in an hermitage so distant from the dwellings of men as that he could not conveniently go forth to beg, mindful of Him Who on that day had appeared unto the disciples going unto Emmaus in the guise of a pilgrim, he, as a pilgrim and beggar, did ask alms from the Brethren themselves. And, having humbly received them, he taught them in holy discourse that while passing through the wilderness of the world as pilgrims and strangers, and Israelites indeed, they might celebrate continually, as those poor in spirit, the Lord's Passover, to wit, His departure from this world unto the Father. And since in asking alms he was moved, not by desire for gain, but by a free spirit, God, the Father of the poor, seemed to have an especial care of him.

10. It chanced once that the servant of the Lord had been

weighed down by sickness in the place called Nocera, and was being brought back unto Assisi by an honourable escort, sent for this purpose by the devotion of the people of Assisi. And they, escorting the servant of Christ, reached a poor little hamlet, Satriano by name, whither, since their hunger and the hour demanded it, they went to seek food, but, finding naught that they could buy, returned empty handed. Then the holy man said unto them, "Naught have ye found, for that ye put more trust in your flies than in God"—for he was wont to call money *flies*. "But go back (saith he) among the houses that ye have visited, and, offering the love of God as your payment, humbly ask an alms. And do not by a false reckoning esteem this a thing shameful or base, since the great Almsgiver hath in His abounding goodness granted all things as alms unto the worthy and unworthy alike, after we have sinned." Then those knights laid aside their shamefastness, and of their own accord asked for alms, and bought more for the love of God than they had been able to for money. For the poor inhabitants of the place, stricken to the heart by a divine impulse, freely proffered not only their goods, but their very selves. Thus it befell that the necessity, which money had not availed to relieve, was supplied by the rich poverty of Francis.

11. On a time when he was lying sick in an hermitage nigh Rieti, a certain physician did oft visit him with welcome ministries. And since the poor man of Christ was unable to give him a recompense meet for his toil, the most bountiful God, on behalf of His poor, rewarded his kindly service by this singular benefit, that he might not depart with no immediate fee. The house of the physician, which he had at that time built anew with the whole of his savings, by a gaping cleavage of the walls from top to bottom threatened so speedy a collapse as that it seemed impossible that any mortal skill or toil should avert its fall. Then the physician, entirely trusting in the merits of the holy man, with great faith and devotion besought from his companions the gift of some thing that that same man of God had touched with his hands. Accordingly, having with much importunity of pleading gained a few of his hairs, he laid them at even in the cleavage of the wall; then, rising next morn, he found the opening so firmly sealed as that he could not withdraw the relics he had placed therein, nor find any trace of the former cleavage. Thus it came to pass that he who had diligently tended the frail body of God's servant was able to avert the danger from his own frail house.

12. On another time, when the man of God was fain to betake him unto a certain solitude, where he might more freely give himself up unto contemplation, he rode, being weak in body, upon the ass of a poor man. While this man was following the servant of Christ in the summer heat, and up mountain ways, he became worn out by the journey, as the path grew ever rougher and longer, and, fainting with exceeding and burning thirst, he began to cry aloud with importunity after the saint, "Lo! (saith he) I shall die of thirst, if I be not at once refreshed by the help of some draught!" Without delay, the man of God got off the ass, fell on his knees, and, raising his hands unto heaven, ceased not to pray until he knew that he had been heard. His prayer at length ended, he said unto the man, "Hasten unto yonder rock, and there thou shalt find a spring of water, that Christ in His mercy hath at this hour caused to flow from the rock for thee to drink." O marvellous condescension of God, that doth so readily incline unto His servants! The thirsty man drank the water produced from the rock by the power of him that prayed, and drained a draught from the flinty rock. Before that time there had been no flowing water there, nor from that time—as hath been carefully ascertained—hath any been found there.

13. Now in what manner, by the merits of His poor one, Christ multiplied provisions at sea, shall be related in its own place hereafter; suffice it to note this only, that by the scanty alms brought unto him he saved the sailors from the peril of famine and of death during many days; thus it may be clearly seen that the servant of God Almighty, as he was made like unto Moses in the drawing of water from the rock, was made like also unto Elias in the multiplying of food. Wherefore let all anxious thought be far removed from the poor ones of Christ. For if the poverty of Francis was of such an abundant sufficiency as that it supplied by its wondrous power the needs of them that assisted him—so that neither food, nor drink, nor house failed them, when the resources of money, of skill, and of nature had proved of none avail—much more shall it merit those things that in the wonted course of the divine providence are granted unto all alike. If, I say, the stony rock, at the prayer of one poor man, poured forth a copious draught for another poor man in his thirst, naught in the whole creation will refuse its service unto those who have left all for the sake of the Creator of all.

CHAPTER VIII

OF THE KINDLY IMPULSES OF HIS PIETY, AND OF HOW THE CREATURES LACKING UNDERSTANDING SEEMED TO BE MADE SUBJECT UNTO HIM

1. THAT true godliness which, according unto the Apostle, is profitable unto all things, had so filled the heart of Francis and entered into his inmost parts as that it seemed to have established its sway absolutely over the man of God. It was this piety that, through devotion, uplifted him toward God; through compassion, transformed him into the likeness of Christ; through condescension, inclined him unto his neighbour, and, through his all-embracing love for every creature, set forth a new picture of man's estate before the Fall. And as by this piety he was touched with kindly feeling for all things, so above all, when he beheld souls redeemed by the precious Blood of Christ Jesus being defiled by any stain of sin, he would weep over them with such tenderness of compassion as that he seemed, like a mother in Christ, to be in travail of them daily. And this was with him the chief cause of his veneration for the ministers of the word of God, to wit, that with devout care they raise up seed unto the Brother which is dead, that is, unto Christ crucified for sinners, by converting such, and cherish the same seed with careful devotion. This ministry of compassion he maintained was more acceptable unto the Father of mercies than all sacrifice, in especial if it were performed with the zeal of perfect charity, so that this end might be striven after by example rather than by precept, by tearful prayer rather than by eloquent speech.

2. Accordingly, he would say that that preacher should be deplored as one without true piety, who in his preaching did not seek the salvation of souls, but his own glory, or who by the sins of his life pulled down that which he built up by the truth of his teaching. He would say that the Brother simple and unready of speech, who by his good example inciteth others unto good, should be preferred before such an one. That saying, moreover, "The barren hath borne many," he would thus expound, "The barren (saith he) is the little poor Brother, who hath not the function of begetting sons in the Church. He in the Judgment shall bear many, for that those whom he now converteth unto Christ by his secret prayers shall be then added unto his glory by the Judge. And 'she that hath many children

is waxed feeble,' for that the empty preacher of many words who now boasteth in many begotten, as it were, by his power, shall then perceive that there is naught of his own in them."

3. Since then with heartfelt piety and glowing zeal he sought after the salvation of souls, he would say that he was filled with the sweetest fragrance and anointed as with precious ointment whensoever he heard of many being led into the way of truth by the sweet savour of the repute of the holy Brethren scattered throughout the world. Hearing such reports, he would rejoice in spirit, heaping with blessings most worthy of all acceptance those Brethren who, by word or deed, were bringing sinners unto the love of Christ. In like wise, those who were transgressing against holy Religion by their evil works, fell under the heaviest sentence of his curse. "By thee," saith he, "O Lord most holy, by the entire company of heaven, and by me, Thy little one, be they accursed who by their evil example do bring unto naught and destroy that which through the holy Brethren of this Order Thou hast built up, and dost not cease to build." Ofttimes he was affected by such sadness, by reason of the stumbling-block unto the weak brethren, that he thought his strength would have failed him, had he not been sustained by the comfort of the divine mercy.

But when once on a time he was disquieted because of evil examples, and with troubled spirit was beseeching the merciful Father for his sons, he obtained an answer on this wise from the Lord, "Why dost thou fret thee, poor little mortal? Have I set thee as shepherd over My Religion that thou shouldst forget I am its chief Protector? I have appointed thee, simple as thou art, for this very end, that the things that I shall perform through thee may be ascribed, not unto man's working, but unto grace from above. I have called this Religion, I will keep it and feed it, and, when some fall off, I will raise up others in their place, yea, so that, were none born, I would even cause them to be born. And by whatsoever shocks this little poor Religion may be shaken, it shall always abide unscathed under My guard."

4. The vice of slander, hateful unto the fount of goodness and grace, Francis would shrink from as from a serpent's tooth, declaring it to be a most hateful plague, and an abomination unto the most holy God, forasmuch as the slanderer feedeth on the blood of those souls that he hath slain by the sword of his tongue. Hearing once a certain Brother blacken the repute of another, he turned unto his Vicar, and said, "Rise, rise,

make careful enquiry, and, if thou findest the accused Brother to be guiltless, with stern discipline make the accuser to be marked of all." At times, indeed, he would sentence him who had despoiled his Brother of the praise of his good repute to be himself despoiled of his habit, and deemed that he ought not to be able to lift up his eyes unto God unless first he had exerted himself to restore, as best he might, that which he had taken away. "The sin of slanderers," he would say, "is more heinous than that of robbers, inasmuch as the law of Christ—that is fulfilled in the observance of godliness—bindeth us to desire more the salvation of the soul than of the body."

5. Unto them that were afflicted with bodily suffering of any sort he would condescend with a marvellous tenderness of sympathy; if he perceived in any aught of destitution, aught of lack, he would in the gentleness of his devout heart carry it unto Christ. Mercy, verily, was inborn in him, and redoubled by the shedding upon it of the piety of Christ. Thus his soul was melted over the poor and the weak, and, when he could not open his hand unto any, he opened his heart. It chanced on a time that one of the Brethren had made somewhat harsh reply unto a poor man that importunately asked an alms. When the devout lover of the poor heard it, he bade that Brother throw himself, naked, at the poor man's feet, declare himself in fault, and beg the favour of his prayer and his pardon. When he had humbly done this, the Father gently added, "When thou seest a poor man, O Brother, a mirror is set before thee of the Lord, and of His Mother in her poverty. In the infirm, do thou in like manner think upon the infirmities that He took upon Him." In all the poor he—himself the most Christ-like of all poor men—beheld the image of Christ, wherefore he judged that all things that were provided for himself—were they even the necessaries of life,—should be given up unto any poor folk whom he met, and that not only as largesse, but even as if they were their own property.

It befell on a time that a certain beggar met him, as he was returning from Siena, when by reason of sickness he was wrapped in a cloak over his habit. Beholding with pitiful eye the poor man's misery, "It behoveth us," said he unto his companion, "to restore the cloak unto this poor man, for his own it is. For we received it but as a loan, until it should be our hap to find another poorer than ourselves." But his companion, having regard unto the need of the kindly Father, did urgently seek to refrain him from providing for another, leaving himself uncared for. Howbeit, "I think," saith he, "the great Almsgiver would account it a theft in me did I not give that I wear unto one needing it more." Accordingly he was wont to ask from those that had given him necessities for the succour of his body permission to give them away, did he meet a needier person, so that he might do so with their sanction. Naught would he withhold, neither cloak, nor habit, nor books, nor the very ornaments of the altar, but all these he would, while he could, bestow upon the needy, that he might fulfil the ministry of charity. Ofttimes whenas he met on the road poor folk carrying burdens, he would lay their burdens on his own weak shoulders.

6. When he bethought him of the first beginning of all things, he was filled with a yet more overflowing charity, and would call the dumb animals, howsoever small, by the names of *brother* and *sister*, forasmuch as he recognised in them the same origin as in himself. Yet he loved with an especial warmth and tenderness those creatures that do set forth by the likeness of their nature the holy gentleness of Christ, and in the interpretation of Scripture are a type of Him. Ofttimes he would buy back lambs that were being taken to be killed, in remembrance of that most gentle Lamb Who brooked to be brought unto the slaughter for the redemption of sinners.

On a time when the servant of God was lodging at the monastery of San Verecondo in the diocese of Gubbio, an ewe gave birth unto a lamb one night. There was hard by a very fierce sow, and she, sparing not the innocent life, slew him with her greedy jaws. When the gentle Father heard thereof, he was moved with wondrous pity, and, remembering that Lamb without spot, mourned over the dead lamb in the presence of all, saying, "Woe is me, little brother lamb, innocent creature, setting forth Christ unto men! Cursed be that evil beast that hath devoured thee, and of her flesh let neither man nor beast eat." Marvellous to relate, the cruel sow forthwith began to languish, and in three days paid the penalty in her own body, and suffered death as her retribution. Her carcase was cast forth into a ditch near the monastery, and there lay for a long time, dried up like a board, and food for no famished beast. Let human evil-doing, then, take note by what a punishment it shall be overtaken at the last, if the savageness of a brute beast was smitten by a death so awful: let faithful devotion also consider how in the servant of God was shown a piety of such marvellous power and abundant sweetness, as that even the nature of brute beasts, after their own fashion, acclaimed it.

7. While he was journeying nigh the city of Siena, he came on a great flock of sheep in the pastures. And when he had given them gracious greeting, as was his wont, they left their feeding, and all ran toward him, raising their heads, and gazing fixedly on him with their eyes. So eagerly did they acclaim him as that both the shepherds and the Brethren marvelled, beholding around him the lambs, and the rams no less, thus wondrously filled with delight.

At another time, at Saint Mary of the Porziuncula, a lamb was brought unto the man of God, the which he thankfully received, by reason of the love of guilelessness and simplicity that the lamb's nature doth exhibit. The holy man exhorted the lamb that it should be instant in the divine praises, and avoid any occasion of offence unto the Brethren; the lamb, on its part, as though it had observed the piety of the man of God, diligently obeyed his instructions. For when it heard the Brethren chanting in the choir, it too would enter the church, and, unbidden of any, would bend the knee, bleating before the altar of the Virgin Mother of the Lamb, as though it were fain to greet her. Furthermore, at the elevation of the most holy Body of Christ in the solemn Mass, it would bend its knees and bow, even as though the sheep, in its reverence, would reprove the irreverence of the undevout, and would incite Christ's devout people to revere the Sacrament.

At one time he had with him in Rome a lamb, by reason of his reverence for that Lamb most gentle, and it he entrusted unto a noble matron, to wit, the lady Jacoba di Settesoli, to be cared for in her bower. This lamb, like one instructed in spiritual things by the Saint, when the lady went into church, kept closely by her side in going and in returning. If in the early morning the lady delayed her rising, the lamb would rise and would butt her with its little horns, and rouse her by its bleatings, admonishing her with gestures and nods to hasten unto church. Wherefore the lamb, that had been a pupil of Francis, and was now become a teacher of devotion, was cherished by the lady as a creature marvellous and loveworthy.

8. At another time, at Greccio, a live leveret was brought unto the man of God, the which—when set down free on the ground that it might escape whither it would—at the call of the kindly Father leapt with flying feet into his bosom. He, fondling it in the instinctive tenderness of his heart, seemed to feel for it as a mother, and, bidding it in gentle tones beware of being recaptured, let it go free. But albeit it was set on the ground

many times to escape, it did alway return unto the Father's bosom, as though by some hidden sense it perceived the tenderness of his heart; wherefore at length, by his command, the Brethren carried it away unto a safer and more remote spot.

In like manner, on an island of the lake of Perugia, a rabbit was caught and brought unto the man of God, and, albeit it fled from others, it entrusted itself unto his hands and bosom with the confidence of a tame creature.

As he was hastening by the lake of Rieti unto the hermitage of Greccio, a fisherman out of devotion brought unto him a water-fowl, the which he gladly received, and then, opening his hands, bade it depart; howbeit, it would not leave him. Then he, lifting his eyes unto heaven, remained for a long space in prayer, and, after a long hour returning unto himself as though from afar, gently bade the little bird depart, and praise the Lord. Then, having thus received his blessing and leave, it flew away, showing joy by the movement of its body.

In like manner, from the same lake there was brought unto him a fine, live fish, which he called, as was his wont, by the name of *brother*, and put back into the water nigh the boat. Then the fish played in the water nigh the man of God, and, as though drawn by love of him, would in no wise leave the boat-side until it had received his blessing and leave.

9. On another time, when he was walking with a certain Brother through the Venetian marshes, he chanced on a great host of birds that were sitting and singing among the bushes. Seeing them, he said unto his companion, "Our sisters the birds are praising their Creator, let us too go among them and sing unto the Lord praises and the Canonical Hours." When they had gone into their midst, the birds stirred not from the spot, and when, by reason of their twittering, they could not hear each the other in reciting the Hours, the holy man turned unto the birds, saying, "My sisters the birds, cease from singing, while that we render our due praises unto the Lord." Then the birds forthwith held their peace, and remained silent until, having said his Hours at leisure and rendered his praises, the holy man of God again gave them leave to sing. And, as the man of God gave them leave, they at once took up their song again after their wonted fashion.

At Saint Mary of the Porziuncula, hard by the cell of the man of God, a cicada sat on a fig-tree and chirped; and right often by her song she stirred up unto the divine praises the servant of the Lord, who had learnt to marvel at the glorious handiwork of the Creator even as seen in little things. One day he called her, and she, as though divinely taught, lighted upon his hand. When he said unto her, "Sing, my sister cicada, and praise the Lord thy Creator with thy glad lay," she obeyed forthwith, and began to chirp, nor did she cease until, at the Father's bidding, she flew back unto her own place. There for eight days she abode, on any day coming at his call, singing, and flying back, according as he bade her. At length the man of God said unto his companions, "Let us now give our sister cicada leave to go, for she hath gladdened us enough with her lay, stirring us up these eight days past unto the praises of God." And at once, his leave given, she flew away, nor was ever seen there again, as though she dared not in any wise transgress his command.

10. Once while he was lying ill at Siena a fresh-caught pheasant was sent unto him, alive, by a certain nobleman. The bird, so soon as it saw and heard the holy man, pressed nigh him with such friendliness as that it would in no wise brook to be parted from him. For, albeit it was several times set down in a vineyard outside the abode of the Brethren, so that it might escape if it would, it still ran back in haste unto the Father as though it had alway been brought up by his hand. Then, when it was given unto a certain man who was wont out of devotion to visit the servant of God, it seemed as though it grieved to be out of the sight of the gentle Father, and refused all food. At length, it was brought back unto the servant of God, and, so soon as it saw him, testified its delight by its gestures, and ate eagerly.

When he had come unto the solitudes of Alverna, to keep a Lent in honour of the Archangel Michael, birds of divers sort fluttered about his cell, and seemed by their tuneful chorus and joyous movements to rejoice at his coming, and to invite and entice the holy Father to tarry there. Seeing this, he said unto his companion, "I perceive, Brother, that it is in accord with the divine will that we should abide here for a space, so greatly do our sisters the little birds seem to take comfort in our presence." While, accordingly, he was sojourning in that place, a falcon that had its nest there bound itself by close ties of friendship unto him. For always at that hour of night wherein the holy man was wont to rise for the divine office, the falcon was beforehand with its song and cries. And this was most acceptable unto the servant of God, the more so as that the great concern which the bird showed for him shook from him all drowsiness of sloth. But when the servant of Christ was weighed down beyond his wont by infirmity, the falcon would spare him, and would not mark for him so early an awakening. At such times, as though taught of God, he would about dawn strike the bell of his voice with a light touch. Verily, there would seem to have been a divine omen, alike in the gladness of the birds of myriad species, and in the cries of the falcon, inasmuch as that praiser and worshipper of God, upborne on the wings of contemplation, was at that very place and time to be exalted by the vision of the Seraph.

11. At one time while he was sojourning in the hermitage of Greccio, the natives of that place were plagued by manifold evils. For an herd of ravening wolves was devouring not beasts alone, but men also, and every year a hailstorm laid waste their corn and vineyards. Accordingly, when the herald of the Holy Gospel was preaching unto them under these afflictions, he said, "I promise you—pledging the honour and glory of Almighty God—that all this plague shall depart from you, and that the Lord will look upon you, and multiply your temporal goods if only, believing me, ye will take pity on your own selves, and will first make true confession, then bring forth fruits worthy of repentance. But again, I declare unto you that if, unthankful for His benefits, ye shall turn again unto your vomit, the plague will be renewed, the punishment will be redoubled, and greater wrath will be shown upon you." Then from that very hour they turned at his admonition unto repentance, and the disasters ceased, the perils passed over, nor was aught of havoc wrought by wolves or hailstorms. Nay more, what is yet more marvellous, if a hailstorm ever fell upon their neighbours' lands, as it neared their borders it was there stayed, or changed its course unto some other region. The hail observed, yea, and the wolves observed, the pact made with the servant of God, nor did they essay any more to break the law of natural piety by raging against men that had turned unto piety, so long as men in their turn, according unto the agreement, did not act wickedly against the most holy laws of God.

With holy affection, then, must we think on the holiness of this blessed man, that was of such wondrous sweetness and might as that it conquered wild beasts, tamed woodland creatures, and taught tame ones, and inclined the nature of the brutes, that had revolted from fallen man, to obey him. For of a truth it is this piety which, allying all creatures unto itself, is profitable unto all things, having promise of the life that now is, and of that which is to come.

CHAPTER IX

OF HIS ARDENT LOVE, AND YEARNING FOR MARTYRDOM

1. Of the ardent love that glowed in Francis, the friend of the Bridegroom, who can avail to tell? He seemed utterly consumed, like unto a coal that is set on fire, by the flame of the love divine. For, at the mere mention of the love of the Lord, he was aroused, moved, and enkindled, as though the inner chords of his heart vibrated under the bow of the voice from without. He would say that it was a magnificent largesse to offer such wealth in exchange for alms, and that those who esteemed it of less worth than money were verily fools, for that the priceless price of the divine love alone availeth to purchase the kingdom of heaven, and His love Who hath loved us much is much to be loved.

That he might by all things be stirred up unto the divine love, he triumphed in all the works of the Lord's hands, and through the sight of their joy was uplifted unto their life-giving cause and origin. He beheld in fair things Him Who is the most fair, and, through the traces of Himself that He hath imprinted on His creatures, he everywhere followed on to reach the Beloved, making of all things a ladder for himself whereby he might ascend to lay hold on Him Who is the altogether lovely. For by the impulse of his unexampled devotion he tasted that fountain of goodness that streameth forth, as in rivulets, in every created thing, and he perceived as it were an heavenly harmony in the concord of the virtues and actions granted unto them by God, and did sweetly exhort them to praise the Lord, even as the Prophet David had done.

2. Christ Jesus Crucified was laid, as a bundle of myrrh, in his heart's bosom, and he yearned to be utterly transformed into Him by the fire of his exceeding love. By reason of his chief and especial devotion unto Him, he would betake him unto desert places, and seclude himself in a cell, from the Feast of the Epiphany until the end of the forty days following, to wit, for the space of time wherein Christ had sojourned in the wilderness. There with all the abstinence from food and drink that he might compass, he devoted himself without interruption unto fasting, prayer, and the praises of God. With such glowing love was he moved toward Christ, yea, and with such intimate love did his Beloved repay his, that it seemed unto the servant

of God himself that he felt his Saviour almost continually present before his eyes, even as he once revealed unto his companions in intimate converse.

Toward the Sacrament of the Lord's Body he felt a glowing devotion that consumed the very marrow of his bones, marvelling with utmost amazement at that most loving condescension and condescending love. Oft did he communicate, and so devoutly as to render others devout, while, as he tasted of the sweetness of that Lamb without spot, he became like one inebriated in spirit, and rapt out of himself in ecstasy.

3. He loved with an unspeakable affection the Mother of the Lord Jesus Christ, forasmuch as that she had made the Lord of Glory our Brother, and that through her we have obtained mercy. In her, after Christ, he put his chief trust, making her his own patron and that of his Brethren, and in her honour he fasted most devoutly from the Feast of the Apostles Peter and Paul until the Feast of the Assumption. He was bound by ties of inseparable affection unto the Angelic spirits that do glow with wondrous fire to approach God, and in the kindling of elect souls, and out of devotion unto them he would fast for forty days from the Assumption of the glorious Virgin, remaining instant in prayer throughout that time. Unto the Blessed Michael Archangel—inasmuch as his is the ministry of bringing souls before God—he cherished an especial love and devotion, by reason of the ardent zeal that he had for the salvation of all such as should be saved. When he called to remembrance all the Saints, he was kindled afresh, as if they had been stones of fire, with the flame of heavenly love; he regarded with the utmost devotion all the Apostles, and in especial Peter and Paul, by reason of the glowing love that they bore toward Christ, and out of reverence and love for them he dedicated unto the Lord the fast of an especial Lent. The poor man of Christ had naught save two mites, to wit, his body and soul, that he could give away in his large-hearted charity. But these, for the love of Christ, he offered up so continuously as that at all seasons, through the rigour of his fasting, he made an offering of his body, and through the fervour of his yearnings, of his spirit, sacrificing in the outer court a whole burnt-offering, and within, in the Temple, burning sweet incense.

4. Now this exceeding devotion of love uplifted him into the divine in such wise as that his loving goodwill extended unto those that had received with him a like nature and grace. For it is no wonder if he, whose affectionate heart had made him

kin unto all created things, was by the love of Christ drawn into yet closer kinship with such as were sealed with the likeness of their Creator, and redeemed by the Blood of their Maker. He esteemed himself no friend of Christ did he not cherish the souls that He had redeemed. He would say that naught was to be preferred before the salvation of souls, proving this chiefly by the fact that the Only-Begotten Son of God deigned to hang on the Cross for the sake of men's souls. Unto this end he wrestled in prayer, this was the theme of his preaching, and this the cause of his exceeding zeal in setting an example. Wherefore, whensoever some excessive austerity was blamed in him, he would make answer that he had been given as an example unto others. For albeit his guileless flesh had already voluntarily subjected itself unto his spirit, and needed no chastisement by reason of transgressions, nevertheless, for the sake of example, he was ever renewing in it punishments and penances, walking in hard paths for the sake of others. For he would say, "Though I speak with the tongues of men and of Angels, and have not charity, I shall set no example of virtues unto my neighbours, I shall profit others little, and mine own self naught."

5. He emulated, with an ardent flame of love, the glorious victory of the holy Martyrs, whose burning love could not be quenched, nor their constancy broken down. Accordingly he too, kindled by that perfect love that casteth out fear, yearned to offer himself up as a living sacrifice unto the Lord in martyr flames, that he might pay back somewhat in his turn unto Christ Who died for us, and might stir up others unto the love of God. Wherefore, in the sixth year from his conversion, burning with desire for martyrdom, he was minded to cross unto the regions of Syria to preach the Christian faith, and penitence, unto the Saracens and other infidels. When he had embarked on a ship that he might voyage thither, contrary winds prevailed, and he had perforce to land on the coasts of Slavonia. When he had delayed there some time, nor could find any ship that was then crossing the sea, feeling himself cheated of his desire, he besought some sailors that were making for Ancona to take him aboard, for the love of God. When they persisted in their refusal because of his lack of money, the man of God, putting all his trust in the goodness of the Lord, embarked secretly on board the ship with his companion. A certain man was present—sent, as is believed, from God on behalf of His poor one—and he took with him the necessary

victuals, and, calling unto him one on the ship that feared God, spake thus unto him, "Keep faithfully all these things for the poor Brethren that lie hid on the ship, and in their hour of need deal them out unto them as a friend." It befell that, owing unto strong winds, the sailors were unable for many days to touch land anywhere, and had consumed all their own provisions, and only the alms brought for the poor man Francis were left. These, though they had been but scanty, were by the divine power so multiplied as that, during many days' delay at sea by reason of incessant storms, they fully supplied the needs of all until they made the port of Ancona. Then the sailors, seeing that through the servant of God they had escaped manifold agonies of death—like men that had known the dire perils of the sea, and had seen the works of the Lord and His wonders in the deep—rendered thanks unto Almighty God, Who doth ever show Himself marvellous and loveworthy in His friends and servants.

6. When, leaving the sea behind, Francis began to travel through the land, sowing therein the seed of salvation, he gained rich sheaves. Then, because the fruit of martyrdom had so enchanted his heart that he preferred above all merits of virtues a costly death for Christ's sake, he took his way toward Morocco, that he might preach unto Miramolin and his people the Gospel of Christ, if by any means he might avail to gain the coveted palm. For he was borne along by so mighty a desire that, albeit weak in body, he outran the comrade of his pilgrimage, and flew with all speed to fulfil his purpose, like one inebriated in spirit. But when he had advanced as far as Spain, by the divine will, that reserved him for other ends, a very heavy sickness fell upon him, and hindered him so that he could not fulfil his desire. Then the man of God—perceiving that his life in the body was still needful for the family that he had begotten, albeit he deemed that for himself to die was gain—returned to feed the sheep that had been committed unto his care.

7. Howbeit his glowing charity urged his spirit on unto martyrdom, and yet a third time he essayed to set forth toward the infidels, that by the shedding of his blood the Faith of the Trinity might be spread abroad. Thus in the thirteenth year of his conversion he set forth for the regions of Syria, continually exposing himself unto many perils that so he might win entrance into the presence of the Soldan of Babylon. For at that time there was relentless war between the Christians and the Saracens,

and the camps of both armies were pitched each over against the other in the plain, so that none might pass from one unto the other without peril of death. Moreover, a cruel edict had gone forth from the Soldan that any who should bring the head of a Christian should receive a gold bezant as reward. Nevertheless, the undaunted soldier of Christ, Francis, hoping that he was shortly about to gain his end, determined to continue on his way, not dismayed by the fear of death, but urged on by his yearning therefor. And as he prepared himself by prayer, he was strengthened of the Lord, and boldly chanted that verse of the Prophet, "Yea, though I walk through the valley of the shadow of death, I will fear no evil, for Thou art with me."

8. Then, taking the Brother that was his companion, Illuminato by name, a man verily of illumination and virtue, they started on their way. And, meeting two lambs, the holy man was gladdened at the sight, and said unto his companion, "Put thy trust, Brother, in the Lord, for in us that saying of the Gospel is fulfilled: Behold, I send you forth as sheep in the midst of wolves." When they had gone on further, the bands of the Saracens met them, and they, like wolves making haste to fall upon sheep, brutally seized the servants of God, and cruelly and despitefully dragged them along, casting abuse at them, vexing them with stripes and binding them in fetters. Thus in manifold wise tormented and beaten down, they were brought before the Soldan, the divine counsel so disposing as the holy man had desired. When that prince demanded of them from whom, and for what purpose, and after what manner they had been sent, and how they had come thither, the servant of Christ, Francis, made answer with undaunted heart that he had been sent not by man, but by God Most High, that he might show unto him and his people the way of salvation, and might preach the Gospel of truth. With such firmness of mind, with such courage of soul, and with such fervour of spirit he preached unto the Soldan aforesaid God Three in One and the Saviour of all, Jesus Christ, that in him was manifestly and truly fulfilled that saying of the Gospel, "I will give you a mouth and wisdom, which all your adversaries shall not be able to gainsay nor resist." For, as the Soldan beheld the marvellous fervour of spirit and valour of the man of God, he heard him gladly and did right earnestly invite him to tarry with him. Then the servant of Christ, taught by the heavenly counsel, said, "If thou, together with thy people, wilt be converted unto Christ, for the love of Him I will right gladly tarry among you.

But if thou art hesitating whether to give up the law of Mahomet for the faith of Christ, do thou command that a great fire be kindled and I will enter the fire with thy priests, that even thus thou mayest learn which faith is the surer, and holier, and most worthy of being held. Unto whom the Soldan made answer, "I do not believe that any of my priests would be ready to expose himself unto the fire in defence of his faith, or to undergo any sort of torture." For he had seen that, so soon as mention of this was made, one of his priests, an aged man and one in authority, had fled from his presence. Unto whom the holy man replied, "If thou wilt promise me, on behalf of thyself and thy people, that thou wilt embrace the faith of Christ, if I come forth from the fire unscathed, I will enter the fire alone; if I am burned, let it be set down unto my sins, but if the divine might protect me, ye shall know that Christ, the power of God and the wisdom of God, is the true God and the Lord and Saviour of all." Howbeit, the Soldan replied that he dare not accede unto this proposition, for that he feared a revolt of his people. But he offered him many costly gifts, all of which the man of God, hungering, not for worldly goods, but for the salvation of souls, contemned like mire. The Soldan, perceiving the holy man to be so absolute a despiser of worldly things, was moved with amazement and conceived a greater devotion for him. And, albeit he would not, or perchance dared not, go over unto the Christian faith, he did nevertheless devoutly pray the servant of Christ to receive the gifts aforesaid, for his own salvation, and to bestow them upon Christian poor folk, or on churches. But Francis, for that he shunned the burden of money, and could not see in the soul of the Soldan any root of true piety, would not agree thereunto.

9. Seeing, then, that he could neither make progress in the conversion of that people, nor attain his purpose, warned by a divine revelation, he returned unto the regions of the faithful. Now the mercy of God so ordained, and the virtue of the holy man merited, and mercifully and marvellously it befell, that the friend of Christ—who with all his might sought a death for His sake, and yet in no way could find it—nevertheless did not lose the coveted merit of martyrdom, and was reserved to be signalled out unto posterity by an especial distinction. Thus it befell that that divine fire glowed ever more hotly in his heart, so that afterward it was openly manifested in his flesh. O truly blessed man, whose flesh, albeit not stricken by the tyrant's steel, was nevertheless not left without the likeness of

the Lamb that was slain! O fully and truly blessed, I say, whose life, albeit not cut off by the sword of the persecutor, did yet not lose the palm of martyrdom!

CHAPTER X

OF HIS ZEAL AND EFFICACY IN PRAYER

1. Francis, the servant of Christ, feeling himself in the body to be absent from the Lord, had now through the love of Christ become wholly untouched by earthly desires, wherefore—that he might not be without the consolation of his Beloved—he prayed without ceasing, striving ever to manifest a spirit present with God. Prayer was a consolation unto him in contemplation, while, being already made a fellow-citizen with the Angels in the circle of the heavenly mansions, with ardent yearning he sought his Beloved, from Whom the wall of the flesh alone parted him. It was, moreover, a defence unto him in his labours, while in all that he did, distrusting his own working, and relying on the heavenly goodness, he cast all his care upon the Lord in earnest prayer.

He would confidently affirm that the grace of prayerfulness should be more desired than all others by the religious man, and—believing that without it no good could be wrought in the service of God—he would stir up his Brethren unto zeal therefor by all means that he could. For, whether walking or sitting, within doors or without, in toil or at leisure, he was so absorbed in prayer as that he seemed to have devoted thereunto not only his whole heart and body, but also his whole labour and time.

2. Nor was he ever wont to pass over heedlessly any spiritual visitation. When it came unto him, he followed after it, and, for as long as the Lord granted it unto him, he rejoiced in its proffered sweetness. If, while absorbed in thought on a journey, he felt some breathings of the divine Spirit, he would let his companions go on before, and would himself stay his steps, and turn the new inspiration into fruitfulness, not receiving the grace in vain. Ofttimes he was rapt in such ecstasies of contemplation as that he was carried out of himself, and, while perceiving things beyond mortal sense, knew naught of what was happening in the outer world around him.

Thus, when he was passing on a time through Borgo San Sepolcro, a very populous town, riding on an ass because of his bodily weakness, he met crowds of folk that ran together out of devotion unto him. Yet albeit they touched him, and delayed his progress, crowding round him and in many ways pressing upon him, he seemed as one that felt naught, and, even as though he had been a dead body, perceived no whit what was being done around him. Accordingly, when they had long since passed through the town and left the crowds behind them, and had come unto a certain leper settlement, that contemplator of heavenly things, like one returning from another world, anxiously enquired when they would draw nigh unto Borgo. For his mind, intent on heavenly glories, had not perceived the changes of place and time, nor of the folk that met them. And that this oft befell him, the repeated experience of his companions attested.

3. Moreover—as he had experienced in prayer that the longed-for presence of the Holy Spirit vouchsafed itself by so much the more intimately unto suppliants as it found them removed from the noise of worldlings—he would seek lonely places, going to pray by night in solitudes and in deserted churches. There ofttimes he endured dire assaults from demons, who, struggling with him in perceptible form, strove to disturb him in his exercise of prayer. But he, furnished with heavenly arms, the more desperate his enemies' attack, was rendered by so much the more strong in might and fervent in prayer, saying with confidence unto Christ, "Hide me under the shadow of Thy wings, from the wicked that oppress me." But unto the demons he would say, "Do unto me aught that ye can, evil and false spirits. For ye have no power, save that which is granted you from the divine hand, and here am I, ready to bear with all gladness all things whatsoever that has decreed to inflict upon me." Then the proud demons, not able to brook this constancy of mind, retreated in confusion.

4. But the man of God, remaining alone and at peace, filled the woods with his sighing, bedewed the ground with his tears, and beat his breast with his hands, and, like one who hath gained a secret and hidden thing, spake familiarly with his Lord. There he made answer unto his Judge, there he made supplication unto his Father, there he held converse with his Friend, there too he was at times heard by the Brethren, who out of filial piety watched him, to invoke the divine mercy for sinners with cries and wailings, yea, and to lament aloud as though the Lord's Passion were set before his eyes. There he was beheld praying by night, his hands stretched out after the manner of

a Cross, his whole body uplifted from the earth, and wrapt in a shining cloud, as though the wondrous illumination of the body were a witness unto the wondrous enlightenment of his mind. There, moreover, as is attested by sure signs, the unknown and hidden things of the divine wisdom were laid bare unto him, albeit he did not publish them abroad, save in so far as the love of Christ constrained him, and the profit of his neighbours demanded. For he would say, "For a trifling gain, one may chance to lose a priceless thing, and may easily provoke him that gave it to give no more."

When he returned from his private prayers, in the which he became changed almost into another man, he endeavoured with all diligence to make himself like unto others, lest perchance that which was shown outwardly should by the breath of popular applause depart from the gain within. Whensoever he was rapt on a sudden in public, and visited of the Lord, he would always make some pretext unto them that stood by, lest the intimate visitations of the Spouse should be published abroad. When that he was praying among the Brethren, he utterly avoided coughings, groanings, hard breathing, and outward gestures, either because he loved secrecy, or because, shutting himself up within himself, he was wholly borne away unto God. Ofttimes he would speak on this wise unto his intimate companions, "When the servant of God is visited of God in prayer, he ought to say 'This comfort, O Lord, Thou hast sent from heaven unto me, a sinner and unworthy, and I commit it unto Thy care, for that I feel me to be a thief of Thy treasure.' When, therefore, he returneth from praying, he ought thus to show himself as a little poor one and a sinner, not as one who hath attained unto any new grace."

5. Once when the man of God was praying at Saint Mary of the Porziuncula, it chanced that the Bishop of Assisi came to visit him, as was his wont. He at once on entering the place betook him unto the cell wherein the servant of Christ was praying, with more boldness than was seemly, and, knocking at the door, was about to enter; but, as he thrust in his head, and beheld the Saint in prayer, a sudden trembling gat hold of him, his limbs became rigid, and he lost the power of speech; then suddenly he was driven forth by force, by the divine will, and with returning steps was led afar off. All astonished, the Bishop hastened unto the Brethren with all the speed he might, and, God restoring unto him his speech, with his first words he declared his fault.

It befell on a time that the Abbot of the monastery of Saint Justin in the diocese of Perugia met the servant of Christ. Beholding him, the devout Abbot with all speed alighted from his horse, that he might both do reverence unto the man of God and hold some converse with him concerning his soul's welfare. At length, their sweet conference over, the Abbot, as he departed, humbly besought that prayers should be offered on his behalf. Unto whom the man dear unto God made answer, "I will pray for thee with goodwill." Accordingly, when the Abbot had departed a little space, the faithful Francis spake unto his companion, "Tarry for me awhile, Brother, for I am minded to pay the debt that I have promised." While, then, he was praying, on a sudden the Abbot felt in his spirit an unwonted glow and a sweetness hitherto unknown, in such wise as that he was carried out of himself in an ecstasy, and wholly loosed from himself and absorbed in God. This lasted but for a brief space, after which he came unto himself again, and recognised the efficacy of the prayer of Saint Francis. Thenceforward he did alway burn with greater love toward the Order, and recounted this event unto many as a miracle.

6. The holy man was wont to say the Canonical Hours before God not less reverently than devoutly. For albeit he suffered from infirmities of the eyes, the stomach, spleen, and liver, yet would he never lean against an outer or inner wall, while he was intoning them, but alway said the Hours standing upright, and with lowered hood, not letting his eyes roam about, nor cutting short his words. If he were on a journey, he would, when the time came, stay his steps, nor would he omit this reverent and holy habit for any storm of rain. For he would say, "If the body needeth quiet when it partaketh of the bread that, like itself, shall become food for worms, with how much peace and calm doth it behove the soul to receive the Bread of Life?" Grievously did he consider himself to have stumbled if ever, while giving himself unto prayer, his mind was led astray of empty fantasies. When anything of the like happened, he made mention thereof in confession, that he might forthwith atone for it. This earnestness he had so turned into an habit that right seldom did he suffer from flies of this sort.

One Lent, he had made a little vase, that he might fill up his spare moments, and they not be utterly wasted. But forasmuch as while saying Tierce this came into his memory and a little distracted his mind, he, moved by the fervour of his spirit, burnt the little vase in the fire, saying, "I will sacrifice it unto the

Lord, Whose sacrifice it hath hindered." It was his wont to say the Psalms with mind and spirit as attentive as though he saw God present before his eyes, and when the Name of the Lord occurred therein, he seemed to refresh his very lips with the savour of its sweetness. He was fain that that same Name of the Lord, not alone when it was meditated upon, but also when it was uttered or written, should be honoured with an especial reverence, and at times he would prevail on the Brethren to collect all papers with writing upon them, wheresoever they might find them, and to lay them in some seemly place, lest perchance that sacred Name might happen to be written thereon, and so trodden underfoot. And when he uttered or heard the Name of Jesus, he was filled with an inward rejoicing, and seemed all transfigured outwardly, as though some honey-sweet taste had soothed his palate, or some melodious sound his ear.

7. Now three years before his death it befell that he was minded, at the town of Greccio, to celebrate the memory of the Birth of the Child Jesus, with all the added solemnity that he might, for the kindling of devotion. That this might not seem an innovation, he sought and obtained licence from the Supreme Pontiff, and then made ready a manger, and bade hay, together with an ox and an ass, be brought unto the spot. The Brethren were called together, the folk assembled, the wood echoed with their voices, and that august night was made radiant and solemn with many bright lights, and with tuneful and sonorous praises. The man of God, filled with tender love, stood before the manger, bathed in tears, and overflowing with joy. Solemn Masses were celebrated over the manger, Francis, the Levite of Christ, chanting the Holy Gospel. Then he preached unto the folk standing round of the Birth of the King in poverty, calling Him, when he wished to name Him, the Child of Bethlehem, by reason of his tender love for Him. A certain Knight, valorous and true, Messer John of Greccio, who for the love of Christ had left the secular army, and was bound by closest friendship unto the man of God, declared that he beheld a little Child right fair to see sleeping in that manger, Who seemed to be awakened from sleep when the blessed Father Francis embraced Him in both arms. This vision of the devout Knight is rendered worthy of belief, not alone through the holiness of him that beheld it, but is also confirmed by the truth that it set forth, and withal proven by the miracles that followed it. For the example of Francis, if meditated upon by the world, must needs stir up sluggish hearts unto the faith of Christ, and the hay that was kept back

from the manger by the folk proved a marvellous remedy for sick beasts, and a prophylactic against divers other plagues, God magnifying by all means His servant, and making manifest by clear and miraculous portents the efficacy of his holy prayers.

CHAPTER XI

OF HIS UNDERSTANDING OF THE SCRIPTURES, AND OF HIS SPIRIT OF PROPHECY

1. UNTO such a tranquillity of mind had his unwearied zeal for prayer and continuous practice of virtue brought the man of God that—albeit he had no instruction or learning in the sacred writings—yet, illumined by the beams of eternal light, he searched the deep things of the Scriptures with marvellous intellectual discernment. For his genius, pure from all stain, penetrated into the hidden places of the mysteries, and, where the learning of a theologian tarrieth without, the feelings of the lover led him in. At times he would read in the sacred books, and whatsoever had once been presented unto his mind became indelibly imprinted on his memory, for it was not in vain that he comprehended by hearing and by an attentive mind that which he ever meditated upon with the love of an unceasing devotion. Once when the Brethren asked whether it were his will that the clerks that had been already received into the Order should devote themselves unto the study of Holy Scripture, he made answer, " It is indeed my will, yet for so long alone as they follow the example of Christ, Who, we read, prayed more than He read, and for so long as they do not lose their zeal for prayer, nor study only that they may know how they ought to speak; rather let them study that they may be doers of the word, and, when they have done it, may set forth unto others what they too should do. I am fain (saith he), that my Brethren should be learners of the Gospel, and thus make progress in knowledge of the truth, that they should grow in the purity of guilelessness, so that they sever not the harmlessness of the dove from the wisdom of the serpent, which twain the greatest Teacher hath joined together with His blessed mouth."

2. Being asked at Siena by a certain devout man, a doctor of sacred theology, concerning sundry problems hard of understanding, he laid bare the hidden things of the divine wisdom with such luminous exposition that that learned man was

mightily astonished, and exclaimed in amazement, "Verily, the theology of this holy Father, borne aloft by purity and meditation as though by wings, is as a flying eagle, while our learning creepeth on its belly on the earth." For, albeit he were unskilled in speech, yet, full of learning, he unravelled the knots of problems, and the thing that was hid he brought forth into the light. Nor was it unfitting that the holy man should receive from God an understanding of the Scriptures, seeing that by the imitation of Christ he fulfilled and set forth in his deeds their perfect truth, and by the abundant anointing of the Holy Spirit had within him, in his own heart, an instructor therein.

3. So mightily did the spirit of prophecy shine forth in him that he both foreknew what was to come, and beheld the secrets of men's hearts, and perceived absent things as though they were present, and in wondrous wise manifested his own presence unto them that were absent. For on a time when the Christian army was besieging Damietta, the man of God was present, fortified not by arm but by faith. When on the day of battle the Christians were preparing them for the conflict, and the servant of Christ heard thereof, he groaned bitterly, and said unto his companion, "If they attempt to join battle, the Lord hath shown me that it will not fare well with the Christians; but, if I say this, I shall be accounted a fool; if I keep silence, I shall not escape the reproaches of my conscience. What, then, dost thou advise?" His companion replied, "Brother, do thou esteem it but a light thing to be judged of men, for that thou dost not now make a beginning of being accounted a fool. Unburden thy conscience, and fear God rather than men." Hearing this, the herald of Christ hastened forth, and approached the Christians with salutary warnings, forbidding the battle, and prophesying its issue. The truth was unto them as a vain tale, they hardened their hearts and would not turn back. They went into the field, they joined battle, they fought, and the entire Christian host was put to the rout, thus winning shame, not triumph, as the ending of the warfare. In this dread defeat, the Christian host was so diminished that there were about six thousand slain or captured. Thereby was it clearly made manifest that the wisdom of the poor man, Francis, had not been worthy of contempt, for the mind of a righteous man is sometime wont to tell him more than seven watchmen, that sit above in an high tower.

4. At another time, when he was returned from beyond seas, and had come unto Celano to preach, a certain Knight with

humble devoutness and great importunity invited him to dine with him. He came accordingly unto the house of the Knight, and the whole household rejoiced over the coming of their poor guests. Before they partook of the meal, Francis, as he was wont, stood with eyes uplift to heaven, with a devout mind offering unto God prayers and praises. His prayer ended, he called aside his kindly host in familiar wise, and thus addressed him, " Lo, my brother and host, yielding unto thine importunity I have come unto thy house to eat. Do thou now yield speedily unto my exhortations, forasmuch as thou shalt eat not here, but elsewhere. Confess now thy sins, and be contrite with the grief of a true repentance, nor let aught abide in thee that thou dost not lay bare in sincere confession. The Lord will reward thee this day for that thou hast received His poor with such devoutness." The Knight yielded forthwith unto the words of the holy man, unto whose companion he disclosed all his sins in confession, and then set his house in order, and prepared himself, in so far as he might, for death. At length they sat down to table, and, while the rest were beginning to eat, the host on a sudden gave up the ghost, carried off by a sudden death according unto the word of the man of God. And thus it befell, by the merits of his gracious hospitality, that, according unto the Word of truth, " He that receiveth a prophet shall receive a prophet's reward; " for by the prophetic prediction of the holy man that devout Knight made himself ready against the sudden onset of death, inasmuch as, fortified by the weapons of penitence, he was able to escape eternal condemnation and enter into the everlasting tabernacles.

5. Once on a time, while the holy man was lying sick at Rieti, a prebendary, Gideon by name, a man unstable and worldly, that had been stricken with a sore disease and was lying in his bed, was brought unto him, and with tears besought him—as did the bystanders—that he would make over him the sign of the Cross. Unto him he said, " Since aforetime thou wert living after the lusts of the flesh, not fearing the judgments of God, how can I sign thee with the Cross? Howbeit, for the sake of the devout prayers of these that plead for thee, I will make over thee the sign of the Cross in the name of the Lord. Yet be thou well assured that a worse thing will befall thee if, when thou hast been set free, thou shalt return unto thy vomit. For the sin of ingratitude ever bringeth with it worse evils than were suffered afore." Then, when the sign of the Cross was made over him, at once he that had lain paralysed rose up

whole, and, breaking forth into God's praises, "I," saith he, "am set free!" His bones cracked within him, in the hearing of many, even as when dry wood is broken by the hand. Yet when but a short time had passed by, he forgat God, and again yielded his body unto unchastity. When one evening he had supped in the house of a certain Canon, and was sleeping there that night, on a sudden the roof of the house fell in above them all. But while the rest escaped death, that wretched man alone was overtaken and cut off. Thus by a righteous judgment of God the last state of that man was worse than the first, by reason of his sin of ingratitude, and contempt of God, since it had behoved him to be grateful for the pardon that he had gained, and since a crime when repeated is twofold an offence.

6. On another time, a devout woman of noble birth came unto the holy man to unfold her grief unto him and to ask a remedy. Now she had a right cruel husband, from whom she suffered opposition in the service of Christ, wherefore she besought the holy man that he would pray for him that God would deign to soften his heart with His own mercy. Hearing this, Francis said unto her, "Go in peace, and confidently await from thine husband the comfort that he shall speedily afford thee." And he added, "Say unto him from God and from me that now is the day of mercy, hereafter that of justice." When he had blessed her, the woman returned, found her husband, and declared what had been spoken. Then the Holy Spirit fell upon him and changed him into a new man, making him in all gentleness reply thus, "Lady, let us serve the Lord, and save our souls." Then by the persuasions of his devout wife for many years they lived a life of continence, and both on the same day departed unto the Lord. Of a truth, we must marvel at the might of the spirit of prophecy that was found in the man of God, through the which he restored unto withered limbs their power, and impressed on hard hearts godliness; albeit no less must we be astonished at the clear perception of that spirit, whereby he so foreknew the issue of future events that he could search even the secret things of men's consciences, having obtained, like another Elisha, a double portion of the spirit of Elias.

7. Once when at Siena he had decisively foretold unto a certain friend some events that should come to pass, that learned man—of whom mention hath been made above as to his conferring with him about the Scriptures—heard thereof, and, doubting, asked the holy Father whether he had said the

things that he had heard from the narration of that other. Then Francis not only declared that he had so spoken, but also foretold by prophecy that man's own end, who was thus asking concerning another. And that he might the more surely impress this on his heart, he revealed unto him a certain hidden scruple of his conscience, which that man had never laid bare unto any living, and by thus marvellously revealing the same he explained it, and by his salutary counsels laid it low. To confirm the truth of all this, it befell that that same devout man came unto his end at the last in the manner foretold him by the servant of Christ.

8. Once, moreover, when he was returning from beyond sea, with Brother Leonard of Assisi as his companion, it chanced that, worn out and weary as he was, he was riding on an ass. His companion, as he followed him—himself no little wearied—began to say within himself, with a touch of human weakness, "This man's family was not of equal standing with mine own. And now, look you, he rideth, and I on foot lead his ass." Even as he thus reasoned, the holy man forthwith dismounted from the ass, saying, "It is not fitting, Brother, that I should ride, and thou walk afoot, for that in the world thou wert of nobler birth and more standing than I." Then the Brother was dumb with amazement, and blushed for shame, and, perceiving his fault, fell at the other's feet, which he bedewed with tears, and laid bare what had been his thought, and implored pardon.

9. A certain Brother, devoted unto God, and unto the servant of Christ, oft meditated in his heart how that one must be meet for the divine grace whom the holy man embraced with intimate friendship, yet nevertheless he thought himself considered of God as a stranger, outside the number of the elect. Being, then, ofttimes harassed by the oncoming of such thoughts, he ardently desired the intimate friendship of the man of God, yet did not lay bare unto any the secret of his heart; him the kindly Father called gently unto him, and thus addressed, "Let no thoughts disturb thee, my son, for I hold thee most dear, and amongst those most especially dear unto me I do gladly bestow upon thee the gift of my friendship and my love." Thereat the Brother marvelled, and from being devout became ever more devout, and not only increased in love of the holy man, but was also laden, through the gift of the grace of the Holy Spirit, with greater endowments.

Now while Francis was sojourning on Mount Alverna, secluded in his cell, one of his companions did mightily desire to possess some of the words of the Lord written by his hand, and with brief notes thereupon. For, having it, he believed that he might escape a grievous temptation, not of the flesh, but of the spirit, by the which he was distressed, or assuredly might be enabled to bear it more easily. While he was pining with such a desire, he suffered torments within, being overcome with shamefastness, nor daring to lay the matter before his venerated Father. But though man told it not unto him, the Spirit revealed it. For he bade the Brother aforesaid bring unto him ink and parchment, and according unto the desire of the Brother he wrote with his own hand the praises of the Lord thereon, and finally, a blessing for him, saying, "Take unto thyself this parchment, and keep it with care until the day of thy death." The Brother received the gift he had so desired, and forthwith that temptation utterly departed from him. The writing was preserved, and forasmuch as in later days it wrought miracles, it became a witness unto the virtues of Francis.

10. Now there was a Brother eminent, in so far as outward appearance went, for his sanctity, distinguished in his converse, yet somewhat singular in bearing. Devoting his whole time unto prayer, he observed silence with such rigour as that he was wont to make his confession not by words, but by nods. Now it chanced that the holy Father came unto that place and beheld the Brother, and spake concerning him with the other Brethren. When they all praised and glorified him, the man of God made answer, "Beware, Brethren, lest ye praise unto me in him the deceitful semblances of the devil. Know in truth that this is a temptation of the devil, and a deceitful snare." The Brethren were loth to believe this, judging it almost impossible that the devices of a false seeming should adorn themselves with so many evidences of perfection. Yet of a truth, on his leaving the Religion not many days after, it was manifestly seen with what clearness of inward vision the man of God had discerned the secrets of his heart.

After this manner he would predict with irrefragable truth the fall of many who seemed to stand, but also the conversion unto Christ of many who were turned aside, so that he seemed to have approached unto the mirror of eternal light to gaze therein, and by its wondrous radiance the sight of his mind surely perceived things that were absent in bodily form, even as though they were present.

11. Thus, on a time when his Vicar was holding a Chapter, and he himself was in his cell praying, he was a mediator between

the Brethren and God. For when one of them, sheltering himself under some cloak of defence, would not yield himself up unto discipline, the holy man beheld this in spirit, and called one of the Brethren, and said unto him, "I saw, Brother, the devil sitting upon the back of that disobedient Brother, holding his neck gripped, for he, driven by such a master, spurning the bridle of obedience, had given the reins unto his instincts. And when I besought God for the Brother, at once the devil withdrew in confusion. Go then and bid the Brother yield his neck with all speed unto the yoke of holy obedience." The Brother, exhorted by the messenger, forthwith turned unto God, and humbly threw himself at the feet of the Vicar.

12. Again, it befell on a time that two Brethren had come from afar unto the hermitage of Greccio, that they might behold the man of God, and carry away with them his blessing, the which they had long time coveted. They came and found him not, for that he had returned from the common dwelling-place unto his cell, wherefore they were departing disconsolately. Lo, as they were withdrawing, Francis, who could have known naught by human perception of their arrival or departure, contrary unto his wont came forth of his cell, called after them, and, according unto their desire, made the sign of the Cross over them, blessing them in the name of Christ.

13. Once two Brethren were come from Terra di Lavoro, the elder of whom had given some offence unto the younger. But when they came before the Father, he asked of the younger how the Brother that was his companion had behaved toward him on the way. On his making answer, "Well enough," he responded, "Beware, Brother, that thou lie not under pretext of humility, for I know, I know—do thou wait a while and thou shalt see." The Brother was mightily astonished in what wise he had perceived in spirit what had taken place so far off. Accordingly, not many days after, he that had given the offence unto the Brother, spurning the Religion, went out utterly, not seeking pardon from the Father, nor submitting unto the discipline of correction that was his due. Thus two things were made manifest at the same time in the ruin of this one man, to wit, the justice of the divine judgments, and the clear vision of the spirit of prophecy.

14. In what wise Francis showed himself present unto them that were absent, by the working of the divine power, is clearly apparent from what hath been afore related, if we recall unto mind how in his absence he appeared unto the Brethren as one transfigured, in a chariot of fire, and how at the Chapter of Arles

he showed himself with arms outstretched after the likeness of a Cross. This we must believe to have been wrought by the divine ruling, that by the miraculous appearance of his bodily presence it might be abundantly evident how that his spirit was present in and penetrated by the light of the eternal wisdom, which is more moving than any motion, and goeth through all things by reason of her pureness, and entering into holy souls maketh them friends of God, and prophets. For the most exalted Teacher is wont to reveal His mysteries unto the babes and simple, as was first seen in David, the most lofty of the Prophets, and afterward in the Prince of the Apostles, Peter, and lastly in Francis, the little poor one of Christ. For these, albeit they were simple, and unskilled in letters, were made famous by the teaching of the Holy Spirit; the first a shepherd, to feed the flock of the Synagogue that was brought forth out of Egypt; the second a fisher, to fill the great net of the Church with a multitude of believers; the last a merchantman, to buy the pearl of Gospel life, when that he had sold and disposed of all things for the sake of Christ.

CHAPTER XII

OF THE EFFICACY OF HIS PREACHING, AND OF HIS GIFT OF HEALING

I. THE truly faithful servant and minister of Christ, Francis, that he might faithfully and perfectly fulfil all things, strove most chiefly to exercise those virtues that he knew, by the guidance of the Holy Spirit, were most pleasing unto his God. Wherefore it came to pass that he fell into great striving with himself by reason of a doubt, the which that he might end—on his return after many days of prayer—he set before the Brethren that were his intimates. "What," saith he, "do ye counsel, Brethren, what do ye commend? Shall I devote myself unto prayer, or shall I go about preaching? Of a truth, I that am little, and simple, and rude in speech have received more grace of prayer than of speaking. Now in prayer, there seemeth to be the gain and heaping up of graces, in preaching, a certain giving out of the gifts received from heaven; in prayer, again, a cleansing of the inward feelings, and an union with the one, true, and highest good, together with a strengthening of virtue; in preaching, the spiritual feet wax dusty, and many things distract a man, and discipline is relaxed. Finally, in prayer, we speak with God and hear Him, and live as it were the life of Angels, while we converse with Angels; in preaching, we must needs practise much condescension toward men and living among them as fellow-men must think, see, say, and hear such things as pertain unto men. Yet one thing is there to set against these, the which in God's sight would seem to weight more than they will, to wit, that the only-begotten Son of God, Who is the highest wisdom, left His Father's bosom for the salvation of souls, that, instructing the world by His example, He might preach the word of salvation unto men, whom He both redeemed at the cost of His sacred Blood, and cleansed in a laver and gave them to drink, keeping back naught of Himself, but for our salvation freely bestowing all. And forasmuch as we ought to do all things after the pattern of those things that was shown us in Him as on the lofty mount, it seemeth that it might be more acceptable unto God that, laying aside leisure, I should go forth unto the work." And albeit for many days he pondered over such sayings with the Brethren, he could not of a surety discern whether of the twain he should choose as more truly pleasing unto Christ. For albeit he had known many wondrous things through the spirit of prophecy, he was not able thereby to resolve this question clearly, the providence of God better ordaining, so that the merit of preaching might be made evident by an heavenly oracle, and the humility of Christ's servant be kept intact.

2. He, a true Friar Minor, was not ashamed to ask little things from those less than himself, albeit he had learnt great things from the greatest Teacher. For with an especial zeal he was wont to enquire after what way and manner of life he might most perfectly serve God accordingly unto His will. This was his highest philosophy, this his highest desire, so long as he lived, so that he would enquire of wise and simple, of perfect and imperfect, of young and old, in what wise he might with most holiness attain unto the summit of perfection. Therefore, calling unto him two of the Brethren, he sent them unto Brother Silvester—he that had seen the Cross proceeding from his mouth, and was at that time giving himself up unto continuous prayer in the mountain above Assisi—that he might seek an answer from God concerning this doubt, and announce it unto him from the Lord. This same bidding he laid upon the holy virgin Clare, that through some of the purer and simpler of the virgins that were living under her rule, yea, and through

her own prayers united with those of the other Sisters, she might ascertain the will of the Lord touching this matter. The reverend priest and the virgin vowed unto God were marvellously in agreement concerning this, the Holy Spirit revealing it unto them, to wit, that it was the divine will that the herald of Christ should go forth to preach. When, therefore, the Brethren returned, and, according unto what they had heard, pointed out the will of God, Francis forthwith rose and girded himself, and without any delay set forth on his journey. And with such fervour did he go, to fulfil the divine behest, and with such speed did he hasten on his way, that he seemed—the hand of the Lord being upon him—to have put on new power from heaven.

3. When he drew nigh unto Bevagna he came unto a spot wherein a great multitude of birds of divers species were gathered together. When the holy man of God perceived them, he ran with all speed unto the place and greeted them as if they shared in human understanding. They on their part all awaited him and turned toward him, those that were perched on bushes bending their heads as he drew nigh them, and looking on him in unwonted wise, while he came right among them, and diligently exhorted them all to hear the word of God, saying, "My brothers the birds, much ought ye to praise your Creator, Who hath clothed you with feathers and given you wings to fly, and hath made over unto you the pure air, and careth for you without your taking thought for yourselves." While he was speaking unto them these and other like words, the little birds—behaving themselves in wondrous wise—began to stretch their necks, to spread their wings, to open their beaks, and to look intently on him. He, with wondrous fervour of spirit, passed in and out among them, touching them with his habit, nor did one of them move from the spot until he had made the sign of the Cross over them and given them leave; then, with the blessing of the man of God, they all flew away together. All these things were witnessed by his companions that stood awaiting him by the way. Returning unto them, the simple and holy man began to blame himself for neglect in that he had not afore then preached unto the birds.

4. Thence, while going among the neighbouring places to preach, he came unto a town named Alviano, where, when the folk were gathered together and silence had been bidden, he could yet scarce be heard by reason of the swallows that were there building their nests, and twittering with shrill cries. The

man of God, in the hearing of all, addressed them, and said, " My sisters the swallows, 'tis now time that I too should speak, seeing that until now ye have said your say. Hearken unto the word of God, and keep silence, until the preaching of the Lord be ended." Then they, as though gifted with understanding, on a sudden fell silent, nor moved from the spot until the whole preaching was finished. All they that saw it were filled with amazement, and glorified God. The report of this marvel spread on all sides, and kindled in many reverence for the Saint, and devotion unto the faith.

5. Again, in the city of Parma, a scholar of good disposition that with his comrades was busily intent on study, was troubled by the importunate twittering of a certain swallow, and began to say unto his comrades, " This swallow is one of those that troubled the man of God, Francis, on a time when he was preaching, until he bade them be silent." Then, turning unto the swallow, with all confidence he said, " In the name of Francis, the servant of God, I bid thee come hither to me forthwith, and keep silence." Then the bird, hearing the name Francis, like one instructed by the teaching of the man of God, at once fell silent, and withal gave herself up into his hands as though into safe keeping. The scholar, in amazement, forthwith set her free again, and heard her twittering no more.

6. On another time, when the servant of God was preaching on the seashore at Gaëta, crowds gathered about him out of devotion, that they might touch him; whereupon the servant of Christ, shrinking from such homage of the folk, leapt alone into a little boat that was lying by the beach. And the boat, as though impelled by a reasoning power from within, without any rowing put out unto some distance from land, while all beheld it and marvelled. But when it was withdrawn some little distance into deep water, it stayed motionless among the waves, while the holy man preached unto the waiting crowds upon the shore. When the discourse was ended, and the miracle perceived, and his blessing given, the throng gave place, in order that they might no more disturb him, and the little boat of its own guidance put in again unto land.

Who then could be of so obstinate and wicked mind as to despise the preaching of Francis, by whose wondrous might it came to pass that not only creatures lacking reason were amenable unto his correction, but that even lifeless objects, as though they had life, ministered unto him while preaching?

7. Thus there was ever present with His servant Francis,

in whatsoever he did, He Who had anointed him and sent him, the Spirit of the Lord, yea, and Christ Himself, Who is the power of God and the wisdom of God, that he might abound in words of saving doctrine and shine in the light of miracles of great power. For his speech was as a burning fire, penetrating the secrets of the heart, and he filled the minds of all with amazement, since he set forth no adornments of men's invention, but savoured of the breath of divine revelation. Thus on a time, when he was about to preach in the presence of the Pope and the Cardinals, at the suggestion of the lord Bishop of Ostia he had committed unto memory a certain carefully prepared sermon, and, standing in the midst to set forth the words of edification, found that he had so utterly forgotten it all as that he knew not how to speak a word thereof. When with fruitful humility he had confessed this, he set himself to invoke the grace of the Holy Spirit, and forthwith began to pour forth words so mighty in effect, and of such wondrous power to move the minds of those illustrious men unto repentance, as that it was manifestly seen that it was not himself that spake, but the Spirit of the Lord.

8. And forasmuch as he did himself first practise that which he afterward preached unto others, he feared none that might blame him, but did most faithfully preach the truth. It was not his way to smooth over the faults of any, but to smite them, nor to flatter the life of sinners, but rather to aim at it with stern reproofs. Unto great and small alike he spake with the same firm spirit, and he would as joyfully address him unto few as unto many. Folk of every age and either sex hastened to see and to hear this man, newly given unto the world from heaven. He, indeed, as he went throughout divers districts, preached the Gospel with fervour, the Lord working with him and confirming the word with signs following. For in the power of His Name Francis, the herald of the truth, did cast forth demons, heal the sick, and, what is more, by the might of his preaching did soften and make penitent hard hearts, restoring health unto body and soul at the same time, even as the instances of his working to be cited below give proof.

9. In the city of Toscanella, he was devoutly entertained as guest by a certain Knight, whose only son was crippled from birth; at his own urgent entreaty, he raised him with his hands, and so suddenly made him whole that, in the sight of all, his limbs were all forthwith strengthened, and the boy, made whole and strong, rose up at once, walking and leaping and praising God.

In the city of Narni, when, at the entreaty of the Bishop, he had made the sign of the Cross from head to foot over a certain paralytic who had lost the use of all his limbs, he restored him perfectly unto health.

In the diocese of Rieti, a boy that from the age of four had been so swollen that he could in no wise look on his own legs, was brought unto him by his mother with tears, and forthwith, when the Saint touched him with his holy hands, was healed.

In the city of Orte, a boy was so deformed that his head rested on his feet, and some of his bones were broken; he, when Francis at the tearful entreaties of his parents had made the sign of the Cross over him, on a sudden stood upright and was from that moment unloosed.

10. A certain woman in the city of Gubbio had both her hands so withered and paralysed that she could do no work with them; she, when Francis had made the sign of the Cross over her in the name of the Lord, gained such absolute healing that, returning home forthwith, she prepared with her own hands food for him and for the poor, even as Peter's wife's mother did.

A girl in the town of Bevagna had lost her sight, but when her eyes had been thrice anointed with his spittle in the name of the Trinity she regained her longed-for sight.

A woman in the city of Narni, stricken with blindness, when the sign of the Cross was made over her by Francis, recovered the sight she yearned for.

A boy in Bologna had one of his eyes so clouded by a spot that he could see nothing therewith, nor find relief by any remedy; howbeit when the servant of the Lord had made the sign of the Cross over him from head to foot, he recovered his sight perfectly, insomuch as that, entering the Order of Brothers Minor thereafter, he affirmed that he saw far better with the eye that aforetime was clouded than with the eye that had been alway sound.

In the town of San Gemini, the servant of God was received as guest by a certain devout man whose wife was tormented by a demon; after he had prayed, he commanded the demon on obedience to go out from her, and by the divine power put him so instantly to flight as that it became clearly evident that the audacity of demons availeth not to resist the power of holy obedience.

In Città di Castello, a raging and evil spirit possessed a woman; he, charged on obedience by the holy man, went out in wrath, leaving the woman that had been possessed free alike in mind and body.

11. One of the Brethren was afflicted with such an horrible disease as that it was asserted of many to be rather a tormenting from demons than a natural sickness. For ofttimes he was quite dashed down on the ground, and wallowed foaming, with his limbs now drawn up, now stretched forth, now folded, now twisted, now become rigid and fixed. At times he was quite stretched out and stiff, and with his feet on a level with his head, would be raised into the air, and would then fall back again in dreadful fashion. The servant of Christ, full of compassion, pitied him in his so lamentable and incurable sickness, and sent unto him a morsel of the bread wherefrom he had been eating. When the sick man had tasted the bread, he received such power as that never thenceforward did he suffer trouble from that sickness.

In the province of Arezzo, a woman for many days had laboured in childbirth, and was now nigh unto death; she was utterly despairing of her life, and no resource was left her but in God. Now the servant of Christ, by reason of his bodily weakness, had travelled on horseback through those regions, and it chanced that the beast was led back through the village wherein the woman lay suffering. The men of the place, seeing the horse whereon the holy man had sat, took off the bridle, that they might lay it on the woman, and at the marvellous touch thereof all danger was banished, and the woman forthwith was delivered in safety.

A certain man of Città della Pieve, devout and one that feared God, had by him a cord wherewith the holy Father had been girt. Whereas a great number of men and women in that city were afflicted by divers diseases, he went among the homes of them that were sick, and, dipping the cord in water, gave drink therefrom unto the sufferers, and thus by this means very many were cured. Moreover, the sick who tasted of bread touched by the man of God, by the efficacy of the divine power obtained right speedily healing cures.

12. Forasmuch as the preaching of the herald of Christ was illuminated by these and many other portents and miracles, the words that fell from him were listened for as eagerly as though it were an Angel of the Lord speaking. For there was in him a surpassing excellence of the virtues, the spirit of prophecy, power of miracles, an eloquence in preaching inspired from heaven, the submission unto him of the creatures that lack

reason, a mighty moving of men's hearts at the hearing of his words, a learning given him of the Holy Spirit beyond all human teaching, licence to preach granted him by the supreme Pontiff as the result of a revelation, yea, and the Rule too, wherein the manner of the preaching was set forth, confirmed by that same Vicar of Christ, and, finally, the signs of the King Most High imprinted on his body after the manner of a seal; these gave unanswerable evidence unto the whole world, as it were by ten witnesses, that Francis the herald of Christ was worthy of reverence in his ministry, was of authority in his teaching, and was to be marvelled at in his saintliness, and that through these virtues he had preached the Gospel of Christ like one that was indeed a messenger of God.

CHAPTER XIII

OF THE SACRED STIGMATA

1. It was the custom of that angelic man, Francis, never to be slothful in good, but rather, like the heavenly spirits on Jacob's ladder, to be ever ascending toward God, or stooping toward his neighbour. For he had learnt so wisely to apportion the time granted unto him for merit that one part thereof he would spend in labouring for the profit of his neighbours, the other he would devote unto the peaceful ecstasies of contemplation. Wherefore, when according unto the demands of time and place he had stooped to secure the salvation of others, he would leave behind the disturbances of throngs, and seek a hidden solitude and a place for silence, wherein, giving himself up more freely unto the Lord, he might brush off any dust that was clinging unto him from his converse with men. Accordingly, two years before he yielded his spirit unto heaven, the divine counsel leading him, he was brought after many and varied toils unto an high mountain apart, that is called Mount Alverna.[1] When, according unto his wont, he began to keep a Lent there, fasting, in honour of Saint Michael Archangel, he was filled unto overflowing, and as never before, with the sweetness of heavenly contemplation, and was kindled with a yet more burning flame of heavenly longings, and began to feel the gifts of the divine bestowal heaped upon him. He was borne into the heights, not like a curious examiner of the divine majesty that is weighed down by the glory thereof, but even as a faithful and wise servant, searching out the will of

[1] Called La Verna in *The Little Flowers*.

God, unto Whom it was ever his fervent and chief desire to conform himself in every way.

2. Thus by the divine oracle it was instilled into his mind that by opening of the Book of the Gospels it should be revealed unto him of Christ what would be most pleasing unto God in him and from him. Wherefore, having first prayed very devoutly, he took the holy Book of the Gospels from the altar, and made it be opened, in the name of the Holy Trinity, by his companion, a man devoted unto God, and holy. As in the threefold opening of the Book the Lord's Passion was each time discovered, Francis, full of the Spirit of God, verily understood that, like as he had imitated Christ in the deeds of his life, so it behoved him to be made like unto Him in the trials and sufferings of His Passion before that he should depart from this world. And, albeit by reason of the great austerity of his past life, and continual sustaining of the Lord's Cross, he was now frail in body, he was no whit afeared, but was the more valorously inspired to endure a martyrdom. For in him the all-powerful kindling of love of the good Jesu had increased into coals of fire, which hath a most vehement flame, so that many waters could not quench his love, so strong it was.

3. When, therefore, by seraphic glow of longing he had been uplifted toward God, and by his sweet compassion had been transformed into the likeness of Him Who of His exceeding love endured to be crucified—on a certain morning about the Feast of the Exaltation of Holy Cross, while he was praying on the side of the mountain, he beheld a Seraph having six wings, flaming and resplendent, coming down from the heights of heaven. When in his flight most swift he had reached the space of air nigh the man of God, there appeared betwixt the wings the Figure of a Man crucified, having His hands and feet stretched forth in the shape of a Cross, and fastened unto a Cross. Two wings were raised above His head, twain were spread forth to fly, while twain hid His whole body. Beholding this, Francis was mightily astonished, and joy, mingled with sorrow, filled his heart. He rejoiced at the gracious aspect wherewith he saw Christ, under the guise of the Seraph, regard him, but His crucifixion pierced his soul with a sword of pitying grief. He marvelled exceedingly at the appearance of a vision so unfathomable, knowing that the infirmity of the Passion doth in no wise accord with the immortality of a Seraphic spirit. At length he understood therefrom, the Lord revealing it unto him, that this vision had been thus presented unto his gaze by the

divine providence, that the friend of Christ might have foreknowledge that he was to be wholly transformed into the likeness of Christ Crucified, not by martyrdom of body, but by enkindling of heart. Accordingly, as the vision disappeared, it left in his heart a wondrous glow, but on his flesh also it imprinted a no less wondrous likeness of its tokens. For forthwith there began to appear in his hands and feet the marks of the nails, even as he had just beheld them in that Figure of the Crucified. For his hands and feet seemed to be pierced through the midst with nails, the heads of the nails showing in the palms of the hands, and upper side of the feet, and their points showing on the other side; the heads of the nails were round and black in the hands and feet, while the points were long, bent, and as it were turned back, being formed of the flesh itself, and protruding therefrom. The right side, moreover, was—as if it had been pierced by a lance—seamed with a ruddy scar, where from ofttimes welled the sacred blood, staining his habit and breeches.

4. Now the servant of Christ perceived that the stigmata thus manifestly imprinted on his flesh could not be hidden from his intimate friends; nevertheless, fearing to make public the holy secret of the Lord, he was set in a great strife of questioning, to wit, whether he should tell that which he had seen, or should keep it silent. Wherefore he called some of the Brethren, and, speaking unto them in general terms, set before them his doubt, and asked their counsel. Then one of the Brethren, Illuminato by name, and illuminated by grace, perceiving that he had beheld some marvellous things, inasmuch as that he seemed almost stricken dumb with amaze, said unto the holy man, " Brother, thou knowest that at times the divine secrets are shown unto thee, not only for thine own sake, but for the sake of others also. Wherefore, it seems thou wouldst have reason to fear lest thou shouldst be judged guilty of hiding thy talent, didst thou keep hidden that which thou hast received, which same would be profitable unto many." At this speech, the holy man was moved, so that, albeit at other times he was wont to say, " My secret to me," [1] he did then with much fear narrate in order the vision aforesaid, adding that He who had appeared unto him had said some words the which, so long as he lived, he would never reveal unto any man. Verily we must believe that those utterances of that holy Seraph marvellously appearing on the Cross were so secret that perchance it was not lawful for a man to utter them.

5. Now after that the true love of Christ had transformed His lover into the same image, and after that he had spent forty days in solitude, as he had determined, when the Feast of Saint Michael Archangel came, this angelic man, Francis, descended from the mountain, bearing with him the likeness of the Crucified, engraven, not on tables of stone or of wood, by the craftsman's hand, but written on his members of flesh by the finger of the Living God. And forasmuch as it is good to keep close the secret of a King, the man that shared this so royal secret did ever hide those sacred signs as best he might. Howbeit, since it pertaineth unto God to reveal the great things that He doth for His glory, the Lord Himself, Who had imprinted those seals upon him in secret, wrought divers miracles openly by means thereof, that the hidden and wondrous power of those stigmata might be demonstrated by the well-known fame of the signs that followed.

6. Thus, in the province of Rieti, there had prevailed a very grievous plague, the which devoured all oxen and sheep so cruelly that no succour had been of any avail. But a certain man that feared God was warned at night by a vision to go in haste unto an hermitage of the Brethren, and obtain some water that had washed the hands and feet of the servant of God, Francis, who at that time was sojourning there, and to sprinkle it over all the animals. Accordingly, he rose at dawn, and came unto the place, and, having secretly obtained this water from the companions of the holy man, he sprinkled therewith the sheep and oxen that were diseased. Wondrous to relate, so soon as the sprinkling, were it but a drop, fell upon the sick animals as they lay on the ground, they recovered their former strength, and got up forthwith, and, as though they had felt no sickness, hastened unto the pastures! Thus it befell, through the marvellous virtue of that water that had touched the sacred wounds, that the whole plague was at once stayed, and the contagious sickness banished from the flocks and herds.

7. In the neighbourhood of the aforesaid Mount Alverna, before that the holy man had sojourned there, a cloud was wont to arise from the mountain, and a fierce hailstorm to lay waste the fruits of the earth. But after that blessed vision, to the amazement of the inhabitants, the hail ceased, that the excellence of that heavenly apparition and the virtue of the stigmata that were there imprinted might be attested by the very face of the heavens, made calm beyond its wont.

Moreover, it befell one winter season that, by reason of his bodily infirmity, and of the roughness of the roads, he was riding on a poor man's ass, and was obliged to pass the night under the edge of an overhanging rock, that he might by any means escape the inconveniences of the snow and night that had overtaken them, the which hindered him so that he was not able to reach the place wherein he was to lodge. And when Francis perceived that this man was muttering, sighing, and complaining, and was tossing himself to and fro, like one thinly clad, and unable to sleep by reason of the bitter cold—he, kindled with the glow of the love divine, touched him with his outstretched hand. Marvellous to relate, so soon as that holy hand that bore the burning of the live coal of the Seraph touched him, his sense of cold was utterly banished, and as great a warmth came upon him within and without as if the flaming breath from the mouth of a furnace had blown upon him. Strengthened thereby in mind and body, he slept more sweetly until the morning among the rocks and snow than he had ever done resting in his own bed, even as he himself did thereafter declare.

Wherefore it is proven by sure tokens that those sacred seals were imprinted by the might of Him Who doth by the ministry of Seraphs purify, enlighten, and kindle, seeing that they brought health out of pestilence by driving it forth, and with wondrous efficacy bestowed ease and warmth upon men's bodies, even as after his death was shown by yet more clear portents that shall be related hereafter in their own place.

8. Francis himself, albeit he strove with great diligence to hide the treasure found in the field, could nevertheless not so conceal it as that some should not behold the stigmata in his hands and feet, although he almost always kept his hands covered, and from that time forth wore sandals on his feet. For, while he yet lived, many Brethren saw them, who, albeit they were men worthy of all trust by reason of their especial holiness, did yet for the removal of all doubt swear a solemn oath, laying their hands on thrice-holy things, that so it was, and that they had seen it. Moreover, some Cardinals, during the intimate intercourse that they held with the holy man, beheld them, and these composed truthful praises of the sacred stigmata, in prose, and verse, and antiphons, which they published in his honour, giving their witness alike in word and in writing unto the truth. The Supreme Pontiff, moreover, the lord Alexander, whenas he was preaching in the presence of many Brethren, myself among them, declared that he, during

the lifetime of the Saint, had beheld with his own eyes those sacred stigmata. At the time of his death, more than fifty Brethren beheld them, as did Clare, that virgin most devoted unto God, with the rest of her Sisters, and countless seculars, many of whom, as shall be told in its own place, both kissed them with devout emotion, and touched them with their hands, to confirm their witness.

Howbeit, the wound in his side he so heedfully concealed as that during his lifetime none might behold it, save by stealth. Thus one of the Brethren, who was wont solicitously to tend him—having prevailed on him with holy caution to doff his habit that it might be shaken out—by looking closely, beheld the wound, and moreover, by laying three fingers upon it with an hasty touch, learnt the extent thereof alike by sight and by touch. With a like precaution the Brother that was then his Vicar beheld it. And a Brother of wondrous simplicity, that was his companion, while he was rubbing his shoulder-blades by reason of a pain and weakness that he suffered therein, put his hand within his hood, and by an accident let it fall on the sacred wound, inflicting great pain on him. Thenceforward he wore his under-garments so made as that they reached right unto his armpits, to cover the wound in the side. Moreover, the Brethren who washed these, or shook out his habit as occasion demanded, finding them stained with blood, by this manifest token arrived at an assured knowledge of the sacred wound, whose appearance, revealed thereafter at his death, they too, in company with very many others, gazed upon and venerated withal.

9. Up then, most valiant knight of Christ! Bear the armour of that most invincible Captain, equipped and adorned wherewith thou shalt overcome all enemies. Bear the standard of the King Most High, the which to look upon inspireth all the warriors of the host of God. Bear no less the seal of the High Priest, Christ, whereby thy words and deeds shall be deservedly received as blameless and authoritative by all men. For from henceforth, by reason of the marks of the Lord Jesus, which thou dost bear in thy body, let no man trouble thee, nay rather, let whosoever is the servant of Christ be constrained unto deepest devotion and love for thee. For now by these most clear tokens—proven, not by the two or three witnesses that be enough to establish a matter, but by a multitude, over and above what was necessary—the witness of God in thee, and the things wrought through thee worthy of all belief, take from the

infidels every pretext or excuse, while that they strengthen believers in faith, uplift them by confidence of hope, and kindle them with the fire of charity.

10. Now, verily, is that first vision fulfilled, which thou sawest, to wit, that thou shouldst become a captain in the warfare of Christ, and shouldst be accoutred with heavenly armour, marked with the sign of the Cross. Now that vision of the Crucified, that, at the outset of thy conversion, pierced thy soul with a sword of pitying sorrow, yea, and the sound of the Voice from the Cross, proceeding as though from the exalted throne of Christ and His hidden place of atonement—as thou didst declare in thy holy converse—are shown to have been true beyond a doubt. Now, too, the Cross that, as thou madest progress in thy conversion, was seen of Brother Silvester marvellously coming forth from thy mouth—the swords, too, that the holy Pacificus saw laid crosswise upon thee, piercing thine heart—and thine appearance uplifted in the air with arms outstretched after the manner of a Cross, while the holy Anthony was preaching on the title of the Cross, as that angelic man, Monaldo, beheld;—these all are verily shown and proven to have been seen, not in imaginations of the brain, but by revelation from heaven. Now, finally, that vision that was vouchsafed thee toward the end of thy life—to wit, the exalted likeness of the Seraph, and the lowly image of Christ shown in one—kindling thee inwardly and marking thee outwardly as another Angel ascending from the sunrising, having the seal of the Living God in thee—giveth a confirmation of faith unto those visions aforesaid, and likewise receiveth from them a witness unto its own truth. Lo, by these seven appearances of the Cross of Christ in thee and about thee, marvellously set forth and shown in order of time, thou hast attained, as though by six steps, unto that seventh, where thou dost make an end, and rest. For the Cross of Christ was at the outset of thy conversion both set before thee, and taken up by thee, and thenceforward as thou madest progress in thy conversion, it was unceasingly sustained by thee throughout thy most holy life, and was shown as an ensample unto others with such clearness and certainty that it demonstrateth that at the end thou didst arrive at the summit of Gospel perfection; thus none that is truly devout will reject this showing-forth of Christ-like wisdom written in thy mortal dust, none that is a true believer will impeach it, none that is truly humble will lightly esteem it, seeing that it is verily set forth of God, and right worthy of all acceptation.

CHAPTER XIV

OF HIS SUFFERINGS AND DEATH

1. FRANCIS, now crucified with Christ alike in flesh and in spirit, while glowing with seraphic love toward God, did also thirst, even as did Christ Crucified, for the multitudes of them that should be saved. Wherefore, being unable to walk by reason of the nails protruding from his feet, he caused himself to be borne round cities and castled villages, emaciated as he was, that he might incite others to bear the Cross of Christ. And unto the Brethren also he would say, "Let us begin, Brethren, to serve our Lord God, for until now we have made but little progress." So mightily did he yearn to return unto the first beginnings of humility that he would serve the lepers as he had done at the outset, and would recall unto its early ministries his body that was now broken down by toils. Under Christ's leadership, he was minded to do mighty deeds, and, albeit his limbs were waxing feeble, yet, strong and glowing in spirit, he hoped in this new contest to vanquish the foe. For there is no room for languor or sloth where the spur of love ever urgeth on unto greater things. Yet in him the flesh was so much in agreement with the spirit, and so ready to obey, as that when the spirit strove to attain unto perfect holiness, the flesh not only refrained from thwarting it, but did even hasten to forestall it.

2. Now in order that the merits of the man of God might be increased—merits that of a truth do all find their consummation in endurance—he began to suffer from divers ailments so grievously that scarce one of his limbs was free from pain and sore suffering. At length by divers sicknesses, prolonged and continuous, he was brought unto such a point that his flesh was wasted away, and only as it were the skin clave unto his bones. While he was afflicted by such grievous bodily suffering, he would call his pangs not punishments, but *sisters*. And when once he was harassed more sorely than usual by sharp pains, a certain simple Brother said unto him, "Brother, pray the Lord that He deal more gently with thee, for meseemeth that His hand is laid more heavily on thee than is right." Hearing this, the holy man groaned, and cried out, saying, "Did I not know the simple purity that is in thee, I would from henceforth have shunned thy company, for that thou hast

dared to deem the divine counsels concerning me meet for blame." And albeit he was wholly worn out by the long continuance of his grievous sickness, he cast himself on the ground, jarring his frail bones in the hard fall. And, kissing the ground, he cried, "I give Thee thanks, O Lord God, for all these my pains, and I beseech Thee, my Lord, that, if it please Thee, Thou wilt add unto them an hundredfold; for this will be most acceptable unto me if laying sorrow upon me Thou dost not spare, since the fulfilling of Thy holy will is unto me an overflowing solace." Thus he seemed unto the Brethren like another Job, whose powers of mind increased even as his bodily weakness increased. But he himself knew long before his death when it should be, and, when the day of his departure was at hand, said unto the Brethren that he was about to put off the tabernacle of his body, even as it had been revealed unto him of Christ.

3. When, therefore, during the two years after the impression of the sacred stigmata, to wit, in the twentieth year from his conversion, he had been shaped by many trial blows of painful sicknesses, like unto a stone meet to be set in the building of the heavenly Jerusalem, and as it were an hammered work that under the mallet of manifold trials is brought unto perfection—he asked to be borne unto Saint Mary of the Porziuncula, that he might yield up the breath of life there, where he had received the breath of grace. When he had been brought thither—that he might give an example of the truth that he had naught in common with the world—in that most severe weakness that followed after all his sickness, he prostrated himself in fervour of spirit all naked on the naked earth, that in that last hour, wherein the foe might still rise up against him, he might wrestle in his nakedness with that naked spirit. As he lay thus on the ground, his habit of haircloth laid aside, he lifted his face, as was his wont, toward heaven, and, wholly absorbed in that glory, covered with his left hand the wound in his right side, that it might not be seen, and said unto the Brethren, "I have done what was mine to do, may Christ teach you what is yours."

4. While the companions of the Saint were weeping, stricken with keen pangs of pity, one of them, whom the man of God had said should be his Warden, knowing by divine inspiration his wish, rose in haste, and taking an habit, with the cord and breeches, brought it unto the little poor one of Christ, saying, "These I lend unto thee, as unto a beggar, and do thou receive them at the bidding of holy obedience." At this the holy man rejoiced, and exulted in gladness of heart, for that he saw that

he had kept faith with the Lady Poverty even unto the end, and raising his hands unto heaven, he glorified his Christ for that, freed from all burdens, he was going unhindered unto Him. For all this he had done in his zeal for poverty, being minded to possess not even an habit, unless it were lent him by another. He was verily minded in all things to be made like unto Christ Crucified, Who had hung on the Cross in poverty, and grief, and nakedness. Wherefore, as at the outset of his conversion he had stood naked before the Bishop, so in the ending of his life he was minded to quit the world naked. He charged the Brethren that stood around him, on their loving obedience, that when they saw that he was dead, they should leave him lying naked on the ground for so long time as a man would take leisurely to compass the distance of a thousand paces. O truly Christ-like man, who strove alike in life to imitate the life of Christ; in dying, His dying; in death, His death, by a perfect likeness, and was found worthy to be adorned with an outward likeness unto Him!

5. Then, as the hour of his departure was fast approaching, he made all the Brethren that were in the place be called unto him and, consoling them for his death with words of comfort, exhorted them with fatherly tenderness unto the love of God. He spake long of observing patience, and poverty, and fidelity unto the Holy Roman Church, placing the Holy Gospel before all other ordinances. Then as all the Brethren sat around him, he stretched his hands over them, crossing his arms in the likeness of the Cross, for that he did ever love that sign, and he blessed all the Brethren, present and absent alike, in the might and in the Name of the Crucified. He added, moreover, "Be strong, all ye my sons, in the fear of the Lord, and abide therein for ever. And, since temptation will come, and trials draw nigh, blessed are they who shall continue in the works that they have begun. I for my part make haste to go unto God, unto Whose grace I commend you all." When he had made an end of gentle exhortations after this wise, this man most beloved of God asked them to bring him the book of the Gospels, and to read unto him from the Gospel according unto John, beginning at that place, "Before the feast of the Passover." Then he himself, as best he could, brake forth into the words of that Psalm, "I cried unto the Lord with my voice, with my voice unto the Lord did I make my supplication," and went through even unto the end, saying, "The righteous shall compass me about, for Thou shalt deal bountifully with me."

5. At length, when all the mysteries had been fulfilled in him, and his most holy spirit was freed from the flesh, and absorbed into the boundless depths of the divine glory, the blessed man fell asleep in the Lord. One of his Brethren and disciples saw that blessed soul, under the likeness of a star exceeding bright, borne on a dazzling cloudlet over many waters, mounting in a straight course unto heaven, as though it were radiant with the dazzling whiteness of his exalted sanctity, and filled with the riches of divine wisdom and grace alike, by the which the holy man was found worthy to enter the abode of light and peace, where with Christ he resteth for evermore. Moreover, a Brother named Augustine, who was then Minister of the Brethren in Terra di Lavoro, an holy and upright man, having come unto his last hour, and some time previously having lost the power of speech, in the hearing of them that stood by did on a sudden cry out and say, "Tarry for me, Father, tarry for me, lo, even now I am coming with thee!" When the Brethren asked and marvelled much unto whom he thus boldly spake, he made answer, "Did ye not see our Father, Francis, who goeth unto heaven?" And forthwith his holy soul, departing from the body, followed the most holy Father.

The Bishop of Assisi at that time had gone on pilgrimage unto the oratory of Saint Michael on Monte Gargano, and unto him the Blessed Francis, appearing on the night of his departure, said, "Behold, I leave the world and go unto heaven." The Bishop, then, rising at dawn, related unto his companions that which he had seen, and returned unto Assisi; there, when he had made diligent enquiry, he learnt of a certainty that in that hour whereof the vision had notified him, the blessed Father had departed from this world.

At the hour of the passing of the holy man, the larks—birds that love the light, and dread the shades of twilight—flocked in great numbers unto the roof of the house, albeit the shades of night were then falling, and, wheeling round it for a long while with songs even gladder than their wont, offered their witness, alike gracious and manifest, unto the glory of the Saint, who had been wont to call them unto the divine praises.

CHAPTER XV

OF HIS CANONISATION, AND THE TRANSLATION OF HIS BODY

1. Francis, then, the servant and friend of the Most High, the founder and leader of the Order of Friars Minor, the professor of poverty, the pattern of penitence, the herald of truth, the mirror of holiness, and example of all Gospel perfection—the heavenly grace preventing him—did make progress in ordered course from the depths unto the heights. This wondrous man, in poverty exceeding rich, in humility exalted, in mortification full of life, in simplicity wise, and in every grace of character noteworthy, whom in life the Lord had marvellously made illustrious, was made of Him in death incomparably more illustrious. For as that blessed man departed from this world, his holy spirit entered the eternal mansions and was made glorious by a full draught of the fountain of life, while he left set forth in his body certain tokens that were to be his glory, so that his most undefiled flesh, that had been crucified with its lusts, and had become a new creature, did both set forth the image of Christ's Passion by its unexampled distinction, and prefigure the semblance of the Resurrection by the newness of the miracle.

2. For in those blessed limbs were seen the nails marvellously fashioned out of his flesh by the divine might, and so implanted in that flesh that if they were pressed on one side they at once sprang back unto the other, like nerves that be joined together and taut. Moreover, there was manifestly seen in his body the scar of the wound in the side, nor inflicted nor wrought by man, but like unto the wounded side of the Saviour, the which, in Our Redeemer Himself, afforded us the holy mystery of man's redemption and regeneration. The appearance of the nails was black like iron, but the wound in the side was ruddy, and by a contraction of the flesh shaped as it were into a circle, in appearance like a rose most fair. The rest of his flesh—which aforetime both from his infirmities and from natural complexion had tended toward swarthiness—now shone with a dazzling whiteness, and was a type of the beauty of its second state and royal apparel.

3. His limbs were so soft and pliant when touched as that they seemed to have returned unto the softness of childhood,

and were seen to be adorned by divers clear tokens of innocence. Since, then, the nails showed forth black on this most dazzlingly white flesh, and the wound in the side showed ruddy as a rosy flower in Spring, it is no wonder that so fair and marvellous a contrast filled the beholders with gladness and marvelling. His sons were weeping for the loss of so loveworthy a Father, and yet they were filled with no small joy as they kissed the seals of the Most High King in him. The newness of the miracle changed mourning into exultation, and turned the examination of the reason into dumb amazement. Verily, this sight so unparalleled and so noteworthy was, unto all that beheld it, alike a confirmation of faith and an incitement unto love, while unto them that heard thereof it was a subject for marvelling, and the kindling of a yearning to behold it withal.

4. When the departure of the blessed Father became known, and the report of the miracle was spread abroad, the folk gathered in haste unto the spot, that with their bodily eyes they might behold that which should dispel all doubt from their reasons, and should add rejoicing unto their love. Accordingly, very many of the citizens of Assisi were admitted to behold and to kiss those sacred stigmata. Now one among them, a learned and wise Knight, Jerome by name, a man illustrious and renowned, having had doubts concerning these sacred tokens, and having been an unbeliever like Thomas, did very eagerly and boldly, in the presence of the Brethren and of the other citizens, move the nails, and touch with his own hands the hands, feet, and side of the Saint; and thus it befell that, while touching those authentic marks of the wounds of Christ, he cut away every wound of unbelief from his own heart and the hearts of all. Wherefore he became thereafter a constant witness, among others, unto this truth that he had learnt with such certainty, and confirmed it by an oath, laying his hands on thrice-holy things.

5. Now his Brethren and sons, that had been summoned for the passing of their Father, together with the entire assembly of the folk, devoted that night wherein Christ's dear Confessor had departed unto divine praises, in such wise that they seemed no mourners for the dead, but a watch of Angels. When morning came, the crowds that had come together, carrying branches of trees and many wax lights, brought the holy body unto the city of Assisi, with hymns and chants. Moreover, they passed by the church of Saint Damian, where at that time that noble virgin Clare, now glorified in heaven, abode cloistered with her

Sisters; and there for a space they stayed, and set down the holy body, adorned with those heavenly pearls, that it might be seen and embraced by those holy virgins. Coming at length with rejoicing unto the city, they laid the precious treasure that they were bearing in the church of Saint George, with all reverence. In that very place, Francis as a little boy had learned his letters, and there it was that he first preached in after days, and there, finally, he found his first resting-place.

6. Now the holy Father departed from the shipwreck of this world in the year 1226 of the Lord's Incarnation, on the fourth day of October, at late even of a Saturday, and on the Sunday he was buried.

At once the holy man began to shine in the glory of many and great miracles, the light of the divine countenance being uplifted upon him, so that the loftiness of his holiness that, during his life, had been conspicuous in the world for the ruling of men's lives through its ensample of perfect uprightness, was, now that he himself was reigning with Christ, approved from heaven by miracles of divine power, so that belief might be thoroughly confirmed. And since in divers parts of the world the glorious marvels wrought by him, and the great blessings won through him, were kindling many unto devotion unto Christ, and inciting them unto veneration for the Saint himself—so that men's tongues, as well as these deeds, were loud in his praise—it came unto the ears of the Supreme Pontiff, the lord Gregory the Ninth, what great things God was working through His servant Francis.

7. Of a truth, that Shepherd of the Church had been fully assured of his marvellous holiness, not alone by hearing of the miracles wrought after his death, but also by proofs during his life of what he had seen with his own eyes, and handled with his own hands, and he had put perfect faith therein; so that, by reason of this, he now in no wise doubted but that Francis was glorified of the Lord in heaven. Wherefore, that he might act in accord with Christ, Whose Vicar he was, he was minded, with devout consideration, to make the Saint famous on earth, as one most worthy of all reverence. Moreover, to gain the fullest assurance throughout the whole world for the glorification of that most holy man, he caused the miracles that were known of him to be written and approved by trusty witnesses, and then examined by those of the Cardinals that seemed least favourable unto the business. When they had been diligently discussed and approved of all, with the unanimous counsel and

consent of his Brethren, and of all the Prelates that were then in the Curia, he decreed that he should be canonised. Accordingly, he came in person unto the city of Assisi in the yea of the Lord's Incarnation 1228, on the sixteenth day of July, a Sunday, and with rites exceeding solemn, that it would take long to narrate, he enrolled the blessed Father in the list of the Saints.

8. Now in the year of the Lord 1230, the Brethren assembled for a Chapter-General that was held at Assisi, and his body consecrated unto the Lord was translated unto the Church built in his honour on the twenty-fifth day of May. While that holy treasure, signed with the seal of the Most High King, was being removed, He Whose image it set forth deigned to work many miracles, that by the fragrance of its healing power the hearts of the faithful might be drawn to follow after Christ. Verily, it was right fitting that the blessed bones of him, whom God had made well-pleasing unto Him and beloved of Him in life, and whom He had carried unto heaven by the grace of contemplation, like Enoch, and had borne aloft into the sky in a fiery chariot, by his fervour of love, like Elias—being now among the heavenly Spring flowers of the everlasting planting, should flourish out of their place with a marvellous fragrance.

9. Furthermore, even as that blessed man in life had been distinguished by marvellous tokens of virtue, so too from the day of his departure unto this present time, he doth shine throughout the divers parts of the world in the light of famed marvels and miracles, the divine power glorifying him. For the blind and the deaf, the dumb and the lame, the dropsical and the paralysed, the possessed and the leper, the shipwrecked and the captive, have found succour by his merits, and in all diseases, needs, and perils he hath been an aid. But in that many dead have been miraculously raised through him, there is made manifest unto the faithful the glorious working of the power of the Most High, exalting His Saint, and His is the honour and glory throughout the endless ages of eternity. Amen.

HERE ENDETH THE LIFE OF THE BLESSED FRANCIS